AMERICAN DREAMTIME

WITHDRAWN

AMERICAN DREAMTIME

A Cultural Analysis of Popular Movies, and Their Implications for a Science of Humanity

Lee Drummond

LITTLEFIELD ADAMS BOOKS

LITTLEFIELD ADAMS BOOKS

Published in the United States of America
by Rowman & Littlefield Publishers, Inc.
4720 Boston Way, Lanham, Maryland 20706

3 Henrietta Street
London WC2E 8LU, England

British Cataloging in Publication Information Available

Library of Congress Cataloging-in-Publication Data

Drummond, Lee.
American dreamtime : a cultural analysis of popular movies and their
implications for a science of humanity / Lee Drummond.
p. cm.
Includes bibliographical references and indexes.
1. Myth in motion pictures. 2. Heroes in motion pictures.
3. Motion pictures—Semiotics. I. Title.
PN1995.9.M96D78   1996   791.43'615—dc20   96-3697   CIP

ISBN 0-8226-3046-x (cloth : alk. paper)
ISBN 0-8226-3047-8 (pbk. : alk. paper)

Printed in the United States of America

○∞™ The paper used in this publication meets the minimum requirements of
American National Standard for Information Sciences—Permanence of
Paper for Printed Library Materials, ANSI Z39.48–1984.

This work is dedicated to the memory of my stepfather, Walter Lenore (Lee) Corbett, a true Master of Machines, who taught me that words are not everything — or even most of it.

This work is also dedicated *in memoriam* to Baby Fae and Barney Clark, recipients respectively of the first baboon heart transplant and the first artificial heart transplant, pioneers and martyrs who have pointed the way to . . . Something Else.

The [Australian aborigine's] outlook on the universe and man is shaped by a remarkable conception, which Spencer and Gillen immortalized as the "dream time" or *alcheringa* of the Arunta or Aranda tribe. Some anthropologists have called it the "Eternal Dream Time." I prefer to call it what the blacks call it in English — "The Dreaming," or just "Dreaming."

A central meaning of The Dreaming *is* that of a sacred, heroic time long, long ago when man and nature came to be as they are; but neither "time" nor "history" as we understand them is involved in this meaning. I have never been able to discover any aboriginal word for *time* as an abstract concept. And the sense of "history" is wholly alien here . . .

Although . . . The Dreaming conjures up the notion of a sacred, heroic time of the indefinitely remote past, such a time is also, in a sense, still part of the present. One cannot "fix" The Dreaming *in* time: it was, and is, everywhen . . .

Clearly, The Dreaming is many things in one. Among them, a kind of narrative of things that once happened; a kind of charter of things that still happen; and a kind of *logos* or principle of order transcending everything significant for aboriginal man . . .

The tales are a kind of commentary, or statement, on what is thought to be permanent and ordained at the very basis of the world and life. They are a way of stating the principle which animates things. I would call them a poetic key to Reality . . . The active philosophy of aboriginal life transforms this "key," which is expressed in the idiom of poetry, drama, and symbolism, into a principle that The Dreaming determines not only what life *is* but also *what it can be*. Life, so to speak, is a one-possibility thing, and what this is, is the "meaning" of The Dreaming.

— W. E. H. Stanner, *The Dreaming*

Contents

Preface   xi
Acknowledgments   xiii

Chapter

1. Introduction   1

    Beginning at the Beginning   1

    An Anthropologist Goes to the Movies   2

    Cultural Anthropology and the Movies   6

    Which Movies?   11

    An Anthropologist Goes to the Movies, Take 2   18

2. The Primacy of Myth   23

    What Is Myth?   23

    The Nature of Myth   27

    The Foundations of a Cultural Analysis of Myth   29

    A Semiotic Approach to Modern Culture:
      Myth Today, Totemism Today   36

    Myth and Language   44

3. A Theory of Culture as Semiospace   51

    Before and Beyond Language: Cultural Anthropology,
      Quantum Mechanics, and Cosmology   51

    Metaphor, Quality Space, and Semiospace   56

    Dimensionality in Nature and Culture   59

    Processual Analysis and Cultural Dimensionality:
      Liminality, Social Drama, and Social Field 72

    Intersystem and Continuum   76

    Cultural Generativity   88

    The Semiotic Dimensions of Culture   96

4. The Story of Bond — 127

James Bond: An American Myth? — 127

How to Do — and *Not* to Do — Cultural Analysis:
The Novel-Bond and the Movie-Bond — 130

Gadgets and Gladiators: The Master of Machines — 137

Low Brows and High Stakes:
Bond Movies in a World of Consumer Capitalism — 148

Folklore Past:
James Bond, Wild Bill Hickok, and John Henry — 153

Folklore Present:
Secret Agents, Football Players, and Rock Stars — 160

The Story of America — 167

5. Metaphors Be with You: A Cultural Analysis of *Star Wars* — 169

A Bookstore Browse — 169

Inside the Theatre: Semiosis in *Star Wars* — 172

Outside the Theatre: Luke Skywalker, James Bond, and
Indiana Jones in the Temple of the Technological State — 185

Gone to Look for (Post-Literate) America — 196

6. It and Other Beasts: *Jaws* and the New Totemism — 199

The Fish: An Anthropologist Goes to the Movie Studio — 199

Totemic Animals in a Technological Age — 202

The Fish Takes a Bite:
The Myth of Ecology and the Ecology of Myth — 206

The Middle-Aged Man and the Sea: The Story of
Chief Brody, The Great White Shark . . . and Flipper — 218

The Collapse of a Dichotomy: Mechanistic Animals and
Animalistic Machines in *Jaws* and *Jurassic Park* — 229

7. Phone Home: *E. T.* as a Saga of the American Family — 241

From Creature Feature and Saucer Saga to *E. T.* — 241

What is E. T.? — 243

Machines at Home:
The Suburban Family in a Technological State — 247

Monsters at Home: *E. T.* and *Poltergeist* — 253

Ambivalence at Home: The Myth of Family — 256

8. Conclusions   **261**

Understanding Our Movies and Ourselves:
Cultural Analysis and Film Criticism   261

The Logic of Things That Just Happen: The Sandpile and
Cellular Automaton as Models of Cultural Process   265

Something Else   283

Notes   291

References   311

Index of Movies   319

Index   323

Note on the Author   335

Preface

A conventional self-image Americans hold of themselves and their society in these final years of the twentieth century is that of a practical, realistic people engaged in building an ever larger and more complex technological civilization. At the same time, however, we spend countless billions on activities and products that fly in the face of our supposed commitment to a down-to-earth realism: Our movies, television programs, sports events, vacations, fashions, and cosmetics seem to be the pastimes of a whimsical, fantasy-ridden people rather than of the stalwart folk of our national stereotype. How are these conflicting images to be reconciled? Are we *really* a practical, self-reliant people who simply like to escape our busy lives occasionally by retreating into a fantasy world? Or is our vaunted practicality and common sense actually a mask for a frivolous, wasteful nature intent on partying while Rome burns and the national debt ratchets up another trillion dollars?

This book sets out to explore those conflicting self-images by focusing on the intimate ties our daily activity and thought have with a world of myth. Written from the perspective of a cultural anthropologist, *American Dreamtime* approaches modern culture as an anthropologist does a "primitive" society, seeking in its myths and rituals clues to its fundamental nature.

The theme of the book is that myth is alive and well in America, and that its temples are the movie theatres across the land. Movies and myths, I argue, issue from the same generative processes that have brought humanity into being and that continually alter our lives, our societies, and the ultimate destiny of our species. The "Dreamtime" of the title is taken from a concept documented for certain Australian aboriginal groups, according to which the origins of everything — plants, animals, humans — both occurred and are occurring in a kind of waking dream that is at once past and present. The candidates I propose for Dreamtime status are recent movies whose phenomenal popularity signals their resonance with the modern psyche: James Bond movies, the *Star Wars* trilogy, *Jaws*, and *E. T.*

Inquiring into the status of myth in American culture leads, for an anthropologist, to fundamental questions about the nature of myth and culture generally. In discussing particular movies and particular American social institutions, the agenda before me is always to combine the specific findings of an ethnographic study with a theoretical inquiry into the nature of culture. If a signature of our peculiarly American brand of humanity is the movies we flock to, then a thorough analysis of those productions should contribute to our understanding of what it is to be human, should contribute to a *science of humanity*. That is the project I undertake here.

As the "science of humanity," anthropology should be the ideal discipline within which to conduct the kind of inquiry pursued in this book. Curiously, though, cultural anthropologists themselves are sharply divided over the issue of whether anthropology is a science at all, or what kind of science it is. As the end of the century and of the millenium approaches, we find ourselves drawn up in opposing camps over these very issues. "Positivists" or "materialists" espouse a deterministic credo rooted in a vision of humanity as a product of political, economic, and ecological conditions. "Interpretivists" or "post-modernists" renounce any approach that smacks of science in favor of a vision of humanity as a literary-like ensemble of texts or messages.

A major purpose in writing this book is to dismantle that dichotomy, which I believe to be entirely false, and to replace it with a cultural analysis that does not shun a scientific orientation to mythic and ritual texts. In my view, anthropological positivists and postmodernists alike have seriously misconstrued the enterprise of "science," converting it into a hollow image of itself that serves, on the one hand, as a cult emblem, and, on the other, as a demon to be exorcised. Intent on waging internecine warfare, we have largely ignored the fascinating and profound developments in branches of science that, if their subject matter is very different from our own, bear directly on anthropological thought. An innovation of this book is to search for answers to general anthropological questions in the fields of quantum mechanics, cosmology, and chaos-complexity theory. I do not pretend for an instant to have a working knowledge of those fields or to make rigorous comparisons between them and aspects of anthropological theory. But I find the play of ideas in those fields so intriguing and suggestive that I think it essential to incorporate them, however crudely, into my cultural analysis of myth. I believe I will have succeeded here if I convince you, not of the correctness of my application of physical and mathematical concepts, but simply of the need for you yourself to explore the scientific and mathematical literature with an eye to its culturological implications.

Following the introduction, chapters 2 and 3 take up general questions of myth and culture, attempting to situate an anthropological discussion of them in the context of contemporary scientific thought. Chapters 4–7 then explore the mythic realm of the movie *oeuvres* of James Bond, *Star Wars*, *Jaws*, and *E. T.*, focusing on their significance for diverse areas of American experience — from popular music and sports to family life, the ecology movement, and global economics. Chapter 8 returns to a discussion of the relevance of cultural anthropology for an understanding of modern life, and to the quest for a science of humanity.

Acknowledgments

Grateful acknowledgment is made to the following:

Greg Mahnke, M.A. (Martian Ambassador), Ph.D. (Piled higher & Deeper), whose zany profundity inspired it.

Mike Bisson, whose zeal for "cave man" and "bug-eyed monster" movies fueled it.

Anne Brydon, whose insights into the nature of boundaries illuminated areas of darkness in it.

Michael Herzfeld, whose probing critiques, generously provided over a period of years, made it, if not quite ethnographic, then perhaps at least anthropological.

. . . .

The *American Journal of Semiotics,* for permission to reprint in chapter 2 occasional passages that first appeared in my essay "Movies and Myth: Theoretical Skirmishes." *AJS* 3 : 2: 1–32.

The University of Nebraska Press, for permission to reprint in chapter 4 a greatly revised version of my essay "The Story of Bond," which first appeared in *Symbolizing America,* Herve Varenne, ed., pp. 162–186.

The Joe Steinmetz Studio and The Photography Archive, Carpenter Center for the Visual Arts, Harvard University, for permission to reproduce in the frontispiece the photograph "Bradenton, Florida 1951."

Oxford University Press, for permission to quote selected passages from Roger Penrose's *The Emperor's New Mind,* pp. 176–182 and 256–258, and to reproduce Fig. 5.14.

Doubleday Press, for permission to quote selected passages from Peter Benchley's *Jaws,* pp. 9, 218–219, 277.

Scientific American, for permission to quote selected passages from the following articles:

"Viral Quasispecies," by Manfred Eigen, (July 1993), pp. 42–49.

"Diet and Primate Evolution," by Katharine Milton, (August 1993), pp. 86–93.

"Self-Organized Criticality," by Per Bak and Kan Chen, (January 1991), pp. 46–53.

1

Introduction

It's a dream. That's what we live on. That's what this country's all about.
—Robert Crane, Director of the Massachusetts State Lottery
(on the eve of the $41,000,000 New York State Lottery, August 21, 1985)

Beginning at the Beginning

On a Tuesday or Wednesday afternoon in the spring of 1977, I was driving along a street in downtown Seattle, Washington. On making a turn I discovered that the sidewalk of the next street was thronged with people, all waiting in a line that stretched up the block and around the corner. I was just visiting the city for a few days and had no idea what had attracted the crowd. If I could retrieve the first thoughts I had after catching sight of that queue, they would have to do with a sale or, possibly, a demonstration (although 1977 was not a good year for demonstrations). My curiosity aroused, I forgot my destination for the moment and turned at the next corner, following the line to discover what had brought all those people onto the sidewalk in the middle of a weekday afternoon.

They were waiting to buy tickets at a movie theatre, and the theatre was showing *Star Wars*.

At the time I did little TV watching or even newspaper and magazine reading, so the sight of all those people lining up to see *Star Wars* caught me completely off guard. Why had they turned out in droves to see *that* movie? The question intrigued me, and in the months and years that followed I have searched for an answer. It is probably more an index of my own compulsiveness than of the sheer impact of the movie that the search has led me to formulate ideas about the nature of culture, particularly its modern American variant, as a means of explaining what *Star Wars* and other popular movies are all about. This book offers the explanations I have come up with, and attempts to place them in the framework of a general inquiry into the nature of culture.

An Anthropologist Goes to the Movies

Having seen the queue, I had to see the movie. Circumstances prevented my joining the line that afternoon in Seattle, and it was only several weeks later that I found myself seated in a theatre waiting for *Star Wars* to begin. As the credits scrolled horizontally across the screen into the galactic void and the action started, I felt the first stirrings of a puzzlement or ambivalence that has by now become my lasting impression of the movie.

My first reaction was the intellectual's predictable scorn: I found it incredible that so many people would spend their time and money on a movie whose dialogue is easily surpassed by the Sunday comic strips. Then the space operatic effects began to work on me, and I discovered a realm of curiously stirring fantasy that enveloped the characters and made their banal exchanges less awful. Clearly, the popularity of the movie was tied to its imagery and not to the sparkling repartees of Luke Skywalker, Han Solo, and Princess Leia—not to mention Chewy's grunts and moans. The imagery was so powerful, in fact, that *Star Wars* actually seemed to dispense with the dialogue of human actors, who, with the exceptions of Alec Guinness (Obi-Wan Kenobi) and Peter Cushing (Grand Moff Tarkin), were unknowns anyway, and thereby excuse their narrative flatness. Instead of on people, the camera throughout much of the movie was trained on mechanical or monstrous characters acting in otherworldly scenes that included people only as a kind of prop.

Even if I had been steeped in film criticism rather than cultural anthropology, I don't know how I would have come to terms with these first reactions. The purposeful strangeness of the movie, coupled with the audience's emotional involvement, actually made me think I was on more familiar ground in this theatre than a film critic would have been: I was an anthropologist who had happened onto an important myth/ritual of an exotic tribe known as "Americans."

Observing both performance *and* audience as an anthropologist, it seemed that the real stars of the movie were R2D2 and C3PO, sophisticated machines or "droids" who displayed a far wider range of emotions than the wooden characters of Skywalker and Leia. Action and dramatic tension were provided by an assortment of beings of all descriptions. In addition to the droids, there were Jawas, Tusken Raiders, Imperial Guardsmen, Wookies, bizarre insectean forms in the Mos Eisley cantina, the sinister Darth Vader, and an array of technological gadgets ranging from the immense Death Star to Luke's hot rod landspeeder. While much of the minimal plot was built on a damsel-in-distress theme—Princess Leia's captivity aboard the Death Star—the audience seemed most excited and empathic when R2D2 made an appearance: we were alarmed at its capture by the Jawas, delighted with its gleeful beeps, amused at its electronic put-downs of the effete C3PO, distressed by its injury while serving as Luke's copilot.

Rather than detract from the movie's dramatic impact, the insipid human characters and dialogue actually seemed to highlight complexities in the personalities of droids. *Star Wars* was a fairy tale in which the fairies were robots, machines raised to a level of characterization superior to their human associates and presumed masters. People were flocking to the movie to watch R2D2 go through its endearing displays of beeps and flashes and to agonize over its fate. R2D2 was the Tin Man of *The Wizard of Oz*, but with significant differences: he had completely upstaged Dorothy, or Princess Leia, and pretty much replaced Toto (for a thorough and insightful analysis of the mythic nature of *The Wizard of Oz*, see Paul Nathanson's *Over the Rainbow: The Wizard of Oz as a Secular Myth of America*). Tin Man's appeal rests on his human form and feeling in mechanical guise; he is the Nutcracker, who wants a heart to validate his human emotions. R2D2, however, evokes strong audience response in spite of the fact that it resembles an animated trash barrel more than a person. Although we do not remotely suspect that it has, or even wants, a heart, R2D2's gait, electronic "voice," and agitated displays somehow invest it with the humanity Tin Man so fervently sought. And R2D2's "humanity" definitely eclipses that of the anthropomorphic and English-speaking C3PO, whose human form and cultivated voice merely serve to emphasize its stiff, "mechanical" nature in contrast to R2D2's spontaneity.

Why should so many people be so taken with the doings of a mobile electronic cylinder? Are Americans so disgusted with their lives, so alienated from the world they inhabit, that they seek release by pouring emotion into a machine that exists only in a movie? And, if we find a strong undercurrent of alienation or disorientation in popular movies, is it a vague, diffuse feeling or is there an identifiable cultural framework or *pattern* to it, something that sheds new light on the events in our lives? These are the kind of critical questions that a cultural anthropologist doing a *cultural analysis* of American movies must ask of his material, questions his more traditionally oriented colleagues politely (and, I think, wrongly) refrain from asking of the exotic performances they study in Amazon villages and New Guinea valleys.

I think it is undeniable that *Star Wars* and other popular movies contain and communicate large doses of alienation or, perhaps more precisely, what Gregory Bateson called *schismogenesis*: *the representation of unresolvable dilemmas that lie at the heart of a cultural system, a representation that makes life bearable only by disguising its fundamental incoherence.*[1] Recognizing the schismogenic features of our own cultural productions and those of the "primitive" or exotic peoples anthropologists typically study (and normally exempt from a searching critique) can only be the beginning of a rigorous cultural analysis, which must ground its moral discourse in the signifying *details* of particular cultural productions that appear at particular times and are enjoyed by particular people. Why is *Star Wars* the movie it is, and not some other piece of "escapist" fare? *That* is the question a cultural analysis of the movie must address.

In taking up that question, it is immediately apparent that if *Star Wars* viewers were just looking for a harmless cotton candy adventure, a fairy tale to take their minds off the grim reality of life, then a little melodrama featuring only Luke, Leia, the paternal Obi-Wan Kenobi, and the villainous Grand Moff Tarkin would have sufficed. Dress the story up in futuristic garb if you like, even throw in loads of special effects. But why introduce and give star billing to robots, Wookies, Jawas, insectoids, and other exotics? Unless, that is, the presence of that unearthly menagerie has a great deal to do with the primary message and popularity of the movie.

That is what I would suggest. The space operatic world of *Star Wars*, with its formulaic "long ago in a galaxy far, far away," is not mere window dressing for a syrupy handsome-country-boy-rescues-beautiful-princess-and-they-live-happily-ever-after fairy tale. It is the fantasy world itself, specifically the peculiar "mechanicals" and "organics" that inhabit it, that accounts for the movie's resonance with American audiences.

Star Wars provides Americans an opportunity to work out and to explore their relationships with an extremely important, ever-changing reality in their daily lives: *the machine*. As I sat watching R2D2 beep and twinkle, Darth Vader rasp through his (its?) voice synthesizer, and the Death Star dispense annihilation, I began to realize that here was material fantastic only in a special, mythic sense. The movie's escapist stereotypes came to seem a cushion or palliative for an American public having to face up to some crucial facts about its coexistence with an immensely large and complex population of cars,[2] tools, computers, heavy equipment, appliances, lawnmowers, bicycles, and their secondary products in the built environments that provide the universal background and staging area for human consciousness and social life. And the machines I have named are only the good guys, the ones made, as they say, "for domestic consumption": many would say that the problem of coexistence really begins with the tanks, bombers, nuclear submarines, guided missiles, and, that machine of machines, The Bomb.[3]

Machines, I concluded, were the key both to the plot of *Star Wars* and to its tremendous popularity. But the movie was decidedly not a rehash of that dreary old daytime TV staple "Industry on Parade," updated for Cinemascope and Dolby. What struck me during that first, fateful encounter with what would become a trilogy stretched over six years was that *Star Wars* deliberately turns away from mundane relations between people and machines to explore the extramundane basics of their coexistence. I began, in short, to think of machines in *Star Wars* as I believe a cultural anthropologist should think of myth: *as questions or areas of puzzlement basic to the elaboration of human identity, which get asked and pondered in the course of narration.*

Most "primitive" myths are about people's relations with animals or, more precisely, with totemic ancestors that are both human and animal and that exist in a kind of World Dawn.[4] It is this world of simultaneous past and present, of the origin of all things *and* contemporary events that Stanner, translating from the Australian languages, calls the Dreaming or *Dreamtime*. It makes perfect sense that members of hunting and gathering groups should focus their efforts to understand the world on the animals and plants around them, for their lives are intimately bound up with other species. How human and animal groups came to be and the nature of their present relationships are the subject and substance of their thought. Because those questions contain profound enigmas, they can never be answered in a once-and-for-all way, but the *process* of asking them and trying out possible solutions is an absolutely vital aspect of existence.

That process, as I argue in chapter 2 and throughout this book, is what we term *myth*. The fact that many of us have never even touched a wild animal, and certainly never hunted down, killed, and butchered a kangaroo or emu, places our lives and our reflections on our lives in quite a different context from that of the Australian aborigines. It does not, however, mean that we give up thinking about and relating to animals, or that we abandon the relentless questioning that is the essence of the myth-making process as I describe it here. We simply change the terms of the process, or have them changed for us by the forces of circumstance. The principal change of this sort, and the one most of this work is devoted to, is the prominence of *artifacts* or *machines* in our lives and thought. *Star Wars* did not just fall out of the sky and somehow manage to captivate hundreds of millions of people around the world. The movie, which I maintain focuses on the critical question of the coexistence of humans and increasingly "smart" machines, holds a powerful attraction for audiences because they somehow sense that it deals with issues that lie at the heart of their daily concerns. *Machines* are increasingly important in our lives. They may determine whether or not we are born and when we will die, and they are with most us through virtually every waking moment in between. And *Star Wars* is a myth about machines.

Until my professional interest in *Star Wars* was kindled, I had thought a lot about "traditional" myths the cultural anthropologist typically studies—those told by exotic people in exotic places—but very little about movies (and the idea that the latter had much in common with the former had never crossed my mind). The myths I had been concerned with were mostly those told at one time or another by South American Indians, particularly Arawak and Carib groups of Guyana with whom I lived and worked for about two years during the seventies. What intrigued me about their myths of clan origin and of bizarre sexual liaisons between people and dogs, monkeys, and serpents was the persistence of these tales in the face of centuries of social change that had completely transformed indigenous society and made contemporary Arawak and Carib into persons many of us might run into on the street in the course of our daily lives. While some folklorists and anthropologists would be inclined to minimize the relevance these Indian myths hold for the everyday concerns of the Arawak and Carib who tell them, viewing them as irrelevant leftovers of an indigenous past, I found that the narratives speak directly to the burning social issues engaging Guyanese Amerindians today. The myths' obsession with problems of identity (tribe vs. tribe, human vs. animal) meshes perfectly with present Arawak and Carib fears, desires and, most of all, ambivalences about their place in an emergent (read declining) multiethnic nation of the Third World.

In looking back over the long process of composing the topical essays collected here and of fitting them into the framework of a theory of culture, it strikes me that this project derives its inspiration and direction from my earlier studies of Arawak and Carib myth. The spatial and social gulfs that separate the anthropologist in a South American Indian village, huddled with his aged, trusted informant over transcripts and translated texts of fantastic stories few Westerners have ever heard, from the anthropologist back home, lined up with the masses for a screening of the latest supergrosser, are not as extreme as they might appear. The differences between the two situations are offset for me by the lessons a first-hand encounter with "traditional" myth teaches someone about to embark on a cultural analysis of popular, folk productions of his own society. In the village of Kabakaburi, perched uncertainly between the populous coast and the desolate rain forests of Guyana, I discovered that tribal narratives which should have long since lost their appeal for individuals who were thoroughly "detribalized" and "Westernized" still spoke compellingly to them as they sought to find their bearings in a confused and turbulent national society. I believe that realization prepared me to take seriously the improbable and shallow tales that comprise the bulk of our own popular culture: if seemingly antiquated myth exerts a strong force on the lives of Guyanese Indians, might it also be true that the apparently inconsequential productions of the Hollywood "dream factory" have a significance beyond their self-imposed aesthetic limitations?   That thought is the genesis of the present study.

Cultural Anthropology and the Movies

An anthropologist may indeed go to the movies, but can he take anthropology with him? Are the parallels between aboriginal myth and American movies sufficiently close to warrant an anthropological study of a subject that has already received scrupulous treatment by legions of film critics, cinematologists, and associate professors of English?[5] The daunting prospect of wading into the murky waters of film/literary criticism, where the real predators of academe prowl just beneath the surface, should discourage any reasonably sane anthropologist. Why risk a shark attack (to anticipate my later discussion of *Jaws*) when one can stick to the safe ground of one's own arcane specialty —

Arawak myth, Borneo ritual, Bedouin social organization, or whatever — and watch the big fish thrashing offshore in their feeding frenzy?

The problems raised in considering the possible contribution of anthropology to film studies are simply extreme instances of a general, divisive, and utterly serious debate now underway in the discipline of cultural anthropology. The debate centers on anthropology's role in the modern (some would want to say "postmodern") world, both within the university community and the wider (some would want to say "real") world of everyday life, and is carried on amidst the ruins of a now outmoded, but still conventional image of anthropology.

The conventional image of cultural anthropology as the study of living museum pieces and other social oddities—lost tribes, South Sea islanders, Latin American peasants, quaint subcultures like the Amish and not-so-quaint subcultures like the Hell's Angels—still burdens the field with an insupportable identity. As tribesmen become peasants and peasants the urban poor of the Third World, and as sociological and journalistic treatments of groups like the Amish and Hell's Angels become more substantial and ethnographic, the cultural anthropologist's role diminishes to stereotype. He becomes either the bespectacled and irrelevant old fool who plays a bit part in a B movie or TV drama, or his opposite: a swashbuckling adventurer in the manner of Indiana Jones. Either way, the anthropologist is shut off from the world around him and denied any voice in those forums for commentary and debate (television, newspapers, popular magazines) that monitor and perhaps even influence social trends and events. Since the death of Margaret Mead, cultural anthropology's public presence has shrunk to negligible proportions, creating a crisis of professional identity among practitioners of the craft and effectively silencing their moral voice.

American anthropologists have reacted to this situation in three ways. The first has been simply to ignore the social climate and consequences of research and get on with the work at hand: counting beads on nineteenthth century Oglala moccasins; measuring the daily caloric intake of !Kung Bushmen; deciphering the kinship terminology once used by the Crow; and thousands of other projects that consume the greater part of thousands of professional lives in the discipline. The second kind of reaction to our professional identity crisis is a frontal assault on the stigma of academic irrelevance: if the first sort of anthropologist busies himself with scholarly minutiae, the second rolls up his sleeves, goes into the field, sees what needs doing, and helps get it done. These are the applied or "development" anthropologists who work closely with national and international agencies, such as the Agency for International Development and the World Bank, to ameliorate some of the innumerable problems facing the burgeoning masses of the Third World.

A third response to the crisis in cultural anthropology, which I adopt here, involves a sharp departure from the classical and applied approaches. I propose to examine several recent popular movies from the perspective of *cultural analysis,* or *anthropological semiotics.* The basic idea of cultural analysis is that a group's cultural productions — the whole diverse assemblage of its artifacts, speech, gesture, fashion, cuisine, architecture, art, literature, music, games, sports, television, and, of course, movies — form a system of meanings or interpretations individuals constantly and necessarily employ in leading their lives. "Leading their lives" is not the plodding activity the phrase might imply, for the point of cultural analysis is that movies, fashion, and the rest represent attempts to give form to an enigmatic and inchoate human identity, and in the process to resolve or suspend conceptual dilemmas that would otherwise make ordinary life impossible. Without those cultural productions, in short, there would be no human lives to lead, and the form or pattern inherent in the productions indicates just what sort of lives are led.

The classical approach typically focuses on *the* culture of *the* native society considered as a small-scale, relatively stable, self-contained isolate, and not on the often bewildering conglomeration of cultural productions of a rapidly changing, multiethnic national state. As a consequence, the classical approach tends to treat culture as a sort of ideational baggage that furnishes the trousseaux in which a society wraps itself: the social group is simply *there* and casts about for convenient garments, in the form of cultural productions, to embellish itself. Cultural analysis denies this pat claim to priority of a pre-existing *in situ* "society," and instead goes against the grain of common sense to assert that it is the ongoing struggle to adopt one version or another of the way things are that constitutes what we call a "society." "Culture" is not just baggage; it is the stuff of experience—but, like baggage, it is always having to be sorted out.

Applied or development anthropology generally gives due importance to social transformation and intergroup relations, but then proceeds as though political and economic forces operated independently of ideational, cultural, or "symbolic" phenomena. There is probably no more specious distinction in modern anthropology than this "economic" vs. "symbolic" opposition, and insisting on it vitiates much of the work that applied anthropologists do on social change. Modern capitalist societies have so thoroughly interlinked the commodity value and ritual value of goods and services that it is meaningless to speak of separate social domains of the "economic" and the "symbolic." Our tourism and entertainment industries have elevated the stodgy old Marxian notion of "fetishism of commodities" to the status of a global economic force; more billions go into those "diversions" than into groceries for Mom and Dad and Buddy and Sis.

The anthropological implications of this inseparable link between sup- posedly distinct realms of experience came rushing in on me when I began seriously to consider popular movies as a major source of modern American mythology. Under the guise of studying the practical while disparaging "symbolic anthropologists" who concern themselves with "irrelevant" myth and ritual, applied anthropologists actually turn their backs on much of the on-the-ground daily activity they claim as their special subject.

A great deal of what people, in America as well as Europe and the Third World, spend their time and money on is highly ritualized and mythologized: food that conforms to particular tastes, and not simply to caloric and nutritional requirements; clothes that embody a particular fashion, and not just criteria of warmth and modesty (itself, of course, a highly cultural, mythologized notion); sexual partners who personify standards of beauty and not just convenient orifices; and so on to the television programs and movies that often consume hours of the day and provide the raw material for much discussion and play-acting.[6]   Ordinary people occupy themselves with these and other similarly fantastic, "symbolic" pursuits, and leave the determination of their caloric intake, the efficiency or inefficiency of their agricultural cooperative, and the legal technicalities of their group's land claim to bureaucrats and applied anthropologists, who, if the truth were told, are not all that easy to distinguish when you are on the receiving end of their attentions.

"Real life" is a slippery notion that constantly seems on the verge of becoming "reel life." This telling pun, one of innumerable gems to be found in Edmund Carpenter's amusing yet profound book, *Oh, What a Blow that Phantom Gave Me!*, runs through much of what follows and constitutes one of the main themes of this work. "America" is, interchangeably and inseparably, a political and economic titan *and* a "dream factory" that spews out, in addition to the mountains of consumer goods and armaments, the mannerisms, fashions, games, sports, magazines, television programs, and movies of the Dreamtime. And our Dreamtime, just as the Australian aborigines', is so thoroughly a part of the fatefulness of life—of whom one loves and marries (and probably divorces), of how one coexists (is there any other term for it?) with one's children, of whom one kills (or simply dutifully hates) in the name of God and Country, of what one does as daily toil, even of what one has for dinner — that it is impossible to segregate it from a supposedly objective, material reality. Consequently, the questions I pursue in the following chapters are concerned with *how*, and not *whether*, popular movies like *Star Wars* shape and transform our most fundamental values and most cherished truths. That, in brief, is the goal of this particular exercise in the cultural analysis of American life.

But why movies? If "culture" as I have been describing it seems to be just about the whole ball of wax, encompassing what ecologists, Marxists, and assorted practical types wrongly try to distinguish from culture, then why single out movies for privileged treatment and not, say, the latest blip in the Leading Economic Indicators, or a few hundred hours of scintillating C-Span coverage of congressional debates, or, even staying within the general topic of "popular culture," some other stereotypically "symbolic" phenomenon such as fashion, advertising, or comic books? I offer two reasons, neither likely to satisfy my more conventional colleagues. The first is simply the personal encounter with

Star Wars I have already described. Going to a movie and seeing it as myth was for me a profoundly anthropological experience, different in content but not, perhaps, in kind from that *deracinement* anthropologists recently returned from the field often report in informal conversation with their fellows: it is the disorienting experience of the at-home and familiar become suddenly alien and vertiginous, like opening the door to your house and walking into a story by Kafka. One could really begin anywhere in the vast reservoir of popular culture and emerge with the same themes I find in movies; I simply chose to begin with movies. Having made them my starting point, however, I follow their characters —James Bond, Luke Skywalker, Chief Brody (of *Jaws*), and Elliott and E. T.— outside the theatre into highly diverse areas of social life: football games, rock concerts, tales of the Old West, the environmental movement, gender and sexuality, ethnic relations, and family life. A cultural analysis of movies must move outside its topic if it is to have any hope of identifying the system of meanings that make a particular movie a *generative* source of culture, as detailed in my discussion of cultural generativity in chapter 3.

My second reason for making popular movies the subject of this work is less subjective than the first, but may strike you as even less plausible. Either by coincidence or fate, my interest in movies as myths that would lend themselves to an anthropological approach was kindled during the first years of the *supergrosser era*. Movies had been a fixture of American life for more than sixty years when I began thinking obsessively about *Star Wars*, but it was only with the release of *Jaws* in 1975 that a movie attracted so many people and made so much money that it became a social and economic phenomenon in itself. *Jaws* vastly surpassed previous box office hits, and came along just when movie moguls and media commentators had about concluded that the demon Television really would be the death of Film. Moreover, that movie was not just a flash-in-the-pan sensation, the unique product of a young director named Steven Spielberg. *Jaws* opened the floodgates for a rapid succession of action-packed, fantasy-based supergrossers, many superer and grosser than the last: *Close Encounters of the Third Kind*; *Superman* (I, II, III, IV); *Star Wars*; *The Empire Strikes Back*; *Raiders of the Lost Ark*; *Indiana Jones in the Temple of Doom*; *Return of the Jedi*; *E. T.*; *Rambo* (I, II, III); *Rocky* (1. . .n, where "n" stands for "no end in sight"); *Predator* (I and a half, since II was sans-Arnie); *Terminator* (I and II); *Batman* (I and II); and on to a seemingly endless series of aliens, mutants, cyborgs and time cops.

America rediscovered movies in the mid-seventies, after a decade of bitter involvement in Viet Nam and domestic turmoil that tore apart families and communities. For the first time in years, Americans seemed to be moving in the same direction: toward movie theatres with the latest supergrosser on their marquees. Kids kept going to the movies; baby boomers left the barricades and headed there; and old folks (meaning those has-beens over forty), sensing they could once again enter their neighborhood theatres without being insulted by animated chipmunks or assaulted by sadistic orgies, went to see if the silver screen retained the magic they had found there during their youth. One phenomenal hit and box office record followed another. The era of the super-grosser truly had begun.

The sudden, staggering popularity of movies cannot be dismissed as a fluke. Whatever is behind it — and the causes are doubtlessly complex — it is now established that particular movies have tremendous mass appeal. The entire movie industry (or, as they say in southern California, "*the* Industry") has geared itself to the supergrosser, to finding the right combination of big-name talent and script that will garner the Olympian gold of top ratings in *Variety*. And people go to see those movies, not because they are sheep, but because they expect to find *something there*, something worth seeing, something that genuinely *recreates* them. Movies are not just one genre of popular culture among others; they are at present its Main Vein, in Tom Wolfe's phrase, distillations of American culture, myths of the Dreamtime. Future generations cannot but be impressed by the time and resources devoted to the movie industry in late twentieth century America; the phenomenon will appear as a unique efflorescence, an outpouring and summing up of the collective sentiment of a people—its *eidos*, if you will. The movie is to the twentieth century what the Gothic cathedral was to the thirteenth, and, to expand an analogy that must already appear outlandish to some, Spielberg and Lucas are our Michelangelo and Leonardo. Cultural anthropology, since it searches for what is most basic in the beliefs and expressions of a people, necessarily fixes on popular movies as keys to understanding American culture. And if the movie houses are where culture is happening, that is where cultural anthropologists must go, notebooks in hand (and, just perhaps, audio cassette recorders discreetly tucked in shoulder bags), to map out the framework of our cultural structure, to chart the American Dreamtime.

Which Movies?

But which movies should anthropologists head for, which primitive temples will they visit in Dreamtime America, assuming they are even prepared to go along with my argument up to now? This is one of two critical questions that must be asked in broaching the possibility that some movies are like the origin myths of native peoples. The other question is a major theoretical issue engaged throughout this work: What counts as "myth" and what is myth's place in the world of human experience? In the next two chapters and the subsequent topical essays, I confront that issue by adopting a broadly construed notion of "myth" as the principal dynamic of culture and, therefore, the very content of experience. For now, though, the first question is more pressing: How do you get started at a cultural analysis of movies? How do you know which movies to put on your list?

Where, as anthropology thesis supervisors are fond of asking, will you do your field work?

Because this work is really a scouting expedition, an attempt to move cultural anthropology into areas it has left largely unexplored, I want to be quite conservative in this business of selecting particular movies for extensive analysis. I do not discount the mythic content of any popular movie, and in fact am convinced that a mature cultural analysis would encompass film (or Film) as a whole. But for the present it is best to proceed cautiously, focusing on only a few of those movies that, on the basis of one or two simple criteria, are decidedly "mythic." The litmus test I use here for a movie's mythic content is simply: "Could this be happening to me, or to someone I know?" Is the world described in the movie sufficiently like my own that I can picture myself inhabiting it? Are the action and plot closely enough related to my life that I can view the movie as a dramatization of what I do, or might be doing in the near future? In applying this test, I have identified (no cinematological breakthrough here!) two general types of movie that I would count as unquestionably mythic: the space opera and the incredible adventure (but not, quite yet, *Bill and Ted's Excellent Adventure*). It is convenient to lump these under a generic category of "fantasy movies," and contrast that category with another in which the mythic content is more subtle and ambiguous: "people movies."

The element of fantasy is critical here, for it provides a natural link between at least one type of movie and myth, which we conventionally regard and describe as fantastic. A number of recent movies invite their audiences to inhabit, for a brief two hours, the Dreamtime, a cinematic *alcheringa* in which larger-than-life, nonhuman or superhuman beings perform feats and have experiences outside the realm of possibility in everyday life. These movies create settings, characters, and, in the audience, states of mind that belong to another realm. For me the best example of this fantasy genre is the movie, now trilogy, that started me thinking about all this: the space opera *Star Wars*. It evokes the classic, "once upon a time. . ." of fairy tale with its introductory, "long ago, in a galaxy far, far away. . ." The viewer experiences immediate displacement in time and space with this evocation of a world (or worlds) where the human presence is hemmed in and shaped by unearthly beings of every description.

Although science fiction movies have been a fixture of theatre fare since the early fifties, it is the generic space opera or space fantasy set partly or wholly in space that interests me here.[7] Apart from early Buck Rogers and Flash Gordon serials, the modern space opera began with the 1968 release of *2001: A Space Odyssey* and appeared, after Stanley Kubrick's tour de force, to be dead in its tracks, exhausted by the master's consummate first work. Nine years later, however, George Lucas and *Star Wars* revived the genre with that movie's spectacular success. Following the golden path charted by *Star Wars*, a spate of movies has explored or, more often, exploited the format of space fantasy. A partial list would include *Battlestar Galactica, The Black Hole, Buck Rogers in the Twenty-Fifth Century, Alien(s),* and *Star Trek* (like the *Rocky* movies, another 1. . .n series).

Situated somewhere between these space operas and incredible adventures of an earthly nature are fantasy movies that develop the theme of extraterrestrial contact. The modern classic and holder of the number one spot on the supergrosser list, *E. T.*, released in 1982, exemplifies this group. The movie is set in real life, but the incredible adventure that befalls its characters is a visitation by an extraterrestrial. Elliott and his family are leading stereotypically normal lives (southern Californian suburban life being modern culture's Everyman), when the outlandish literally lands on top of them. Fantasy is a critical element in what follows and, as I discuss in chapter 7, clearly links *E. T.* with the Dreamtime tradition of American movies.[8]

Space operas and their hybrid form, extraterrestrial movies, share Dreamtime billing with incredible adventure movies featuring real/reel-life supermen. James Bond and Indiana Jones are flesh-and-blood characters who do not spend most of their lives in space (although Bond, in *Moonraker*, makes it aboard the space shuttle), nor do they have to confront those bug-eyed monsters from the recesses of the galaxy. Nevertheless, Bond and Jones, in their frenetic, cliff-hanging adventures, inhabit a world more like a comic strip than any that we mere mortals experience. No one lives in their world; it is an artful (or at least, considering its box office appeal, crafty) construction of an imaginary realm in which certain human abilities—to handle machines, engage in combat, escape from mortal danger — are pushed well beyond the limits of everyday life. Because they are at once compelling and systematic exaggerations of human experience, James Bond and Indiana Jones thrillers offer their audiences what I would identify as myth's distinctive contribution to life: *the opportunity to enter a world of virtual experience and to do, vicariously, the undoable.*

But whatever the formal, cinematological characteristics of James Bond movies may be, the most important thing about those movies from the perspective of cultural analysis is that James Bond is indisputably the Hero of Our Age, a literary and cinematic character of unprecedented appeal and staying power. If they hope to join him at the pinnacle of popular culture, Indiana Jones, Luke Skywalker, and even Rambo and Rocky, those beefy sensations of the eighties, will have to hang in there for decades, starring in movie after movie and, when their human actors/avatars begin to get long of tooth and heavy of paunch, will have to shuck those mortal forms for fresh new bodies if they are to preserve their heroic cinematic presence. Will a new, young Roger Moore-type stand-in replace Sly in *Rocky 12*? Not likely, and there would surely *not* be a Timothy Dalton waiting in the wings if the ersatz-Moore began to lose a step in the ring with Apollo Creed's grandson. As the most popular of popular movies, in terms of number of films, years in the theatres, and, that old reliable American yardstick, box office, James Bond epics are an ideal starting place for the cultural anthropologist attempting to ply his eccentric trade in the highly specialized, tinseled world of film studies. I have, therefore, chosen Bond movies as the *Ur-mythe* of this study, beginning the topical essays with a cultural analysis of Bond and tying into it the subsequent essays on *Star Wars*, *Jaws*, and *E. T..* In this way I hope to achieve a comprehensive treatment of that highly variegated and mercurial entity, American culture.

There remain two types of fantasy movie as I am loosely defining that genre: horror and animal movies. You will discover that horror movies, considering their prominence in popular culture, receive far less attention here than they deserve. I attempt only a broad assessment of some of their thematic properties in chapter 7, where I discuss the relationship between *E. T.* and another Spielberg film that features houseguests who are not quite so loveable as E. T.: *Poltergeist*. That movie is, admittedly, rather a special case, far removed from the slasher sleaze of Freddy Kruger (*Nightmare on Elm Street*, 1 to a zillion) and Michael Myers (*Halloween*, also 1 to a zillion), and it would be incorrect to make general statements about *the* horror film just on the basis of themes I might discern in *Poltergeist*. Horror movies demand extensive treatment, for they have become a fixture of modern culture (along with Stephen King's supergrosser novels that have served as the basis for several of these terrifying and grotesque films). The prominence of novels and movies like *The Shining*, *Firestarter*, *Pet Sematary*, *Carrie*, *It*, *Misery*, and all the other shrieker/slasher epics that pour from our publishing houses and movie studios should alert us to a disturbing yet fundamental aspect of that phenomenon, itself wholly mythic, we gloss as *America*: the insistence on finding, at the heart of domestic life, a dark, malevolent presence — the Death Force — always ready to assert itself and transform daily experience into a waking nightmare.[9]

Set in the everyday world, the horror movie introduces malignant super-natural forces, which often take human form and proceed to wreak havoc in the domestic and social spheres. The plot inevitably revolves around victims' attempts to escape, and perhaps destroy, the malignant being. If one discounts the many creature features and vampire movies of the fifties that still sustain late night television (discounts them for reasons I detail in discussing *Poltergeist* in chapter 7), the horror film in its modern form can be dated from Roman Polanski's 1968 box office sensation, *Rosemary's Baby*. Incubi and succubi of that macabre work soon spread through Hollywood, and spawned *The Exorcist*, *Omen* (1. . .n), *Halloween* (1. . .n), *Friday the Thirteenth* (1. . .n), *Nightmare on Elm Street* (1. . .n), and on and on into the dark night of the theatre and the tormented consciousness of Dreamtime America. Apart from their "shock value" (a glib, useless notion for any cultural analysis), what is to account for the phenomenal popularity and staying power of these grotesque and violent films? What is it about life as it is lived in America today that endows these movies with a timeliness and resonance that show no sign of abating? These are precisely the questions a cultural anthropologist must ask of the seemingly frivolous material of popular culture.

My own answers to these difficult questions are incorporated, in abbreviated form, in the section of chapter 7 that deals with what I regard as a critical paradox of modern popular film: how Steven Spielberg, probably the major cinematic genius of our time, could create within a brief two years and using basically the same settings, two movies as profoundly different as *E. T.* and *Poltergeist.* Either we credit Spielberg with a mind of impossible diversity, or we look beneath the surface of the movies to discover what the loveable E. T. has in common with the vengeful spirits of *Poltergeist.* In the process of comparing them, of doing a cultural analysis rather than merely running on about individual creativity and biography, something of the nature of American life will emerge that sustains and binds together, in a fashion itself macabre, the sentimentality of *E. T.* and the horror and revulsion of *Poltergeist.*

The genre of animal movies presents another kind of internal discontinuity, which undermines once again the easy assumption that popular movies, being superficial themselves, admit of only a superficial analysis. Like the jarring contrast between *E. T.* and *Poltergeist,* the large corpus of animal movies embraces diametrically opposed themes: the animal-friend and the animal-killer. Animal-friend movies eulogize animals and our relations with them; animal-killer movies depict animals as dangers to life and community that must be hunted down and destroyed.

This remarkable polarity in the representation of animals in popular movies must be interpreted in the context of our species' ancient ties with them. Since its beginnings (and actually well before), *Homo sapiens* has exercised its developing sapience by contemplating its ties to the somewhat similar, somewhat different animals in its environment. As I discuss in the following chapter, anthropology, that "science of humanity," imitated its subject by launching its own career with studies of the conceptual uses to which "primitive man" put his growing knowledge of animals. Those studies described representations of human-animal ties as examples of *totemism.* Much of the history of cultural anthropology can be read in what various theorists, from E. B. Tylor to Claude Lévi-Strauss, have had to say about this protean but critical concept. In this work I contend that popular culture carries on in the best "primitive" tradition by continually postulating and attempting to resolve the complexities of the human-animal relationship.

Our modern totemism, far from being a relic of the dead past, is a fundamental force in cultural processes now actively shaping our lives, for the simple reason that our relations with animals have undergone major changes during the past decades of (sub)urbanization. Farms have disappeared, and with them have gone the experiences and memories of growing up around an assortment of animals. A tandem process has been the diminution of the family, with children appearing later in the lives of a conjugal pair (itself an increasingly imaginative and problematic entity) and in numbers well below the replacement level of urban populations. Into this double void have stepped a wide array of animals or animal-like figures, principally, of course, pets (dogs and cats) which have effectively taken the place of children in many "families," but also including such diverse characters as Mickey Mouse, Donald Duck, Garfield the Cat, anonymous but valorized dolphins and whales, zoo creatures, and—my primary concern in what follows—the phenomenon of *Jaws*, the book/movies that alone have created a little universe of representations of animals that make our modern totemism as vital as any that inspired the myths of a bona fide, "primitive" society.

Animal movies of every variety, from animated cartoon fantasy to incredible adventures of real/reel-life characters, have flooded our theatres since Walt Disney produced his first Mickey Mouse drawings in 1927. Mickey Mouse, Donald Duck, Dumbo, and Bambi share the billing with a menagerie of naturalistic collies, cats, stallions, deer, falcons, and other even less plausible candidates for intelligence and altruism (but so far no paramecia). Either animated animal characters are invested with stereotypical human identities (*Dumbo*, *Bambi*, *Lady and the Tramp*), or actual flesh-and-blood animals are supplied with syrupy human voice-overs (*Milo and Otis*) and involved in plots (using that term loosely!) that reveal their own deep emotions and perceptions. With few exceptions, animal movies explore one of two opposed themes, friendship and hostility, or, framed in terms of the semiotic dimensions introduced in chapter 3, *kinship* and *ethnicity*. As ideal stereotypes (with the possible exception of a few very clever chimps, they can never speak for themselves), animals lend themselves to representations of our most basic feelings toward other people. And since we do not have to stand on ceremony with animals in quite the way we do with people—although the ground rules *there* are changing rapidly—we can invite pets into our homes and even beds while consigning their biological siblings and cousins to animal "shelters" and slaughterhouses. The symbolic fallout of these erratic behaviors is to be found in movies, where our complex and uncertain relations with other people are dramatically explored in terms of our relations with animals.

A very interesting thing about animal movies is that there is a sharp temporal break between the two types I have identified, with animal-friend movies predominating during what might be called the "Disney period" of 1927–1975 and animal-killer movies from 1975 onward. The year 1975 is critical in a study of animal movies, for it marks the release of *Jaws*. I have chosen to focus exclusively on *Jaws* (really, the *Jaws* quartet) in chapter 6 because the movie represents a fundamental change in the usual cinematic rendering of animals, a change that I think can be tied to important aspects of our cultural identity. *Jaws* in one mighty bite dispatched the dominant genre of animal-friend movies and ushered in a wave of horrific cinematic creatures. The happy view of animals presented for so long in the Disney movies has given ground to a far more somber view, and this transformation must be examined in detail.[10]

Why the sudden popularity of animal-killer movies in the seventies and eighties? Why did American audiences grow tired of weeping with Bambi when the cruel hunter shoots his mother and instead become aroused by the tension and blood lust of the hunt for the Great White Shark? Like my earlier questions about the popularity of *Star Wars* characters, James Bond, and E. T., this one demands an answer that will make some sense of the apparent nonsense of popular movies. This kind of problem is the acid test for cultural analysis. Either movies just come and go, driven by vague "market forces" or "fad," and fickle audiences choose according to their whimsy (which would vitiate any possible cultural analysis of popular film), or there is some connection between movies as cultural productions and the culture that produces them. *Jaws* is an ideal topic for sorting through this fundamental issue, since it represents a novel departure from earlier animal movies that has altered the course of popular cinema. In chapter 6, I attempt to identify the source and meaning of cinematic innovation in *Jaws* and to relate the movie(s) to a deep ambivalence that runs through American attitudes toward animals, an ambivalence that is the heart and soul of myth and its Dreamtime events.

In selecting this improbable collection for analysis — James Bond movies, *Star Wars*, *E. T.*, and *Jaws* — I have kept to a distinction that, if not very high-powered from the standpoint of film criticism, has proved useful in making anthropological sense of the cinematic domain of popular culture. That is the distinction between fantasy movies and people movies. Unlike the several genres of fantasy movies I have outlined, people movies do not happen in space or have an animal "star," and the people in people movies are not Bondesque caricatures of the folks down the block. They do not sprout fangs when the moon is full or tear the flesh from their faces in front of bathroom mirrors (a charming scene from *Poltergeist*). People movies are about people, who lead dramatized but recognizable lives and who behave for all the world as you and I might if we were only more like Robert Redford or Meryl Streep. Woody Allen's bitter comedies, the spate of "relevant" movies about women (*An Unmarried Woman*, *The Turning Point*, and even *The Color Purple*), Robert Altman's cinematic ethnographies (*Nashville*, *The Wedding*) are all people movies, and I therefore leave them and others like them out of consideration in what follows. For present purposes, with cultural anthropology just beginning to direct its ambitious analytical program at popular film, it seems important to examine movies that conform to fairly conventional notions of "myth."

An Anthropologist Goes to the Movies, Take 2

An anthropologist serving notice that he intends to write about movies must explain himself in a way that is seldom required of his colleagues who write about the exotic practices of small, distant societies. The contemporary nature of the material is perhaps not so suspect as its frivolity and commercialism. If we are prepared to abandon the image of the anthropologist as a student of living museum pieces, we are still apprehensive about his studying such lowbrow productions as James Bond movies, *Star Wars*, and *Jaws*. Decades after Edward Sapir's classic essay, "Culture: Genuine and Spurious," anthropologists still have not sorted out the most important distinction between the two sorts of culture. Obsessively open-minded where "primitive societies" are concerned, we still draw an invidious comparison between the "folklore" and "fakelore" of our own culture.[11] Consequently, the most suspect feature of popular movies is not their contemporaneity, or even their unseriousness (jokes have been a recognized topic in the social sciences since Freud's work on the subject), but rather their commercialism. Most academics, anthropologists as well as literary and film critics, are willing to forgive a cultural production anything as long as it does not show a profit. But if, like *The Spy Who Loved Me*, *Star Wars*, *Jaws*, and *E. T.*, it not only shows a profit but is a supergrosser, then it becomes a prime target for sniping by social critics of every persuasion.

Among anthropologists this curiously inverted elitism ("their" folkways are the real thing while "ours" are rubbish) seems to be a simple projection of our prejudices regarding the privileged nature of ethnographic research. In journeying to faraway places with strange-sounding names to do our "field work," we are caught in the curious position of claiming to be nothing like the contemptible tourists who dog our tracks while being, in fact, a kind of super-tourist. Disparaging those superficial hedonists we call "tourists" and only tolerating those slightly more refined types we dignify with the label "traveler," we wrap ourselves in a cloak of expertise that every force in the modern world is proceeding to unravel. Today the ethnographer, after years of exhausting graduate study and months of travel preparation, reaches his destination to find that Club Med is there ahead of him: the naked, dancing savages are not "natives," but young lawyers and secretaries from New York and Toronto there for a week of frenzied rutting and relationship-making. And while the ethnographer is beating the bushes for the Real People, many of their number, having forsaken the impoverished, dead-end villages he has come so far to visit, are themselves in New York, Toronto, and other cities working as immigrant labor and often trying to stay a step ahead of the immigration officer and deportation back to their picturesque homeland.

Even those "natives" who have remained at home take up the pastimes of their emigrant kin: *Dallas*, *Dynasty*, James Bond movies, *Star Wars*, and much of the rest of that global media flood that is American culture have washed over the most remote Peruvian villages, New Guinea river settlements, Amazonian forest camps, and other favorite ethnographic haunts. The Real People know about J. R. Ewing, Sue Ellen, James Bond, and Luke Skywalker, and they work those media personalities into their own habits and conceptions of life, often blending the new myths of Hollywood with the old tribal tales of equally fantastic goings-on and forming in the process a fascinating synthesis of media-myth that can only artificially be segregated into "intrusive" and "indigenous" elements. The American Dreamtime I explore in the following chapters has no clear-cut boundaries; it certainly does not stop at the territorial borders of the United States. The traditional role of ethnography, to provide detailed descriptions and analyses of far-flung societies must therefore be subordinated to the original grand design of anthropology as that "science of humanity" which encompasses all prehistory and all ethnographic variation and strives constantly to make out, through the swirling clouds of data and debate, the outlines of a general theory of culture.[12]

The following chapters represent a departure from mainstream cultural anthropology in another respect. Throughout the brief history of what is known variously as "symbolic anthropology," "cultural analysis," or "anthropological semiotics," practitioners of those esoteric approaches, as well as their detractors, have identified their subject matter with the immaterial, ideational side of things: the airy fairy end of the spectrum at the opposite pole from the solid, down-to-earth topics of politics and economics that lend themselves to empirical research. According to this stereotype, symbolic anthropologists study symbols, and symbols, as everyone knows, are those fluffy, figurative meanings tacked onto the meat-and-potatoes reality of social existence. Every argument and example in this work seeks to overturn that easy assumption and to expose it for the threadbare obfuscation it is. Myth and reality, symbol and substance are seductive but mistaken dichotomies that have, as a fixture of Western thought since the "Enlightenment," led the human sciences into paralyzing contradictions. An integrated approach that details the interworking of ideology and practice, of myth and act, is the only way out of the blind alley into which cultural anthropology has blundered, or been pushed.

The commercialism of popular movies and their deep roots in both the economy and ideology of American life are precisely what make them of critical interest to cultural anthropology. That the fantasy worlds of film are for sale and are consumed avidly by millions of movie-goers situates them at the juncture of idea and experience, of make-believe and everyday life, that is the core of American culture and therefore the problematic of its anthropological investigation. Movies and money are inseparable because movies are a principal cultural production of American society, and American society runs on money. A truly dispassionate observer of that society (perhaps a Martian anthropologist visiting the planet) would soon recognize the importance of money in American life and would devote much of his research to activities in which money flows like water. And movies, being big business, would doubtlessly merit his close attention.

The cultural anthropologist intent on studying modern American culture really cannot avoid going to the movies. Far from being an interesting sidelight on social reality, they are one of the main events. What Americans spend their money on (or allow their government to spend it on) is instructive and rather surprising. The major American industries throughout the eighties included, in addition to the predictable armaments and petrochemical multi-nationals, the complex of entertainment and tourism. And though it is only possible to estimate its revenues, a third industry that shares the pinnacle with these giants is the trafficking in drugs and illegal pharmaceuticals. The combined revenues of the legitimate tourism/entertainment sector and the illegitimate drug trade quite probably exceed those of the industrial complex. Hundreds of millions of people are ready to pay hundreds of billions of dollars for *images*: images of themselves taking their kids to Disneyland, basking in a tropical sun, dining in splendid restaurants, wearing elegant clothes, driving luxurious automobiles; images on film, on television, in print; images in their hallucinating minds. The Dreamtime temples that are our movie theatres do not disguise the real world; as William Stanner observed among the Australian aborigines the Dreamtime actively participates in and occupies the routine of daily life, whose imaginative nature we, unlike Stanner's Australians, struggle to conceal.

The very nature of commercialism and consumption in America puts the lie to both the capitalist ethic and Marxist theory. Even before the collapse of the Evil Empire, the average guy out there was concerned about much more than keeping the Russians out of his back yard, keeping his car gassed up so he could get to work, and keeping his family secure and comfortable. Besides what he has or thinks he should have, he wants and needs something else: vicarious experience, a whole kit of *virtual lives* among which he can move and within which he can experience adventure, excitement, sex, violence. . .the whole seamy, steamy package. And, just perhaps, as well as all this vicarious thrill-taking, he also wants, in those moments just before sleeping or just after waking, to know what it's all about. He wants a form of release *and* self-knowledge that aren't supplied by the two-week vacation or the once-a-week trip to church or therapist. When he looks for that total package, the most complete, engrossing, convincing, *theatrical* source readily at hand is. . . the movie. The theatre is a house of images, at once recreational and edifying, where, after lining up and paying, he is free to traverse the cinematic Dreamtime in search of a reality whose presence and outlines he already perceives.

Far from being an escapist retreat, the Dreamtime of the theatre is often a sobering and terrifying forum where the muted and partially concealed threats to existence we live with every day are given free expression. There is no better example of the inextricable tie between movie-myth and "real life" than the double meaning the name "Star Wars" acquired during the eighties. Luke Skywalker's quest for Jedi mastery of The Force and Ronald Reagan's striving for nuclear supremacy in space through the Strategic Defense Initiative both unfolded within a tableau of American culture that continually searches for and confronts representations of unthinkable possibilities, ranging from the ultimate horror of nuclear holocaust or some other form of ecocide through the mass slaughter and extinction of animal and plant species, and on to the obliteration of simple warmth and caring in human relations. Whether it is in real or reel life, we persist in letting the world scare us stiff. And with good reason.

In comparison with the stark, gripping images of struggle and destruction that pour from our popular movies, novels, songs, and TV shows, the interminable, woolly debates politicians conduct over which constricting, dehumanizing dogma is preferable exert a minuscule influence on public opinion. "Political reality" in the United States today is not to be discerned from close readings and discussions of the *Declaration of Independence*, the *Constitution*, the *Communist Manifesto*, the *Congressional Record*, or even *New York Times* editorials (Noam Chomsky's conspiracy theory notwithstanding). It is rather to be found in a hodgepodge of exceedingly soft, anecdotally cute "news" sources like *Time* and *Newsweek* magazines, of TV anchormen and women like Dan Rather, Connie Chung, Barbara Walters, and perky Katie Couric, of commentators and columnists like Rush Limbaugh and George Wills, and, last but not most, of the politicians themselves, congressmen and women and presidents whose effectiveness, and certainly whose continued presence in office, is a product of their own relative success as TV personalities and of their "spin doctors" who further manage the images their politician bosses generate. The line between myth and reality, stage and street, symbol and substance, Dreamtime and common sense is hopelessly tangled and blurred where the "political reality" of American life is concerned. To argue otherwise — and here is the crushing paradox for any form of "realism" — is to grasp at yet other mythic forms and ritual behaviors, to prop up hopelessly caricatured images (the "real American," the "patriot," the "national defense," and the "American family") as self-evident truths somehow present and directly perceptible in social life.

The dawning of the era of the supergrosser coincided remarkably with the rise to political power of an individual, Ronald Reagan, who is to date the best, and worst, example of the power of myth in American life. Himself a product of the then maturing movie industry, it is not surprising that Reagan seemed always to inhabit an America produced in Hollywood and to conduct his office as though from a director's chair. A lifelong resident of the Dreamtime, Reagan's career on both Hollywood and Washington stages attests to the impossibility of separating "symbolic" from "real" life. With Death Stars circling not only Tatooine but also the planet Earth, it becomes imperative that every thinking person take a long, deep look at the role myth plays in our lives. Anthropologists and others wary of committing themselves to the kind of uncompromising cultural analysis attempted in what follows cannot defend their professional preferences with that old cliche of "working in the real world," for that world, if it ever existed (and I am convinced that it did not) has, in the contemporary United States, drifted or been dragged, kicking and screaming, deep into the territory of the Dreamtime.

2

The Primacy of Myth

Banks and tariffs, the newspaper and caucus, methodism and uni-
tarianism, are flat and dull to dull people, but rest on the same
foundations of wonder as the town of Troy and the temple of Delphos, and
are as swiftly passing away. Our log-rolling, our stumps and their
politics, our fisheries, our Negroes and Indians, our boats, our re-
pudiations, the wrath of rogues and the pusillanimity of honest men, the
northern trade, the southern planting, the western clearing, Oregon and
Texas are yet unsung. Yet America is a poem in our eyes; its ample
geography dazzles the imagination, and it will not wait long for metres.
— Ralph Waldo Emerson, *Essays*

What Is Myth?

The premise of this work is that certain popular movies have a great deal in common with myths. Since anthropologists have developed analytical frameworks for studying the social relevance of myths told by their traditional ethnographic subjects — the "natives" — it follows that an anthropologist interested in the natives of America in the approaching twenty-first century can expect to find important clues to their culture in the movies they attend.

But if movies are myth, what is myth? No question is more crucial to this inquiry, and yet few questions are more intractable. Although anthropology and comparative religion have produced a great many studies of the subject, the extent of fundamental disagreement over the nature of myth, among scholars as well as the lay public, is remarkable. Part, but only part, of the problem arises from the fact that "myth," like notions of "kinship," "family," and "race," is an idea scholars have borrowed from ordinary language and forced to conform to their own specialized usages. Even in the wider public arena, however, the concept of myth is a deceptively simple notion that embraces contradictory meanings. Sorting out those discrepant everyday meanings and reconciling them with an anthropological understanding of myth is a large part of the project before us. As we proceed it will become apparent that a theory of myth and a theory of culture are inseparable, and may be basically identical.

The idea of "myth" is so deceptive because it is so commonplace; everyone uses the word in everyday contexts and has no trouble with its meaning. The term occurs repeatedly in newspaper articles, television news programs, and in casual speech: the myth of male superiority; the character of Santa Claus; "I know people who claim they've seen Bigfoot, but I still think he's just a myth." *Just a myth*—the phrase captures the popular mood wherever myth is invoked: it is a falsehood that may be quite harmless or terribly insidious in its deception, but that in either case should not be allowed to mask the good, old-fashioned pragmatic reality that every mother's son and father's daughter recognizes as the bedrock of existence.

The strongest challenge to this study of American mythology, and its strongest appeal, consists precisely in the tremendously schizoid, paradoxical, *ambivalent* attitudes toward myth that characterize the thinking of those mothers' sons and fathers' daughters. Americans cherish the image of themselves as a practical, down-to-earth people who, for that very reason, stand out in a world of older societies mired in complex social refinements and bizarre, otherworldly religious traditions. According to this collective self-image, we do not venerate royal lineages as our European cousins do.[1] Nor, again keeping to this self-image, do we sacrifice our lives for Allah or take a rice bowl and wander off into the woods to seek enlightenment. Yet there has never been a people so committed to projecting, on so massive and global a scale, an idealized, stereotypical, high-contrast image of themselves. I am not referring here specifically to movies or other forms of leisure, which might be expected to traffic in stereotype, but to the values that presumably figure in our daily lives, from the breakfast cereal and aerobic routine that start the day through everyday interactions with family, friends, and workmates, to the major events and decisions that punctuate and define our lives: marriage and divorce, childbirth and abortion, the purchase and sale of a home, getting and changing jobs.

At least since Tom Wolfe chronicled the appearance of the Me Generation, in a series of brilliant essays collected in *The Purple Decades* and *Mauve Gloves & Madmen, Clutter & Vine*, the lives of "ordinary" Americans have been anything but that: we do not simply *do* something, like get married, have a baby, buy a house, change jobs, or even choose new wallpaper; rather we *agonize* endlessly over the significance, the implications of what we do for *who we are*, for which character on the great silver screen of life we may find ourselves playing. Divorce lawyers, plastic surgeons, personal trainers, and family therapists, amid a growing swarm of other "facilitators," are always there to help us stir the tea leaves of our psyches in the vain hope of coming up with an answer to the most engaging question in America: "Who am I?" And, as Wolfe mercilessly observes, we tackle that question through what has become an almost religious quest in itself: the obsessive, insatiable plea, "Let's talk about *me*!"

America, a supremely mythic construct always rendered here within implicit inverted commas, is dedicated to the antithetical principles that its men and women are the equivalent of living, breathing cartoon characters, imbued with all the virtues of the founding fathers (mothers supposedly weren't big on founding in those days), *and* that these same walking gods and goddesses are good, sensible down-to-earth folk who believe in practicality above all else. The individual, archetypical "American" thus becomes an impossible collage of Rambo and Benjamin Franklin, Calamity Jane and the Little Woman.

While every grade school history book, magazine advertisement, TV commercial, and movie insinuates the *myth of America* into the consciousness, not just of United States citizens but of most persons alive on the planet today, the primary audiences of those mythic texts—Mom and Dad and Buddy and Sis, going about their daily routines in Wichita Falls, Memphis, Rapid City, and points north, east, south, and west—take them all in and somehow, through some amazing, magical transformation, turn them into the stuff of a down-to-earth, bread-and-butter, myth-denying, "real life"-embracing existence. Unable to live with the idea that myth is an active force in their lives and unable to do without its fantastic productions for more than a few minutes at a time, Americans lurch from pole to pole of the improbable symbolic/semiotic landscape they have created, now deriding the "unrealistic" qualities of myth, now reveling in them.

This profound ambivalence toward the role of myth in our lives is not, however, just an idiosyncratic trait of Americans. It is so prominent in the United States, once one begins to notice it, because American society, with its movies, TV, advertisements, and mountains of consumer goods projects a larger-than-life image onto the entire planet, fashioning an immense web of experiences and meanings that comprise a global culture of consumer capitalism. The absolutely fundamental point I want to make here is that the powerful ambivalence that haunts our thoughts and feelings about myth is a *general condition of human experience*, that the ambivalence, operating in a particular symbolic/semiotic framework described in the following pages, is the primary force that makes human culture what it is. While undertaking a cultural analysis of popular American movies here, I approach them as especially striking examples of mythic processes which I see operating at the deepest level of *all* societies, all human experience, and which constitute that flash-in-the-pan phenomenon we have come to call "humanity." According to this view, the enormous corpus of myths composed by the native peoples of the Americas, Asia, Africa, and Australia are substantially comparable with our James Bond movies, *Star Wars, Jaws, E. T.*, and the like. The obvious cross-cultural differences within this disparate global corpus, I would claim, have to do in large part with the highly varying situations the peoples of the world find themselves in vis-à-vis artifacts or machines, animal life, kin and ethnic groupings, and natural or man-made forces of creation and destruction, and *not* with inherent differences between "modern" and "native" thought.

If anything distinguishes "us" from "them" in these waning years of the twentieth century, it is our more pronounced and often desperate efforts to deny myth a place in our lives. Those doomed efforts contrast sharply with the willingness of native peoples, as documented repeatedly by anthropologists in the field, to view the Dreamtime world of myth and the everyday world of mundane affairs as inseparably linked, so that life unfolds, as William Stanner notes in the epigraph, not from one discrete historical moment to another, but within an *everywhen* of mythic/"real" events.

Questions of profound importance arise when we confront our pressing need to keep myth at bay. A fundamental point I seek to establish in this work is that the "everywhen" world of native peoples actually accords better with physical reality as represented in the mathematics of quantum mechanics, cosmology, and complexity theory than does the myth-denying "realism" so dominant in the American self-image. As I discuss in chapter 3, those scientific and mathematical theories describe a world of *virtuality* in which multiple possibilities of states of existence are simultaneously present, and in which "what happens next" is inherently unpredictable, undecidable, up for grabs. These powerful scientific theories of physical reality advance a "logical" picture of the world, in the sense of mathematical rigor and experimental confirmation of their bizarre findings, but it is *a logic of things that just happen.*

The both-feet-on-the-ground realism that dominates the American self-image—the myth of America—thus conflicts, in a stunning bit of irony, with the best models of physical reality modern science can provide. Those models describe, in the most elaborate and intimidating mathematical terms, a seemingly mystical world in which things can be in two places at once, travel backwards in time, and even pop into existence from nowhere. The implication I think can be drawn from this striking disparity between the "science" of American myth and that practiced by living, breathing scientists is that we harbor, at the base of our consciousness, a compelling, fearful need to believe that our cultural values and social institutions *make sense*, a need threatened by a vision of a world of stark contradictions and shifting, multiple realities. However disorganized and out of control our individual lives may become, we want to believe that these are inadvertent missteps, departures from a human existence solidly grounded on a foundation of good, true values. Hence the tremendous ambivalence toward "science" in American life: we hold it, or rather our mythical version of it, up as the embodiment of the sense and rationality we yearn for in daily life, and yet simultaneously reject it for the dark, unwelcome truths we fear it may hold.

The paradox, perhaps the definitive, crippling paradox of our age, is that we yearn for (and even proclaim as doctrine) a world of consistency and continuity, for a society *that is a certain way*, just at a period in history when technological change and population growth are utterly transforming the very basis of what it means to be human, and in the process ushering in a being, a "form of life" in Wittgenstein's phrase, as different from ourselves as we are different from our hominid ancestors of a million years ago. Humanity's tortuous movement toward that Something Else is the stuff of myth, as I propose myth's nature to be in these pages. That movement, however, is both tortuous *and* contested. Against the irreversible tide of change, and against the profound generativity of myth (which directs that change), we erect hopeless, hateful institutions to proclaim that life, after all, *is* a certain way, that things are unquestionably this rather than that, and that we should think and act accordingly or suffer the consequences. Our classrooms, law courts, and government offices are all variations of an institution that, following Foucault, has come to embody the spirit of our age: the prison. Yet despite the best efforts of our wardens to suppress the mercurial truths of myth, the intensity and persistence of our forbidden longing for the Dreamtime world of the movie theatre or of the simple momentary reverie bear witness to our desire to abandon the doomed effort to impose meaning and uniformity on an enigmatic and diverse humanity.

The Nature of Myth

In coming to terms with our ingrained ambivalence toward myth, it may be helpful here to chart some of the twists and turns our thinking takes on the subject as we simultaneously deny myth's place in our lives and cling to a rich mythic experience. Ambivalence, wanting to have it both ways, at once accepting and rejecting basic aspects of our lives: this is the powerful force, itself paradoxically both crippling and enabling, that we must comprehend.

The popular equation of myth and lie flies in the face of other, dictionary-sanctioned meanings of the term that influence the reception myth receives in daily life and complicate attempts to explain its cultural significance. For example, my *Random House Dictionary of the English Language, College Edition*, offers the following definitions:

1. a traditional or legendary story, usually concerned with deities or demigods and the creation of the world and its inhabitants.

2. a story or belief that attempts to express or explain a basic truth; an allegory or parable.

3. a belief or a subject of belief whose truth or reality is accepted uncritically.

4. such stories or beliefs collectively.

The internal contradictions are patent in this list. Definition 3 corresponds with popular usage (males are naturally superior, there is a Santa Claus, Bigfoot exists) in which the true complexities of a situation are glossed over by facile prejudice and stereotype. Definitions 1 and 2 reflect an earlier, classical understanding of myth that has been largely repudiated by modern American practicality and scientism: myths are attempts to grasp the fundamental problems of human existence by framing them in narrative. The two perspectives, placed side-by-side in definitions 2 and 3, are impossible to resolve: How can "a story or belief that attempts to express or explain a basic truth" be identified with a simple prejudice or stereotype "whose truth or reality is accepted uncritically"? Allegories, parables, and other narrative devices in myth function to call attention to difficulties in thought and action, and not to silence the inquiring mind at its source. A myth simply cannot be simultaneously a simple stereotype and an enigmatic statement of life's intellectual and moral dilemmas. Yet it is precisely on that note that my dictionary hopelessly concludes, with its definition 4 facilely conjuring an impossible semantic complex of "such stories or beliefs collectively." Going to the dictionary here solves nothing; the act merely confirms the pronounced ambiguity, and ambivalence, that surround the notion of myth in the modern world.[2]

Everything I have to say (or, rather, electronically text) in this work about the nature of modern culture and the mythic role of movies in American life is predicated on my belief that myth is a fundamental, generative force in human existence, that it operates as a set of signifying practices which actually bring humanity into existence and continually modify what we suppose to be an "elementary" human nature. This view, quite obviously, is directly opposed to the conventional assumption that myth is some variety of falsehood, and hence opposed to the kind of theoretical program that seeks to brush aside the "irrelevant" and "superficial" productions of mythic thought to discover the "hard core," "bedrock" layer of social reality underlying that frothy overburden.

I have come by this view by combining my more or less traditional anthropological work on "primitive" myth with several years' thinking and writing about popular movies as manifestations of an emergent global cultural system of consumer capitalism that can be called, for want of a better term, "American culture." In what follows, I hope to show that movies bring to the fore aspects of everyday life that are at once basic and fantastic, from making love to making war, from growing up to raising a family, from driving a car to watching a football game. The thread that connects these and countless other activities of daily life is the *cultural production*.[3] People do all these things within complex frameworks of understandings they have of their own and others' actions, and of artifactual processes — interacting with *made* things, sometimes to make other things, sometimes to accomplish an end in itself, sometimes to effect or influence an interaction with another person. A particular ensemble of their understandings and artifactual activities is an enacted piece of culture, a set of meanings or representations that may be called, taking some liberties with MacCannell's original idea, a "cultural production."

The endless list of cultural productions that make up social life would include such obviously "staged" events as movies, TV shows, rock concerts, football games, graduation ceremonies, and such highly constructed but seemingly unchoreographed activities as wearing a particular outfit of clothing, serving a particular set of dishes for a meal, driving a particular kind of car, performing a handshake, and gesturing to a friend. In focusing on several of these cultural productions in succeeding chapters, I hope to establish a single, crucial point: virtually every social action involves an effort to establish a meaningful and tolerably unambiguous relationship with others in a situation normally charged with considerable potential ambiguity, ambivalence, and conflict.

Cultural productions create a little piece of culture by saying or showing something about the individuals interacting and the world that frames their interaction. The task of analysis for any particular set of cultural productions is therefore to ascertain how specific representations of various human, animal, and machine identities are marshalled to create the effect of coherence in an intrinsically incoherent world. Put a little more starkly, the job before us is to make sense of actions, situations, states of being that are, at best, fraught with ambiguity or, more commonly, so polarized by conflicting principles that they simply do not make sense, do not resolve themselves into any consistent, rational pattern. Claiming that movies are myths and that myths are primary cultural productions opens the way to a line of thought that departs radically from whatever mainstreams have formed in the still young discipline of cultural anthropology. The main purpose of this work is to develop that line of thought and, in the process, attempt to extend the range of cultural analysis or anthropological semiotics as that analytical program strives to comprehend the nature of culture and humanity's probably all too brief role in it.

The Foundations of a Cultural Analysis of Myth

It is important to recognize from the outset, then, that my approach to the cultural analysis of myth does some violence to the assumptions about myth that dominate our commonsense. My approach also rejects that peculiar orthodoxy which renounces imagination and creativity—the axis mundi of the Dreamtime —in favor of a world, both unreal and decidedly unreel, made up of "facts" that can be pinned down, labeled, counted, and trotted through the ludicrous acrobatics of a naive positivism that has come to dominate the classrooms, law courts, and even research institutions of the world's most powerful nation states.

The concept of myth I want to promote here is an intriguing conjunction of the internally inconsistent commonsense view and a perspective that emphasizes the classical definition of myth as an expression of fundamental truths. As a commonsense notion, everyone knows what a myth is: a fantastic story, an account of a make-believe, fairy-tale world in which imaginary beings do impossible things. Myth, indeed, is just that. The last thing I want to do here is reduce the fantastic Dreamtime imagery of recent movie-myths to prosaic lessons on current events. But it is also a great deal more. The situations myth presents us with are not only improbable in the fantastic, cow-jumped-over-the-moon sense; they possess a cerebral and emotional improbability that is both profound and disturbing.

Myth's improbability is a species of the unthinkable, or just barely thinkable. Where did things come from before there were things? How could something originate from nothing? Where did people come from? From animals? If so, how did they become different from animals? How did animals and, more importantly, people come to be sexually differentiated? Were people once androgynous, somehow acquiring their sexual natures along the way? And if sexuality was a later acquisition, did only a very few people acquire it at first? And wouldn't it stand to reason that those first sexual beings were members of a single family? How did people pass from a seemingly unavoidable period of incest, during which there were very few first people and sexuality was a recent acquisition, to an established social order in which incest is an abomination? If people are different from animals, how did they acquire those attributes of humanity (language, fire, clothing, tools and weapons, rules of social behavior) that now distinguish them from the animals? And, having acquired all those talents and things, how do they interact with their own plastic and incomplete physiological organisms to produce human experience?

Far from being a silly little story, a fanciful embroidery on the durable fabric of social reality, a myth exposes the seams and flaws in what is actually the gossamer of strands holding people to other people and to the things in their lives. The story it narrates is often too profound, threatening, and embarrassing to make easy social chat. For example, Prometheus and Oedipus are two conventionally mythic figures (that is, cultural heroes now safely confined to musty tracts on "classical mythology") whose stories chronicle radical disruptions in the religious and moral order of society. Prometheus did not simply give people fire, like a helpful neighbor loaning a cup of sugar: he disobeyed a command of the gods and, as a consequence of his action, destroyed the harmony that had prevailed in the relationship between humanity and divinity. And Oedipus, through a remarkable series of coincidences that would strain the credulity of the most gullible sitcom audience, managed to murder his father, marry his mother, blight his city, and destroy a supernatural being in the course of an adventure story that, cast in another mode, could claim supergrosser billing on the downtown marquee rather than languish on Humanities 101 reading lists (provided, of course, that Oedipus have phenomenal pecs and an Austrian accent).

Myth attempts to answer questions people would rarely think, or dare to think, of asking. In making that attempt, one of its primary functions is to pose —through spoken narrative and the visual imagery of movies—alternative or *virtual worlds* in which experience departs radically from the everyday. Hence the odd conjunction of convention and innovation in the approach I propose that cultural analysis take to myth: myths *are* fantastic, bizarre stories, but they nevertheless pose fundamental questions about human existence. Whether Amerindian myths of clan origin, "classical" myths of antiquity, or modern movie-myths, all are simultaneously outlandish, crazy tales that nonetheless speak to essentials of the human condition. James Bond and Luke Skywalker, if not quite the tragic figures that Prometheus and Oedipus are, share with them and with Lodge Boy, Spring Boy, and other cultural heroes of Amerindian myth the ability to transport their audiences from a world of gritty little concerns to a Dreamtime *real-m* of fateful action and consuming emotion.

No one lives in Bond's or Skywalker's worlds, just as no one lived in those of Prometheus or Oedipus, but the Greek myths still find an audience (even if it is primarily reluctant and undergraduate) and the movie theatres of Dreamtime America still receive their hordes. Why? My answer, the central argument of this work, is that myths provide distillations of experiences which define humanity and which, because the virtual world of experience is forever changing (our Dreamtime is not that of classical antiquity), provide a glimpse into possible futures, into alternate realities unstably contained in everyday life and awaiting birth as flesh and blood (or, increasingly, as silicon and yttrium) constructions.

A cultural analysis of myth, whether movies or traditional oral narratives, must strive to be faithful to both disparate features of myth by retaining the sense of the bizarre myth projects while keeping to its utterly serious subject matter (humanity's uncertain place in a changing world).[4] In its efforts to keep both these avenues open, cultural analysis differs significantly from the varieties of materialist interpretation that inform both the popular (mis)understanding of myth and academic approaches to the subject in anthropology and other fields.

Describing movies as myth rests on an understanding of myth that owes a great deal to the works of Claude Lévi-Strauss. In the next section I examine a few of the major contributions Lévi-Strauss has made to the study of myth, limiting specific discussion to his early *Totemism* while drawing generally on the immense corpus of *The Savage Mind, Structural Anthropology* (I and II), *Mythologiques* (I - IV), *The Jealous Potter*, and *The Story of Lynx*. Any particular criticisms I have to make of his work should not obscure the great debt I owe this immensely impressive scholar. For the foundation of his argument is the central theme of this work: in understanding myth we understand what is truly human.

In his vast analysis of South and North American mythology, Lévi-Strauss reverses the practice of an earlier generation of anthropologists, who treated myth as a kind of frosting on the cake of their descriptive accounts of social organization and ritual. For those anthropologists, ranging from Franz Boas through A. R. Radcliffe-Brown, the myths told by a group of people could be conveniently listed in an appendix at the end of a monograph whose principal divisions were organized around such topics as kinship, ecology, political organization, and social structure.

In Lévi-Strauss's perspective myth has primacy, since it serves as the vehicle for a human intelligence that is continually assigning meaning to actions and events, including those that get categorized by anthropologists as somehow belonging to domains of "kinship," "religion," and the like. Rather than being an epiphenomenon, an embroidery on an existing sociocultural reality, mythic thought is in fact a precondition of that reality. A major paradox of culture is that a framework of conceptual relations, a set of possibilities for thought and action (what in chapter 3 I call a *semiospace)*, must be in place *before* a living being can have what we would be willing to call a human experience. In short, *culture precedes humanity*, wrapping the protocultural hominid in the enveloping folds of its topologically complex space. Myth does not validate experience; it makes it possible.

Broadly speaking, if one is uneasy with Lévi-Strauss's argument that myth constitutes the foundation of culture, then two alternative perspectives remain. One is to view myth as essentially reflective or repetitive: sociocultural reality is already constituted, people's lives already are what they are, and for the sake of rationalization or just to hear an amusing story we think up myths that will dress up our everyday lives. This dismissive, commonsense perspective on myth completely disregards the questions of where and how we acquired the conceptual framework necessary for articulating our experience, for conferring on particular thoughts and actions the dubious mantle of the "natural."

How, for example, do individuals acquire and formalize in language the idea that they belong to a particular "group" of people who possess the same qualities and substance as themselves? Where do they get this idea of "belonging"? Where do they get this idea of "group"? These are obviously the very sort of uncommon questions that common sense does not take up—that's why it's called "common sense." A cultural analysis informed by Lévi-Strauss's insight, however, regards these questions as imminently worth asking. And its response is that the concept of "group" is simply one of several key constructs that emerged during the very genesis of culture, semiospace, or whatever we choose to call it. But how did culture or semiospace, a unique and highly complex phenomenon, originate? The answer to *that* ponderous question is that it did not simply happen; somebody or Something had to think it up.

Because the circumstances of those somebody's or Something's lives are forever changing, in continual feedback with cultural forces already set in motion, their most basic understandings about what is involved in being *this* rather than *that*—a somebody rather than a Something—are subject to continual revision. Culture thus has to be continuously rethought; the conceptual parameters that define the system must accommodate new and ever more complex perturbations. Thinking and rethinking culture, folding and refolding, pushing and pulling the parameters of its semiospace is what myth is all about. It is therefore impossible for myth to be simply reflective or repetitive of human society, for prior to the creative intervention of a symbolization/conceptualization process there was no human presence to reflect or repeat.

The second, more sinister perspective that affords what I take to be an inadequate alternative to the kind of cultural analysis attempted here is to regard myth as a deliberate and oppressive distortion of a sociocultural order formed and maintained by independently acting economic or environmental processes. Myth is mystification, and needs to be denounced to prevent our analysis of culture being sidetracked from the true, hardcore, nitty gritty infrastructural nature of things. Churches, shopping malls, football games, fashion magazines and, not least, movies exist, not to mirror reality, but to distract us from what the generals, the corporate magnates, the Daddy Warbucks of this world are doing on the sly to keep us down.[5]

At its most charitable, the materialist critique of mythic thought reduces to the commonsense notion of myth as fanciful tale — a pleasant and perhaps reassuring diversion, but not to be taken seriously if we are searching for a scientific or social scientific "explanation" of human behavior. How God created man from the clay of a riverbank, how death and suffering originated with the original sin, how birds came to fly and the tiger got its stripes are all tales we have heard at some point in our lives, but not material most of us would bring up at a job interview or include in an answer to an exam question on human evolution or zoology

There are several difficulties with the *uncharitable* materialist perspective, which puts a hard edge on the fantasy element in myth by viewing myth as dangerous distortion or mystification. The main difficulty is the one that also undermines the reflectivist perspective: if sociocultural reality, now defined as economic or class conflict, exists prior to or independently of myth, then what has served as the vehicle or *device* for conceptualizing and communicating notions of *value*, of what the powerful possess and the powerless lack? Specifying the differences between powerful and powerless, superior and subordinate appears an easy task at first, but it becomes incredibly difficult if one looks for answers without first invoking (pre)established categories of a cultural (mythic) system.

Suppose that a nascent human culture already exists in which relationships of inequality are firmly established.[6] If I am one of the powerful, then by definition I have the ability to impose my will on the less powerful, to dispose of their time, resources, and physical selves as I desire. But what will I desire? Obviously, you might say, I will desire the best food, shelter, sex, and, depending on how Hobbesian you want to be, the suffering of others. But if I am to continue working my will on the powerless for any length of time, then they must also have access to most of these necessities of life. How, then, are my satisfactions as one of the powerful to be distinguished from those of the powerless? The obvious answer here must refer to quality and quantity: I will demand and receive abundant portions of the *best* food; I will live in *luxurious* surroundings; I will have the *most attractive* sexual partners; I will *amuse* myself at the expense and pain of others.

At this point an unresolvable inconsistency arises in the materialist account of cultural origin. How did you and I come by ideas about one food being *better* than another, about potential sexual partners being *attractive* or *unattractive*, about certain activities being *more amusing* than others? I may dine on filet mignon while you subsist on corn meal mush, but how have these equally edible substances acquired their relative merit or *value*? How do chemical substances —proteins and carbohydrates—somehow indicate or signal that the ingester of one is superior to the ingester of the other? Discriminating physical objects and actions on the basis of quality depends on the prior existence of a standard of values, a sociocultural yardstick. And where or how did this standard, this yardstick originate? Surely *not* as an automatic response to some hypothetical set of "natural" economic activities — "relations of production" — for social differentiation on such a basis would depend on you and I already having a shared understanding of what is worth more and what less, of what is desirable and undesirable.

The desirability of a food, of a person, of a dwelling is not simply given in the nature of things, not just sitting there waiting to be fitted into a system of social relations based on economic activities. Nor does desirability follow from a convenient principle like the "law" of supply and demand. If that were true, then, as Marshall Sahlins notes in *Culture and Practical Reason*, we would "naturally" value the scarce organs of a food animal—its heart, kidney, tongue, brains, and liver—over its more abundant steaks and roasts. The fundamental point is that desirability is the *effect*, and not the cause, of a *system of understandings* about the nature of human existence and the entities — plants, animals, machines, and inanimate objects—that figure in that existence. That system of understandings is *culture* (or, as we may come to know it, *semio-space*). Before a materialist approach to myth can hope to produce meaningful statements, therefore, it must first identify the elements of culture and the order or disorder, the configuration and dynamics, of their arrangement.

It is precisely at this point that myth reasserts its primacy, for the organization of culture, the system of meanings that are central to a notion of human identity, is the problematic of myth. Why there are powerful and powerless, why one food is inherently better than another, how beauty and ugliness came to be — all these questions are the stuff of myth. The Lévi-Straussian perspective on myth as the primary vehicle of cultural experience thus overturns materialist perspectives that would dispense with myth as a distorting, mystifying force in society.

Approaching popular movies as myths in the Lévi-Straussian sense means that they can neither be dismissed as redundant nor denounced as mystification. Movies have to be examined in a direct, empirical, anthropological fashion that pays close attention to their concrete detail and that identifies the positions those details have within an encompassing cultural system. My argument is that the popularity of movies like *Star Wars* and *E. T.* is due to their peculiar resonance with fundamental questions about human existence in the late twentieth century, questions that can only be formulated within the framework of a cultural system articulated by the conceptual device of myth. Materialist approaches would pull that cultural system out of a hat, claiming (half-heartedly) that the most powerful human sentiments—whom we love and want to be with versus whom we loath and want no part of; what we cherish seemingly as much as life itself (the most coveted *objects* in our lives) versus what we find hideous and detestable—either just happen "naturally" or, nonsensically, derive from economic activities which are themselves predicated on those very sentiments.

Movies and myths are alike in another respect: both are partially independent of their creators and audiences. Once shown or told they acquire a life of their own, a kind of semiotic inertia, and break free from the constraint of being precisely, definitively understood or interpreted by either the narrator or the viewer/listener. Note that this independence allows directors, actors, and audiences to assign a variety of (often contradictory) meanings to a particular movie, or, in the case of many moviegoers, no meaning at all: try asking a seventeen-year-old exiting from *Rambo* or *Predator* about the movie's cultural significance and see what incisive commentary you will receive! Most people, including our seventeen-year-old, don't come out of a movie theatre prepared to take an exam on it (for a few, though, that will come later, when the baby lit-crits file into their Contemporary Film classes).

What is imparted in the Dreamtime temples of our movie theatres is a kind of *implicit understanding* of aspects of life rarely, if ever, discussed around the family dinner table or in the classroom. In this movies are like myths as well, for the primary audience of myth-telling, at least in some South American Indian villages, is a large, extended family household of adults and children who are drifting in and out of sleep in their hammocks late at night while some old insomniac sits by the central fire, stirring its embers and rambling on about the doings of the creator-god Makunaima and how people sprung from the seeds of the silk-cotton tree. Like these native Americans, many of us learned the stories of Humpty Dumpty, The Little Old Woman Who Lived in a Shoe, Mickey Mouse, Bugs Bunny, and Bambi when we were very young, uncritical, and completely uninterested in whether they "reflected" or "distorted" reality.

The really distressing aspect of perspectives that view myth as escapism, banal reflection, or distortion is the lackluster quality they impart to our existence, for all such perspectives basically deny that human life is meaningfully linked with the fantastic imagery of recent movies, that all their imagination and creativity do not touch our own inexorably drab lives. I reject that view in favor of one that marries elemental dilemmas of existence to the fantastic and powerful imagery of popular movies. The hundreds of millions of people who have turned out to see Luke and Princess Leia defeat the Empire, Bond take on megalomaniac scientists, Chief Brody hunt the Great White Shark, Admiral Kirk command the *Enterprise* on its ultimate adventure (or its *next* ultimate adventure?), and other modern epics are not just buying a few hours of diversion and rotting their minds on trivia. Through all the popcorn crunching, drink slurping, flesh kneading, and idle chatter that goes on in the theatre, enough of the singular drama of popular movies penetrates to warrant serious consideration by students of culture.

A Semiotic Approach to Modern Culture: *Myth Today, Totemism Today*

An anthropological approach to popular movies that seeks to explain their content, and not merely to explain it away, has to proceed by identifying the constituent elements or themes of the movies and the relationships that bind elements together in some kind of framework or system. This, loosely described, is the Lévi-Straussian perspective I have contrasted with other, less helpful approaches that anthropologists and others have taken toward the phenomenon of myth.[8]

Rather than increase the murkiness the notion of structuralism has acquired since its introduction to social thought in the fifties, I prefer to identify the approach I take to popular movies here simply as a piece of cultural analysis, or anthropological semiotics: the search for patterns of meaning in cultural productions. Movies either mean nothing or they mean something in relation to their cultural milieu, and the task of discovering what, if anything, they mean falls to cultural analysis or anthropological semiotics.

Following Ferdinand de Saussure, Charles Peirce, Thomas Sebeok, and Umberto Eco, among others, I study movies' cultural significance semiologically or semiotically. As envisaged and practiced by these theorists, semiotics is the *science of signs*. Popular movies considered as a system of signs thus fall under the rubric of the semiotics of modern cultural productions. A comprehensive semiotics of modern culture would include analyses of such prominent forms as food and clothing preferences, work habits and values, as well as the whole gamut of institutions we loosely describe as "leisure activities": sports, musical concerts, pulp literature, television, tourism, and, of course, movies. I am thus concerned with only a small part of the total field of cultural phenomena, but I would maintain that the system of signs identified in movies is generic to American culture as a whole.

Reasoning from the particular to the general is characteristic of earlier semioticians whose work I would like to discuss in framing this topic of the semiotics of modern culture. I am thinking here of Claude Lévi-Strauss and

Roland Barthes, both of whom have combined topical monographs with the most elevated theory. In 1957 Barthes published *Mythologies*, a collection of brief, incisive essays on aspects of popular culture in France at the time ("La nouvelle Citroen," "Strip-tease," "L'homme jet," and fifty others). *Mythologies* concludes with a long theoretical essay that has become a milestone of contemporary semiotic theory: "*Le mythe, aujourd'hui*" ("Myth Today"). Five years later, in 1962, Lévi-Strauss published *Le totemisme aujourd'hui* ("Totemism Today"), a brief but incredibly powerful theoretical work that set the stage for his later treatise on the nature of indigenous thought, *The Savage Mind*, and the monumental four-volume series, *Mythologiques*. While Barthes was a literary critic writing about popular culture and Lévi-Strauss an anthropologist writing about American Indians, Australian aborigines, and the like, the complementarity of their work is suggested by the intriguing similarity of their titles and themes: "Myth Today" and "Totemism Today."

Barthes's analysis of popular culture was inspired by his reading the work of the founder of modern descriptive linguistics, Ferdinand de Saussure, who visualized "a general science of signs," or *semiology*: "a science that studies the life of signs within society."[9] As a literary critic Barthes was primarily concerned with systems of meaning in language, but Saussure's call for a *general* science of signs led him to apply essentially literary critical tools to the analysis of nonlinguistic material items and actions like cars, drinks, meals, strikes, and vacations. Consequently, the exciting methodological program that emerges in *Myth Today* is to treat diverse aspects of modern culture as conceptual representations approachable in much the way that a literary critic would proceed to interpret a *text*. Saussure's call for a science of signs thus elicited from Barthes a wide-ranging study of cultural productions, all of which he identified as "myth."

Totemism represents an analogous expansion of intellectual boundaries. In that essay, Lévi-Strauss's first goal is to invalidate the assumption held by anthropologists from Sir James Frazer through Bronislaw Malinowski and A. R. Radcliffe-Brown that "totemism" represents a distinct type and stage of religious thought. Prior to Lévi-Strauss's work, the accepted interpretation of "totemism" was that it consisted of a circumscribed set of beliefs and practices of particularly "primitive" (or technologically simple) peoples, based on the idea that animals were the ancestors of humans: if groups of American Indians or Australian aborigines identified themselves as "Bear" and "Eagle," or "Kangaroo" and "Emu," it was because they believed that those species were actual genealogical forebears of their social groups. Thus according to this interpretation, societies whose members called themselves after animal species and observed food taboos related to their emblematic animal were *totemic*, whereas societies in which these practices did not occur possessed a fundamentally different, nontotemic belief system.

Lévi-Strauss exploded this narrow definition of totemism by pointing out that the particular phenomenon of naming human groups after animals is simply one aspect of the universal human faculty of *classificatory thought*. Totemism is not a separate religion of very primitive societies; it is rather one means of expressing, in the concrete terms of daily experience, conceptual relations that other, technologically complex peoples also employ in giving meaning to their lives. Classifying social groups according to perceived divisions in the animal world—bears and eagles, kangaroos and emus—is one manifestation among many of the general human disposition to classify everything, to pick out features of things and people that put them in separate categories and that invest them with distinct identities. "Totemic" thought thus becomes the springboard for Lévi-Strauss's searching inquiries into the underlying structure of the human mind and culture.

If Barthes maintains that myth exists in the modern world, taking the form of popular culture, and Lévi-Strauss argues that "traditional" myths about people descending from animals simply represent one aspect of the human mind's proclivity for classificatory thought, then it would seem possible to marry the two studies of "myth" and arrive at a very useful framework for an anthropological semiotics of myth in modern culture. Aborigines living in the Australian bush have myths connecting them to animals, but then so do contemporary urban dwellers who leave their apartments (after saying "goodbye" to their pets) to take elevators down to subterranean garages where their Mustangs, Falcons, Jaguars, and Hornets are waiting, like *kachina* figures in a Hopi *kiva*, to envelop them in metallic clouds of totemic imagery and carry them away. Unfortunately, however, Barthes's and Lévi-Strauss's ideas do not mesh quite so nicely, for each arrives at conclusions that seem to undermine the other's.

My view is that the similarities between "Myth Today" and *Totemism* need to be emphasized, even when their authors would disagree, for a synthesis of the two provides a foundation for a comprehensive semiotics of modern culture as visualized in the present work. In this spirit of rapprochement, I would agree wholeheartedly with Barthes that myth plays an active role in modern societies (if you can find it thriving among rational Parisians, you can find it anywhere), and is not just some outmoded relic of cultural expression that "primitives" have and we do not. And I would also endorse Lévi-Strauss's view that myth represents a fundamental constituent of human thought, that it is not just an isolated, exotic oddity. The mythic qualities I ascribe to popular movies in these pages possess a Barthesian modernity and a Lévi-Straussian profundity. Before elaborating on those qualities, however, it is necessary to attend to some problems raised by coupling the approaches of Barthes and Lévi-Strauss in this apparently straightforward way. These problems will have a familiar look, for, despite the fact that both thinkers focus on ideational systems in myth, Barthes's approach incorporates the flaws of the materialist perspective discussed earlier.[10]

In what strikes me as an exceedingly peculiar transposition of Saussure's key ideas, Barthes argues that myth is like language in that it consists of signifier and signified, but differs from language in that myth is built upon it in a superficial, parasitic fashion. Myth is, in fact, stolen or misappropriated language: ". . .myth is always a theft of language" (*Mythologies*, 217).

> It can be seen that in myth there are two semiological systems, one of which is staggered in relation to the other: a linguistic system, the language (or the modes of representation which are assimilated to it), which I shall call the *language-object*, because it is the language which myth gets hold of in order to build its own system; and myth itself, which I shall call *metalanguage*, because it is a second language, *in which* one speaks about the first. When he reflects on a metalanguage, the semiologist no longer needs to ask himself questions about the composition of the language-object, he no longer has to take into account the details of the linguistic schema; he will only need to know its total term, or global sign, and only inasmuch as this term lends itself to myth. (*Mythologies*, 115, emphasis in original)

This argument is seriously flawed. Its acceptance would contradict the premise on which Barthes's, or any other, semiotic is based: relations of meaning in language are not part of a naturalistic order of things, but the result of the same cultural processes that generate myth. There is nothing intrinsic in the rush of air over tongue and teeth to form the sound "tree" that indicates "that thing in the yard with apples growing on it." Nor are there intrinsic levels of meaning to a word, so that "the thing with apples on it" and the "Tree of Life" in Genesis stand in a primary:secondary, language:metalanguage relationship. To claim that myth is a secondary semiological system which uses language as its raw material (its signified) implies that everyday speech, which now becomes a primary semiological process, somehow conveys meaning in the absence of or prior to a *cultural system* of values, identities, behaviors. Barthes's "language-object" becomes a device for naming objects, independent of cultural determinations those objects may have acquired as elements in long-standing human (and protohuman) interaction systems. "Myth Today" makes out myth and language to be sequential processes, so that the world is first somehow endowed with named things (through language) and then those named things acquire cultural associations (through myth). It is both ironic and distressing that this classic essay should insist on distinguishing myth and language in this fashion, for its effect is to separate the significative content of any utterance into two categories and to make one of those categories—the linguistic—impervious to cultural or semiotic analysis. It is as if to say that we first acquire language through a natural process of establishing utterance-concept pairs and only later proceed with the cultural process of orienting things in the (named) world within a framework of meaning.

The problem with Barthes's distinction between myth and language is best illustrated with one of his own examples, for a critical examination reveals the impossibility of scraping away the mythic overburden of an image to reveal its simple, descriptive denotata.

> And here is now another example. I am at the barber's, and a copy of *Paris-Match* is offered to me. On the cover, a young Negro in a French uniform is saluting, with his eyes uplifted, probably fixed on a fold of the tricolor. All this is the *meaning* of the picture. But, whether naively or not, I see very well what it signifies to me: that France is a great Empire, that all her sons, without any colour discrimination, faithfully serve under her flag, and that there is no better answer to the detractors of an alleged colonialism than the zeal shown by this Negro in serving his so-called oppressors. I am therefore again faced with a greater semiological system: there is a signifier, itself already formed with a previous system (*a black soldier is giving the French salute*); there is a signified (it is here a purposeful mixture of Frenchness and militariness); finally, there is a presence of the signified through the signifier. (117, emphasis in original)

Barthes perceives distinct levels of meaning in the magazine photograph. A black soldier giving the French military salute is for him the reduced core of the image, its denotative message, which serves as the signifier in a separate, mythic expression. That metalinguistic, mythic message consists of intertwined ideas of French imperial might and the brotherhood of Frenchmen.

But in what sense are the "youth" and "blackness" of the soldier, or the "Frenchness" of his uniform elementary, naturalistic constituents of meaning? I would argue that they are no less complex than the notions of empire and racial harmony which are supposedly based on them. All these concepts (age, gender, race, occupation, nationality) are *categories of identity*, instances of the representational process of classificatory thought as elucidated by Lévi-Strauss. The meaning those categories take in particular situations is always complex, shifting, and charged with emotion; it is definitely *not* an automatic response, like reciting the alphabet, that Barthes maintains it to be. Categories of identity contain densely packed symbolic associations that can only artificially, and uselessly, be dissected into "primary" and "secondary" elements. What Barthes assumes are "givens" in the photograph are, for the cultural anthropologist, the very material that calls for interpretation.

For example, there is certainly nothing denotative or given about the "blackness" or "Negro-ness" of the individual in the photograph, as anthropologists who have worked in racially heterogeneous societies have repeatedly demonstrated. Physical features and skin coloration that may indicate an ethnic identity of "*negre*" or "*noir*" to a Caucasian Parisian academic may be interpreted quite differently by a person "of color" from a society in which fine gradations of hair texture and skin coloration make the difference between an individual's having one ethnic identity rather than another. If a Martiniquais had been seated next to Barthes in that barbershop, for instance, and glanced at the same photo, he may well have seen an individual with skin color significantly lighter than his own, whom he would automatically categorize as a member of a different ethnic group.[11]

Nor is the "Frenchness" of the soldier's uniform self-evident. Barthes and his immediate audience can easily "read" that message into the image because of its familiarity, but someone from another country taking up a copy of *Mythologies* thirty or forty years after its publication might well form an extremely vague notion of that picture in *Paris-Match* which Barthes found at his barber's (and which, unfortunately, he did not reproduce in "Myth Today"). As for the "age" of the soldier—that topic is at least as contestible and agonizing as "race" for an American audience steeped in the advertising hype and social pressure of a youth-obsessed culture whose fitness instructors, diet counselors and plastic surgeons dedicate their careers to thwarting the processes of physical maturation and aging. Show the *Paris-Match* photo to a Beverly Hills High School senior who has just recovered from his rhinoplasty procedure in time for the class photos and prom (but don't expect to find him in a barbershop!), and compare his critical impressions of the soldier's appearance with Barthes's easy attribution of "youthfulness" to the individual in the photo.

The point of these examples is to illustrate how exceedingly difficult it is to interpret the signs or symbols that figure in the cultural meanings (and that is the only sort of "meaning" we know) that flow from even the simplest social action, such as glancing at a magazine cover while waiting for a haircut. Any attempt to parse the instantaneous flood of impressions that accompany that glance into "primary" and "secondary" or "linguistic" and "metalinguistic" meanings seriously distorts the very phenomenon under study. The only way to obtain some kind of reasonably value-free physical data in the present example of the photo would be to compile photocell readings of skin reflectivity and measurements of all kinds of indices of body structure (distance between the eyes, ratio of forearm to upper arm, etc.). Those measurements would, of course, contribute nothing to the task before anthropological semiotics in this case, which is to identify the synthesis of perceptual and conceptual cues involved in glancing at the photo and then to describe how that synthesis, the *meaning* of the photo, affects an individual's thoughts and actions in a wider social context. In short, the only way to salvage something of Barthes's argument here is to conscript him, or his writings, as ethnographic subject: the savant becomes the native.

Barthes's efforts to draw the mythic elements of popular culture into Saussure's semiology thus risk subverting its principles by erecting a specious distinction between language and myth. Language would become an inanimate object on which myth acts but which itself carries none of the symbolic associations of myth. Correspondingly, myth would become a distant, nonparticipating commentary (a metalanguage) on the semantic processes of language. Construed in this way, it is difficult to see why and how myth would have originated at all. What impetus would have driven speakers of a value-neutral and representationally correct language, one that they could use perfectly well to describe what was going on in the world (young Negro soldiers saluting French flags and so on), to subject themselves to the parasitism of myth? My answer to this rhetorical question, developed in the following section, would not have pleased Barthes: I want to claim that Barthes has got things turned around, that the meaning inherent in language derives from the Dreamtime of myth, and that, if any prioritizing were to be done, then myth would become the "primary" and language the "secondary" process.

In *Totemism* Lévi-Strauss launches anthropological semiotics and sets it on a very different course from Barthes's literary semiotics. The most critical difference for present purposes is that Lévi-Strauss does not introduce notions of primary and secondary processes to account for the relation of myth to experience, as Barthes does in relating myth and language. "Totemic" thought properly understood does not relate a particular animal species to a particular human group; it establishes a *system of differences* that provides a framework for conceptual representations of animals and humans, their natures and behaviors, and the myriad of associations, similarities, and differences between them. The animal species is not simply out there, in the real world, waiting to become the totemic emblem of a pre-existing human group, for it is only by reflecting on perceived differences among animals, by using these essentially as the "raw material" of thought, that humans (whose "humanity" is a rather dubious status at this juncture) are led to formulate distinctions among themselves.

> The animals in totemism cease to be solely or principally creatures which are feared, admired, or envied: their perceptible reality permits the embodiment of ideas and relations conceived by speculative thought on the basis of empirical observations. We can understand, too, that natural species are chosen not because they are "good to eat" but because they are "good to think." (89)

The fundamental, definitive nature of human thought (and cultural origin) involves two interlinked, simultaneous processes: (1) investing animals, including here their appearance, habits, behaviors, and interaction with their environment, with a set of orderly, discontinuous properties; and (2) using those properties to establish the characteristics and conceptual boundaries or identities of human groups. The importance of these interlinked processes cannot be overemphasized, for in producing a conceptual order of Nature in the first instance, the users of symbols (who have been "human" through some, but not all, of this period of processual interplay) also created in the second instance a self-conscious realization of themselves, and thus produced Culture, produced themselves as sentient, human subjects.

It is crucial to recognize how radically this analysis of totemism differs from Barthes's approach to myth. In assigning myth the status of a metalanguage, Barthes denies its direct effects on the basic structure of the world around us: myth is essentially reactive and reactionary, a seductive and deceitful cover-up, a bit of "stolen language" appropriated by the powers-that-be in bourgeois society. While keeping his intellectual Marxist credentials in good order, and thereby keeping favor with Parisian cafe society, Barthes frustrates the principal goal of semiology or semiotics, which is to explain how a conceptual system works and not just explain it away. In sharp contrast, Lévi-Strauss's project of dissolving "totemism" as an isolated, exotic phenomenon culminates in an understanding of myth as the concrete embodiment of the human spirit.

> The alleged totemism pertains to the understanding, and the demands to which it responds and the way in which it tries to meet them are primarily of an intellectual kind. In this sense, there is nothing archaic or remote about it. Its image is projected, not received; it does not derive its substance from without. If the illusion contains a particle of truth, this is not outside us but within us. (104)

Curiously, although Lévi-Strauss asserts that "there is nothing archaic or remote" about totemic processes of symbolization, he has consistently denied that his structural analysis of myth has any direct application to modern cultural productions. This is the one fly in the ointment in drawing on Lévi-Strauss's work to usher in my cultural analysis of movies, for despite his soaring statements about the universality of totemic thought, Lévi-Strauss would probably decline to pull in the same harness as James Bond and Luke Skywalker (not to mention the Ewoks!). I must confess I have never followed his reasoning on this issue, and it would serve little purpose to go over it here. The great shame, as I see it, is that if we were to take him at his word on this point, then the powerful procedures he has developed for the analysis of myth would be useless for all but the most arcane investigations of preliterate societies, the stereotypical "living museum pieces." And as those societies are increasingly "contaminated" by the outside world with its media-saturated, movie-infested civilization, the structural analysis of myth would find more and more doors closed to it. I propose to avoid that impasse by blithely ignoring Lévi-Strauss's sage demurral (fools rush in) and proceeding to use his insights into the nature of myth and human thought to extend an anthropological semiotics of modern culture.

Myth and Language

The whole question regarding the nature of myth has to do with the relation between thoughts and things, and with the little understood processes of symbolization/conceptualization that operate in what is, for the time being, the "human" mind/brain. One way to begin to unpack this pithy (or, for the sceptical, vacuous) statement is to consider the associations we conventionally make between the concept of myth and the institutions of language and narrative. Myth, we say automatically (and along with my dictionary), is a "story" or "narrative" that relates particular sorts of episode in a particular way. As such, it is framed in language, an instance of that greater, encompassing form and hence subject to all that can be said by linguists, philosophers, literary critics, even anthropologists, about the nature and principles of language.

During the years I spent devouring the works of Lévi-Strauss and writing some pieces of my own about South American myth, it never occurred to me to question that fundamental assumption. It was not until 1977, when I walked into a screening of *Star Wars* and, about the same time, of the James Bond epic *The Spy Who Loved Me* that a glimmer of doubt began to spread across the nicely tailored landscape (the grounds groomed at a couple of America's better institutions of higher learning) of my mind. In short, I began to question whether myth is actually *in* language and, after letting that gnaw at me for a while, whether language/culture/symbolization is quite such a cozy trio as cultural anthropologists like to suppose.

Consider my initial response to *Star Wars*, described in chapter 1. To me, the remarkable thing about the movie wasn't its transparent, cliched plot — not the story considered as text — but its gripping imagery, breakneck pace, and phenomenal array of quasi-human, quasi-mechanical, quasi-animal characters. *Star Wars*, as I came to think, is about *machines* as much as it is about people,[12] and about people's relationships in the face of a rapidly changing technological order of droids, tie-fighters, and Death Stars. After long reflection, it now seems to me that R2D2, C3PO, and the Death Star are not mere characters, but mythic entities in themselves: they are representations of identities or states of being that figure prominently in human experience, so prominently that they transform the grounds for any possible human experience.

In this new perspective, the figures of myth do not live solely by virtue of the operation of a collection of sentences woven into a "plot." The machines in *Star Wars* and in daily life are quite capable of interacting directly with humans and thus contributing to a course of meaningful action without benefit of script. The critical thing about the doings of Luke Skywalker, Princess Leia, Darth Vader,

R2D2, C3PO, and the rest is the elemental level of crisis—identity crisis—that lies right at or just beneath the surface of their actions: Will The Force or its Dark Side triumph? Will R2D2 survive? Will Luke discover the awful truth of his paternity?

I believe that the crises, or elemental dilemmas, represented in *Star Wars* are not primarily dependent on their place in a narrative structure because those crises, including our life-and-death encounters with machines, falling in and out of love, and coping with irreversible changes in our famil are at least as old, and very probably far older, than the narrative structures of contemporary languages. Long before *Homo sapiens* emerged in the course of hominid evolution—long before people were people; long before there were folks — intelligent, tool-making, social, symbol-using beings were employing their nascent technology, forming conjugal unions, living in the close proximity of particular individuals over considerable periods, in short, were organizing a society on the basis of cultural or protocultural (the hair really doesn't need splitting here) principles.

In its grossest recognizable form, fully developed human language dates back perhaps about 40,000 years; hominid artifact production extends at least fifty times as far, to australopithecine base camps with their simple pebble choppers. However dearly we treasure our linguistic heritage (and the academicians who write about myth and human nature treasure it more than most), the inescapable fact is that much of that heritage has come to us from a past that lacked any recognizable language. I would suggest that the evolution of language and the refinement of technology were inseparably linked in the hominid chain leading to *Homo sapiens*, that machines are as much at the origins of language as language use is the basis for the development of a technological society. There is no tenable question of priority: both language and tool use are basic constituents of the symbolization/conceptualization processes that comprise the human mind/brain.

If this argument seems rather implausible, I think that is because those of us who read and write a lot have simply not noticed, or have forgotten, how much our fellows do with things without embedding what they do in words. It takes going to a movie like *Star Wars*, immensely popular with folks who spend far more time waiting on tables, working on cars, and watching Monday night football than on reading and writing, to appreciate how easily language can be dealt out of the deck of myth.

A striking example of the habitual obliviousness scholars visit on such pursuits is a recent work by the linguist Philip Lieberman, *Uniquely Human*. Having followed my discussion in this section, you will not be astonished to learn that Lieberman, after sagely weighing the factors at work in human evolution, concludes that it is the faculty of language that makes us "uniquely human." Major changes in primate social organization (including patterns of mating and infant care), the morphological transformation of the primate body, and, most importantly for the present discussion, the dramatic emergence of an *artifactual intelligence* capable of fashioning and using tools according to a preconceived plan — all these landmarks of hominid evolution pale for Lieberman when compared with the advent of language. This is, I think, an instance of finding what one is looking for in a subject, and it is not at all unusual for this topic. The little community of liberal arts scholars tolerated by American society is rigorously self-selected for individuals good with words, who naturally put a (perhaps unwarranted) premium on their ability. We usually do not have much balance in discussions of the role language has played in human evolution, because cabinet makers, photographers, ranchers, mechanics, chefs, musicians, and a host of other, often highly intelligent, practitioners are rarely asked for their opinions. Mechanics don't write many books, and if they do those are manuals about how to use machines. In charity to Lieberman and other linguistically oriented scholars, then, we should perhaps not object too much if they write about language in the proprietary, wistful style of temple priests facing the barbarians at the gates (who arrive, not on horseback wielding swords, but on skateboards and plugged into their Walkmans and SuperNintendo sets).

The little heresy I find so attractive here, at a time when cultural anthropologists have about decided that culture is a text, and even that one sits down and writes culture, is that myth may not so much be in language as language is in myth. The symbolization/conceptualization processes we have come to regard as distinctively human and to link indissociably with the present structure of language had to come from somewhere, from some prior state of mental and artifactual activity among protocultural hominids struggling to organize their experience of a world itself in the process of fundamental transformations which they could only dimly perceive. The creation or generation of a symbolic/conceptual map, or holograph, of a world one simultaneously inhabits (what Thomas Sebeok, developing an idea of Alfred Schutz's and other phenomenologists, calls an *Umwelt*) is the fundamental project of culture. The processes of *cultural generativity* did not, and do not, derive solely or even primarily from language; they rather impel its use and change the nature of language along the way. It is those processes of cultural generativity, explored in detail in the following pages, that make up the Dreamtime.

The deeply rooted prejudice that myth is in language is tied to a confusion over the nature and history of narrative. That confusion is manifest in our easy equation of "narrative" with "story," and the two with a sentence-by-sentence spoken or, more often, written account of events (do you spend more time reading novels or listening to storytellers?). This narrow view of myth is the product of a few highly unusual centuries of human symbolization, during which a rich gestural-aural-visual semiotic complex of largely public myth-making was pared down to the impoverished arrangement of a solitary writer laboriously putting words on paper and having those words, after months or years of negotiation and production, being consumed by an anonymous reader. Without impugning the great creations of the literary imagination, it is necessary to point out that these have been made possible by a combination of short-lived social and technological circumstances, and by a crushing rejection of faculties of human understanding and expression that could not be accommodated by the new order of writing-printing-reading.

The crucial point here is that narration, as a fundamental activity of an emerging symbol-making and symbol-using being, long preceded writing and reading, and was probably responsible for the development of speaking. The conceptual origins of our notion of "narrative" may be traced to a Greco-Latin verbal complex in which "to narrate" refers to a "way of making known or becoming acquainted with." *Knowing*, and not "telling" or "speaking," is the primary meaning of that complex, which etymologically links the Latin *narrare*, *narus*, *gnarus*, and the Greek *gnosis* as closely related conceptualizations of how, as Sebeok might say, humans acquire their *Umwelt*.

Myth as a way of knowing or becoming acquainted with the elemental dilemmas of existence can only briefly and artificially be confined to linguistic systems of speech and writing. This is why the lengthy debate over what kind of language myth is (of whether, for example, it is a lot or a little like poetry) hopelessly obscures its nature. I believe there have been numerous modalities or theatres for myth in the long transition from protoculture to culture. These included those caves of Upper Paleolithic Europe (Altamira, Lascaux, and numerous others) in which recently evolved modern *Homo sapiens*—people who had just become people—combined an early speech with chant, song, gesture, dance, drawing, and painting in elaborate ritual forms dedicated to representing their experience of the world and of themselves (or, as Clifford Geertz has said, explaining themselves to themselves).

Throughout the long history of narrative in this sense of the term, vision and performance in the form of kinesthetic involvement, ritual display, and social interaction have been its principal characteristics. We should not be misled by the brief impoverishment of narrative represented by the ascendance of the writing-printing-reading complex, which paralleled exactly the origin of nations and the establishment of standing armies. Long before Gutenberg and presumably long after the widespread use of multimedia-capable personal computers, the impetus to a holistic narrative has prevailed and will prevail. Storytellers, like John Bennett, Charlie Lowe, Joe Hendricks, Charles Williams, and Lynette Bennett from the Arawak village of Kabakaburi in the Guyanese forest, who shared with me their profound understanding of narrative art, and countless others like them in Third World villages, rural communities, and urban neighborhoods around the world, demonstrate every day the preeminence of social interaction and performance in narrative. It is a fact intuitively grasped by the millions who line up to see Luke Skywalker, James Bond, and other superheroes undertake impossible feats in impossible worlds, and who thus fill to overflowing the temples of the Dreamtime.

The sounds, visual images, and almost tactile sensations of the movie overwhelm the sentence-by-sentence development of the plot and push to the forefront a set of mythic beings whose qualities the individual member of the audience grasps and wrestles with directly (again, largely without benefit of script). The droids and Darth Vader in *Star Wars*, Bond's endless supply of deadly gadgets, the animal-alien-friend-brother that is E. T., the great fish in *Jaws*, and other human, mechanical, animal, and somewhere-in-between supergrosser heroes are not merely characters fleshed (?!) out by a script; they are myths in themselves, embodied visions,[13] communicative forms that provoke immediate thought and feeling in their human audiences.

A myth, then, is not necessarily a story composed by someone else and told to you at some particular time; it is a kind of conceptual field, a mental vortex, that envelopes and attracts certain things, people, and actions at certain times (akin both to the *strange attractor* of chaos theory and to vectorial movements in the phase and Hilbert spaces of mathematical physics). A myth of that sort comes alive, not just when you sit down to consume a scripted tale, but whenever the things and people in your life take on, often in the blink of an eye, an uncommon significance that sets off a chain of thoughts, feelings, associations, and you find yourself transported to a *virtual* world that lacks the signposts and landmarks of daily life. It is, in short, one of the innumerable forays each of us takes into the Dreamtime during our lives.

You pass someone on the sidewalk and that person is not just another face, the 999th obstacle you have circumvented that day, but an attraction or hook — sexual, humorous, nostalgic, antagonistic — that grabs you, focuses your attention, and causes you to tie that fleeting encounter into a web of experiences, of personal stories, that are always with you, slotted away somewhere in the grey matter, and that make up who you are. Or, on another occasion, you are out driving and see a perfect, immaculate '57 Chevy convertible go by. If you are a certain age and, probably, gender (I can only speak personally here), watching that car go by is a completely different experience from the routine monitoring you do of the plastic blobs of the eighties and nineties that choke the road in a gridlock of pastel monotony. That '57 Chevy machine, like the R2D2 machine, has something special about it. It casts a spell, provokes a rush of thoughts and feelings, sets in motion little eddies of narrative—real/reel narrative—around it. In both these encounters you have come face-to-face (or face-to-grille) with genuinely mythic beings, who or which make little openings in the gates of the Dreamtime and allow you, probably for the most fleeting moment, to suspend yourself in the rich world of memories, associations, and longings that is always there, alongside you as you go about your daily round of immediate, get-the-job-done-and-get-on-with-it routines.

If people, machines, and events in the world can be myths in themselves, gates of the Dreamtime, it is clear that the whole nature of language and its relation to culture has to be rethought. The convenient fiction cultural anthropologists have employed up to now, according to which myth is in language and language is a model of culture (or at least a particularly important example of a cultural system), will no longer serve to describe a world in which symbolization/conceptualization processes link mind and object, word and thing, in a complex set of auditory, visual, and tactile experiences. Those experiences intersect and *tilt* our daily lives, bringing us in and out of synch with a Dreamtime world of virtuality which, as William Stanner reveals (see epigraph), the native people of Australia are perceptive enough to recognize even if we have almost lost that critical human faculty. We are capable of living in several worlds at once, of participating in multiple realities in which we can have the most detailed and intense virtual experiences, and, our final credential as mythic beings ourselves, of integrating those virtual experiences into daily lives lived in the walking-around-in world.

According to this perspective on myth, the mind/brain is not the linguistically determined instrument it has been held to be in much of anthropological theory. It is a *holographic engine*, a multidimensional network of measureless neural complexity in which an *Umwelt* is continuously under construction and rearrangement through the mixing of virtual experiences (which are themselves the stuff of myth). If reality/reelity is an exceedingly complex holograph, its "structure" is not that of Lévi-Strauss or Chomsky, not the encoded principles of language. Its "structure" is rather that of a tremendously complex and dynamic vectorial system, which has affinities with the astonishing, sentience-infused quantum world now being mapped by theoretical physicists and cosmologists, and with the "self-organized criticality" discovered in other natural and social systems (such as clouds, blood vessels, population distributions, and cotton prices) by Benoit Mandelbrot, Edward Lorenz, and others.[14]

3

A Theory of Culture as Semiospace

The mind is a very strange place.
— Gregory Mahnke, *Signs of the UnSelf*

Before and Beyond Language:
Cultural Anthropology, Quantum Mechanics, and Cosmology

The affinity between the cultural productions of human societies/minds and so-called natural systems such as subatomic particles, black holes, clouds, blood vessels, plants, and neural networks is the theoretical foundation of this work. It is a view I have come to after years of reflection, and from a very great conceptual distance. For anthropologists of a "symbolic" persuasion like myself, that is, those of us who spend much of our time studying myth and ritual rather than "realistic" topics like subsistence practices and kinship relations, generally try to avoid what we consider the shortcomings of a "scientific," positivist approach. Symbolic anthropologists tend to reject (rather vigorously!) suggestions that their esoteric craft has much in common with the natural and physical sciences, people presumably being so much more complicated and interesting than photons, weather systems, or (God forbid) *bugs* (such as ants). In the brief four or five decades that symbolic anthropology, which is really synonymous with "cultural anthropology" in this regard, may be said to have existed as a subdiscipline, its practitioners have tended to associate their work with that of linguists, literary critics, and philosophers. It is from this peculiar alliance of eccentrics (one of the better definitions of the field of anthropology is "the study of the exotic by the eccentric") that the doctrine or perspective of *interpretivism* was forged. The watchword of this orientation in cultural anthropology is the call for a "postmodern" anthropology that rejects a supposedly simplistic objective analysis of culture in favor of a literary notion of cultures as "texts" that are infinitely interpreted and reinterpreted by everyone under the sun, from the individuals directly involved (the "natives") to a theoretician in a university office thousands of miles and decades removed from the events shaping those individuals' lives.

Productive as this view has been (and I have done my own small part to foster it), I now believe that it actually impedes cultural analysis by drawing back, even turning away from the fundamental nature of culture (and its current host, humanity) as a creative, *generative* system that does far more than endlessly stir its ashes by interpreting and reinterpreting itself. As a generative system, culture *makes things*, and also *makes things happen*. Most importantly, those made things, from australopithecine pebble choppers and Acheulian hand axes to James Bond's lethal gadgets and Luke Skywalker's droids, are not inert objects that plop into our lives and, once arrived, just sit around until we are ready to pick them up and use them in some unthinking, routine task. Those objects — the machines in our lives — are interactive beings themselves, and in conjunction with our own activity focused on them they create a new presence and force in the world, what Gregory Bateson called an "ecology of mind." And when I say that culture "makes things happen," I refer to our most powerful sentiments and the acts, sometimes beautiful but too often horrible, they inspire. The heroic sacrifice of one's life to save another and the hateful taking of another's life because he embraced the wrong ideal or was the wrong color, are both unintelligible outside an encompassing framework of beliefs and values that is culture.[1]

If we reject the usual view that myth and cultural productions generally are somehow derived from language, that is, if we beg to differ with Philip Lieberman about what is "uniquely human," then where do we look for an appropriate framework for the daunting tasks of cultural analysis, for something that might begin to lend credence to my upstart suggestion that the human mind and its attendant cultural productions are a kind of holographic engine? Remarkably, a powerful theoretical framework that fuses sentient behavior and a spatiotemporal world of randomness, uncertainty, and multiple realities (the attributes I was ascribing to myth earlier) has existed for decades, since the mid-twenties to be precise, and flourishes on the same university campuses, a couple of buildings over or across the quad, where cultural anthropologists proclaim the ascendancy of postmodernism and the decline of a scientific worldview. I refer to quantum mechanics, or rather to that small and predigested portion of it I have managed to pick up without the requisite training or mathematical ability. The essential point here is that, despite its vastly different subject matter (subatomic particles versus human beings and their productions) and approach (rigorously mathematical versus anthropologists' prosaic ramblings), quantum mechanics appears to emphasize some of the very things I have been saying about the nature of myth and the symbolization processes of culture. A critical affinity is the phenomenon of *virtuality* and its corollary, the coexistence of very different, mutually exclusive arrangements of a system, what may be described by the terms *multiple realities* or *intersystems*.

These preliminary remarks about the spatiotemporal nature of myth and culture are not quite the place to engage the reader in the details of the correspondence I see among cultural analysis, quantum mechanics, and recent work in cosmology. For now I merely wish to make two general but, I think, highly telling points.

First, even my amateurish acquaintance with quantum mechanics, gained over a lifetime of being a kind of "science groupie" and reading lots of *Scientific American* articles and books written for the lay (meaning mathematically ignorant) public, has instilled in me a deep sense of awe (as close as I come, actually, to a religious sensibility) at the pervasive mystery of the physical world. Particles, or rather particle pairs, can just appear from nothing in a vacuum — the "oscillation of the void" — and then annihilate each other. A particle, through its wave function, can be in two places at once, perhaps light years apart. Particles separated, again perhaps by light years, can instantaneously affect each other if an intrusive measurement is made on one of them. Elementary particles such as quarks, gluons, mesons and the rest are not just out there, bouncing off one another in the time-honored tradition of those junior high school ping-pong models, but rather are surrounded by and interact with a menagerie of ghostly characters like *virtual quarks, virtual antiquarks, virtual gluons*, etc., so that what is actually observed of "the particle" is the woolly cloud of virtuality surrounding it. Of such nebulous stuff are the "building blocks" of matter composed! Francis Bacon, the late-sixteenth-century philosopher often credited with promulgating the modern scientific method, would not be happy with this turn of events.

Perhaps most appositely here, the simplest physical system, say a few particles confined within a magnetic field, exists between intrusive measurements as countless *virtual systems* — a "quantum linear superposition" of states — in which all the innumerable combinations of locations of individual particles are equally possible, equally real, existing in what some (but not all by any means) physicists describe as the particles' being "smeared" across space. These tantalizing, mysterious features of physical reality as described by quantum mechanics have prompted theoretical physicists and cosmologists most involved in this research to remark on the eerie, mystical nature of their subject. Fritjof Capra's *The Tao of Physics*, Paul Davies' search for *The Mind of God*, Stephen Hawking's description of an "anthropic universe" in *A Brief History of Time*, and Roger Penrose's lengthy discussion of "quantum magic and quantum mystery" in *The Emperor's New Mind* exemplify the keen awareness these prominent thinkers have of the intrinsic strangeness and complexity of physical reality.[2]

The second general point I would like to make about the proposed fit between quantum mechanics, cosmology, and cultural anthropology is that developing the analogy offers a way out of the language-centered theories of myth and culture that have dominated anthropological thought for so long. I find the image of the mind and culture as a holographic engine so appealing because it unites the world of human experience with the complex and dynamic, sentience-infused physical world of spacetime described by quantum mechanics and cosmology. Long before its recent retooling for a linguistic capability, the (for the time being) human mind/brain was "hardwired" to produce convincing, compelling experiences of a life lived in a web of interlinked spatial and temporal *dimensions*. Life is lived somewhere, and that somewhere is the thoroughly cognitized surround — Sebeok and Schutz's *Umwelt* again — of a social world. Because this world generated by the holographic engine of the mind is both infused with meaning *and* spatiotemporal, I would like to call it a *semiospace*. "Culture," as conceptualized in the present work, *is* semiospace, and since the former term has acquired some very weighty and unwelcome baggage during the brief century of anthropology's existence as a field of study, I would happily see it replaced by the latter, or, not to be too proprietary here, by *some* term that would capture the unique fusion of *meaningfulness*, *generativity*, and *dimensionality* that is the signature of human existence.[3] The Dreamtime world of virtual experience and multiple reality is a (very large) domain of semiospace, and as such is inherently dimensional. That domain's *semiotic dimensions* are composed of the opposing concepts that generate culture, as described in the following sections, rather than of the familiar physical opposites of up/down, right/left, earlier/later, etc.

Conceptualizing the mind/brain and its cultural productions as a tremendously intricate, self-generating holograph opens the way for a cultural analysis based on a notion of culture as a fundamentally spatial and dynamic system, again, as a *semiospace*. The notion that culture possesses a fundamentally spatial nature or *dimensionality* is a minor, regrettably neglected theme in anthropology. Over thirty years ago, however, the brilliant anthropologist Edmund Leach (who was originally trained as an engineer) proposed, in a work fittingly entitled *Rethinking Anthropology*, that his prominent colleagues stop typologizing ("butterfly collecting") and psychologizing indigenous societies and begin applying a mathematically-inspired structuralism to them.

> My problem is simple. How can a modern social anthropologist, with all the work of Malinowski and Radcliffe-Brown and their successors at his elbow, embark upon generalization with any hope of arriving at a satisfying conclusion? My answer is quite simple too; it is this: *By thinking of the organizational ideas that are present in any society as constituting a mathematical pattern. . . .*

I don't want to turn anthropology into a branch of mathematics, but I believe we can learn a lot by starting to think about society in a mathematical way.

Considered mathematically society is not an assemblage of things [i.e., not a butterfly collection] but an assemblage of variables. A good analogy would be with that branch of mathematics known as topology, which may crudely be described as the geometry of elastic rubber sheeting.

If I have a piece of rubber sheet and draw a series of lines on it to symbolize the functional interconnections of some set of social phenomena and I then start stretching the rubber about, I can change the manifest shape of my original geometrical figure out of all recognition and yet clearly there is a sense in which it is the *same* figure all the time. The constancy of pattern is not manifest as an objective empirical fact but it is there as a mathematical generalization. . . .

The trouble with Ptolemaic astronomy [with its endless typologies of cycles and epicycles] was not that it was wrong but that it was sterile — there could be no real development until Galileo was prepared to abandon the basic premiss that celestial bodies must of necessity move in perfect circles with the earth at the centre of the universe.

We anthropologists likewise must re-examine basic premises and realize that English language patterns of thought are not a necessary model for the whole of human society. (2–27, emphasis in original)

Oddly, after making this bold call for a mathematical-logical basis for anthropology, Leach did not pursue it vigorously in his later work.[4] His ideas, though not developed explicitly, run through the structuralist literature associated with Claude Lévi-Strauss, with its extensive use of "structural models" that display relationships in cultural systems in terms of spatial arrays. For some reason, and I have never been sure just why, cultural anthropologists have largely ignored the manifestly spatial, geometrical nature of Lévi-Strauss's models, which attempt to pose the elemental features of a cultural system in a framework of linked oppositions, situated in (semio)space and connected by algebraic (+/-) signs. Encouraged by Lévi-Strauss himself, who was greatly impressed by advances in structural linguistics in the forties and fifties, anthropologists have chosen to regard the manifestly spatial orientation of structural models as merely a heuristic device, a convenient means of displaying what are held to be essentially *linguistic* relations (binary opposites) produced by a language-dominated intelligence. The possibility that Leach's and Lévi-Strauss's profound and original analyses of myth, which rely heavily on their pioneering use of structural models, are so powerful *because* they invoke a semiospace, a dimensionality inherent in the mind and culture, has, again for reasons largely unexplained, been dismissed by anthropologists committed, like their colleague Philip Lieberman, to the notion of a humanity dominated and defined by its faculty of language.

Metaphor, Quality Space, and Semiospace

> *Perhaps every science must start with metaphor and end with algebra; and*
> *perhaps without the metaphor there would never have been any algebra.*
> — Max Black, *Models and Metaphors: Studies in Language and Philosophy*

Another cultural anthropologist who has explicitly based a theory of symbolization/conceptualization on a spatial model of culture is James Fernandez, whose essay "Persuasions and Performances: Of the Beast in Every Body . . . And the Metaphors of Everyman" has become a modern classic. Fernandez advances a theory of metaphor conceived as "a strategic predication upon an inchoate pronoun (an I, a you, a we, a they) which makes a movement and leads to performance." Metaphor, a supremely important concept in cultural anthropology, is here given a unique interpretation as a vectorial, semantic operation, not upon known objects but upon the intrinsically unknown and ultimately fascinating beings in the experiential world: ourselves and those with whom we interact.

> In the intellectual sense the movement accomplished by these metaphors is from the inchoate in the pronomial subject to the concrete in the predicate. These are basic if not kernel predications in social life which enable us to escape the privacy of experience. For what is more inchoate and in need of a concrete predication than a pronoun! Personal experience and social life cries out to us, to me, to you, to predicate some identity upon "others" and "selves." We need to become objects to ourselves, and others need to become objects to us as well. (45–46)

The matrix within which these strategic predications make their movements is what Fernandez calls the "quality space" of culture.

> Behind this discussion, as the reader will have perceived, lies a topographic model of society and culture. I am inordinately attracted to it, but it may be useful. Culture from this view is a quality space of "n" dimensions or continua, and society is a movement about of pronouns within this space. (47)

In this statement is the cornerstone of the present work. What follows is my attempt to describe the continua within that quality space identified by Fernandez, to specify the extremities of those continua (what are the names/ values of the semiotic axes or variables?), and to explore in detail the semiotic processes through which particular movies, by creating a world of myth/metaphor, manage to predicate identities on the inchoateness of existence.

Forward-looking as I find Fernandez's essay to be, however, it is also an unfortunate example of the tenacity of the linguistic model in contemporary cultural anthropology. While Fernandez advances the idea that culture is "a quality space of 'n' dimensions or continua," he needlessly restricts that model to movements of *metaphors* acting on *pronouns* through *predications*: his tentative foray into semiospace keeps to the safe confines of a language-dominated mind and world. What I have in mind here is a less confining vision of a multidimensional quality (semio)space that began to develop, to construct an *Umwelt*, long before hominids acquired a functional grammar and polite vocabulary, and will likely continue to develop long after Word and Word-Perfect versions 5000.1 have utterly transformed the nature of our present language.

In my view, the basic "predications" Fernandez identifies — how the inchoate I, you, we, they are given form — have a powerfully visceral, sensory nature that overwhelms or circumvents language even as they are given metaphoric expression. One is speechless before beauty or speechless with rage precisely because physical and aesthetic attraction or a flash of anger is a *perceptual* operation, a nearly instantaneous event within a multidimensional neural organization, which occurs without the prompting of language. If you happen to be a male heterosexual (from a bygone era), do you remember what it was like asking a girl out on your very first date? In that bewildering mix of emotions, I would wager that the vaunted dominance of language was not much in evidence, even though you were engaged in a specifically linguistic task. If I am strongly attracted or repelled by someone, it is not because the associative areas of my cerebral cortex have obligingly provided an apposite metaphor to start things off — gem, doll, pig, dog, fox — and then proceeded to interpret my experience for me in terms of that metaphor. Quite the contrary: my visual, visceral reaction (which stood my hominid ancestors in good stead for hundreds of thousands of years before they became adroit with metaphor) is primary, and provides a metaphorical interpretation only after the fact. When you first glimpse a dear friend you haven't seen in years, when a gourmet first tastes a sumptuous dish, when a bigot first spots someone of the wrong color, religion, or nationality on "his" street, the reaction is immediate, powerful, and, I would claim, essentially non-linguistic. The primacy of this kind of perception, borrowing on Merleau-Ponty, is also the *primacy of myth*: it is the creation and organization of experience within the multidimensional world of a quality (semio)space that I, solidly with Fernandez here, would call *culture*.

An excellent example of what I mean by the "primacy of myth" comes from another source anthropologists have scrupulously avoided (and I am definitely *not* alluding here to quantum mechanics and cosmology): the novels of William Burroughs. Perhaps the most antilinguistic of modern writers, Burroughs (a Harvard-trained anthropologist!) describes language and the society built on it as an enormous con game that sucks us in and dupes us with its false promise of meaning in a fundamentally enigmatic, meaningless world.

In his early work, *Naked Lunch*, Burroughs proposes what is an impossible task: to clearly see what is on the end of your fork. The substance on the end of your fork, although seemingly just-what-it-is in its physical immediacy, is already, even in its lowly inert state, imbued with a mythic significance: it is *food*, or, horribly, some revolting, inedible non-food thing that has become impaled on youry fork. The distinction between food and non-food, elemental and alimental as it seems, is not given in the substance itself; it emerges from other mental constructs of the world that differentiate types of living things and associate particular human behaviors with those types. If I can work my way one forkful at a time through a medium-rare sirloin steak, the bleeding flesh of a fellow mammal that died horribly to accommodate my appetite, it is because I have previously "ingested," in the process of becoming a human being, a particular holographic image or arrangement of the edible and inedible things in the world — a *dietary system* in the anthropological parlance, which, in this example, happens to be loosely and generically "American."

Note that I proceed happily through my meal, without a conscious thought that my actions are situated in something as abstruse and bloodless (unlike my steak) as an "American dietary system," *unless*, that is, you tell me, even jokingly, that the substance *on the end of my fork* is actually cat meat or rat meat, cleverly disguised to resemble beefsteak. Then things come to a jarring halt; I throw down the now offensive fork, push the plate away, and perhaps even run gagging from the table (make the offensive substance *human* flesh and you will definitely get the latter reaction). A little tinkering with the holographic arrangement, however, a few pushes and pulls of some vectors in semiospace, and you might obtain a dietary system, as exists in a number of places (including neighborhoods of American cities), in which cat or rat meat makes quite a palatable dish. In such a context, my immediate "natural" revulsion would be bizarre and unseemly, rather like that of a flu-wracked president from Texas being presented with a plate of sushi delicacies at a Japanese state dinner.

The important point here is that my instant revulsion, whether appropriate or inappropriate given the context, would seize me *without benefit of an interceding metaphor* supplied by a language-dominated intelligence. Horrible things, like beautiful things, issue from a consciousness, a semiospace, that is not primarily built up from linguistic operations. They possess a powerful immediacy that is the wholly consuming sensory and visceral *primacy of myth*, which originates in the movements, not of metaphors, but of semiotic fields twisting and turning through the semiotic dimensions of the quality (semio)-space of culture.

Another basic difficulty with Fernandez's emphasis on metaphor and his implicit identification of language with culture is its ignoring the principal topic of this work: machines and their emerging ascendancy in the semiospace of an American Dreamtime. If you are fortunate enough to climb behind the wheel of that '57 Chevy convertible evoked earlier and pull out onto Palm Canyon Drive one Saturday night, or even if you just crank up the Hoover for the weekly run over the Berber carpet and around the potted ferns, the little action systems of person-machine-environment thus created (Bateson's ecologies of mind again) owe very little to metaphor or any other operation of language. For if you are at all experienced at driving or vacuuming, then your actions are a vibrant synthesis of your motor skills and the components of the machine as both respond to the elements of a particular environment. The finest irony, which captures exactly the spirt of this work, is that we often say of the experience of our human flesh bonding with machine parts — a wheel, a joystick, a pair of skis, a baseball bat, or Ms. Howard's bowling ball (see chapter 4) — that it is a delightfully *natural* feeling, meaning that our plodding, language-shackled consciousness is temporarily liberated by the primal rush, the mythic exhilaration of an unmediated, hands-on mastery of the machine.

Dimensionality in Nature and Culture

Poems are made by fools like me, but only an algorithm can make a tree.
　　　—California Institute of Technology, rest room graffiti

In putting the language-dominated theory of metaphor behind us, I would suggest that what remains of Fernandez's quality space is a model of culture as semiospace that must be rather like the analytical concepts of "phase space" and "Hilbert space" that figure importantly in physics and, particularly for the latter concept of Hilbert space, in quantum mechanics.[5]

The first lesson I would like to draw from Roger Penrose's erudite presentation of these truly mind-boggling concepts is that Fernandez's terse assertion that culture "is a quality space of `n' dimensions or continua" now acquires new meaning and substance. The fact that mathematical creatures like phase space and Hilbert space exist and, moreover, have great explanatory power for what goes on in the physical, "real" world gives a cachet to the notion of a "quality space" of culture. Without these stunning models from mathematical physics, we would, I think, be inclined to take Fernandez's work on metaphor metaphorically, that is, to fall back into the old habit of anthropologists of regarding the elegant geometrical compositions of structural analysts like Leach and Lévi-Strauss as mere teaching tools, helpful illustrations of what a language-bound intelligence is up to. Penrose's exposition offers a promising alternative, for while the "spaces" he describes are highly abstract (far more so than the pedestrian structural models anthropologists devise), I'm sure he would claim that they are nonetheless "real" in the sense of describing the physical properties of matter.[6]

The outstanding contribution Penrose makes to the present discussion may be drawn from his words of encouragement to his nonmathematical readers, whom he knew would be doing mental cartwheels trying to visualize phase space: Don't even try; it's impossible to visualize and wouldn't help much if you could. A space that one cannot visualize — now *that* is a tall order for most of us, anthropologists included, who, even if we've had umpteen years of schooling, still cling to a core of commonsense beliefs about what we will (and can) see when we open our eyes in the morning. It seems more a Zen exercise than a science project, and for that very reason is helpful in disrupting our habitual pattern of thought just enough to let the seed of doubt, and imagination, slip in: suppose there *are* "spaces" that we can't visualize . . . and suppose that culture is such a space. . . . That is what I propose. The quality space of culture, or semiospace, *is* dimensional, *is* a "world" (hence the tremendously suggestive power of the term, "*Umwelt*", the "world-around"). The fact that we don't get up in the morning, go to the window, and see vistas of semiotic dimensions stretching off into the distance does not mean that they don't exist. It takes something like Penrose leading us on a forced march through some of the thornbush of contemporary mathematics to alert us to the fact that dimensionality, our old clear-as-day, straight-as-an-arrow acquaintance from high school geometry classes is in fact an elusive, difficult, and tremendously complex subject.

I will discuss aspects of that complexity presently, but would first like to note that it is probably our commonsense beliefs, augmented by a little high school geometry, that have made us ill-disposed toward those who would introduce mathematics into a discussion of social relations or cultural values. For there is a dominant belief (and here the *myth of America* with its ambivalence-fraught stereotype of science reasserts itself) that the truths of mathematics apply to a pristine, cut-and-dried, artificial world of straight lines, right angles, and perfect circles but do not fit the convoluted, emotional, real world of people's lives. Our collective psyche again dips into the deep well of American myth, and draws forth the sentiment, both cherished and crippling, that the rational world of scientists and mathematicians is cold and even cruel — like the scientists and mathematicians themselves — and cannot describe or explain the emotion and subtlety of human experience.[7]

But what is this supposed "complexity of dimensions" I insisted on earlier? Perhaps theoretical physicists and cosmologists *have* abandoned their rulers and compasses, but why should that ameliorate the hopelessly sterile attempt to draw lines and boxes around people's lives, the attempt so dreaded by humanistic anthropologists? Whatever the high-powered physical theory behind them, aren't lines just lines and boxes just boxes? Well, no. There is a major problem with this retreat into common sense, which hits us in the face as we slog through the Penrose passages above: the world served up to us by our common sense (and its fellow travelers, elementary math and science courses) is simply not realistic. It is a rough gloss of how things actually work, enough to get by with on a day-to-day basis, but one that lets us down hard from time to time.

Concerning the dimensionality of lines, for example: We all know that a straight line is the shortest distance between two points, and that if you have two straight lines going in different directions in something called a "plane" you have a two-dimensional, "flat" figure. Add another straight line travelling away from the first two, out of the "plane," and you have a three-dimensional solid. The problems — big problems — start dropping out of the sky right away and landing on top of this tidy view. For starters, it's hard, or actually impossible, to find a straight line. The ruler, or "straight edge," on your desk lets you down right away because of the little detail that the space on which you inscribe the line (the paper, blackboard or football field) happens to be curved, so that if you extend your line a bit, say a few billion light years, it actually curves back on itself or describes a weird, saddle-shaped hyperbola. For that matter, your ruler itself, just lying there in your hand taking up space, is also curved, but just by, as Maxwell Smart says, "that much." You might object that this is something of a cosmic quibble; you aren't measuring light years in drafting a floor plan or even composing a structural model in anthropology, and your trusty ruler does a pretty good job. True enough, but notice that even this tiny discrepancy has upset the apple-pie, smile-button reality of common sense: things are supposed to *be* what they seem, not *almost* what they seem. What has happened here is what I described earlier as a critical attribute of myth: it introduces a vertigo, a tilt to everyday life that, be it ever so slight, still serves to announce its presence, to crack open the gates of the Dreamtime.

But worse is to follow. Let us say you opt to give up the high ground of cosmic distances, and let Einstein have his curved space, bent light rays, elastic rulers, and clocks that speed up or slow down depending on who is reading them. You take your nice, solid, nonelastic ruler and retreat into the practical world, where the cosmic scale does not alter the results you expect to find. Once there, however, you find there is very little to measure with your "straight edge" except other straight edges that have been put there earlier by someone who made them with his "straight edge."

Looking around you in this practical, real world and discounting all the "artificial" straight edges of buildings, sheets of paper, pieces of furniture, tennis courts, and even the video borders on your word processing screen, you see the silhouettes of hills and mountains, the outlines of clouds, the path of a river, the branches of a tree, the veins of a leaf, and so on. "Real" lines are almost invariably curved, and therein lies the rub: how will you measure them with your ruler? Also, a quick inspection of some of these "real" lines shows you that there is great variation in their amount of curvature or twistedness. For example, there is the rare, straight-as-an-arrow line described by — what else? — an arrow.[8] While the people in white coats at the National Bureau of Standards wouldn't be happy with its "straightness," preferring their lasers instead, the lowly arrow serves as a good, practical index of what a straight line should look like. Then there are gently curving lines that still have an obvious directionality about them: the graceful track a skier makes down a gentle slope, for example. But then things, as always, get complicated and messy: many, many "lines" we encounter wander so much that they lose all sense of directionality and begin to fill up a lot of the area traversed, like an ant on a sidewalk or a five-year old crossing the yard on an errand, for example (see Figure 3.1). A very interesting variety of this kind of complicated line is the great number of lines that describe *boundaries*: the silhouette of a mountain range that marks the boundary of earth and sky, or a coastline that separates land and sea.

Figure 3.1. Meandering ant path on sidewalk.

When you proceed to measure one of these complicated lines with your ruler, some very peculiar, noncommonsense factors rapidly come into play. Take the path of the ant on your sidewalk, for example. You've watched the little creature for a few minutes, then gone into the house and come back with your trusty camcorder, which is a deluxe model equipped with a super-fast tape speed for ultra-slow-motion effects (you use it to study and improve your tennis serve). After taping the electrifying event of the ant crossing your sidewalk for a few minutes (your neighbors are now looking at you like Richard Dreyfuss's neighbors in *Close Encounters*, when he was tearing up his nice suburban yard to use in his sculpture of the aliens' mountain rendezvous), you go back inside and put the tape in your VCR. Taking several pieces of transparency the size of your TV screen and a fine-tipped felt pen, you sit down beside the set with the VCR remote. You place a transparency over the screen and, for the first run, set the equipment to play at normal, real-life speed. When the ant appears on the screen, you position the tip of your pen over its image and trace its path as it wanders across the screen. Because you are new to this ant path tracing business, on this first effort you miss many of its twists and turns, glossing over them with gently curving lines that lack the squiggles of the ant's motion.

To improve your chart, on successive runs with fresh pieces of transparency you increasingly slow the motion, until you reach the molasses-world of Sunday football's "instant replay," and even resort to the "coach's clicker" freeze-frame button on your remote, so you can catch the ant in mid-stride. Even though the transparencies are now piling up, you are still not content: your TV has a "zoom" function, which you crank up to the max, so that the ant now looks like a Volkswagen driven by a lunatic, crazily veering across an endless patch of concrete. At this high-powered setting, with the set zoomed to the max and the tape at ultra slow motion, you make one more chart, feverishly hitting the freeze-frame control so you can follow the ant's every motion with your pen (see Figure 3.2).

Figure 3.2. Extreme close up of ant path.

Exhausted at the end of this session, you spread out your transparencies (there are now a couple of dozen) and proceed to inspect them, trusty ruler in hand. The differences between early and late charts are considerable: gentle, meandering lines gradually become frenetic, static-like squiggles. While you are contemplating this disparate collection, your long-suffering spouse or roommate comes in and says, "Well, now that you've spent the day on this stupid project, tell me: How far did the ant travel? *How long is your line?*" And *these* are tough questions to answer. If you sit down with your ruler and the stack of transparencies and begin to measure the first chart,the one with the gentle curves, you can probably come up with a fair approximation by, say, marking off one-inch gradations on the ant-line and then adding these up. Of course, there will be plenty of places where the ant-line curves within the one-inch distance, but you've already discounted Einstein's curved space, so why not the ant's curved path?

In this way, you can come up with one answer to your companion's question. But if the two of you are standing there surveying the charts spread out around you, it will be clear to both of you that you have only flirted with an answer to your companion's question. Suppose you take your final, ultra-fine-grain transparency and begin to measure it. It will be clear from the outset that you cannot get away with marking this line off in one-inch segments, since whole mountain ranges of squiggles will lie within some of those segments. So you break out a draftsman's ruler marked off in sixteenth-inch gradations (and a good magnifying glass) and begin the tedious chore of measurement. Even at this scale, there will still be plenty of squiggles between the marks whose lengths are glossed over by the measurement procedure. Still, you come up with a result. The problem is, the length of the line you now announce to your companion is different from the first measurement you gave: it is considerably longer, because of all those squiggles.

Which is the better measurement? How far did the ant *really* travel? Again, not easy questions. If you're after an ant's eye view of its travels, perhaps your last, fine-grained chart is a more accurate representation. But note the extremely important consideration that this detailed chart does not represent what you, or any other human standing beside you, saw as you watched the ant's motions on the sidewalk. The better representation of the human's eye view is your first, and most impressionistic or sensory chart with its gentle, meandering line. After all, there is nothing "natural" or authoritative about trying to represent the ant's eye view of its travels (which, if you could actually bring *that* off would "look" absolutely otherworldly and unintelligible to those other, human eyes). The crew cuts at the Bureau of Standards, for instance, might find even the ant's scale of things much too indiscriminate for their purposes, and insist on trotting out their lasers and micrometers in order to nail down the length of the squiggles in Angstrom units. That procedure would yield something on the scale of a microbe's eye view (if the microbe happened to possess organs) as it clung, say, to the ant's left antenna. A measurement at this microbial scale would yield a much larger result (in fact, very much larger since it begins to approach infinity) than obtained from your initial, carefree foray into what now turns out to be an impenetrable thicket of ant path measurements.

Dismayingly, the result of this last measurement is substantially different from your first results obtained with an ordinary ruler, since lots of those previously glossed-over squiggles now get figured into the final result. And, depending on whose equipment you choose to use, subsequent measurements you might make would differ from all these results. The unwelcome conclusion to be drawn from this little brush with an obsession neurosis (sometimes called "laboratory science") is that the "same" line, which you actually drew with your very own felt pen, has different lengths depending on how you go about measuring it.

Benoit Mandelbrot, mathematician and cult figure, makes these same points about the length of a line, more eloquently and with far deeper mathematical understanding than I, in his famous essay, "How Long is the Coast of Britain?" (see his *The Fractal Geometry of Nature*). Basically, Mandelbrot's answer to his own question is: as long as you want to make it. You can fly along the coast in an airplane and record the air miles traveled; you can drive along it on a coastal highway and take odometer readings; you can walk along it on a foot trail or even jump from rock to rock at the shoreline; or you can set a mouse — or our ant friend — to traversing it pebble by pebble. The coastline of England, like the lines we have been examining, has an infinite number of lengths. Mandelbrot's surprising finding is not just mental sleight-of-hand done with smoke and mirrors to distract us from the hard-edged reality of things; it is a mathematically correct description of reality — as real as it gets, the Platonists among us might say. Our difficulty in reaching the same conclusion, our reluctance to take this paradoxical stuff seriously, is due to the fact that the smoke and mirrors involved here are frantically deployed, not by the evil scientists and mathematicians of the

Dreamtime, but by our own common sense in a hopeless attempt to cling to a simple vision of a world in which an ant crawling on a sidewalk covers a certain, measurable distance, in which *a* line has *a* length. Myth and reality: Is there any way to unscramble these categories we habitually separate? If so, which is the source of delusion?

Mandelbrot has even more disturbing news in store for us than this business of the indeterminacy of a line, and it bears directly on the matter of dimensionality. Even though the inoffensive line has become a treacherous serpent in our grasp, we might hope to salvage something of our common sense (and our faith in schoolday memories of Euclid) by supposing that however long lines may be, they still serve to mark off and define the one-two-three dimensions of line, plane, and solid which we see, like the nose on our face, right before our very eyes, stretching out around us. We might grant Penrose his infinite dimensions of phase space and Hilbert space in the same, save-the-women-and-children-first spirit in which we granted Einstein his curved space and elastic rulers, while insisting that for all practical purposes (a phrase already sounding hollow as a gourd) we see and walk around in a world of three clear-cut dimensions. Yet Mandelbrot has denied us even that practical refuge, in a stunning theoretical development that has transformed contemporary mathematics and, amazingly, inspired a large cult following of spinoffs of his work. His thesis, like that in the essay on the coastline of England, is brilliantly simple: There are no clear-cut boundary markers that separate lines, planes, and solids from one another as elementary dimensions of space; instead there are any number of transitional or fractional dimensions (hence the popular term, "fractal") that connect the three classical dimensions and that are fundamental to a description of physical objects.

Examples may be found in our now-treasured archive of ant path charts. Take one of the fine-grained, zoomed close-up charts in which your felt pen line wanders all over the place and fills up a lot of the chart (see Figure 3.2). Tack this chart to the wall and inspect it at a "normal" reading distance of eighteen inches or so. Although your line is definitely more squiggly and messy than those found in your old high school geometry textbook, it is still, just as Euclid said, a one-dimensional line meandering over the two-dimensional plane of the transparency sheet. But now step backward a few feet and examine the chart again. Much of the squiggly detail has begun to blur together because the resolution power of your on-board optical equipment has been pushed past its limit, so that some individual line segments now form clots or islands surrounded by relatively open areas transected by lines that still retain their individual identity. In Mandelbrot's terms, this simple change of perspective has altered the geometry of the chart from that of a one-dimensional line on an open plane to that of an object of a fractional dimension, say 1.2 or 1.3, which is transitional between line and plane.

This highly original perspective on geometry also allows our experiment to proceed in the opposite direction: instead of stepping back from the chart, you zoom in on it, probably with the help of a magnifying glass or low-powered microscope. Now your felt pen lines grow and expand to fill much of the visual field; their one-dimensionality is again seen to be an ephemeral, contingent attribute and you are back to contemplating an object of dimension 1.2 or 1.3. Dimensionality does not lose its mathematical stature as a fundamental property of things, but it does lose its one-two-three, pigeon-hole determinacy. The scale or region of space involved in the observation of a particular object now becomes a primary criterion in describing its physical properties. Mandelbrot, in essence, chucks out the ruler and compass we were fretting about earlier, and installs in their place the zoom lens, particularly in its modern form of adjustable coordinates on the screen of a computer monitor (as hundreds of thousands of Mandelbrot set trekkies will attest).

Mandelbrot's arguments, when allied with the works of chaos and complexity theory partly inspired by his pioneering discoveries, lead to conclusions as unsettling, and as productive, as those Penrose highlighted in the field of theoretical physics. If a line has no fixed length and if the dimensionality of a figure depends on the scale selected for its observation, it becomes exceedingly difficult for anyone — mathematician, anthropologist, politician, evangelist — to maintain that the elementary truths of existence, in this case the physical properties of objects as apprehended by the human mind, are fixed, unambiguous propositions that affirm the central tenet: *things are a certain way.* It is this tenet, applied to the areas of social relations and cultural values, that has been responsible for the strident denial of a Dreamtime world of mythic virtuality, and for a very great many horrible things done to people by other people in the name of the way, the truth, and the light.

Theoretical physics as presented by Penrose acts conjointly with Mandelbrot's mathematics in eroding this cherished but vicious dogma of certainty and fixedness. The "nuts and bolts" of existence turn out to be true phantoms: elusive "virtual particles" that may be here, there, or both places at once, and that inhabit, together with their shadowy companions, the dynamic, vector-driven, many dimensional worlds of "phase space" and "Hilbert space," worlds, as Penrose says, that we have no hope of ever "seeing." Contemporary mathematics and physics thus seem to have developed rigorous models of physical reality that correspond on crucial points, and that together paint a very different picture of the "real world" from that usually presented by "normal" folks (and by not-so-normal folks, like anthropologists).

From my vantage point as a distinct outsider to fractal geometry and mathematical physics (their anthropologist, if you will), I find it astonishing that these fields have for so long pursued topics of the sort most anthropologists and other social thinkers have not only ignored but shrilly rejected: the virtuality or multiple possibilities of experience; the coexistence of incompatible, contradictory states of being; the complexity and importance of dimensionality in a cultural system; and the indispensable role of the knower (the sentient presence) in fixing the properties of the known. Quantum mechanics and relativistic cosmology, as I noted earlier, have been around for most of the century. And, while fractal geometry and the hacker cult of the Mandelbrot set are quite recent, non-Euclidean geometry and nonlinear mathematics, developed by giants in the discipline — Gauss, Bolyai, Riemann, Cantor — are even older than the field of quantum mechanics.

The truly impressive, and bewildering, thing to me in the peculiar conjunction of the success of contemporary physical theory and the widespread rejection of its findings by laymen and social thinkers alike is that the theory, while smacking of "weirdness" all the way, miraculously serves up an image of the world that is far more familiar, and really far more comprehensible, than that of earlier theories of both physical and social reality. Classical mechanics presented us with a clockwork world in which everything followed in a perfectly determinate manner from what came before, provided only that you confined your attention to actual clocks, projectiles, ball bearings on inclined planes, or, best of all, the distant stars and planets. If, however, you foolishly let your attention wander to the swirl of cream in your cup of coffee, the movement of clouds across the sky, the traffic clogging the freeway around you, or the tropical storm bearing down on your town, then classical mechanics, along with William Burroughs's Nova Mob (colloquially known as "civilization"), abruptly check out of the Mind Motel.[9]

When we stop to look at the things around us, to smell the roses,[10] we see a world of ebb and flow, of twists and turns, of pushes and pulls, of change that is sometimes gradual and subtle and sometimes bewilderingly dramatic, but overall, a world of great diversity, vitality, and, as basic a property as all the rest, a world of much confusion. To say that it is otherwise, that the subtlety and turbulence of everyday life may be harnessed by the deterministic shackles of a science that is not really science (a "science" that flows from the dark forces of the Dreamtime) is, perhaps, to express a wistful longing for certainty in an uncertain life, or, all too often, to foist off a lie concocted by those who do or should know better, who find it convenient to bend the mercurial human spirit of their subjects, employees, followers, or students to the yoke of an order that can be inscribed in the report cards, spreadsheets, and law books of a blighted civilization.

The clockwork world of classical mechanics parallels that of Euclidean geometry and linear equations, and, just as it has been superceded by a world of quantum mechanics and relativity, so the old mathematics has yielded, decades ago for the most part, to the inroads of non-Euclidean geometries (with an emphasis on the plural), set theory, and nonlinear equations. Here, too, as with theoretical physics, the seeming off-the-wall weirdness of contemporary mathematics actually describes a much more livable, believable world than that promulgated by our old high school textbooks. The great problem with the public perception of mathematics in the United States is the very widespread and accurate sentiment that the math most of us learned in school has almost no relevance to our daily lives. Euclid's compulsively tidy, axiomatic world of points, lines, triangles, and circles is hardly to be found when we raise our eyes from the text and confront the things around us, whose shapes are of the meandering, fragmented, complex kind we encountered in our ant path exercise. The things in our lives, like our lives themselves, are not measurable or determinate in the Euclidian or commonsense meaning of those terms. Remarkably, it turns out not to matter all that much if we acknowledge that we cannot fix the length of our ant path, or even of the coastline of England (except, perhaps, to tourism promoters who advertise "x hundreds of miles of lovely, pebble-strewn, cloud-shrouded beaches"). And whether we want to believe that we can come up with some kind of satisfying answer to vexing little problems of the ant path variety, we know we cannot answer apparently straightforward questions of the most pressing urgency, like "When will the Big One level L. A. (and issue in the post-apocalyptic world of *Blade Runner*)?" or "When will a hurricane finish levelling Miami?"

The tremendous appeal of chaos and complexity theory lies in its restoration of the familiar world around us as the object of scientific inquiry: for the first time those of us who are not mathematicians (which, after all, is almost all of us) have an immediate grasp of what the subject matter is and why it is important, if not how to go about modelling it in the difficult nonlinear equations of complexity theory. Earthquakes, weather patterns (including hurricanes), traffic flow, the shapes of plants and insects, even what the stock market is up to, all become the subject matter of what James Gleick, in his popular work on chaos theory, has fittingly called a "new science." These subjects replace the hopelessly artificial, impoverished ones of lines, planes, triangles, and circles, which we all somehow knew, as we suffered through Mr Dork's geometry class, were *way* off base.

The most important aspect of this revolution in mathematics and science and, particularly, of its impact on the Dreamtime world of a global, Americanized psyche, is that it installs *unpredictability* and *undecidability* as distinguishing features of the physical world, which must be accommodated rather than arbitrarily expelled. It is first necessary to know the inherent limitations of earthquake or hurricane prediction before those dramatic, turbulent events can be put into a framework of "real-life" phenomena like daily weather patterns, the smell of coffee (or a rose), or the neural events associated with your reading these words. Where earlier mathematics carved out a small, precise area for itself and pretended its deductive power in that area could be extended to the actual physical phenomena of daily experience, contemporary mathematics abandons the deterministic posture as regards those events and considers them on their own terms, in all their complexity and changefulness.

As I have noted, most of this is old news in the mathematical community, as evidenced in a work by Morris Kline, *Mathematics: A Cultural Approach*, published over thirty years ago and detailing developments much earlier still.

The very fact that there can be geometries other than Euclid's, that one can formulate axioms fundamentally different from Euclid's and prove theorems, was in itself a remarkable discovery. The concept of geometry was considerably broadened and suggested that mathematics might be something more than the study of the implications of the self-evident truths about number and geometrical figures. However, the very existence of these new geometries caused mathematicians to take up a deeper and more disturbing question, one which had already been raised by Gauss. Could any one of these new geometries be applied? Could the axioms and theorems fit physical space and perhaps even prove more accurate than Euclidean geometry? Why should one continue to believe that physical space was necessarily Euclidean?

At first blush the idea that either of these strange geometries [Gauss's and Riemann's] could possibly supercede Euclidean geometry seems absurd. That Euclidean geometry is *the* geometry of physical space, that it is the truth about space is so ingrained in people's minds that any contrary thoughts are rejected. The mathematician Georg Cantor spoke of a law of conservation of ignorance. A false conclusion once arrived at is not easily dislodged. And the less it is understood, the more tenaciously is it held. In fact, for a long time non-Euclidean geometry was regarded as a logical curiosity. Its existence could not be denied, but mathematicians maintained that the real geometry, the geometry of the physical world, was Euclidean. They refused to take seriously the thought that any other geometry could be applied. However, they ultimately realized that their insistence on Euclidean geometry was merely a habit of thought and not at all a necessary belief. Those few who failed to see this were shocked into the realization when the theory of relativity [with its curved space] actually made use of non-Euclidean geometry. . . .

Perhaps the greatest import of non-Euclidean geometry is the insight it offers into the workings of the human mind. No episode of history is more instructive. The evaluation of mathematics as a body of truths, which obtained prior to non-Euclidean geometry, was accepted at face value by every thinking being for 2000 years, in fact, practically throughout the entire existence of Western culture. This view, of course, proved to be wrong. We see therefore, on the one hand, how powerless the mind is to recognize the assumptions it makes. It would be more appropriate to say of man that he is surest of what he believes, than to claim that he believes what is sure. Apparently we should constantly re-examine our firmest convictions, for these are most likely to be suspect. They mark our limitations rather than our positive accomplishments. On the other hand, non-Euclidean geometry also shows the heights to which the human mind can rise. In pursuing the concept of a new geometry, it defied intuition, common sense, experience, and the most firmly entrenched philosophical doctrines just to see what reasoning would produce. (563–577)

Kline's balanced, not to say charitable, account of the late development and reluctant acceptance of a new paradigm for conceptualizing space is a fitting point to conclude, on a similarly balanced note, that the seemingly obvious ideas we have of dimensionality, of the lines and boxes in our lives, warrant close scrutiny outside the hermetic realms of contemporary mathematics and physics. In simply going about our daily lives, we are not immune to the *deracinement*, or sense of uprootedness, conventional mathematicians experienced toward the end of the last century when they began to confront the stunning implications of a non-Euclidean geometry that could no longer be treated as a mental diversion, but had to be accepted as a representation, however bizarre, of the physical world. And our daily lives, as I argue throughout this work, wander, like our ant path, in and out of the shallow depth of field of common sense, in and out of an enveloping Dreamtime consciousness. The critical question before us now is how this new understanding of dimensionality may be applied to the cultural world around us, and particularly to an anthropology of the cultural productions of the American Dreamtime, in the form of popular movies.

If mathematicians and physicists have taken two thousand years to come up with the concepts embodied in non-Euclidean geometries and quantum mechanics, then anthropologists may perhaps be forgiven for having spent their first meager century engaged in the sorts of butterfly-collecting activities Edmund Leach criticized three decades ago. Nevertheless, as Kline and numerous others have pointed out, once the spurious certainties of Newtonian mechanics and Euclidean geometry had been unmasked (a process substantially completed by the 1930s), there followed a diffuse but widespread acknowledgement among intellectuals that the world had shifted underfoot, that the solid ground of science and moral order had given way to a morass of unknowns and, worse, unknowables. What was happening in anthropology, that upstart new "science of humanity," while this major transformation in worldview was underway? Did anthropologists, like Newton's pygmies standing on the shoulders of giants, absorb the new intellectual climate purportedly inspired by the mathematicians and physicists and proceed to build it into their tentative theories of culture (literally from the ground up, since they were just starting work on their own disciplinary edifice)?

Actually, no. You see, a funny thing happened on the way to anthropology.

This is not the place to attempt to chart the parade of *isms* and social movements that accompanied and embodied the fundamental change of perspective ushered in by such unlikely revolutionaries as Gauss, Riemann, Einstein, and Heisenberg. It suffices to note that the grand themes, the basic principles and problems of aesthetics, of political and moral discourse, of philosophical debate and literary creation have changed in ways that would have been unthinkable to educated persons of the nineteenth century. The place of anthropology and the other social sciences in this time of ferment and change is one of the major paradoxes of contemporary intellectual history, a monstrous curiosity that leads repeatedly into scandal. For the role anthropology has played in pursuing the implications the new perspective of Einstein, Riemann, Schroedinger, and company holds for the cultural world has been essentially that of Uncle Remus's tarbaby: "De tarbaby, he jus' sit dere, and he don' say *nuthin'*!"

In truth, that assessment is too charitable, for anthropologists had a great deal to say about the nature of culture, both before and after the second world war, but almost nothing they said indicated an understanding of the tremendous dynamism and multiplicity of their subject. In a staggering absurdity, while the world was coming apart at the seams and would never be the same again, pre- and early post-war sociologists and anthropologists labored mightily and produced a grand theoretical scheme, "structural functionalism," that proclaimed, according to various versions, that societies were like organisms, possessing a morphology (structure) of parts that all nicely worked together (function), or were "integrated systems" whose institutional subsystems articulated to form cohesive, stable wholes.[11]

The easy successes of structuralist-functionalist arguments indicate that here, in the storm-tossed world of post-war, post-colonial, and pre-God-only-knows-what uncertainty, the line supposedly separating anthropology as scientific discourse from anthropology as Dreamtime "science" is, as so often the case, perilously thin and crooked (we already know something about such lines). As I have discussed in other essays,[12] the anthropology *of* myth must often be interpreted as anthropology *as* myth, for the images we anthropologists conjure up of our disciplinary Other, the "native," have disconcerting resemblances to ourselves. It is far from established that in doing anthropology we are engaging in some sanitized, intellectual undertaking that is heaven-and-earth removed from what we normally think and say about the other people in our lives. As I have argued here and elsewhere, the impetus and process of doing anthropology are so compelling precisely because they are also the bases of "doing humanity": what we think and say as degreed, bona-fide social scientists is intimately tied to how we think of people as a function of being human ourselves. Thus in employing the Dreamtime "science" of structural-functionalism to describe and analyze "natives," we contribute more to the rapidly growing *myth of humanity* than to some (mythical!) body of carved-in-stone, objective fact.[13]

Processual Analysis and Cultural Dimensionality:
Liminality, Social Drama, and Social Field

> *Liminality may perhaps be regarded . . . as a realm of pure possibility*
> *whence novel configurations of ideas and relations may arise.*
> —Victor Turner, *The Forest of Symbols*

In the early sixties Edmund Leach's *Rethinking Anthropology* was only beginning to make small dents in the armored behemoth of structural-functionalism, which nevertheless lumbered along for decades and is still to be found, alive and living, not in Argentina but in the monographs and seminars of "development anthropology." As we have seen in discussing Leach's and Lévi-Strauss's contributions to cultural analysis, Leach's call for a *topological* anthropology that would issue in a new meaning of dimensionality in the emergent field of structuralism went mostly unanswered or misinterpreted. Up-and-coming, hard-charging young structuralists, not unlike Lévi-Strauss himself, were anxious to take up questions of symbolism and meaning without acquiring the stigma of being thought mathematical "reductionists."

In addition to Leach's work at this phase of his thought (he tried on some very different hats during his long and illustrious career), a striking and profound departure from the general background noise of structuralist-functionalist accounts of culture was provided by a team of highly productive and prolific ethnographers: Victor and Edith Turner. The Turners conducted extensive field work among the Ndembu of northwestern Zambia, beginning in 1950 and continuing, with Edith carrying on alone after Victor's death, into the eighties, thus making theirs one of the more impressive ethnographic projects in the history of anthropology. In a series of brilliant theoretical works on ritual symbolism initiated in the late fifties, Victor Turner unveiled a new perspective, processualism or processual analysis, that broke radically with an already tired structural-functionalism and with the new fashion of Lévi-Straussian structuralism, and that has much to contribute to our present discussion of dimensionality in culture.

In fact, without saddling Turner's memory with the peculiar mix of ideas in the present work, I want to emphasize that the fundamental attributes I believe I have identified for culture in general and for the Dreamtime world of American movies in particular — virtuality, multiple reality, internal contradiction, intersystem, and even a vector-driven semiotic dimensionality — are strikingly reminiscent, to the point of being translations in some instances, of Turner's tremendously seminal concepts of *liminality, multivocality, polarization of meaning*, and *field*. As with other thinkers cited here, I borrow (steal, actually) as needed to put together a framework of a theory of culture as semiospace, without attempting a scholarly review of their work (*im*balance being, after all, the watchword of the theory under development).[14]

Considered just as on-the-ground anthropology, i.e., out in the field working with the "natives," the Turners' ethnographic work could not be more different from that of Lévi-Strauss or many of the structuralist studies inspired by him. Lévi-Strauss's approach is magisterially eclectic: rather than go and live with a particular community of people for any length of time, he draws on his encyclopedic knowledge of the ethnographic literature, principally of the Americas, to construct vast comparative studies of hundreds of myths told in dozens of different "societies." The Turners exemplify (and greatly exceed) the "old school" approach to doing anthropology: select a particular group of "tribal" or at least "ethnic" people, establish residence among them, and get to know them intimately on a day-to-day basis. What distinguishes the Turners' work is that they kept returning to and writing about the Ndembu, amassing a tremendously detailed collection of material and a lifetime of impressions and memories. In today's fast-paced and under-funded academic world, by contrast, cohorts of anthropology graduate students fan out to exotic locales in the rural Third World or, increasingly, ethnic neighborhoods of American cities, try to get in a year's dissertation field study, and subsequently spend only a few months, at most, living with "their" people. The depth of the Turners' ethnographic understanding of Ndembu society and ritual symbolism is thus quite extraordinary, and made it possible for them to interpret their material in terms of the long-term, ebb and flow of experience. In sharp contrast, Levi-Strauss's long-distance comparisons of groups scattered over two continents and using ethnographic material gathered by others give his work, monumental as it is, an oddly stroboscopic effect of tiny slices of text or behavior frozen in place and time, and juxtaposed through a bewildering set of "structural transformations" with other tiny slices of life taken from here, there, and everywhere.

These pronounced differences in ethnographic method are tied to profound differences in theoretical orientation, for Victor Turner's analytical writings are unique in their unrelenting concern for *process* and *event* as opposed to *structure* and *text*. Having known the Ndembu, collectively and as individuals, over a major portion of his and their lives, Victor Turner recognized the importance of the transitions that punctuate an individual's life and that impel the rich symbolism of life-crisis rituals which accompany those transitions. Moreover, he extended this theme of a life crisis ritual focused on an individual initiate (he called this person an "initiand") to the cathartic *social dramas* (political and religious movements) that mark major transitions in the life of an entire community. Hence Turner's call for a processual analysis of society or culture as a whole, that would emphasize the "antistructure" of periods of great turbulence and effervescence in social life (a very rough gloss for what he termed "communitas") and focus on the large issue of how those abnormal periods of life are knit together with normal, structured periods.

Yet through all these changes [associated with social drama], certain crucial norms and relationships — and other seemingly less crucial, even quite trivial and arbitrary — will persist. The explanation for both constancy and change can, in my opinion, only be found by systematic analysis of *processual* units and temporal structures, by looking at phases [of social dramas] as well as atemporal systems. For each phase has its specific properties, and each leaves its special stamp on the metaphors and models in the heads of men involved with one another in the unending flow of social existence. In keeping with my explicit comparison of the temporal structure of certain types of social processes with that of dramas on the stage, with their acts and scenes, I saw the phases of social dramas as culminating to a climax. I would point out too that at the linguistic level of "parole," [that is, speech as opposed to the rules of language] each phase has its own speech forms and styles, its own rhetoric, its own kinds of nonverbal languages and symbolisms. These vary greatly, of course, cross-culturally and cross-temporally, but I postulate that there will be certain important generic affinities between the speeches and languages of the crisis phase everywhere, of the redressive phase everywhere, of the restoration of peace phase everywhere. Cross-cultural comparison has never applied itself to such a task because it has limited itself to atemporal forms and structures, to the products of man's social activity abstracted from the processes in which they arise, and, having arisen, which they channel to a varying extent. It is much easier to prop oneself on the "paradigmatic" crutch, coolly remote from the vexatious competitiveness of social life. Such cross-cultural comparison, moreover, cannot be made until we have many more extended-case studies. An extended-case history is the history of a single group or community over a considerable length of time, collected as a sequence of processual units of different types, including the social dramas and social enterprises mentioned already. This is more than plain historiography, for it involves the utilization of whatever conceptual tools social anthropology and cultural anthropology have bequeathed to us. "Processualism" is a term that includes "dramatistic analysis." Processual analysis assumes cultural analysis, just as it assumes structural-functional analysis, including more static comparative morphological analysis. It negates none of these, but puts dynamics first. (43–44, emphasis in original)

Turner's processual analysis, formulated here in his 1974 work *Dramas, Fields, and Metaphors: Symbolic Action in Human Society*, is an elaboration of ideas first presented in a 1964 essay, "Betwixt and Between: The Liminal Period in Rites de Passage," one of the most original and evocative works in anthropology's brief history. The key concept of the essay, and really the key to understanding Turner's work as a whole, is *liminality*. Liminality is, quite literally, that experience of being "betwixt and between" phases of life or states of consciousness which possesses the initiate during a life-crisis ritual and plunges him or her into an interstitial realm where the rules and values of everyday life cease to apply, where the structure of normal life gives way to the antistructure (which I would call the Dreamtime) of initiatory experience.

> The essential feature of these symbolizations [of the seclusion and "rebirth" of initiates] is that the neophytes are neither living nor dead from one aspect, and both living and dead from another. Their condition is one of ambiguity and paradox, a confusion of all the customary categories. Jakob Boehme, the German mystic whose obscure writings gave Hegel his celebrated dialectical "triad," liked to say that "In Yea and Nay all things consist." Liminality may perhaps be regarded as the Nay to all positive structural assertions, but as in some sense the source of them all, and, more than that, as a realm of pure possibility whence novel configurations of ideas and relations may arise. . . .
> We are not dealing with structural contradictions [i.e., like those in Levi-Strauss's structural models] when we discuss liminality, but with the essentially unstructured (which is at once destructured and pre-structured) and often the people themselves see this in terms of bringing neophytes into close connection with deity or with superhuman power, with what is, in fact, often regarded as the unbounded, the infinite, the limitless. . . .
> The arcane knowledge or "*gnosis*" obtained in the liminal period is felt to change the inmost nature of the neophyte, impressing him, as a seal impresses wax, with the characteristics of his new state. It is not a mere acquisition of knowledge, but a change of being. His apparent passivity is revealed as an absorption of powers which will become active after his social status has been redefined in the aggregation rites. (97–102, emphasis in original)

The individual's profound psychological experience of liminality feeds, on a social level, into the social dramas experienced by communities of individuals caught up in turbulent social, political, or religious movements. The dual processes of liminality and social drama thus provide a powerful model, not just of ritual symbolism, but of culture as a whole. In my efforts to describe the Dreamtime world evoked in popular movies, I could not produce a better statement of the crucial theme of *virtuality* than Turner's description of liminality as "a realm of pure possibility whence novel configurations of ideas and relations may arise." Moreover, Turner's insistence that cultural processes occur in a *field* of paradigm movement [a concept he took from the work of the psychologist, Kurt Lewin, himself inspired by mathematical physics] is closely tied to the importance I attach to the operation of vector forces in the semiospace of cultural dimensionality. The critical factors in liminality, like those in the theory of culture as semiospace being developed here, are movement and interstitiality within some specifiable domain of symbolic or semiotic space. The initiate in a life-crisis ritual is first traumatically separated from his or her ordinary, daily surroundings, then secluded in an extreme fashion that often involves induced hallucinations, and finally reincorporated, as a new, postliminal person in a community that has now itself changed, redefined by the addition of a new member.

But, you may ask, is it really feasible to draw a close analogy between Turner's initiate, an individual from a "primitive" culture who experiences a major, once-in-a-lifetime transformation of his entire being, and the more mundane and urban situations we are concerned with here? Can a Topeka teenager checking into the local theatre for a couple of hours of Spielberg or Lucas even begin to be compared with an Ndembu initiate entering the sacred seclusion hut to undergo his tribe's initiation ritual? The answer to this question requires a closer look at the fit between Turner's "ritual process" and the idea of cultural dimensionality at issue here. This particularly involves considering just what kind of "interstitial" phenomenon Turner has identified and how it meshes with the interstitiality of virtual experience and the rest of the Dreamtime toolkit, as I present it in this work. In pursuing these issues, the concepts of *intersystem* and *continuum*, attributes of true Dreamtime cultural dimensionality, assume critical importance.

Intersystem and Continuum

> . . . *monstrosities cannot be separated by any distinct line from slighter variations.*
>
> — Charles Darwin, *The Origin of Species*

It is clear that Turner's insights into ritual symbolism and the nature of culture assign considerable importance to concepts of process and transformation in a social world that is inherently *spatial*.[15] In my obviously biased view, Turner's concepts of liminality, process, and field take us to the verge of a new theoretical formulation, which he may well have rejected had he had an opportunity to examine it. That formulation is the model of culture as semiospace: a world of virtual experience, ambivalence, and contradiction, all of which are movements or vectorial processes within a number of identifiable semiotic dimensions. In short, I am proposing that Turner's work points the way toward a cultural analysis informed by concepts of physical reality — phase space, Hilbert space, vector fields, etc. — so admirably elucidated by Roger Penrose. At the very least, I find it remarkable that Turner's processual analysis, like the quite divergent views of Levi-Strauss, Leach, and Fernandez examined earlier, incorporate at a fundamental level such constructs as a topologically active cultural space (Leach), geometrical relations among sets of structural elements which undergo structural transformations (Levi-Strauss), and metaphorical movements, or predications, on inchoateness within a quality space of culture (Fernandez). These major theorists of culture, who approach their topic from very different conceptual and methodological premises, nevertheless seem drawn to a cluster of diffuse ideas about culture as a dimensional entity in which directional processes, movements, or transformations are paramount.[16]

If Turner's ideas lead us toward formulations of the semiotic dimensionality of culture, do they furnish a complete framework for such a theory? For example, would an astute application of his concepts of liminality and social drama enable us to understand (if we feel we even *need* to understand) the content and phenomenal popularity of movies like *Star Wars*, *Jaws*, and *E. T.*, and, more importantly, the culture that spawned those bizarre creations? Again, as with Fernandez's provocative notion of culture as a "quality space," I believe that Turner's ideas of liminality and social drama stop short (he would doubtlessly have been relieved to know!) of the broccoli-like labyrinths of phase space (see Penrose's Figure 5.14, reprinted in footnote 5) and the bewildering quantum elusiveness of Hilbert space as these concepts might be deployed in cultural analysis. Despite his emphasis on liminality and drama, Turner does not commit his processual analysis to the kind of situations and constructs we have been considering throughout this work. The problem with his approach may be examined by way of introducing two concepts that are fundamental to the model of cultural dimensionality: *intersystem* and *continuum*.

A few nights ago, in a moment of unthinking weakness, I turned on the TV to watch the late evening news on one of the L. A. stations (actually, several stations, since this is the age of the remote, the perfect device for orchestrating a little Gong Show of your own). Sitting there clicking channels, half asleep, I learned that nothing unusual had happened that day — just the usual atrocities — when an item came across the tube that pierced even my postmodern, desensitized hide. It went pretty much like this: "This just in. A five-year-old Compton boy was killed earlier this evening in a drive-by shooting, apparently gang-related. More from the scene live later in this broadcast. And now in sports. . ." *And now in sports* — this jarring change of frame delivered, in the announcer's rushed Calspeak, with hardly a pause. And it was this vertiginous break, this *tilt* of consciousness I have described earlier, in more sanguine contexts, that got me, that sank the hook. For drive-by shootings are a commonplace occurrence in Los Angeles, where the term had to be invented by some of those very TV news people to describe the latest barbarity, following on an earlier spate of "freeway shootings," to befall the City of Angels. And it is just as common for children to be the victims of these senseless acts, since the intended victims — other gang members — are often hanging around school yards, maybe even attending class when they are not dealing crack, or on the streets outside apartments where children congregate and play. The low-rider car cruises by, a smoky-tinted window glides down with the touch of a button, the snout of a Mac-10 pokes out, a trigger is pulled and held, a random spray of bullets ricochets in the street, and a five-year-old boy dies, within a block of his school or home, his life probably already horribly blighted by a childhood in South Central L. A., and we hear about it an hour or so later, between Bosnia and the Bulls, with details on the death to follow "live."

This world of random, senseless violence that comes to us on the evening news, that many of us inhabit on a daily basis as we drive the same streets and freeways as killers, that the five-year-old boy knew before his life was snuffed out without warning, is it like the world of Turner's Ndembu initiates and their parents, the world of the Zambian countryside as Turner knew it years ago? Or, to turn the question around, can we apply Turner's ideas of liminality and social drama, which, as we have seen, are unique in their emphasis on process and change, on the dynamics of culture, in attempting somehow to make comprehensible the grisly business of drive-by shootings and the sprawling megalopolis that breeds these episodes? I think not. The grim vignette of urban life and death we have been considering throws a harsh light on Turner's ideas, revealing problems with them. Despite their innovative emphasis on process and change, "liminality" and "social drama" as Turner employs these ideas are simply too sedate, too refined, civilized, and, if you will, gentlemanly — like Turner himself — to accommodate the randomness and frenzy of the "initiations" of urban gang life (which may involve "making your bones" by killing a child) or of modern "dramas" like the Los Angeles riots of 1992, Jonestown, and David Koresh's Waco cult. Turner's "ritual process," for all its dynamism, has a thoroughly predictable, orderly flow, as do his "phases" of social drama; they take the individual or community from an initial rupture or conflict in daily life through stages of isolation, transition, resolution, and reincorporation or reaggregation of the psyche and the collective spirit. The *wholeness* of life is briefly lost, only to be restored at the end of the ritual or drama.

In the physical science analogy I have been proposing here, Turner's is very much a "classical" theory of the properties of culture. Things change, but in a fairly tidy, directed manner much like, as Turner emphasizes, the acts of a stage play. For that reason, I believe his theory cannot accommodate the undirected turbulence and near randomness — the *self-organized criticality* — of the cultural processes that control our fates today. *Those* have more to do with Penrose's multidimensional broccoli sprouting in phase space or with the elusive quantum multiplicity of Hilbert space. There is really no way to tell where things are going, but you know they're getting there in an awful hurry. The wholeness Turner attributes to Ndembu lives is overwhelmed by the frag-mented nature of contemporary existence. Have you ever had the experience of flicking a few droplets of water on a hot grill or, heaven forbid, spitting on a hot rock around a campfire at night? The frenzied, skittering, frying motion as the droplets hissed away into nothingness, or into Something Else, is a fair, if not flattering analogy of modern life, of our lives. It is not a happy notion. It will not get a smile-button award from the local chapter of the Jaycees, and I doubt that it would have sat well with Turner as he pondered Ndembu ritual. But it is probably a bit closer to the way things happen than we, or Turner, would readily admit.

Hence the problem I have with Turner's account of the "interstitial" phenomena of liminal experience. While the "inter-ness" of the concept is extremely attractive for a model of cultural dimensionality, the term evokes thoughts of interstices between existing, concrete structures. And as I have just argued, that is indeed the sense in which Turner employs it. In its place I would propose the linked concepts of *intersystem* and *continuum* (ideas stolen in this case from the unlikely field of creole linguistics, with a healthy dollop of pop mathematical physics).[17] The idea of an "intersystem" as developed by Derek Bickerton and other creole linguists involves a profoundly revolutionary departure from the tenets of an earlier, "structural linguistics" (which is implicated in the now-dreaded "structural-functionalism" I was lambasting earlier).

At the time creole linguistics entered the academic fray ("hit the fan" is a more apt metaphor), the field of linguistics was on a roll. The work of the first generation of structural linguists before the second world war, including that of Troubetzkoy, Lobachevsky, and Jakobson, which, as we have seen, so impressed Levi-Strauss, promised to transform the tedious business of describing sound patterns and documenting historical changes in languages into a powerful science which would identify structural principles to account for the features of language and language change. Following the war, Zellig Harris, Noam Chomsky, and a growing cohort of M.I.T.-trained linguists extended this program tremendously, so that they began to speak of the "deep structure" of a language (usually English) as a set of generative and transformational rules which produced the actual speech of persons whose brains had unconsciously assimilated those rules in early childhood (and whose brains were genetically programmed for language acquisition). A popular image of the relationship between this deep structure and actual speech was the *camshaft* of an engine, which is hidden away in the recesses of the machine but which produces, through its precisely engineered form, all the mechanical operations of pistons moving up and down at exact intervals that cause us to say the engine is "running."[18]

In the sixties and early seventies, just as linguistics was seeming to mature into a truly scientific discipline (unlike those messy social sciences, including anthropology, which were still mired in endless description and historical anecdote), a small group of linguists began asking difficult questions about the coherence of individual languages. These linguists, including Douglas Taylor, William Labov, David DeCamp, B. L. Bailey, S. Tsuzaki, Gillian Sankoff, and Derek Bickerton himself, were prompted to formulate the questions on the basis of their various field researches in speech communities of West Africa, the Caribbean, New Guinea, and other Pacific islands. In those locations particularly, the historical processes of colonialism, slavery, mass migration, and very rapid cultural change have fashioned highly diverse societies whose members speak "creolized" versions of some international language (English and French being prominent examples).

The fascinating thing about creoles is that they typically incorporate extremely heterogeneous features of two or more conventional "languages" as different from one another, for example, as English and indigenous languages of West Africa such as the Kwa group. Those disparate elements are fused into a coherent and functional language, or *creole*, which nevertheless embraces a tremendous amount of *internal variation* within the speech community as a whole. There is nothing "contaminated," "reduced," or "inadequate" about creole speech; in fact it is often far more eloquent than the printspeak of educated Americans (one accessible source, although very spruced up for an international audience, is the calypso lyrics of "The Mighty Sparrow"). The internal variation within the speech community takes the form of a *continuum*. One person's speech may contain more African-derived grammatical features (as in the formation of verb tense markers) than another's, but — and here is the vital point — *each speaker can understand and communicate perfectly well across a certain band or swatch of the linguistic continuum.* Thus John may converse easily with Mary and Mary with Angela, but John and Angela will have some difficulty in communicating; whereas a fourth individual, Frank, who has wide ties in the community, may readily converse with all three by shifting his speech accordingly. This process is much more than a mere facility with "dialects," for the internal variation within the creole speech community is *greater* than that found in the "standard" language (since English, for example, does not contain West African grammatical features). The particular pairs of speakers in the above example thus constitute or produce *intersystems* within the total speech community, which can only be described as a *continuum* of linguistic parameters that frame the disjoint collection of intersystems. While no single individual will be fluent across the entire continuum, different speakers are competent within narrower or wider bands of it. The totality of their speech or competencies comprises the "dynamic system" of, say, Guyanese Creole English or Hawaiian Creole.

The research papers and theoretical essays of that small group of creole linguists began to make the linguistics of "natural" languages appear rather contrived.   If Chomskyian structural linguistics is a set of engineer's specifications for the "camshaft" that drives the "engine" of a particular language, then what does the "engine" itself look like?   What are its boundaries?   Since a language such as "English" is not an actual piece of machinery you can reach over and tap with a wrench, how do you know when you are hearing, or even speaking, English and not some other language with a somewhat differently engineered "camshaft"?

These questions have that vertiginous feel to them you may have experienced earlier, when simple questions about the length of an ant path or the dimension of a figure led into some very rough terrain for our commonsense understanding of the world. If you are a "native speaker" of English, your first, exasperated response might be something like: "What kind of question is that? Of course I know when somebody is speaking English! Except for a few words of Spanish I can't understand any other language — and I certainly know when *I'm* speaking English!" If an engine is a separate physical object, so your reasoning might go, then a language is a separate set of words and grammar that together form a *system* of parts much like an engine.

The problem with this seemingly straightforward argument has to do, once again, with the now familiar and terribly complex issues of boundary and scale (Mandelbrot rides again, only this time in the guise of a linguist). In the practical-minded outlook we have come to take as a signature of the myth of America, you may well think of language as a *tool* you use among others, including the engines of cars, to accomplish a particular task, to get the job done. A little reflection, however, begins to tease apart this little piece of the Dreamtime and to reveal the essential, if disturbing symbiosis of common sense and myth.

If you drive a Ford and I drive a Chevy, our two cars can go in different directions and places because they have two separate engines. However, if you and I want to talk about our cars, or anything else, we have to use the *same* language or, by definition, we will be unable to communicate anything through speech. And if we persist in using the analogy of language as a tool, then we will have to say that each of us may have different handles, different competencies with that tool. Your fifth grade English teacher, when she was not busy coercing you to diagram sentences (when is the last time you diagrammed a sentence?), probably taught you that there was one correct way to use the "tool" of the English language and that all other usages were "poor" English, including the dreaded "slang," and the "dialects" that, if not eradicated from your speech, would later tell your adult peers that you were a hillbilly or from an undesirable neighborhood (And keep you from being president one day? Not at all!). Translated into the terms of structural linguistics, which, when you get down to it, differ little in spirit from the homelies of your old English teacher, the English language comprises a system, and that system possesses invariant properties, or rules, which together have the capability of generating all possible utterances in "English."

It is on this point that creole linguistics' concepts of intersystem and continuum are so appropriate, even if they fly in the face of much accepted wisdom regarding the cohesiveness of language. The *boundary disputes* associated with intersystems come rushing in, rudely elbowing their way into the tidy world, desks all arranged in straight little rows, of the English classroom and the M. I. T. lecture hall. For although your fifth grade teacher, if confronted with the outlandish examples of Guyanese creole or New Guinea pidgin, might claim that those "alien" forms have little to do with "correct English," *there is really no difference in kind between the linguistic experiences of a "native speaker" of Guyanese creole and your own experiences with language as a son or daughter of Dreamtime America.*

Suppose, for example, that you live in southern California, where you moved after growing up in the Midwest (perhaps *you* were that movie-going teenager from Topeka). You were never very interested in or particularly good at foreign languages, and when your cretinous guidance counselor at Topeka High advised you to take a year of German because you were interested in science and planned to go on to college, you dutifully but unenthusiastically obliged. A few years passed, you went to college for a couple of years, took no more language courses, worked at a few different jobs, and then, tiring of Topeka (or *Sleepless in Seattle*), wound up in sunny California, hoping to find the American Dream at its source. Once settled in Anaheim, you quickly discover that, although you didn't need a passport to get there, you seem to have moved to another country. Buying groceries, getting gas, finding an apartment, and working at your new job, all these aspects of daily life bring you into contact with people who are clearly *not* from Topeka and who probably wouldn't have a clue about where to find it, assuming you were able to ask them.

Although this swarming multitude seems to speak dozens of languages, you soon find that a great many residents of this new Babel are Hispanics, themselves from all over the western hemisphere, who speak, not English (and definitely not German) but Spanish as their "native language." Of course, some Hispanics you meet speak English that would have pleased your fifth grade teacher more than your own Topeka twang, but others are recent immigrants with little formal education whose English is minimal and almost unintelligible to you.   The majority fall somewhere in between, speaking English that you, recalling the wisdom imparted by your teacher, regard as "incorrect," "ungrammatical," and heavily "accented."   After a while, you develop a disconcerting sense that almost all your conversations with Hispanics are somehow affected by a perceived "language barrier," that makes it difficult to use relaxed speech, to kid around, to tell jokes, to make friends.

As a sensitive individual with a social conscience, and as an organism adapting to its new environment, you decide to ameliorate the difficulties and embarrassments of this language barrier by enrolling in a Spanish immersion course. At the end of a summer of fairly intense study (when you were not out there having fun in that warm California sun), you have acquired a new ability to understand some of the Spanish spoken around you and even to conduct parts of simple conversations in Spanish. Do you now "speak Spanish"? In all fairness and modesty you have to admit that you do not, that most of what you hear on the street and on Spanish TV stations completely passes you by.

Oddly enough, you discover, as have countless language students before you, that your most gratifying experiences with the language, when you feel you are right on top of what is being said, come in conversational sessions with fellow students in your immersion course, or in slightly more or less advanced courses. You find that you can spend a good part of an afternoon conversing in a fairly relaxed manner "in Spanish" with these fellow language-learners, only to leave class, stop at a gas station on the way home, and, your mind still working "in Spanish," make a simple, casual remark "in Spanish" to the station attendant, whereupon you receive a blank-faced "*Que?*" in response.

Does this deflating experience mean that you still haven't learned Spanish, that several more summers of immersion courses will be necessary before you can confidently pull into that gas station and have a pleasant little chat with the attendant? While you are pondering this discouraging scenario, a strange thing happens. An acquaintance of yours from the office, a real *angeleno* Hispanic, pulls up to the pumps, jumps out of his TransAm, says "Hello" to you, and barks a command in rapid-fire Spanish to the attendant — whereupon *he* gets the same, blank-faced, uncomprehending "*Que?*" that greeted your effort at communicating in *la lengua*. But your office-mate is far from cowed: with a look of disgust he does not bother to conceal, he turns to you and mutters, "These damn Cubans can't even speak the Spanish language!"

Welcome to the world of intersystems. You don't have to be eaves-dropping on Rastas in a Jamaican rum shop or on Guyanese rice farmers in a Georgetown bus to experience the kaleidoscopic play of intersystems within a linguistic continuum; your local Anaheim Mobil station will do nicely. Clearly, there are things about the language-learning business that your fifth grade teacher and your immersion course instructors have not told you, and would become quite uncomfortable over if questioned closely about little episodes like the gas station incident.

The big question, of course, is "What counts as speaking Spanish?" Is Spanish like what your fifth grade teacher told you about English, that there was one correct way — her way — to speak it and any number of incorrect ways? In that case, what were you and your fellow immersion course students speaking during all those afternoon sessions? Was it some pathetic, reduced version of a true "Spanish" that was just good enough for the limited com-municative purposes to which you put it? And even if you bow to the authority of those long-ago English classes and self-effacingly reject those pleasant, chatty afternoons of "Spanish" as something shamefully inauthentic, what are you to say about the little scene your officemate threw at the gas station? Did this *angeleno*, who had never been south of his Rosarito vacation condo in his life and who grew up with the innumerable anglicisms of L. A. Spanish ringing in his ears, somehow have a lock on the "true" Spanish language that seemed to be eluding you and, evidently, the hapless *cubano* station attendant?

Suppose, to compound the example, a diplomat from the Spanish consulate, a native Barcelonan, had pulled into the pumps right behind your rude acquaintance. What would he think (but, being a diplomat, would not say) about the Americanized speech of the brash *angeleno*? About the speech of the *cubano* attendant? And would the attendant, for his part, have more or less difficulty understanding the diplomat than understanding the *angeleno* — or even you, since, after all, you had weighed in with a little "Spanish" discourse of your own?

In such complex, fluid situations, which are about the only kind around these days, even your old, ruler-thwacking fifth grade teacher (who, bless her heart, probably thought her ruler was straight and measured lines accurately) might find it difficult to insist on the procrustean standard of a single, correct speech. Perhaps she might backpedal a bit and say some vague things about a language having "dialects" that issue from regional or class differences and impede communication, sometimes to the point of unintelligibility. That, of course, *is* just backpedaling from the awful truth, for it leaves the really vexing questions completely unresolved. Is there a "standard" Spanish and several dialects, or just a collection of dialects? And if, in that collection, you find two dialects that seem to be mutually unintelligible (like the speech of our *angeleno* and *cubano*), then how in the world can you say that speakers of those dialects are speaking the *same* language? And what about the fruits of your immersion course(s)? Had you, or at least some of your more advanced colleagues, not managed to cross over that putative "barrier" (which looks more and more like our ant path) separating "English" and "Spanish," so that you could make yourself understood to *some* "native speakers" of Spanish and *at the same time* could converse "in Spanish" with beginning immersion students whose own efforts *en Espanol* were painfully inadequate?

Do you have that unsettling feeling that we have hit this wall before? That we have reached much the same impasse we encountered in trying to shore up and salvage other seemingly obvious, objective notions like "line" and "dimension"? Do you sense that the common and terribly important idea of "*a* language" is now being sucked into the vertiginous maw that swallowed those other concepts in its churning, murky depths? Concepts that we rely on habitually to tell us that things are "on the level" and running "true to form"? If you are having any of these thoughts, then my little vignette of our Topekan friend has served its purpose.

For the moral of the story, just as in that of the ant path, is that no amount of backing and filling (making *more* measurements, using *finer* instruments, identifying *better* grammatical rules, firing up *faster* computers) will preserve our commonsense notions (line, dimension, language) once we have begun to question them from the perspective presented here. Just as it proved impossible to salvage the simple idea that an ant path or a stretch of shoreline has a certain fixed length, so it is impossible to save the idea of a cohesive, unitary, "standard" language. Invoking *ad hoc* explanations such as "slang" or "dialect" to account for the tremendous amount of internal variation within a speech community is really only to clutch at straws. For if the measurements of a line or the scalings of a dimension proliferate endlessly, depending on our approach and instruments, then so do the intersystems of language. The linguistic system we call "Spanish" or "English" does not consist of a core, "standard" set of rules ("invariant properties") for generating speech and three or four, or even ten or twenty, subsidiary sets that kick in to describe dialectal or regional variation. The system that we might gloss as "American English" ("Ah kyan't speak Anglish too good, but I shore know how to tawlk Amuricun") actually contains millions — or tens of millions or hundreds of millions; the choice is yours; you hold the ruler — of intersystems that taken together establish the parameters of what we are pleased to call "the English language."

This perspective on the highly variegated composition of *a* language is quite close to the molecular chemist, Manfred Eigen's, mathematical analysis of *a* virus as a *quasispecies* whose great genomic variability can best be modeled as a spreading, sprawling thing in a multidimensional semantic ("sequence") space, much like Penrose's broccoli sproutings in phase space (see Figure 3.3).[19]

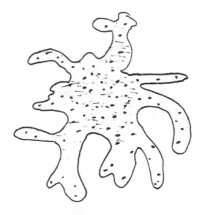

Figure 3.3. Tendrils of Identity. (A Cross-Section)
Virus, Language, Humanity: Internal Variation Within a "System."

It follows that each of us, even if we have no "foreign language" skills, speaks several languages: how you address *your* gas station attendant differs significantly from the speech you use with your spouse or "life companion" or lover, with your five-year-old, with friends, business associates, etc. This is not just a quibble or a mischievous toying with the sacred concept of language. The vast number of speech events that occur in the United States in the course of a single day are all little nudges (that vectorial process of pushes and pulls again) that *move* "American English," or whatever we decide to call it, in directions whose destinations we can only guess at.

One little example, one little nudge stronger than most of ours because it has made it onto the silver screen of the Dreamtime, is Pauly Shore's "dude," a form of speech that seems, to these tired old ears, to be an amalgam of surfer lingo, (San Fernando) Valley-speak, and L. A. black street talk. Try going to his *Encino Man* (which has an explicitly anthropological topic!) or *Son-in-Law*, or listening to his clever audio tape *The Future of America* (which he claims to be, along with his fellow "dude" speakers). Can you follow Pauly's speech readily? Probably not. Are some of the things he says totally incomprehensible to you? Probably. Does it matter, you may ask with understandable irritation, since the stuff *is* so silly? Again, probably not, for in twenty years "dude" may have vanished without a trace: the "future of America" in the domain of speech may have taken an entirely different, unanticipated turn. But the point is that *it will take a turn, and one that we cannot foresee*. "Dude" may vanish without a trace, or it may leave a minor but recognizable imprint on American English in the twenty-first century (when we would find a few linguistics graduate students meticulously transcribing the dialogue from *Encino Man* for analysis in their dissertations!). In twenty years, or fifty years, or one hundred years, or five hundred years there will have been discernible changes in American English, changes that are increasingly noticeable as the time scale lengthens. But the *direction* of those changes, what the future of American speech will sound like, is as indeterminate as the next hop our water droplet makes as it sizzles away on the grill.

We don't, however, even have to wait for those changes. If you, like me, are in that state of physical and social obsolescence euphemistically dubbed being "over-forty," then just slide into a booth at McDonald's some day and eavesdrop on the teenagers in the next booth.[20] Or, God forbid, if you *have* a teenager of your own, then reflect on how you and your teen converse — if that is what you want to call it. Better yet, make an audiotape of a few of those "conversations," so you can study them later, after your feeble old heart has stopped fibrillating from your latest encounter with your flesh-and-blood, with the real/reel-life "future of America." What you will hear is much more than biographical anecdote or confirmation of your good sense in the face of flakiness; you will hear, live and under way, instances of the complex process of *linguistic change*, which is as inexorable as the flowing of a mighty river.[21]

Linguistic change, like cultural change and all other processes, is clearest when viewed through hindsight. Wind the clock back a couple of centuries to when George and Tom and the other founding fathers were putting "America" together (again, little was said about "founding mothers" except for that heavily mythologized seamstress, Betsy). While we can read their writings perfectly well and admire their (archaic) eloquence, if George and Tom had possessed audio tape recorders (and a little of Dick's trickiness) we might find ourselves listening to excerpts of their two-hundred-year-old conversations (trying to get to the bottom of Cherry Tree-gate or Monticello-gate) and having a hard time understanding their speech. Certainly if those time-warped tape recorders had captured conversations between, say, George and his cook, William ("Can you bake a cherry pie, Billy boy, Billy boy. . ."), or his stable hand, or especially between the cook and stable hand when George had left the room, we would be hard pressed to follow what was being said.

If you choose to believe that the "English" of American speech is more coherent than I suggest here (and who can really say, since we don't have those time-warped tapes?), then it is only necessary to wind the clock back further, another four hundred years, say, to Chaucer's "Middle English" or another eight hundred years to the "Old English" of Anglo-Saxon, until we encountered "English" speech that would be completely unintelligible to our modern ears. If we had a tape of Chaucer's miller sporting with his milkmaids (which would definitely not get the Tipper Gore seal of approval) we would be able to understand little more than, shall we say, the more elementary exclamations.

The critical point here is that historical changes in American English occur only because our own everyday speech already embraces a tremendous diversity or internal variation which, radiating chaotically in this direction and that, provides the springboard for transformations that alter our speech, sometimes even as we utter it, beyond recognition. It is also crucial to note that the diversity or internal variation is not the result of a simple clumping of the population according to some convenient sociological criteria: children speak one way, adults another, and similarly for men and women, blacks and whites, rich people and poor folks, urbanites and farmers, and so on. The whole point about intersystems and the multidimensional continua that frame them is that it is the peculiar *pairings* — or three-ings or four-ings, etc. — of a child and adult speaking to each other, of a man and a woman,[22] of a black single mother and her white welfare counselor, and so on that constitute the linguistic system.

The individual speaker, you or I, is not a mere pawn in this proliferation of intersystems, but the *source* of them: each of us "speaks several languages" *because each of us is a multiplicity of selves*, a whole repertoire of virtual beings who, not unlike the photons in a Hilbert space, may appear at an infinity of locations within an unchartable labyrinth of complex dimensions. Walt Whitman wrote in *Leaves of Grass* (appropriate metaphor!) that each of us contains multitudes. I doubt that he had quantum mechanics, creole linguistics, or anthropological semiotics in mind when he composed that line, but its sense could not be nearer the meaning of "intersystems" operating in "semiospace" as I have tried to describe that process here.

It is a fundamental point of this work that our linguistic competencies, summarized under the rubric of "language," are far from being a privileged model of culture, of what, again, is "uniquely human," for the very good reason that those competencies are the interactive *product* of an extremely variegated, multiplex identity of the individual speaker. And the individual "self" or, in the abstract, personal identity — whatever it is that counts as being a *particular* human being — is an inexplicable cipher, a meaningless term, without some understanding of the *cultural processes* that have brought humanity into being, that continuously transform it, and that may well end its career, not necessarily with a bang *or* a whimper, but with an undirected, wandering series of minor transitions that take us, along with that water droplet, across the line into the domain of Something Else.

Cultural Generativity

> *I have come to believe that the whole world is an enigma, a harmless enigma that is made terrible by our own mad attempt to interpret it as though it had an underlying truth.*
>
>   — Umberto Eco, *The Limits of Interpretation*

Up to this point we have seen that many things we take to be simple truths of everyday life have a disturbing tendency to shred or fragment on close inspection. Lines have no fixed length, dimensions are pretty much what you want them to be, and even the notion of a "language," which, after all, is what most of us depend on to communicate what we know about lines, dimensions, and everything else, turns out to be a surprisingly slippery entity. Much more disturbing than these rather arcane issues, however, are the implications that follow from applying the notions of intersystem, continuum, and semiospace to individuals — folks like you and me — considered as social beings and not just as speakers of a language or as reluctant students of geometry.

For a cherished belief and anchor of the myth of America is *the individual*: independent, practical, self-reliant, and with a distinct presence and wholeness — an integrity — about him. To propose, as I have just done, that the individual is actually a multiplicity of selves, a set of virtual beings (not unlike quantum wave-particles) spread (or smeared) out across a little domain of semiospace, is to make a frontal assault on the commonsense belief that, probably more than any other, is the ideological foundation of Dreamtime America. That assault, however, is not just a perverse little campaign I have mounted to shake up the good burghers of the land; at most I can take credit only for struggling to articulate here a truth that each of us (perhaps I should say "some of each of us"!) already recognizes but keeps locked up inside, permitting only an occasional Whitman to voice it outright. That truth is the agonizing tension, a palpable, wrenching force like binary stars of consciousness locked in a death struggle of centrifugal-centripetal motions, between our somehow intuited realization of Whitman's multitudes within each of us and our compelling need to stand up and wave the flag of our individual, unique, personal identity, to proclaim that "This is me!" That tension pervades the Dreamtime, flooding our theatres and our lives with images of beings who *are* this rather than that, who are John Waynes rather than Gregor Samsas.[23]

The terrible *ambivalence of myth* we encountered earlier, in trying to make sense of the contradictory meanings "myth" possesses, is nowhere more evident than in the conceptions we frame and attempt to maintain of our fundamental natures, of what we, as individual human beings, are like. We strive mightily to act as though each of us were a coherent, unitary being, and, as part of that valiant but doomed attempt, even contrive a notion of *truth* that possesses, as its very essence, the coherence and unity we long to discover in ourselves. If the universe around us is whole, then so must we be. But when the universe, or what little we can see and say of it, *turns out to be quite ambivalent about itself*, when the building blocks of matter are sometimes particles and sometimes waves, maybe here and maybe there, maybe even existent or only "virtual," then the coherence and unity of individual identity teeters vertiginously on the edge of chaos.

While this may all sound quite drastic (or to the sceptical, at least melodramatic), I submit that most of us have already learned to live with Whitman's multitudes, even as we struggle to keep those "others" within us sorted out. For the one constancy in an individual's life is change: you are not the being you were as a five-year-old, although that five-year-old is still with you, one of the voices of your multitudes. And as adults you and I are probably much like our friend from Topeka, who may well be another voice in our respective multitudes, in that we have experienced a number of those wrenching dislocations that are part and parcel of (post)modern existence: our family of childhood far away, dispersed, irretrievably lost; our spouses or lovers departed, turned bitter or indifferent; our children become aliens; our surroundings, even if they began as a Norman Rockwell pastoral of corn-on-the-cob shared at the family reunion picnic, become the fragmented, often terrifying existence of the drive-by shooting last night at Tony Wu's teriyaki taco stand on Sepulveda. As the homily runs, you can take the boy out of the country, but you can't take the country out of the boy. Whether trying out his Spanish at that Anaheim Mobil station or dodging hot lead when he decided at just the wrong moment to indulge his newfound appetite for low-budget Cal cuisine, our Topekan friend still carries around a lot of Topeka with him, of Topekan selves who jostle in the tumult of the megalopolitan present to be heard among the cacophony of new, tentative voices, new selves stirring within their multiplex subject.

The clearing house or processing unit for those multitudinous selves struggling within the individual is a small cluster of beliefs we hold about what "people" or "humanity" or, more academically, "culture" is like. We don't have to go around psychologizing about the depths of our individual psyches (all this stuff about "multitudes within") because we believe deeply that people, apart from their idiosyncratic differences, are basically and uniformly people, human beings fundamentally distinct from anything else on the planet and the possessors of a unique facility: culture. We may not follow all the twists and turns in their relationship *When Harry Met Sally,* but we assume without question that Harry and Sally *as people* have a familiar presence, a solidity about them that makes it possible for us to know them: their psychological acrobatics are anchored in the familiar bedrock of a "human nature."

As I indicated in chapter 2, there is a fundamental difficulty with the conventional view that people are a known quantity, i.e., ordinary people leading ordinary lives, upon which we merely embellish a decorative motif of stories or myths to entertain and instruct ourselves. At the heart of the conception of culture as semiospace — as a dynamic, dimensional, semiotic entity — is the principle of cultural generativity: the seemingly paradoxical, rather heretical notion that humanity itself is far from an established fixture of consciousness, a presence possessing a "human nature," but is instead a shifting, drifting complex of identities and artifacts, a complex that is the (vectorial) product of cultural processes acting within a set of semiotic dimensions. Perception and language, as we have seen, can play tricks on us, and perhaps the most outrageous trick of all is our easy acceptance that the "people" or "humans" or, more grandly, "humanity" invoked in our casual thought and speech are a given, a natural feature of our experience that we can simply point to with an exasperated "There!" if ever we encountered someone perverse enough to question their integrality. The several versions of a materialist critique of myth examined in chapter 2 fall prey to this trick, for they insist on some pre-established order or scheme, such as ecology, history, economy, that fixes humanity in place as a sort of dependent variable and only later allows in, by the back door, myth and its imaginative play of Dreamtime beings who are part-human, part-animal, and part-god. Cultural analysis, in working through the principle of cultural generativity, flies in the face of those approaches because it replaces the "." behind "humanity" with a "?"

At the conclusion of chapter 2, I presented what is the underlying theme of this work: that myth has primacy because it is our means of working through elemental dilemmas that arise in the course of specifying who or what we are and of situating ourselves within a cognitized world, or *Umwelt,* which we construct and continually modify through our invention and use of artifacts. In short, myth is about human identity and its ever-changing nature in a world at whose bootstraps we are constantly tugging even as we march, or stagger, along. The relentless classificatory force that is the human mind, as described by Levi-Strauss in *Totemism,* is such only because it is forever trying to place itself as subject within its framework of experience, which, not incidentally, it transforms as it goes along. *Culture* is the name we give to these inexorable processes of myth as it builds up, tears down, pushes and pulls at the very sense of who and what we are and what kind of a world we inhabit. Culture is the accumulating, shifting residue of ongoing conceptual *and* artifactual systems people have developed over the ages, on their way to becoming people and, quite probably, something other than people.

If this seems an odd way of thinking about humanity, which, after all, consists of "just plain folks," then consider the alternative. We can relegate myth and its current vehicle, the supergrosser movies of Dreamtime America, to the back burner of human evolution only by supposing that "human nature" or "identity" or "culture" somehow just popped out of blue sky and gelled immutably at a particular time in the prehuman, precultural past.

In fact, a cinematic version of this just-suppose "theory" of human origins already exists: the opening scene of *2001: A Space Odyssey*, in which dim-witted apes headed for extinction are zapped with a smart ray from the mysterious obelisk that has appeared outside their wretched cave dwelling, all to the thundering kettle drums of "Also Sprach Zarathustra." A few aficionados of popular movies may object that Kubrick's scene was anticipated by the work of another director given to epic themes: John Huston's *The Bible*.[24] And still others, of a fundamentalist if not fundamental turn of mind, may wish to argue vigorously that the book (or The Book) is a lot more important than either Huston's or Kubrick's movie, that it establishes once and for all exactly how and when humanity appeared on Earth and what its true, immutable nature is.

Now although anthropologists tend to get rather snappish when confronted with Bible-pounding creationists who want to stamp out the pernicious lie of evolution being spread by the nation's heathen schoolteachers, I must admit to being fascinated, if ultimately saddened, by the uproar they have generated. What fascinates me about creationism, and what kept me riveted to the screen when I first saw *2001* despite the nagging little anthropologist's voice in the back of my mind saying "This is a crock!", is the great emphasis both give to creativity, to the awesome power involved in taking up a handful of mud or just a dull ape and transforming it into a soulful, sentient being. What deeply saddens me about both creationist dogma and Kubrick's film is that, while seeming to celebrate the germ of divine (or at least extraterrestrial) creativity within the human spirit, they deny humanity any creativity after the fact: we are doomed to plod along in the path laid out for us until The Second Coming or until the next obelisk shows up on the moon. Both have come to bury culture, not to praise it.

I maintain, and would even hope to convince you through this work, that a special kind of creativity, which I insist pedantically on calling *cultural generativity*, is indeed the most powerful force behind the origin of humanity. But unlike the creationists and Kubrick's film, I see that force continuing to operate, to shape and reshape humanity in fundamental ways. Things change, to be sure, but those changes are the result of processes within the system, within the semiospace of culture, and not of an external puppeteer jerking on the strings. The biblical creation as interpreted by our coiffed and mascaraed TV evangelists turns away from the spirit of creativity itself and, in my opinion, insults whoever might be up there, or out there, with the demeaning image of a humanity so constricted and lifeless that bringing it into being would not be such a grand accomplishment. In contrast with that diminished vision of what we humans are and may become, I would suggest that our very being is a consequence of and testimony to ongoing, generative cultural processes.

The best evidence for cultural generativity, for a continually evolving (or at least shifting) humanity, is the prominence or, as I have called it, primacy of myth itself. My argument here is extremely simple, which you may take as a plus or a minus. Suppose (we have supposed things before in preceding sections that have got us into trouble; so watch out!) that cultural generativity and its vehicle, myth, in fact played little or no role in human origins. Instead, natural forces of the environment and biology or outright divine intervention (the choice is yours) operated on the planet and its emergent biota for billions of years (or six days), with the result that a particular species, *Homo sapiens*, appeared that possessed an intelligence born of adaptive response (or the breath of God). Without the elemental dilemmas of cultural generativity to fret about, that is, without Gregory Bateson's *schismogenesis* or what I have called the *ambivalence of myth* in the picture, *Homo sapiens* could proceed directly with the chore of putting together culture. It would have warmed the heart of an early day "management training" specialist sent out from the head office to fire up the troops. And so the new species employed its facility of sapience in an exceedingly tidy, straightforward way: the plants, animals, human relatives and groups, and artifacts it found in its environment needed names (since with sapience they were now concepts, information embedded in a consciousness) and it set about expeditiously naming and classifying them. This task was not difficult, since everything corresponded closely to its intuited nature: lions were dangerous and to be avoided; fruits were sweet and good to eat (except the apple!); sex with parents or siblings wasn't a good idea; the folks in the next valley were revolting beings to be killed on sight; you could knock a rock in a certain way to make a cutting tool.

If you find this a parodying treatment of "environmental determinism" or whatever label we give it, you are quite correct, but I would argue that any claim for an environmental (or divine) basis for the origin of a full-blown human consciousness is already self-parodying. In fact, you can find a similar collection of just-suppose stories that account for cultural origins in a text avidly read by anthropologists (at least embryonic ones) in the late sixties and prominently displayed in leading graduate departments of anthropology at the time: *Anthro* comic books.[25]

The problem with the just-suppose approach to cultural origins as outlined in our sketches above is that a world without something very like cultural generativity would look a lot like a real (but not reel!)-life version of *Anthro* comics. Consciousness, and specifically an *artifactual intelligence*, what I would call the true signature of humanity and culture, would be unrecognizable, and quite useless, in that world. The first hominids (who, it is important to bear in mind, lived over four million years before the appearance of modern *Homo sapiens*) would have sorted out themselves and their surroundings right at the start, assimilated the classificatory order of things they had imposed, and settled into a social life that varied little from eon to eon. Movement, process, change, vectorial semiotic forces, all would have been of negligible or non-existent significance in that protocultural world, which would have possessed the dreary timelessness of a colony of algal pond scum. *Homo sapiens*, and our comic book hero, Anthro, would never have made an appearance: they would not have been needed. The creationists notwithstanding, humanity as presently constituted in *Homo sapiens* has continuously and fundamentally transformed itself throughout its more than four million years of hominid speciation. And the predominant agent of transformation, the impetus behind the big brain, the erect posture, the dexterous hands, the early, foetalized birth, has been incipient culture, or protoculture: patterns of behavior (diet, division of labor, establishing a "home base," infant care, sexuality, con jugal bonding, intergroup relations) *and* artifact production whose adaptive value demanded more and more "computer time" and "RAM space" from the emergent consciousness.

The fundamental point here is that, even with four-plus million years to work on it, humanity has still not "got it right." With all its newfound cognitive skills and its very recently acquired industrial and electronic technologies, *Homo sapiens* is still very much a project underway. In fact, the transformational processes of culture, after proceeding at a leisurely rate for 99.9% of the hominid past, have now shifted into overdrive. If cultural processes influenced the course of biological speciation in the past, selecting for big brains with linguistic capabilities, for example, that is nothing compared with our developing ability to alter the human genome directly: biological speciation and cultural processes have been a synergistic complex for eons; they are now becoming one and the same. Whatever wrinkles biotechnology may introduce to this ancient mix of biology and culture, however, the important thing is that none of the high-tech wizardry would be happening were it not for the fact that the project of culture is intrinsically incomplete. If we had sorted things out with the invention of the Acheulian hand ax, or the wheel, or the Model T, or the computer, then not only technological change would have ground to a halt but cultural processes of identity formation, of establishing the shifting differences between this and that, would also have ceased. That people are still sorting out the basics of their existence attests to the intrinsically unfinished nature of culture and to the vitality of the mythic processes that accomplish that sorting-out. We wouldn't have myths, including the current rash of supergrosser movies, if we didn't need them.

Having made a general argument supporting the principle of cultural generativity, it is important, before moving on to the specific operations of that principle, to make clear what I do *not* mean by "cultural generativity." As heirs of a tradition of "humanism" that extends back at least to the Enlightenment of the eighteenth century, we have become comfortable — *too* comfortable, I would argue — with a diffuse, self-congratulatory attitude toward ourselves as the "architects of our own experience," the masters, for better or worse, of our destiny. Cultural anthropologists routinely endorse this general outlook on "the wonder that is man," which is not surprising since they owe their disciplinary existence to the ascendancy of humanism over the past two centuries. And in an excess of zeal, some anthropologists have even called explicitly (if redundantly) for a "humanistic anthropology" and enshrined that mission in the name of a professional association. I find this outlook, particularly when embraced by anthropologists, far too constricting. In fact, it is directly contrary to the perspective of a semiotic of culture, of an anthropological semiotics. Humanism, however well-intentioned (and it seems rather sacrilegious and "inhumane" to come out against it), installs "humanity" at the center of things, a splendid icon to be marveled at and relished.

Anthropological semiotics, perhaps regrettably, takes a less exalted, and certainly less complacent, view of "humanity." Its radical premise is that the generativity of culture, the ceaseless arranging and rearranging of things, issues from humanity's contingent, *circumstantial* existence, and *not* from humanity's privileged occupancy of center stage in the universe. For me this premise, unflattering though it may be, is indispensable; it is certainly the foundation of this study. Since the world began long before *Homo sapiens* appeared on the scene and will end long after our species has vanished, a naive humanism that insists on a ptolemaic conception of humanity is an insupportable conceit. People, as a whole and as individuals, have issued from something, some prior state that was not of themselves, have undergone major changes in the course of their careers, and will relinquish their place in the scheme of things to heirs that differ fundamentally from themselves. In this radical sense of cultural generativity, humanity not only produces itself and its experiences, as a naive humanism would have it, *but is itself produced* by cultural processes that began long before *Homo sapiens* walked the earth and will quite probably continue after our version of sapience has transmuted into Something Else. Humanity, like languages and ant paths, occurs on a continuum, and can be understood only by following some of the pushes and pulls that continuum receives on its twisting, turning (vectorial) odyssey through the semiospace of culture.

The only way of retaining even a vestige of a spent humanism is to subvert drastically its most crucial principle: that Man (which was what they called humanity back in the bad old days) is at the center of things — what I have termed humanism's ptolemaic conception of humanity. Nowhere is that conception stated more forcefully or with greater conceit than in Rene Descartes's famous dictum, *cogito ergo sum* ("I think, therefore I am"). In a remarkable bit of what Nietzsche called "world historical irony," Descartes proclaimed that the proof of existence itself ("How can I know that anything exists?") hinged on his apperception of his own consciousness, while a few hundred miles away his contemporary Galileo was busily sketching the first outlines of a vast cosmos, an ultimate Being, which existed quite nicely, thank you very much, while relegating Descartes and his epistemology to the far-flung reaches of a nondescript galaxy scattered like a dust mote among billions of other galaxies.

In the spirit of Galileo, if not with his rigor, I would suggest that the anthropocentric Cartesian *cogito* holds only if, invoking the principle of cultural generativity, we conceive of humanity *as an absence at the center of things*, a cipher to be filled with meaning through the operations of an artifactual intelligence. The fact that people think at all, that they are cultural beings who do things and effect changes in their surroundings, is due to the pronounced uncertainty, the relentless unclarity of their lives. The reason that we tell myths, that our minds continue to turn over at a frantic rate after a hundred thousand years or so as *Homo sapiens* and do not just sink into that immortal algal ooze, is that the fundamental characteristic of human identity is its ceaseless, tormented struggle with elemental dilemmas that issue from our particular brand of sentient existence.

Those dilemmas, themselves the product of the semiotic dimensions of culture, operate as movements around the absent center that is humanity: they are parameter-setting, identity-testing, semiotic processes that function in the non-Euclidean domain of semiospace, and not in a tidy world of clearly delineated, preconceived categories that we, following Descartes's seductive example, have popped out of a metaphysical hat. It follows that the (unavoidable) subversion of Descartes's *cogito* is precisely to reverse its terms and negate its second premise: *"I am not, therefore I think"* is much closer to the provisional truths revealed by anthropological semiotics than the classic formulation. Thinking is an emergent, generative process leading to self-consciousness only if the thinker is itself inherently incomplete, an intersystemic multiplicity of beings, a pastiche of lines and shadows that requires something, some form of consciousness to attempt to integrate those disparate elements, to connect the dots.

How, then, does humanity attempt to connect its dots (an activity whose fundamental importance artists from the pointillist Georges Seurat to the neo-conceptualist Brooke Larsen have understood)? The incompleteness inherent in the from-Something Else, to-Something Else nature of humanity is its distinguishing feature, and is therefore the primary focus of a semiotic of culture. The critical question for that developing field of inquiry then is: What are the continua, or semiotic dimensions, through which the generative phenomenon of humanity moves?

The Semiotic Dimensions of Culture

> *Animal* <------------> *Artifact/Machine*
> *Us/Self* <------------> *Them/Other*
> *Life Force* <------------> *Death Force*

> *. . . I count as an aesthete since Sartre applies this term to anyone purporting to study men as if they were ants. But apart from the fact that this seems to me just the attitude of any scientist who is an agnostic, there is nothing very compromising about it, for ants with their artificial tunnels, their social life, and their chemical messages, already present a sufficiently tough resistance to the enterprises of analytical reason. . . So I accept the characterization of aesthete in so far as I believe the ultimate goal of the human sciences to be not to constitute, but to dissolve man. The preeminent value of anthropology is that it represents the first step in a procedure which involves others. . . This first enterprise opens the way for others. . . which are incumbent on the exact natural sciences: the reintegration of culture in nature and finally of life within the whole of its physico-chemical conditions.*
>
> — Claude Levi-Strauss, *The Savage Mind*

> *Enjoy your humanity. . . while it lasts.*
> — Chief Supreme Being, *My Stepmother Is an Alien*

I have said that this work is a scouting expedition, an attempt to try out some theoretical ideas new to cultural anthropology on some material — popular movies — generally neglected by anthropologists. Nowhere is that remark more appropriate than in this section, in which I attempt what an artist could only call a gesture drawing: a quick, impressionistic sketch of a subject that aims at capturing, in passing, something of its essential nature. The "subjects" in this case are the semiotic dimensions of culture, of that semiospace on which I have been harping for scores of pages. And while the sketch I offer here is undeniably provisional, I can assure you that it has not come as easily to me as a gesture drawing: thinking it through even at this rough stage has been for me a long, grueling, and truly mind-altering experience.

But the basics of my argument are quite simple. If our essential nature as cultural beings is generative and processual, and if myth as I have described it here is the vehicle for those generative processes of identity formation, then a close inspection of our myths will reveal the parameters, or dimensions, of semiospace. So where, according to our myths, have we come from, and where are we going? What are our myths about?

In wrestling with this simple question for some years, I have come up with three pairs of answers, three semiotic dimensions of culture that infuse our myths with meaning. It is doubtlessly possible to add to this number; it is certainly possible to take the three pairs or constructs and produce a model of semiospace with multiple, even infinite dimensions, much as Penrose has described for phase space and Hilbert space and Eigen for the sequence space of viral quasispecies. But those are refinements that may be added to the gesture drawing after the fact, provided only that the drawing has any vitality to it. And though there may be more than three constructs, I am convinced that there are no fewer than three, that the movements I identify in our movie-myths involve at a fundamental level the three constructs.

The three constructs are:

Animal <------------> *Artifact/Machine*
Us/Self <------------> *Them/Other*
Life Force <------------> *Death Force*

As semiotic dimensions of the semiospace of culture, these constructs describe the vectorial forces or movements operating on every social action in our lives and on every element of every cultural production. The system, a sort of spacetime of consciousness, which these constructs form may be very roughly visualized in two ways (see Figures 3.4 and 3.5). Figure 3.4 is a kind of schematized "little picture" of the anti-Cartesian perspective on humanity as an absence at the center of things. Its point is that what we are willing to call "humanity" at any one time is the sum of generative processes acting on individuals, so that humanity is a shifting, convoluted entity suspended within the field or semiospace formed by the three dimensions of culture. The identities or forces of animal, artifact/machine, us/self, them/other, life force, and death force impinge on that shifting entity with differing intensities, depending on the particular cultural production involved. For example, the contours of humanity that emerge from James Bond movies (which pay little attention to animals) are quite different from those that emerge from *Jaws*.

Figure 3.5 is my adaptation of Penrose's multidimensional broccoli sprouting in phase space; it is the "big picture" that incorporates Figure 3.4, the detailed contours of "humanity," as but one of a very large number of other complexly bounded units. One point of Figure 3.5 is that every scene in a popular movie, every utterance and gesture we make in the course of a day, every minute piece of culture, has an orientation, a movement with respect to the six poles of the semiotic axes. As with our ant path and our Topekan friend's adventures in language-learning, we may choose to focus on relatively large or small chunks of experience. With increasingly fine-grained detail, semiospace is seen to be a *froth* of minute bits of culture, each with its vectorial movement. In the topical essays that follow, I adopt a decidedly rough-grained focus or scale, selecting a lengthy and complex production such as *Star Wars* and treating that as a large chunk or domain of semiospace whose vectorial movement can be treated as a unit.

But Figure 3.5 is meant to represent another, and far more imposing feature of semiospace. This has to do with the all-important issue of *boundaries* between domains of semiospace. How do boundaries function in semiospace,

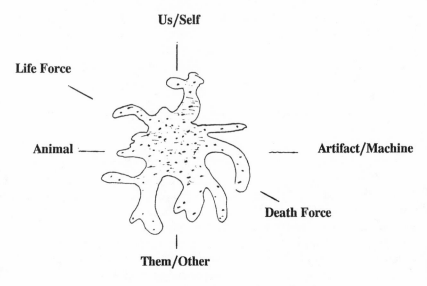

Us/Self

Life Force

Animal

Artifact/Machine

Death Force

Them/Other

Figure 3.4. The Semiotic Dimensions of Culture
as Parameters of a Quasispecies called "Humanity."

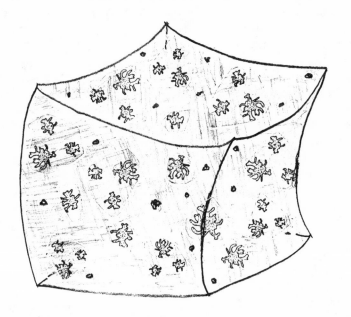

Figure 3.5. The Frothiness of Semiospace: A Cosmos of Consciousness(es).

and what are the properties of the domains they separate? These questions are far more complicated than conventional notions of "text" and "context" would suggest, for in my view this is precisely the point where cultural anthropology comes bump up against quantum mechanics and cosmology (hopefully to their mutual enrichment). The following analogy aims at establishing some very rough correspondences among those disparate fields, at sketching the outlines of a *cosmology of consciousness* (and, just perhaps, of the consciousness of that Being we call the cosmos).

Here is a recipe or model for constructing a somewhat more dynamic version of Figure 3.5. Imagine one of our large stadiums, the Pasadena Rose Bowl, for example, (fittingly enough, just up the road from Cal Tech) filled to the point of overflowing with soap bubbles. These bubbles are made from soaps of different viscosities and surface tensions, so that they vary greatly in size: some are novelty store items the size of basketballs, some are ordinary soap bubbles of an inch or less in diameter, and some are really more of a foam — infinitesimal bubbles like those in shaving cream. All these variously sized bubbles are randomly distributed throughout the vast volume of the Rose Bowl, transforming it into a colossal, frothy sundae composed of billions of the bubbles. Its randomness makes it a fairly lumpy sundae. Here and there the basketball-sized gag store bubbles clump together to give it a large-grained texture; elsewhere, between those pockets of oversized bubbles, whole Wal-Mart stores full of shaving-cream-sized bubbles have accumulated. Besides being remarkably large, this anthro-cosmo sundae is also far more dynamic than the common drug store variety: it has lots of snap, crackle, and pop. For here and there, still completely at random, large bubbles collapse to form smaller ones, while tiny foam-like bubbles fuse to become macroscopic in size.

Now, the prankster who filled the Rose Bowl with these bubbles has pulled another incomprehensible stunt. From the middle row that stretches around the stadium, he has fixed two cables extending clear across the field at right angles, so that they cross above the center of the field to form a gigantic "X". At the ends of these two cables, he has affixed, as though from a half-time show scripted by Magritte, four giant labels: "Animal," "Artifact/Machine," "Us/Self," and "Them/Other." To complete this warped, existential joke, the prankster has erected a towering flagpole right in the middle of the field, which intersects the mid-air nexus of the "X" and soars upward to the very top of the brimming froth. There he has attached a curious banner that reads "Life Force." At the base of the flagpole he has laid out on the ground the (suitably chthonic) inscription, "Death Force."

His prank completed, he exits the scene, leaving the Rose Bowl looking, from the perspective of the baffled pilots of the Met Life blimp who arrive the next morning, like a gigantic confection miraculously deposited in the middle of Brookside Golf Course (truly frosting on the cake of the California Dream) and topped off, not with a cherry, but with some bizarre, quixotic banner.

Now it turns out that the Rose Bowl groundskeepers have done less than their usually meticulous job on that expensive piece of turf: amid the immaculately trimmed blades of grass they have overlooked — you guessed it! — an ant hill. Their negligence is understandable, though, for the ants in this particular ant hill are members of an incredibly tiny species, like those West Indians call "sugar ants" but much, much smaller — mere mites of the ant world. After our prankster has departed, one of these tiny creatures (we will call it Rene) pokes a proboscis out of its little doorway and discovers (*fait incroyable!*) that its world has been transformed. The neat, clipped blades of grass with their lovely aphids have been crushed beneath an enormous mass of frothy stuff. And so, filled with ant angst, Rene sets out to explore its new world of bubbles, like a levitating Lawrence Welk, and abandons the familiar grassy turf for this new, celestial realm.

As with our other ant friend's trip across the sidewalk, Rene's path through the bubble world is tortuously complex, full of zigs and zags as it goes from one bubble to another. Because of its minute size, Rene finds that it is able to enter each bubble it approaches, whether it is an immense basketball-sized affair or a comfy fleck of Gillette foam. It simply pushes through the membrane of one bubble and — hey, presto! — it is inside another, inside its own private capsule. Of course, all this poking and prodding does produce some dramatic changes in its surroundings: on entering a giant bubble, it occasionally bursts and reforms as a smaller, snugger one around it; or a tiny bit of foam it squeezes into may swell by fusing with a couple of adjoining flecks. But large or small, stable or unstable, the end result is the same: Rene finds itself in a hermetically sealed, self-contained bubble world all its own.

Why, you ask, have you had to suffer through another ant parable? My answer, or apology, is that this little story contains most of the elements of culture I have been discussing. The enormous frothy, lumpy mass filling the Rose Bowl represents semiospace, or culture, transected by the three semiotic axes. Its only limit — the edge of the froth — is the limit of that artifactual intelligence I have been insisting on as the *sine qua non* of every cultural system. Or, as Edgar Allen Poe phrased the matter before quantum mechanics and cosmology expanded the scope of things exponentially, "The only limit of the human mind is its own fog."

Now, every one of the billions of bubbles in the stadium, from the largest to the smallest, represents a potential or actual artifactual intelligence. Some of the bubbles, more or less depending mainly on how you choose to confer the title, represent a potential or actual "humanity." Glance back at Figure 3.5 for a moment. The filament-like tendrils snaking off in all directions from just one of our (highly complex) bubbles would, in the real/reel world of the Rose Bowl cultural universe, encounter and twist all around other tendrils of other bubbles representing other intelligences. It would be a commonplace occurrence for a site on the extremity of one of "our" tendrils to be located much nearer the nucleus of some other bubble, some other intelligence. And if we find "humanity" installed at that particular, far-flung site, what are we to say about the intelligences represented by other, more proximate sites which happen to lie on the other side of that complex membrane separating bubbles, sites which are located within some other bubble? Rather than reify what is impossibly complex, the Mandelbrot line of a membrane separating the bubble of "humanity" from all other proximate bubbles, I believe the only workable procedure is to say that "humanity" comprises a region or *domain* of our bubble space. That domain may contain ten bubbles or ten million, depending primarily on the parameters of your observations, of the ruler you choose to use. To simplify this fundamental point greatly, I would suppose that, at the very least, a *large-grained* image of the domain of semiospace representing "humanity" would distinguish separate bubbles for extinct species of the *Homo* genus (including *Homo habilis* and *Homo erectus*).

The bubble Rene happens to find itself in at a particular moment represents the conceptualized world or *Umwelt*, and thus "humanity" as constituted at that time. All the bubbles surrounding Rene, which it really cannot make out until it pushes through the membrane separating its world from those others, represent the Something Else(s) that surround our own world, our own particular version of that artifactual intelligence we have chosen to call "humanity." As for our favorite heuristic ploy, the *ant path* itself, Rene's path from bubble to bubble (really, *through* bubble after bubble) represents a particular career or history of one artifactual intelligence, one *species* if you choose to call it that. That career, as we know from our earlier consideration of ant paths, is one among billions, and is subject to vicissitudes of measurement we had best leave unexplored at this stage. For simplicity's sake, let us just say that *some version* of Rene's wiggly, squiggly path through the sea of froth — the series of bubble worlds it penetrates and exits — represents "our" 4.5 million-year hominid past.

To complete our parable, we would need to endow Rene with a staggering exaggeration of its ant nature: instead of undergoing metamorphosis to adulthood only once in its life, an incredibly versatile Rene would experience that fundamental transformation *each time* it entered a new bubble. Thus the membrane of the bubble it penetrates is indistinguishable from the membrane that separates larva from adult. It is the membrane of birth, whether physical birth or the birth of consciousness, and penetrating it is always a passage from one Something Else to another (rather like what Wittgenstein called *forms of life*).

Through all this, however, Rene remains an adventurous and highly intelligent ant: it was, after all, the first ant out of the gate after the Great Transformation. And, proud of its own courage and intelligence as it pursues its erratic course deeper and deeper into the sea of froth, it recites a little ditty to itself to bolster its spirits: *cogito ergo sum, cogito ergo sum, cogito ergo sum.*

If this parable, simple as it is, already seems to raise too many complex and hypothetical issues, I hesitate to add that even the "frothiness" of semiospace as represented in Figure 3.5 does not begin to capture the complexity of a cultural system. For if there is any correspondence among cultural analysis, quantum mechanics and cosmology, if those multitudinous selves of Whitman are truly dwelling within each of us like particle-waves or baby universes of consciousness, then it is necessary to postulate that each minute piece of culture, each tiny signification, each fleck of anthro-cosmic foam possesses a potentially infinite number of interpretations, of possible locations in semiospace, smeared out across the froth. After all, we do have Rene becoming different ants (or different *antities*) as it goes along, and there are presumably a lot of ants still in the hill where Rene started. What happens when they head out into the froth, creating ant paths of their own and in the process disrupting parts of the bubble-trail "inscribed" by the pioneering Rene? What happens when Rene pops through into the next bubble and finds (*mirabile dictu!*) two little antennae waving in its face, a fellow traveler whose path has crossed its own?

Although the implications of these situations are as mind-boggling as Penrose's account of Hilbert space, with its quantum particles that are anywhere and everywhere at once, they nevertheless surface in familiar aspects of everyday life. For example, you and I may go to *Jaws* and find entirely different messages in that movie and in particular scenes from that movie. Also, if *Jaws* happens to be the late-night creature feature on TV tonight and you decide to watch it, for nostalgia's sake or just out of boredom, it is a certainty that your response to the movie, the articulation of your consciousness and the image frames of the film, will be significantly different now, twenty years down the stretch, than when you lined up with the masses in 1975 to see it in living(?!), gore-dripping Cinemascope and Dolby. When semiospace is regarded as akin to the Hilbert space of quantum mechanics or to the baby universes of recent cosmology, then a decent cultural analysis of *Jaws* would require a chapter from each of the multitudinous selves of each viewer of the movie — say, just to get started, a chapter a month from each of the hundreds of millions of people who have seen it over the past twenty years.

It is daunting considerations like these that have both intrigued and intimidated me as I labored to apply my anthropologist's knowledge of myth to an analysis of popular movies and the peculiar American culture that has created them. I air these abstract considerations at this point, rather than at the end of the section, because I feel it is important for you to keep the analogy or ratio,

quantum mechanics : cultural analysis : cosmology

::

particle : humanity : cosmos,

with all its frothiness, in mind as we examine the construct pairs separately.

Animal < ------ > Artifact/Machine. The dynamic triad of humans, animals, and artifacts or machines comprises one of the foundations of culture, so much so that our species would never have originated without its operating throughout the long, uncertain process leading from the chimp-like australopithecines of over four million years ago to the contemporary "civilized" populations that include you, me, and some six billion of our fellow *Homo sapiens*. The great paradox of human existence issues from our being at once flesh-and-blood — *animals* pure and simple — and an *artifactual intelligence* whose very essence is the production and manipulation of machines. In my view the anti-Cartesian perspective I laid out above could not be demonstrated more clearly than by drawing out the implications of this semiotic continuum. People (even our surfer dude friend, Anthro) did not sit around thinking up culture, until culture matured to such an extent that it begat one Rene Descartes, who promptly proclaimed (in a language he did not happen to invent) that his awareness of his own consciousness was the proof of his existence. People did not do that, and Descartes "proved" a meaningless proposition, for the simple reason that *culture thought them up* (along with the meditative Rene), generated humanity by spurring the australopithecines and their descendants to fabricate tools, extend their diets, expand their social relations. Culture, and the consciousness it has generated, preceded humanity; it is responsible for the very process of self-reflection Descartes held out as some kind of deductive Hot Line to The Truth.

In the anti-Cartesian framework, "self-reflection" comes to mean something entirely different from my leaning back in my chair and having ponderous thoughts about the fact that I am thinking or my gazing soulfully into a mirror and wondering "Who am I?": it becomes synonymous with thinking about what I am *doing*. It is the perspective on the "I" or "me" that is engaged, not in deep meditative thoughts, but in some action: reading these lines, writing these lines, cutting the grass, backing the car out of the driveway, or, winding the clock back a bit, knocking flakes off a flint core to produce a point. We, all those yous and mes, are animals — active, volitional beings — that can make things, and then make other things with those things, until we step back and survey a built environment, an entire world of made things, of artifacts that have fused with our physical beings to the point of becoming part of us. The synthesis in consciousness of the animal's paw-become-hand, the tool it holds, and the object in the environment it fashions is at once what makes such intricate activity possible and the distinctive feature of human identity.

As we saw in chapter 2, the history of cultural anthropology translates to a history of "totemism," of anthropologists' changing interpretations of the powerful, mystical bond between people and animals that they observed everywhere among their "primitive" subjects. The first full-fledged, card-carrying anthropologists, scholars like E. B. Tylor, writing with the shock of Darwinism still reverberating in their heads, tried to insulate that powerful bond with the

animal world from modern human concerns by describing it as an exotic feature of exotic societies, a veritable litmus test of primitiveness. After all, what
could Victorian Englishmen possibly have in common with animals (or with
primitives)? The works of Levi-Strauss, Leach, Fernandez, and others, however, have brought that barrier tumbling down. Primitive or modern, animals
are so much a part of our lives that we constantly refer to them to tell us about
ourselves and others: "He's a pig!"; "I'm in a bitchy mood today!"; and so on.
As Levi-Strauss argued in *Totemism*, the relentless classificatory force of
human consciousness fashions its knowledge of itself by drawing on aspects of
other active, volitional beings — animals — with whom it finds itself in
continual interaction. And although very few of us go out in the woods and
track down, kill, and butcher a deer for the family barbecue, we are still
obsessed with the animals around us and make them a principal focus of some
of our strongest emotions. Testaments to our modern totemism are everywhere: our pets (sales of cat food now exceed those of baby food!); our trips to
zoos and theme parks like Sea World and Busch Gardens; the cuddly stuffed
animal figures we give the few babies we do have; the Garfield dolls we stick
on our car windows; and, of course, our movies. *Jaws* would not have been the
sensation it was, the true vanguard for the supergrosser phenomenon, had we
abandoned our ages-old fascination with animals when we entered the postmodern era of Yuppies, Beemers, and faxes.

But what about those Beemers and faxes, about the other pole of the
Animal <------> *Artifact/Machine* dimension? If the totemism of animals, in
its Levi-Straussian guise, is still with us, is there not a corresponding, if
unheralded, *totemism of machines* that has directed (in a vectorial sort of way,
of course) the flow of human evolution, that has generated culture? That is
precisely what I would suggest. When I walked into *Star Wars* that fateful day
years ago, I found myself in a sacred cave, a temple, functionally identical to
those used by Stanner's aborigines to celebrate the Dreamtime: a place where
images of the most crucial nature are displayed for the spiritual transformation
of those in attendance. *Star Wars* holds the key to our totemism of machines,
to the other pole of the first semiotic dimension. For in situating its human
characters in an advanced technological world, it pursues the joint themes of
people's fundamental involvement with machines and the personalities that
machines themselves possess. Machine personalities and human personalities
are put on a par, and projected on the giant silver screen for all to see and
ponder. And what we ponder is how we are like and unlike these high-tech
wonders, how our fates, like it or not, are inextricably linked with machines —
exactly as a subsistence hunter's life is linked with the game he pursues. This
totemism of machines possesses the very properties Levi-Strauss identifies as
"totemism from within": a system of classificatory processes that simultaneously bestow order on the external world and establish the identities of
human groups and individuals.

Animals and machines are the principal actors in our modern totemism for two reasons: they interact with us in daily life and thereby give substance and content to our behavior; and they are themselves, like us, generative beings. Apart from the hidden or diffuse forces in the natural world that cause the sun and moon to rise and set, the clouds to give lightning, thunder and rain, the rivers to rage and meander, the plants to sprout mysteriously from the soil and bear fruit (Dylan Thomas's "force that through the green fuse drives the flower"), animals and machines are the only discrete entities besides ourselves that are capable of action, of making things happen. The generativity of culture issues from their — and our hominid ancestors' — generativity. Like us, animals and machines are individual entities. They are brought into the world, transform it through creative or destructive acts, and are eventually themselves destroyed. Our own considerable creativity and formidable des- tructiveness are bracketed by the generative powers of animals and machines, so that human identity itself becomes a floating cipher or shifting field in which our myth-making intelligence hunts. On the semiotic continuum of animals and machines, we are a fuzziness, or frothiness, situated somewhere between those poles. We do not author things from scratch; remember that the intersystem and intertextuality have turned out to be the way of things. Consequently, the creativity or generativity of the animate things around us are fundamental ingredients of our own creativity, of our own identity.

It is important to appreciate how deeply these creative forces of animal and machine operate, how they fashion, in a now familiar process through which we are hoisted by our semiotic bootstraps, the very content and context of our experience. Animals and the world of "nature" of which they are a part are not simply "out there," a convenient reservoir from which we pull particular specimens we wish to make part of our experience, to mythologize perhaps. Similarly, the artifacts or machines we create and use are not solely our own, are not just items we can pick up and lay down or put back on the shelf at will. They are not part of a separate, sealed-off "artificial world" that we may choose to enter and leave. As with ant paths and languages, the "worlds" of nature and technology are not that neatly demarcated (Mandelbrot has been fiddling with those lines as well!). For we simultaneously adapt to a natural world by creating it and create a technological world to which we must adapt.

"Nature," including in particular its most dramatic representatives — animals — is a conceptual order or *Umwelt* which we have created and con- tinually modify, and which has the most far-reaching effects on our lives and those of our descendants. Some of us open our eyes in the morning and look out at a world that God put there for us to use, so we wash down six or eight strips of bacon and a stack of pancakes with a pot of coffee or maybe a few brewskies, grab our chainsaws, and head for the timber (and spotted owls be damned!). Others of us jump out of bed, have some religiously nonfat granola (with all the this-saturated, that-unsaturated, beta-this, and omega-that just right) and oh-so-natural fruit juice (uncontaminated by the "unnatural" sugar product of that Satanic mill in green, the sugar cane plant), grab our posters, and go out to picket the hapless lumberjacks on their way to a day's work. Or, if those others of us are not quite so active, we may eschew the animosities of the picket line in favor of sitting down in our wooden chairs at our wooden desks, which are sheltered by our wooden houses, and booting up our computers to fire off a stinging letter to some editor or other denouncing the timber industry.

The contradictions raised in this scenario are not just the stuff of current events and so the preserve of politicians and other opportunistic, lawyerly vermin; they are a manifestation of one of those *elemental dilemmas* that have brought culture into being and that keep it on a rolling boil. Remember: If everything had made sense to the australopithecines, if animals, artifacts and people had fitted into nice, tidy compartments of their very modestly expanded cerebrums, then they would have closed the brain factory at that early stage and we would not be around today. When the animal : artifact semiotic continuum formed in an emergent (proto)human consciousness, it immediately installed an elemental dilemma that is still with us today: We are both like and unlike animals and artifacts; yet those animate, generative entities are seemingly opposites of each other; so what are we?

The paradox that fuels this dilemma is that the operations of consciousness create a sameness-difference, identity-opposition relationship between people and animals on one hand and between people and artifacts on the other. We can know the differences between animals and ourselves (and among animal "species") only by classifying them, by attaching concepts and names to populations of indiscriminate organisms. Yet this operation of the emergent consciousness already culturalizes its biological subjects: in erecting classifications for animal species, we incorporate those biological entities into a semiotic system to which they did not formerly belong. And with those classifications comes a whole set of attitudes and behaviors toward animals, most of which have nothing to do with their empirical qualities: cats are nicer to have around than rats; cows taste better than dogs; killer whales are interesting and smart and fun to watch (you can tell that sea lions didn't come up with culture!). The "naturalness" of animals is thus a function of the generative processes of culture (a defining characteristic of human existence that groups like Greenpeace and the Sierra Club manage to ignore). A reciprocal process yields the same paradox in the case of artifacts. We fabricate artifacts or machines with our own hands, yet those seemingly pure cultural forms assume a life of their own once they enter the world. Like that ultimate artifact, the Bomb, machines are simply *there*, implacable entities that make things happen, and not *there for us*. This implacable there-ness of artifacts naturalizes what might seem to be lifeless bits of material, making machines as much a part of the "natural" environment as spotted owls and killer whales.

At the heart of the dialectic of the generativity of animals and artifacts is the very notion of creation itself. Although we usually do not spend much time thinking about it (about as much time as we spend thinking about infinite ant paths), "creation" and "destruction," birth and death, are not self-evident, objective features of the environment: we can't stick a pin in them. The mythic processes of culture are responsible for formulating the proposition that things are created and destroyed, that we are born and will die. This knowledge of our birth and foreknowledge of our death place an indelible mark on our lives and on the nature of our species. "Creation," "transformation," and "destruction" are concepts and names we attach to events that have no material embodiment apart from the semiotic operations of culture. When proto-humans first came to apply their emergent consciousness to the events of birth and death, they brought the very notions of creation and destruction into being. And the vehicle for that act — the creation of creation, if you will — is the vast and rapidly accumulating corpus of myths about the origins and natures of animals, humans and artifacts, myths that range from the stories of creation told by Amazonian Indians to the more recent, but no less fundamental, productions of *Jaws* and *Star Wars*.

Us/Self <------> Them/Other. Much of the action in action movies like *Jaws*, *Star Wars*, *The Spy Who Loved Me*, and *E. T.* is based on the fact that their characters are divided into sides: there are the good guys and the bad guys, an Us and a Them. Moreover, in watching the movies, each of us is encouraged (or, remembering Whitman and intersystems, some of our multitudinous selves are encouraged) to adopt the persona of the main character, to become the hero, to be, as we are in life, that pivotal Self who confronts the Other. This simple point (which will definitely not place me among the immortals of film studies!), is nevertheless basic to an anthropological understanding of how popular movies operate as myths that create and sustain an American Dreamtime. How the sides are drawn up, how Us is unscrambled from Them and Self from Other, is a function of images, themes, or symbols that specify individual (Self) and group (Us) identity.

But why should it be necessary to specify individual and group identity? Why go to the trouble to produce myths, including major productions like supergrosser movies, just to tell us the obvious? Unless, of course, the obvious truths of self and group identity turn out to possess that deceptive obviousness of ant paths, dimensions, and languages — monoliths we vainly try to prop up on the shifting, heaving ground of indeterminate cultural processes. That, of course, is precisely what I would claim. The anti-Cartesian perspective I introduced in the previous section applies to a far wider range of knowledge than that you or I or Rene can obtain by cerebral navel-gazing. It applies, not only to the process of self-knowledge, but also (and even more strongly) to the process whereby we come to know that each of us is a member of several, extremely important groups: family, relatives or kin, neighborhood, school or factory or office, community, state, religion, race, ethnic group, nation. A cultural analysis of group identity reveals that, far from being a "natural" part of the landscape of life, the phenomenon harbors, like a black hole at the heart of a galaxy, another of those decidedly *un*natural elemental dilemmas that are the unacknowledged powerhouses at the heart of that galaxy called consciousness.

Although the concept of "group," like the concept of "self," turns out to be an exceedingly complex and tricky notion, anthropologists have only belatedly begun to think of it in this way. As we have seen in discussing other subjects, cultural anthropology regrettably has often followed the lead of common sense rather than attempting an admittedly difficult and spiritually painful dissection of it. The turning point was, again, Levi-Strauss's brilliant essay, *Totemism*. What I have called the anti-Cartesian perspective is clearly present in Levi-Strauss's stinging criticism of earlier anthropologists (Emile Durkheim, Radcliffe-Brown, and other late greats) for treating human groups as established, bounded entities whose members decided, for one reason or another, to select animal species as emblems to express and enhance their group identity. The problem with this bland view is the same as that with Descartes *cogito*: groups, like individuals, do not first constitute themselves (through some completely unspecified process) and then cast idly about for images or symbols to enhance their identity. Golly, gee, I seem to be thinking, *ergo* "I" must exist. Or: Hey guys, since we're having so much fun palling around together, why don't we call ourselves "bandicoots" just for the hell of it? My apologies to the scholarly among you, but the point of view invites burlesque. For the Cartesian conception of group is very far off the mark, and it errs on such a fundamental matter, not just for the teacup tempests of anthropological debate, but for what is *the* driving force in human history.

I believe the truth of the matter, as revealed by an anthropological semiotics, is that our humanity itself, including our membership in this or that segment of it, is largely a consequence of our *lacking* clearly defined, "natural" boundaries or markers which would readily distinguish us as this rather than that, which would unambiguously and automatically establish our human-ness. It is this lack, again, this terrifying absence at the center of things, that drives us to do the often frightful things we do to establish and maintain *images* of ourselves as belonging to groups. We belong to groups because we, or, actually, the proto-we who were our hominid ancestors, invented the notion of group.

While our high school basketball coaches, bosses, politicians, and military leaders would find these ideas objectionable (didn't you always suspect that your gym teacher was a dyed-in-the-wool Cartesian?), they are entirely consistent with primatologists' views of how our species launched itself on the path of group identity leading to the nation-state and the arms race. Vernon Reynolds, in *The Biology of Human Action*, puts conceptual or symbolic awareness before any other feature of the process that led from primate to human. Reynolds bases this argument on the behavior of our closest surviving primate relative, the chimpanzees. Their "open-group" organization, in which members are dispersed over a large area during a typical day, represents an important factor in hominid speciation.

> Precisely because of the open-group system it was in the sphere of social relations that conceptualization was most important. Words such as "mother," "brother," "sister," "family," geared to the words for "own" and "other" must be basic to any conceptualization of social relations, and with the distinction "here"/"over there" quite accurate designations of the whereabouts of a large number of the kin of local people could be formulated. At that moment [in the course of hominid evolution] a remarkable thing could be achieved: *the open-group system could be given a structure not based on face-to-face relations but on conceptualized relationships*. For the first time ever group A could be distinguished from group B not on the basis of its whereabouts but purely on the basis of its genealogical connections. We know that monkeys can distinguish between their own and other kin at a behavioural level; now it would become possible for early man to distinguish between them conceptually as well, formulating his ongoing behaviour in symbols. (66, emphasis in original).

Note the staggering paradox that surfaces in Reynold's analysis: the conceptualization of "group-ness" was achieved only because hominids at a particular evolutionary stage had *lost* or were in the process of losing an exclusively physical basis — constant visual or auditory contact — for identifying themselves as members of a group. Our ancestors thus found themselves in the baffling situation of both having and not having a group to which they belonged and on which they could depend for food and protection: the particular individuals in immediate contact with you at a particular time might constitute the entire group, but then again they might not. They might, for example, only be members of a foraging party that intended to return with the day's collection to a base camp, where they would share it with *the* group. The individual's behavior would then depend, for the first time in three-and-a-half-billion years of biological evolution, on a *concept*, on an aspect of the situation that is not present in the situation (just as the mathematical concept of *set* is not lying there on the table with a dozen apples that form a set). The open-group forms, changes, reforms. It has continuity only if it enters onto the level of conceptualization. Like the humanity it anticipated and helped to create, the primate open-group is called into being only through its absence.

In contrast, the closed-group social organization of the more solitary apes such as the gibbon and orangutan depends on maintaining visual or auditory contact with group members at all times. Those species do not have culture or even many of the makings of protoculture because they are too certain of their group's physical boundaries: Mandelbrot's lines do not shrink and expand for them. For them, living and dying in close association with a fixed set of individuals, there is no problem associated with the behavioral reality of group identity. There is none of that terrible ambivalence of myth as it engages the absent center of a human consciousness.

It is not even necessary to engage in this kind of speculation on early hominid evolution to understand the dynamics that created the open-group system and thus served as the springboard to sapience. In an excellent recent study, "Diet and Primate Evolution," the primatologist Katharine Milton compares two species of New World primates, spider and howler monkeys, which are genetically rather distant from chimpanzees and early humans but in which the dividing line between sapience vs. behavioral routine can already be discerned. Having documented significant differences in the diets of the two species — howler monkeys ingest more leaves than fruit and lead quite sedentary lives, whereas spider monkeys eat mostly fruit and have to range further afield to find it — Milton proceeds to tie those differences to brain size and the consequent implications of diet for hominid evolution.

These digestive findings fascinated me, but a comparison of brain size in the two species yielded one of those "eurekas" of which every scientist dreams. I examined information on the brain sizes of howler and spider monkeys because the spider monkeys in Panama seemed "smarter" than the howlers — almost human. Actually, some of them reminded me of my friends. I began to wonder whether spider monkeys behaved differently because their brains were more like our own. My investigations showed that, indeed, the brains of howler and spider monkeys do differ, even though the animals are about the same size. (Same-sized animals generally have like-sized brains.) The spider monkey brain weighs about twice that of howlers.

Now, the brain is an expensive organ to maintain; it usurps a disproportionate amount of the energy (glucose) extracted from food. So I knew natural selection would not have favored development of a large brain in spider monkeys unless the animals gained a rather pronounced benefit from the enlargement. Considering that the most striking difference between howler and spider monkeys is their diets, I proposed that the bigger brain of spider monkeys may have been favored because it facilitated the development of mental skills that enhanced success in maintaining a diet centered on ripe fruit.

A large brain would certainly have helped spider monkeys to learn and, most important, to remember, where certain patchily distributed fruit-bearing trees were located and when the fruit would be ready to eat. Also, spider monkeys comb the forest for fruit by dividing into small, changeable groups. Expanded mental capacity would have helped them to recognize members of their particular social unit and to learn the meaning of the different food-related calls through which troop members convey over large distances news of palatable items. Howler monkeys, in contrast, would not need such an extensive memory, nor would they need so complex a recognition and communication system. They forage for food as a cohesive social unit, following well-known arboreal pathways over a much smaller home range. (90)

As Milton discusses, dietary pressures on now-extinct African primates increased significantly during the period (from four-and-a-half to two million years ago) of early hominid speciation. As warm Pliocene forests gave way to cooler Pleistocene savannas, early hominids' need to forage further and further increased, as did the competition they encountered from herbivores and carnivores that were themselves rapidly evolving to exploit the new open grassland niche. Consequently, there was a strong diet-based selective force favoring even more dispersed open-groups, which possessed even more developed communicative and behavioral repertoires, including artifact production. The tendency already evident at the modest level of spider monkeys to evolve larger brains, which in turn enhance communication and social relations, was thus amplified on the Pleistocene savannas of Africa to the point at which sapience emerged. The use of symbols, and hence the origin of culture, is predicated on the need early sapient beings felt to provide an *image* of themselves, of their group-ness which, by the very process of evolution that spawned them, they could never possess in fact.

As latter-day, perhaps somewhat advanced spider monkeys (though what are we then to think of Milton's friends?), we inhabit an *Umwelt*, a cultural surround, that is decidedly *not* the codification, emblem, or tacked-on label of a pre-established group membership. Our cultural surround is rather a continuously changing and — extremely important — self-contradictory, ambivalent process of erecting and dismantling boundaries between an Us and a Them, a Self and an Other. The primatological findings of Reynolds, Milton, and others thus lead us straight to the (post)modern world with its movie theatres and supergrossers, where, appealing to the spider monkey in all of us, images of who is who and what is what are evoked and pondered.

Of the several boundary conditions or semiotic parameters that situate humanity in the semiospace of culture, the one that holds our interest longest and last is what makes us like and unlike others. People are obsessed with other people. The discipline of anthropology owes its existence to this primordial obsession, which it has elevated to a professional calling. But anthropology, as usual, is small potatoes when compared with the global forces that issue from the same obsession with others: tourism and, that revolting euphemism for ethnic hatred and aggression, "national defense." It is one of the defining paradoxes of our time that our need to establish a political boundary and keep it inviolate, to be a sovereign people qualitatively distinct from those *others* beyond that boundary, is exactly counterbalanced by our need to see how those others live, what their lives are like, to travel over the mountain and across the sea, to breach those very boundaries we create and defend with such care and expense and, moreover, to incorporate those others, through any number of political alliances and international organizations, into new, transient forms of group-ness.[26] Tourist and warrior, the dear little grey head, sensible polyester outfit and sneakers vs the helmet, night glasses and Desert Storm fatigues — these are the disparate uniforms and personae we don in our obsessive, but irredeemably ambivalent efforts to both breach and hold the line we erect around some notion of ourselves, of Us.

The lines, Mandelbrot's lines, we have been considering throughout this chapter here acquire a hard and monetary edge. The savageries of warfare (My Lai, the Khmer Rouge, Desert Storm, Sarajevo) and the extravagances of tourism (Caribbean cruises to former slave islands now tarted up as exotic haunts, gourmet safaris through Europe, and more traditional safaris past the starving villages of Africa to reach the exotic haunts of endangered animals) attest to the tremendous force of attraction-avoidance that surrounds the notion of group-ness. The intensity of emotions that swirl like maelstroms around that notion should not blind us to the fact that all the boundaries it generates are, at bottom, as elusive and shifting as those Mandelbrot has alerted us to. It is a terrible, sickening thing to contemplate, but the conviction and burning hatred that impels the Serb artilleryman to fire the next salvo at the apartment houses of Sarajevo, filled with defenseless civilians, has no more foundation or substance than our choice of one or other of our ant path measurements. Culture, as I maintain throughout this work, is geometrical, but there is nothing about its past or future that precludes an anthropology that is a geometry of horror, a relentless pathologist's study of that enigma which, as Eco laments, "is made terrible by our own mad attempt to interpret it as though it had an underlying truth." As though there really were groups. . .

Cultural anthropology will have begun to mature when it can stare into this abyss, a long, deep, probing stare, and come away from this encounter with a searching analysis that takes full account of both the horror of human existence and its astonishing participation in geometrical orders of existence in the universe as a whole. In my view the starting place or beachhead for such an operation is, again paradoxically, the heartland both of anthropology and of that common sense which we have found to characterize the myth of America: (anthropological) theories and (commonsense) notions of *kinship* and *ethnicity*, of, in other words, Us/Self and Them/Other.

The fundamental nature of the second semiotic dimension, Us/Self : Them/Other, stems from its combining as dialectical or reciprocal terms two concepts that are generally kept apart in both anthropological discourse and everyday life: kinship and ethnicity. Although anthropology has made them pillars of its professional discourse, and although they are basic features of everyday life, the dialectical link between ideas of kinship and those of ethnicity or race is largely ignored. This oversight is quite understandable, since in daily life the line we draw between Us and Them is meant to compartmentalize, and not integrate, our thinking, emotions, and behavior: one set of categories, feelings, and actions for our family and folks; another for those others beyond the pale of kith and kin. In anthropology, which once again enshrines the prejudices of common sense rather than placing them on the pathologist's dissection table, separate chapters or books are given over to the topics of "kinship" and "ethnicity." My view, and the reason I am convinced the second semiotic dimension has kinship and ethnicity as its axes, is that the two are simply complementary ways of establishing group identity, of drawing a line around some collection of people. Establishing a relation of "kinship" involves drawing a line around people on the basis of some principle of *inclusiveness*. Establishing a relation of "ethnicity" involves drawing a line, perhaps the same one in some situations, on the basis of some principle of *exclusiveness*. In the first instance, you and I are related if we share some common substance or property; in the second you are fundamentally different from me because you lack that substance or property which I possess.

The cultural or mythical nature of kinship, of those substances or properties whose shared possession makes us kin, is apparent with but a little inspection, a little dusting off of our cherished images. While peoples in the ethnographic literature single out a variety of things as the definitive marker of kinship — bone, spirit, semen, including even tiny homuncular humans contained in semen — the exotic people of America favor the substance of *blood*. A foundation of the myth of America is this common belief in the importance of blood ties, which asserts, among other things, that "blood is thicker than water" (see David Schneider's modern classic, *American Kinship: A Cultural Account*). If you and I are related "by blood" that means that we share a common substance which is *the* criterion of belonging and which takes priority over nonblood ties we have with others. The mythical nature of this belief, if not the ambivalence it generates at the heart of our strongest value, is already clear from junior high school biology lessons on genetics. You and your mother may indeed be said to be related "by blood," because her blood flowed through your veins in the womb and her flesh and blood literally became the substance of the foetus that was to become you. But it is quite a different state of affairs with your father, Dan Quayle's posturings on "family values" notwithstanding. For Dad's contribution to the organic cocktail that was to become you was a microscopic bit of his nucleic acids, or DNA, nicely split through the process of meiosis and bundled into the head of the single sperm that managed to fertilize Mom's egg. His strands of DNA molecules, as the legions of researchers on the Human Genome Project would tell us, are in fact wondrously complex snippets of computer tape, coded messages so dense that we require, at our present stage of technology, massive hard drives to hold the information wrapped in that single, lucky sperm cell.

But computer code is computer code, regardless of how densely it is packaged, and it is a far cry from the powerful, visceral images evoked by claiming Dad as a "blood relative." For Dad is really no more your blood relative than the pope or the Ayatollah Khomeni, both of whom (if they did not exactly cavort with Mom) are composed of cells containing DNA that is nearly identical with your father's.[27] Yet the particular *ideology* of kinship that is installed in the myth of America makes Dad every bit as much a "blood" relative as Mom. That blood tie is supposedly the basis for those strong family values Dan Quayle used to whine about, and the belief in it is what has led countless Dads to labor, and sometimes to fight and die, for their families.[28]

Ethnicity, like kinship, is both mythical and visceral in the many forms it assumes in the (post)modern world. The attributes we single out to distinguish those others from ourselves, and to justify our often barbarous treatment of them, are as limitless and basically insignificant as Jonathan Swift described in *Gulliver's Travels*. For reasons as diverse as skin color, language, religion, nationality, dress, and even hair length,[29] people exclude and persecute other people. Bigotry turns out to be surprisingly liberal in finding reasons to hate, whether those be religion in the Middle East and Northern Ireland, race and tribe in South Africa, language in Quebec, or, not so long ago, before they became the trendoid haunts of writers and movie people, long hair in Montana bars.

The repugnant fact of ethnic hatred and conflict is so universal and so deeply felt that it must issue from the guts of our being as a species. I suspect it is the other side of the open-group organization described by the primatologists: if your group is habitually dispersed (due to some adaptational imperative such as diet) and you rely on your conceptual abilities to identify it, then there must be a correspondingly strong adaptive value in conceptualizing what and who is *not* a group member. A chillingly suggestive finding in Jane Goodall's pioneering field research among chimpanzees in the wild (*The Chimpanzees of Gombe*) is that bands of male chimpanzees are not only skillful hunters,[30] but that their favorite prey is other primates: hapless monkeys who blunder into their path when they have a taste for meat. While their preference for monkey flesh probably makes good ecological sense — the chimpanzees obtain valuable protein while reducing the competition from other frugivorous primates — it also helps to explain why the *Homo* genus has narrowed to but a single species. The path we have followed to sapience is littered with the fossilized bones of hominid species that have become extinct: several australopithecine and *Homo* lines, including the relatively recent Neandertals, have, instead of radiating like Darwin's finches to exploit different habitats, succumbed to an emergent line whose consuming cleverness wanted it all.

At the core of the seemingly abstract and arid semiotic continuum of kinship : ethnicity there is another of those black holes of consciousness, another elemental dilemma which ensures that our contribution to the project of culture will never be finished until we somehow run off the edge, and penetrate the membrane that separates us (or Us) from Something Else. The dilemma of our animal vs. artifact identity, of being both and thus unable to be either, is expressed in how and where we open-group, conceptualizing hominids situate ourselves on the kinship : ethnicity axis. On the face of it, the task of sorting out Us/Self from Them/Other appears to be a simple matter for clever conceptualizers like ourselves (but by now we have come to despair of simple solutions to any problem!). You are related to a particular group of people by one or other of the ideologies of kinship discussed above, and they are your family, your kin, whom you support and defend. Everyone else falls outside this group and so is an alien Other, to be shunned if not actually hunted down and destroyed.

Now, if it had been possible for our hominid ancestors to follow this unambiguous scenario, to keep the fundamental categories of Us : Them separate, then somewhere in the late Pliocene or early Pleistocene things would have settled into a more or less timeless mold: you would belong to your group; I would belong to mine; and, as the black hustler says to Richard Gere in *American Gigolo*, "I nevah liked you much mah-self." You would go your way, and I would go mine. Only "we" wouldn't be "us," namely, communicating, sapient humans; "we" would be hunchy little ape-things chittering at each other around some East African water hole, dismal extras in an early shoot of *2001*. Distinct hominid groups would have sorted themselves out early on in the evolutionary process and settled down to uneventful eons of *Hangin' with the Homeboys* while keeping the rival *Colors* away from the water hole.

What is wrong with this picture? Why haven't relations of kinship and ethnicity gelled in this tidy, unambiguous fashion? The scenario is hopelessly, disastrously wrong because it omits one of the fundamentals of culture, something more important than the cooking fire: the incest taboo. "Blood" ties cannot be maintained inviolate for the crucial reason that we are not supposed to mate, and certainly not to have children, with our blood relatives. Without the incest taboo, that is, without the carved-in-stone prescription to mate outside the immediate group, our hominid ancestors could indeed have settled into the timeless, algal ooze of a world where everything was tidily arranged, where everything made sense. With the incest taboo, group membership is necessarily a changing, dynamic thing: the fact that you are born into one family requires that you mate into another. This requirement obviously wreaks havoc with efforts to draw any firm, non-Mandelbrotian line between your group and theirs, and by extension it wreaks havoc with any coherent distinction between the powerful forces of kinship and ethnicity. Your membership in a group — the fact that you were born — and all the evocative imagery of "blood ties" with members of that group are made possible only because Mom or Dad broke ranks with the kin group and, in the words of Hank Williams's song, "found somebody new." The ethnic Other is to be found, not lurking outside your village plotting your destruction, but within your immediate family, a nurturing, loving mother, father, sister, brother. *That* is the elemental dilemma of kinship : ethnicity.

But, you may ask, why and whither the incest taboo itself? If early hominid social organization could have sorted itself out nicely without the irksome conundrum of the taboo, why should it have originated at all? Attempts to answer this fundamental question have been a cottage industry in anthropology since the discipline's beginnings, resulting in a wide assortment of interpretations among which we may pick and choose. There are biological arguments, ethological arguments, psychological arguments, sociological arguments, culturological arguments, and any number of hybrid mixes. Sorting these out is far beyond the scope of this chapter, and, in any event, would not really advance this outline of the semiotic dimensions of culture and the elemental dilemmas that power them. The point I have tried to make in this section is that, wherever it came from, the incest taboo functions as the elemental dilemma, the absent center, the black hole of consciousness, around which images and symbols of kinship and ethnicity swirl — galactic-neural debris caught in the grip of a colossal force. As you might imagine, though, I do have some ideas on the subject, and I will take this opportunity to make two points about the incest taboo.

First, although I share my colleagues' interest in the question of the origin of the taboo, I am far more interested in where the taboo is going, that is, where it is taking us, meaning humanity, as culture continues to evolve. Throughout this work I have alluded to that "Something Else" that I see peering, as it were, from under the covers of culture as we know it today (as they say in all the sci-fi movies!). Without meaning to be coy, I have made these references to alert you to the direction in which my own thought is moving, and to prepare for the actual discussion of that Something Else in the conclusion of this work. But there is nothing terribly mysterious or complex about the general point I have been trying to make. Humanity does not "possess" culture in the sense that a traveler has luggage; the opposite is nearer the truth: for the time being, "we" are the baggage of culture (but it was fun while it lasted; we really got blasted!). The semiotic operations of culture I have been describing in this chapter were at work long before humanity in its guise of modern *Homo sapiens* appeared on the scene, and those operations are principally responsible for that species' appearance. "That species" happens to be us, you and me, who are along for the ride, with but a perilous grip on the tiller as our craft heads into the rapids. And somewhere along the next stretch of rapids, or the next, or the next, "we" will have stopped being us. There will be no more you's and me's like the old you's and me's, because the (vectorial) alignment of cultural forces, the *Umwelt* of *Homo sapiens*, if not its actual genetic composition, will have changed fundamentally. "We" will have become Something Else.

In that process of transformation, I see the interaction of artifact and kinship, of technology and family, as playing a major role. The future of the incest taboo is tied to further developments in such diverse technologies as *in vitro* fertilization, cloning,[31] the promise of "virtual sex" already being proffered by developers of virtual reality (VR) video games, and the epidemiology of AIDS. Some of these technologies are already creating excruciating dilemmas for the individuals affected, for example, in the dramas of surrogate parenthood acted out in TV tabloids and law courts across the land. Whatever the outcome of these and other unforeseen twists and turns of technology's impact on family, kinship, and sexuality, they will definitely not leave Mom and Dad and Buddy and Sis cozied down in their house on Elm Street, tuning in the latest episode of *Leave It to Beaver*.

Second, in all that has been said or written by anthropologists and others on the subject of the incest taboo, I find a persistent, underlying, and usually ignored theme. As I have discussed in more detail in an earlier essay,[32] I find the germ of the kinship : ethnicity dilemma already forming in the infant's relationship with its mother (or mother surrogate). While being at one with the mother and depending on her for its every bodily need, the infant is at the same time developing a sense of itself by formulating a sense of its *difference* from the mother, by formulating one, perhaps the first, of those Mandelbrot lines that establish an always illusory boundary between, in this case, Self and Other. The paradox contained in this most elementary of social relations is that Mother, who is the embodiment of sameness, of your own flesh and blood, is also Other, the embodiment of difference, and so the prototype of "those others" separated from you by the boundary of ethnicity. She is mOther.

To this paradox it is only necessary to add the first glow of the consuming fire of human sexuality ("Love is a burning thang, and it makes your heart sayng"), and we have arrived at the incest taboo in full force. The infant's well-being depends entirely on the succoring parent, and so its desire for its own well-being is indistinguishable from its desire for the ministrations of the parent. In this paradisiacal state (the model for all later religious longings for heaven, nirvana, or, especially telling in its imagery, the union of the Breath Within and the Breath Without of the *Upanishads*) self-love and love of the other are indistinguishable. Now for the bad news, junior. This blissful union is severed by the infant's continuing neurological development (remember the evolutionary dictate that it be born in a foetalized state), which brings with it an increasing realization of its organismic integrality. It cannot attain selfhood without first coming to see Mother as Other, which means rejecting the primal one-ness of mother and nursing infant. Yet the infant still has a powerful libidinal attachment — *love*, in short — for the mother. I believe that primal love is severed or split in two (as in the famous split-beam experiment in quantum mechanics!), so that the infant retains a deeply held love of Mother-as-Mother and longing for the visceral one-ness of her nurturance, and at the same time it internalizes a vital need, a desire for Mother-as-Other. And desire for the Other, regardless of age, gender, or sexual proclivity (homo, hetero, or just randy old sheep), is what sexuality is all about.

In the split-beam experiment (see John Gribbin's lucid account in *In Search of Schroedinger's Cat*), a photon is perfectly content to behave like a wave, being spread or smeared out across space, until an act of observation is made on it, whereupon the dispersed wave-function "collapses" into the state of a particle with a particular location. The remarkable thing about this "collapse of the wave-function," as demonstrated in various ingenious arrangements of the split-beam experiment, is that the actual, fundamental physical properties of the system (is it a wave or is it a particle?) are determined by the act of observation itself. *It is only with the introduction of sentience that the physical system acquires its properties.*

I am saying that an analogous process operates in emergent cultural systems: the infant's diffuse identification of self-love and other-love — its conceptual wave-function, if you will — "collapses" with its neurological development, requiring it to situate itself somewhere in semiospace. The emerging cultural intelligence cannot continue to be "in two places at once," and so it must declare its preference: love of Mother-Mother or love of Mother-Other. It is an impossible choice, a classical paradox like Bertrand Russell's barber of Seville:

A man of Seville is shaved by the barber of Seville if and only if the man does not shave himself. Does the barber shave himself?

But it is a choice, a declaration, that must be made (and made by an embryonic intelligence, not the co-author of *Principia Mathematica*).

That declaration takes the form of the kinship: ethnicity conundrum, which pops (or, as the cosmologists would say of a baby universe, "bounces") out of a black-hole-like singularity of consciousness and imposes a dimensionality on semiospace. The self-devouring serpent, Ouroboros, symbol of a primordial One-ness, disgorges itself to form a differentiated world in which there are heads and tails, faces and asses, an Us/Self and a Them/Other.[33] The formulation of the kinship : ethnicity construct is a way out of the impasse an emergent cultural intelligence must face.[34] The solution that intelligence — *our* intelligence — has come up with is a signature of cultural process: My group and I (Us/Self) share some fundamental attribute, some common substance, that others (Them/Other) do not, and so we are fundamentally different. The undifferentiated sameness in which desire for the other was indistinguishable from desire for self is thus fractured by a conceptual sleight-of-hand: Us/Self is *not* the same as Them/Other, and so entirely different sentiments are directed towards the two groups.

This operation, which is vital to the existence of a human culture, is the means we have devised to convince ourselves that each of us does not contain his or her antithesis, does not harbor Whitman's multitudes. And, once again, we find that Whitman stole a march on the theoretical physicists and cosmologists (and "collapsed" my own labored exegesis of this profound subject) with a few lines that seem to issue from the mouth of Ouroboros itself:

Urge and urge and urge,
Always the procreant urge of the world.
Out of the dimness opposite equals advance, always substance and
    increase, always sex,
Always a knit of identity, always distinction, always a breed of life.

The metaphysical wonderment of Whitman's verse, like that of cultural dimensionality itself, appropriately contains its own "opposite equal," its nemesis. Since Whitman ministered to the wounded of the Civil War, and thus experienced firsthand the bloody birth of the American Dreamtime, we may infer that his own multitudes harbored some monstrous beings. He could perhaps have appreciated better than most that the irony and horror of cultural dimensionality, of the kinship : ethnicity construct, are devastating when their implications sink in. The Serb artilleryman in the hills overlooking Sarajevo *is* the mangled child in the collapsed apartment house below; the Khmer Rouge fanatic *is* each of his victims rotting in their mass grave. That Pliocene water hole, with its hunchy, uncomprehending ape-things, begins to look better and better, which brings us to other images of redemption, suspension, and nirvana, of the Life Force and the Death Force.

Life Force < ------ > Death Force. Every human society utilizes and interacts with animals, possesses a technology of more or less complicated artifacts, has a kinship system incorporating an ideology of shared substance and an incest taboo, and harbors deeply held beliefs about ethnic differences separating it from other societies. And every human society embraces a belief system we loosely and parochially refer to as a "religion": notions of supranatural, suprahuman forces of creation and destruction. These are what I designate, impiously following the lead of *Star Wars*, as the *Life Force* and the *Death Force*, the third of the semiotic dimensions of culture postulated in this work.

In concluding my discussion of the first semiotic dimension, animal: artifact/machine, I noted that animals and artifacts provide us, in addition to examples of other creative, generative entities, a basis and source for the very concepts of creation and destruction. In watching an animal move around and do things, in reflecting on our actions as we fashion artifacts and work with them, we are led to conceptualize the principles of creation and destruction. There is, however, a whole class of creative and destructive forces that lack any discrete form or embodiment on anything like the human scale. The Life

Force : Death Force construct subsumes that class of creative and destructive forces; it is a fundamental constituent of culture and source of generativity even though its content may be as elusive as the position of a photon between measurements. Animals, machines, and people are all concrete, identifiable actors. However, creation and destruction often take an anonymous, hidden form. Plants push their way out of the cold, dark earth to flower and bear fruit; clouds release the rain that brings forth that green and growing life; those same clouds sometimes hurl down thunder and lightning that destroy humans and their productions; and earthquakes, volcanos, floods, and hurricanes bring sudden and unforeseen destruction and terror. All these forces of "nature" are in fact supranatural in that the source of their creative or destructive energies is hidden or diffused. It remains, then, for an evolving cultural intelligence to provide those unbounded forces with substance and identity by composing myths of an Earth Mother, the life-giving serpent Ouroboros, the Master of Animals, and culture heroes representing the sun, the moon, and the elements of earth, air, fire and water.

This process of forming representations of unseen, unknowable beings is so critical to the evolution of culture that it may be taken as an index of the presence or absence of a cultural intelligence. Before the development of culture, the sun and moon passed overhead and the ape-things below felt only the warmth and the cold, saw only the light and dark. With the beginnings of (proto)culture, the sun and moon became presences, entities that were *there* and to be pondered and reckoned with. For all its faults, Kubrick's *2001* again comes up with a riveting image of this cerebral Rubicon (it is, after all, a great movie): when the ape-things get smart, the obelisk is seen to glow and shimmer, is *seen* by them for the first time as an object of something other than perceptual interest. The look in their eyes at that moment, just before the scene dissolves and we find ourselves a couple of million years in the future, is the expression of a cultural being. It is the origin of culture, brought to you on the silver screen.

Even placed beside the colossal forces of nature, perhaps the most mysterious and terrifying events of all are human birth and death. Our social institutions and technological innovations testify to the fact that for us soon-to-be residents of twenty-first-century Dreamtime America, nothing is as unnatural as our own birth and death. We insulate ourselves from those events, erecting hospitals, funeral homes (apt euphemism!) and cemeteries, and appointing doctors and morticians to stand in our place and shield us from two of the very few natural events that come into our lives. Animals drop their newborn in the wild; we deliver ours in highly ritualized, engineered social settings. That difference, or how it is conceptualized (animals don't trouble themselves over it) is another Rubicon of culture, another index of the appropriation of biology by a cultural intelligence.

Unlike Kubrick's obelisk, however, this culturization of birth was not a one-shot affair. In order for culture to appropriate the biological function of childbirth, and in the process invest it with mystery and power, it first transformed the very biology and morphology of the human body. The smart ape-thing of the late Pliocene was bipedal, a tricky bit of evolutionary engineering that required, among other things, a reduced pelvic size.[35] The smaller pelvis meant a smaller birth canal. At the same time, however, the smart ape-thing was getting smarter: intelligence turned out to have an adaptive value, so the ape-thing's brain was increasing in size.[36]

The two processes of bipedalism and brain augmentation resulted in the *obstetrical dilemma*, a mainstay of Anthropology 101 curricula across the land. Quite simply, women as they are put together now are not well suited to give birth to their big-brained infants. Proponents of "natural childbirth" conveniently ignore, or never bother to learn, this rather obvious fact of human physiology, which no amount of Lamaze training can appreciably alter. The evolutionary solution to the obstetrical dilemma — and any woman who has given birth can testify that it is a painfully inadequate solution — was to deliver the big-brained infant early, before its cranium had grown even larger. Hence we are born, as physical anthropologists have often observed, less as human beings than as foetalized apes: premature, helpless things whose neurological functions, muscular control, and skeletal formation are woefully incomplete. Childbirth is thus not so much the beginning of a new life as a medical emergency thrust upon a woman and whoever may be assisting her. It is an emergency, however, that is biologically innate, hard-wired into our species at its present evolutionary stage.

Small wonder, then, that we do not think of childbirth in clinical, no-nonsense, naturalistic terms. Even with all the medical equipment at our disposal, the occasion of a birth still involves us in powerful, mysterious forces beyond our control. Those forces represent our most immediate and direct participation in the creative power of life itself — what our friends Luke Skywalker and Obi-Wan-Kenobi would call the Life Force.

The Life Force, though, is only one pole of the third semiotic axis of culture. Both the origin of culture and our daily involvement in it are predicated on the experience, which for us necessarily means the symbolization, of death. As childbirth does with the creative forces in the world around us, so the death of a loved one (if not *The Loved One*) focuses all the destructive, malevolent forces of the world into an intimate, awe-inspiring experience. Although primates and elephants are obviously affected by the death of a group member and even appear to grieve much as we do, it is difficult to believe that those creatures possess, as we regrettably do, a foreknowledge of death, a certainty that those around them and they themselves will one day die.

That terrible certainty is as responsible as any of the other semiotic antipodes of culture — Animal, Artifact, Kinship, Ethnicity, and the Life Force — for the nature and vectorial movement of humanity through the semiospace of culture. It is a principal reason, for example, why computers, if they ever do "take over," will not be taking over our cultural system, our humanity. For computers, at least the current crop, are so differently constituted from us and from the cultural parameters that define us that their ascendancy would move the goal posts of human existence off the present playing field. The Something Else those ascendant computers introduced would radically distort the geometry of culture, propelling "us" and our metamorphosing fellow traveler, Rene, into another, distant bubble of that frothy semiospace we contemplated earlier. Trekkies should relish this prospect, for truly we "would boldly go where no man has gone before," only "we" wouldn't be a paunchy Kirk and wrinkled Spock when "we" got there; "we" would have mutated, along with the versatile Rene, into some unrecognizable cyborg-lobster-thing. But that will not happen quite yet, since, for the time being, computers do not die.

The foreknowledge of death is another of those cerebral Rubicons of culture, a boundary marker (but we know how deceiving those are!) on the route from protoculture to culture, from the smart ape-things to humanity. On one side of that marker death is a natural event, an assault on the mammalian limbic system perhaps, but still just something that happens. The lion lunges at its prey, an antelope falls under its assault, the other antelopes bolt in blind, instinctive fear, then a few minutes later resume their watchful grazing. Similarly, in those distant times of the late Pliocene and early Pleistocene a hominid would be crushed in a cave avalanche, or simply not wake up one morning, and its fellows would remark the fact, perhaps grieve, but then cast the body aside with the rest of the day's refuse.[37] There was no connecting the death to a larger, and already conceptualized, scheme of things, no acting so as to preserve a memory of the fallen individual, no sense that the individual had taken a journey to an unknown place where all his survivors would follow.

The only available evidence for the existence of such considerations among long-extinct hominids is physical: burials that were performed in lieu of casting aside the carcass or butchering it for the family barbecue.[38] While a sense of the sacredness of human death, and by extension the installation of the Death Force in the semiospace of an emergent cultural system, may have preceded actual burials by a hundred millennia, physical evidence of such a behavioral-cum-conceptual transformation first appears in the hominid fossil record only about sixty thousand years ago. The remarkable set of Neandertal burials from Shanidar cave in northern Iraq evidences both purposeful burial, with the bodies arranged in tightly flexed positions, and some form of actual mortuary ceremony: one of the individuals was apparently interred with a covering of wild flowers over his body.[39]

Since the Shanidar burials were already quite elaborate for their time (Forest Lawn and the poodle Taj Mahals of southern California were mercifully still sixty millennia and a *Homo* subspecies away), it is entirely possible that simpler burial practices had begun considerably earlier in the hominid past. However (and this is a big "however") even if the practice of burying the dead began a great deal earlier, say one hundred thousand or one hundred fifty thousand years ago, those time spans would still represent only a tiny slice — no more than two or three percent — of the 4.5 million years that separate us from the earliest hominids, those (sort of) smart ape-things more formally known as australopithecines. These are daunting figures, particularly if you accept even the basics of my argument about the mutability of culture and the corresponding specificity of humanity's domain within culture, of our own little bubble of semiospace. Without a foreknowledge of death, "death" would lack a sense of sacredness, and would have only the fuzziest conceptualization. Without that sense and, perhaps, its ritualization in the form of burial practices, there would be no Death Force as I have described it, no conceptual sense of a set of destructive, malevolent forces loose in the world. Finally, without a Death Force at work in the dynamics of the semiospace of culture, there would, quite simply, be no humanity. There would be something, but it would be Something Else, some hunchy ape-thing, perhaps. The implication is clear: for somewhere around ninety-seven to ninety-eight percent of their career on the planet, hominids wandered through the frothy reaches of semiospace without blundering into that tiny, dancing, outrageously improbable bubble of it we now call "humanity."

Of the four movies (or movie-*oeuvres*) discussed in detail in the following four chapters, only Bond movies lack explicit development or movement along the Life Force : Death Force semiotic axis. *Star Wars*, including its sequels *The Empire Strikes Back* and *Return of the Jedi*, made that axis, in the guise of the Force and the Dark Force, the basis for the pop culture saying of a generation of teeny boppers: "May the Force be with you." While abysmally trite, the saying, and particularly its instant popularity, direct our attention to the whole matter of the role of transcendent experience in our lives, in short, to *religion*. Millions of people who don't go into a church from one year to the next and who only watch the TV evangelists when Jimmy Swaggart is putting on the good viewers with one of his crying jags walked into the Dreamtime temples of theatres showing the *Star Wars* movies and found themselves confronting some heavy metaphysical issues. And yet these same multitudes would hit the remote to zap a talking-heads PBS program on some soporific topic like "The Place of Religion in Contemporary American Life" faster than Luke Skywalker could dust an enemy tie-fighter.

The metaphysical, in its current manifestation of American cinematic folk religion,[40] is similarly prominent in that granddaddy of the supergrossers, *E. T.* As I discuss in chapter 7, it is impossible to disassociate the tremendous appeal of the E. T. – Elliott relationship from the comparable recent appeal of such figures as Reverend Moon, Jim Jones, Guru Ma, David Koresh, and the many maharishis and other cult leaders. Their promise to put their followers in touch with the Divine, the One, the Force is poignantly captured in what have become the two most powerful and lasting images of *E. T.*: the glowing touch E. T. uses to impart life and speed healing; and E. T.'s glowing "heart" that signals its (not "his" or even "her") own connection with the Life Force.

E. T., however, is so good a movie that it eclipses the other, evil side of life: the Dark Force that *Star Wars* depicts with such imagination. The scientist villains of *E. T.* simply cannot hold a candle — or light saber — to Darth Vader and his legion of ersatz-Nazis aboard the Death Star. At the other extreme, the noble Obi-Wan-Kenobi and that huggable mystic, Yota, exemplify with comic book clarity the positive but ineffable presence that many Americans yearn to be a part of their lives, and that sends them off to the reverends and maharishis. As Obi-Wan-Kenobi and his former Jedi pupil, Darth Vader, demonstrate, the Force can be used for good or evil, for Life or Death. The Death Star is more than a technological artifact of the enemy; it is a product of the pathological hatred and evil of its Emperor, the gnarled old anti-Wizard of Oz character who referees Luke and Darth's final showdown. At the other pole of the semiotic dimension, R2D2 is not just Luke's capable robot assistant, for its endearing vitality and spontaneity in the face of its physical droid limitations attest to a Force that is more generative than high technology, that is larger than life.

The benevolent and malevolent supranatural forces of the third semiotic dimension thus operate on and through the other two dimensions of Animal: Artifact/Machine and Us/Self: Them/Other to create characters and actions that overwhelm and terrify the movie audiences of Dreamtime America. Perhaps the crowning achievement in this regard is Steven Spielberg's dramatic amplification in *Jaws* of a shark-fear already deeply entrenched in our consciousness. The Great White of the four *Jaws* movies is far more than an animal, particularly one as anonymous as a fish: like the evil Emperor of the Death Star, the Great White is the living, surging, irrepressible embodiment of the urge to destroy. It is evil incarnate.

As I mentioned earlier, it would be difficult to find in any of the Bond movies the first hint of things metaphysical. Bond, as the archetype of the modern action hero, operates in a cultural landscape that is quite literally flat, since the third semiotic dimension shrinks away to insignificance and leaves a two-dimensional plane formed by the remaining two axes. There are no mystical, glowing touches or hearts, no bad guys whose fingernails arc with blue flame, no robots with great personalities (they have only what Q has given them in his basement lab) in the Bond movies. The Life Force and the Death Force enter the picture only in the logically limiting case that virtually every moment of a Bond movie is a cliff-hanger: Bond is usually to be found dangling just above the waiting jaws of death. And that, perhaps better than a more cinematographic definition of the action film, is what action *movies* are about. For their stark simplicity, then (if not because they are great fun!), Bond movies are the first of the four (post)modern classics to place beneath our cultural analytic lens in what follows.

4

The Story of Bond

The myth is certainly related to given (empirical) facts, but not as a re-presentation of them. The relationship is of a dialectic kind, and the institutions described in the myths can be the very opposite of the real institutions. This will in fact always be the case when the myth is trying to express a negative truth.

—Claude Lévi-Strauss, *The Story of Asdiwal*

I felt so good. I felt just like a machine.
— Brenda Howard, interviewed on *Good Morning, America* on the occasion of her bowling two successive "300" games

James Bond: An American Myth?

Why, in a book on American myth, write about James Bond, a fictional British secret agent in Her Majesty's Secret Service and the creation of a British novelist self-exiled to Jamaica? And if this initial doubt regarding the Britishness of Bond can be put to rest, then we face the more general and certainly more formidable question: Why, considering the evident shallowness of Bond movies and their cheap exploitation of women, foreign places, and people, should we bother with a serious examination of such mindless fare? Despite everything I have said about the "myth of America" and the critical role popular movies have in articulating that myth, surely such lowbrow stuff as James Bond movies contains little to interest the anthropologist searching in his own culture for clues to the fundamental organization of culture? As you might expect, I have what I hope are convincing replies to both these objections, replies that bring us right to the nitty gritty of how — and how not — to do a cultural analysis of American society.

The Britishness of Bond would have been a valid reason for excluding him from consideration had this book appeared thirty-five years ago, before John Kennedy called Bond to the attention of the American public in 1961 by revealing that *From Russia With Love* was one of his ten favorite books.[1] That halcyon time at the dawn of Camelot and the beginning of the sixties was also just before Bond went Hollywood, with the 1962 release of *Dr No*. If there were any question about Bond's transatlantic appeal, the quick succession of Albert Broccoli and Harry Saltzman-produced movies silenced it. The high-tech gadgetry and jet-set characters and locations of those movies negated any lingering, fusty Britishness of Ian Fleming's novelistic Bond, making it all but impossible to interpret his popularity as a function, say, of Americans' interest in things English. The *story of Bond*, his *geste* or *saga*, has become fully incorporated in the larger, ongoing *story of America*, the Dreamtime chronicle of that rich, gimmicky and bizarre land that is less a place than a state of mind.

I would even go further and claim, as I did in the introduction, that James Bond is more than a popular movie character; he is the Hero of Our Age. Since Bond appeared on the world stage in 1954 in Fleming's first novel, *Casino Royale*, Agent 007 has fought and seduced his way through twenty-five books and eighteen movies, in the process drawing on the talents of three novelists (Ian Fleming, Kingsley Amis and John Gardner) and five actors (Sean Connery, Roger Moore, David Niven, George Lazenby, and Timothy Dalton). Over the course of Bond's forty-year career, the novels have sold more than one hundred million copies and the movies collectively have earned far more than the most successful of individual supergrossers. The unprecedented appeal Bond has exercised on the reading and movie-going public is really quite astonishing: this agent — who is anything but "secret" — has outlasted not only the merely mortal writers and actors who gave him life, but major transformations in global history and politics as well. The second world war, the decline of colonies and emergence of independent Third World nations, the Korean and Vietnam "conflicts," the disintegration of the Soviet Union and end of the Cold War, all these and other world-altering events have failed to terminate ("with extreme prejudice," as Bond's cronies say) his career. Instead, Bond has transmuted, chameleon-like, in counterpoint with those transformations in global society. As with other truly mythological figures like Oedipus and Prometheus, no single author or historical period has been able to contain Bond, to make him their agent; his irrepressible (and godawful!) wit and *savoir faire* have kept him free of their constraining embrace. Like Pharaoh, Bond belongs to the ages.

If there were any question about assigning the story of Bond to an American Dreamtime, it would lie in the *universality* of Bond's appeal, and not in a parochial Britishness that, as we will see, others have insisted on ascribing to him. For Bond's career has paralleled, and impelled, the process of media saturation of the planet made possible by postwar technology and the booming sixties. When movie theatres went up and began showing Western films to the burgeoning urban populations of Manilla, Jakarta, Lima, Rio de Janeiro, Mexico City, and points north, east, south, and west, James Bond became a star attraction, perhaps the very first truly global media sensation. Enormous differences in language, social background, and cultural values melted away in the cerebral furnace of the theatre showing a Bond movie, reduced in many instances to the lowest common denominator: Bond was the "kiss, kiss, bang, bang" loved by Third World audiences and immortalized in Pauline Kael's book title. Luke Skywalker, Indiana Jones, E. T., Sue Ellen and J. R. Ewing, Rocky and Rambo — these and other international media sensations would follow Bond into those dingy Third World theatres, some with their wooden benches and dirt floors, and into the sleepy town plazas with their public television sets. But it was Bond who showed the way, and it is Bond who remains at or near the pinnacle of world-wide popularity.

If it were possible to do an impossible survey, we might tabulate the number of retinal images of Bond (whether Sean Connery, Roger Moore, or, God forbid, Timothy Dalton) imprinted on a global cross-section of movie-goers' eyes during the period, say, from 1963 through 1993, and then compare our results with identical surveys using images of Luke Skywalker, Indiana Jones, and other possible candidates. I cannot think of another media creation that might eclipse Bond's popularity as measured in our hypothetical survey. And were we to extend our little *Gedanken-experiment* to other figures whose images are not solely the product of the cinema (but who are decidedly real/reel life characters), I think it likely that Bond would be keeping company with Jesus and Buddha (Mohammed, who spurned icons, would not even be in the running).

It is because the story of Bond, along with the stories of Luke Skywalker and Indiana Jones, are so popular, so universal, that I have insisted from the start that the American Dreamtime is not bounded by, nor does it belong to, a political entity such as the "United States." It is what the physicists call a *nonlocal* phenomenon, diffused or smeared over the physical landscape, simultaneously present in widely separated locations.

If you remain uncomfortable with the elusiveness of an American Dreamtime described in these terms taken from quantum mechanics, I would again suggest thinking of it as an emergent global culture of consumer capitalism. The second half of the twentieth century has been an unbelievably turbulent period in which national boundaries are shuffled like playing cards, enormous numbers of people move from country to city or from continent to continent, and the values and loyalties of an old way of life are jettisoned willy-nilly for those of a dimly perceived modernity. The one constant in this sea of turbulence has been the inexorable growth and spread of consumer economies: money-based systems of exchange that are driven by the desire to possess particular things or experiences more or less for the sake of having them. Old systems of reciprocal exchange, intended to buttress traditional social relations and values (I give you a necklace and next year you give me a bracelet) have pretty much collapsed under the onslaught of consumer goods produced by anonymous workers in faraway places and available to anyone with cash (or plastic) in hand. Malinowski's 1922 ethnographic classic *Argonauts of the Western Pacific*, which details the ceremonial exchange through the institution of the *kula* of those very necklaces and bracelets, could never be written today; it would have to be recast for a generation of Trobrianders more interested in Budweiser, boom boxes, and Nike running shoes than in ceremonial trading alliances.

How has this transition come about? How have centuries of tradition been swept aside by a few feverish decades of modernity? As I have suggested throughout this work, where values and changes in values are concerned it is necessary to look at the systems of images that represent those values and that propose possible, or virtual, worlds in which those values reign — in short, it is necessary to look at myth.

James Bond is an agent, not for a hopelessly outmoded Imperial Britain, but for the new global empire of consumer capitalism. His most important assignment is to spread the word, or rather the images, of that empire and in the process to assess its attractions and pitfalls for individuals the world over. The hundreds of millions who have filed into movie theatres around the world for the past thirty years to watch Bond in action are the citizens, if you will, of this "new world order" (which was definitely not called into being at a George Bush press conference). And these new citizens of the new empire do not swear allegiance first of all to the Stars and Stripes, the Union Jack, or the French tricolor (like Barthes's "young Negro soldier"), but to *things* and *experiences* in themselves: consumer items, images from film and television that have miraculously assumed material form. Quite without the assistance of the United Nations, whose diplomats are themselves busily emulating Bond's expense account lifestyle in the watering holes of Manhattan, these new citizens of the world have forged a global culture in which they are consumers first and members of a polity second. The Bond movies are distillations of this new world of consumption; they package and sell scenes of unattainable luxury filled with beautiful, impeccably tailored and coiffed people. Long before the Berlin Wall crumbled, taking the Evil Empire and the Cold War with it, the world according to Bond had already gained ascendancy.

How To Do — and *Not* To Do — Cultural Analysis: The Novel-Bond and the Movie-Bond

From the preceding it is clear that I am pretty much sold on the cultural significance of James Bond movies; their hedonistic materialism and spirit of light-hearted fun seem to me to be part and parcel of the pleasure-loving Main Vein of American life so brilliantly chronicled by Tom Wolfe. Curiously, however, those very qualities of Bond movies seem to be the reasons social critics and commentators of every political and cultural orientation give for dismissing them — from Bible-thumping fundamentalist Baptist preachers to the *New York Review of Books* mavens Wolfe loves to lampoon. For those critics, the silliness and artlessness of Bond movies seem to lead them to conclude that the movies are at best irrelevant trash and at worst — and more likely — the enemy itself, the cinematic incarnation of that shameless, swaggering, mindless immorality that has brought this once proud land to the brink of ruin.

Clearly there is a great difference of opinion here. I want to claim that a cultural analysis or anthropological semiotics of popular movies, particularly of those as popular as Bond movies, is an excellent if not indispensable means of identifying what is going on in that holographic engine of the modern psyche (which I have chosen to call the *American Dreamtime*, but you are free to call whatever you like). Others would reject the claim that paying serious attention to what they consider sensationalist, chauvinist trash can yield valuable insights into the nature of American culture, let alone culture in general. Among the tribe of anthropologists particularly, choosing to focus on "popular culture" when there are all those authentic natives out there desperately needing to be studied before they are done in or "spoiled" by encroaching civilization is a serious breach of an unspoken professional code.

In my opinion this stark either-or choice is not really viable. If we hope to have anything worthwhile to say about American culture, which really means global culture, we do not have the option of choosing between analyzing and not analyzing popular productions like Bond movies, *Star Wars*, *E. T.* and the rest. We only have the option of analyzing them well or badly. To dismiss Bond and the other supergrosser characters with a few arrogant, sweeping generalities is already to have conducted a cultural analysis — just not a very good one. Such an analysis implies, if it does not say outright, that people are fools for wasting their time and money on such trash, that the mob cannot be trusted to point the way to fundamental insights into the nature of humanity.

As an anthropologist and as a person I find myself strongly opposed to this kind of elitist, dead-end approach. First, as an anthropologist it seems to me that dismissing Bond movies short-circuits the whole enterprise of doing anthropology, which is to try to understand what people are about. If you start out by claiming that things that obviously interest people are not worth studying, you immediately paint yourself into a corner that will require some fancy mental acrobatics to escape. This is in fact the situation of cultural anthropology today, as it thrashes about searching for a public voice while clinging to an obscure academicism that may well silence it forever. My point is that, for better or worse, anthropologists and other members of that shrinking constituency, the "thinking public," have to wake up and smell the coffee (even if it is decaffeinated and served with a twist!), to observe what people are doing and try to figure *that* out.

For the Bond movies have been neither produced nor consumed in a cultural vacuum. Harry Saltzman, Albert Broccoli, Sean Connery, Roger Moore, and their small army of writers, set designers, stunt persons, and special effects technicians did not just fall off the turnip truck and discover they had landed on a gold mine; they deliberately and skillfully created a set of images and stories with genuine appeal. And people did not flock to see the movies because those were one hundred percent cotton candy fluff; they could get enough of that at home with TV sitcoms. They went to see Bond because he was something special, because he had experiences that were exhilarating, vital, seemingly more real than their own occluded lives.

Second, as a person I have always found myself at odds with those who dismiss a topic as trivial without investigating it. Over the past several years it has often happened that I find myself in conversations with educated, intelligent people, who, learning of my anthropological interest in popular movies, make the most scathing, dismissive remarks about the topic and then nervously change the subject (or quickly find another conversational partner!). For some reason this sort of thing usually seems to happen with literary people or with academicians who specialize in literature (associate professors of English being the type case here). Interestingly, these same people are often made nervous by "real" myth as well, that is, the actual stories told by bona fide "primitives" or "natives." They are comfortable enough, and usually even enthusiastic, about "primitive myth" as a general, fuzzy topic, which evokes for them, I suppose, images of primeval man, the world of nature, life in the raw. But try introducing a specific myth for discussion, whose contents are often quite grisly, lurid, and just downright artless, and you will see that enthusiasm vanish with the desert dew.

In my view the really disappointing thing about this oh-so-typical scorn of popular cultural productions is not just that it is intellectually incorrect and will lead to a flawed analysis of those productions, but that it reveals a contempt or fear of the joyful, thrilling, *fun* things in life. If you begin a study of popular movies with a disdain, a gut-level loathing of them, I cannot imagine how anything worthwhile will come out of it. It would be too much like the typical practice of the early ethnographer, who arrived in the "native" village as just another colonial official (pith helmet, scarf, khakis, the whole kit) and summoned the local notables, whom he charmingly called "informants," to the verandah of the Government Rest House, where he took their depositions on their culture.

Note that I am *not* saying that the message of Bond movies is necessarily salutary, that delving deeply into them will make you feel good and will produce a positive, healthy-minded picture of society. Remember my morbid comments earlier about cultural anthropology as a pathological science: the things you encounter may repulse and terrify you, but if you truly have the spirit of inquiry, you will be fascinated by them, will genuinely want to understand them for what they are. Life does not have to be pretty, but at least some of us need to look at it full in the face. It is on this vital point that the dismissive, contemptuous attitude toward popular movies fails so badly.

To begin a cultural analysis, I believe it is essential to be fascinated with the topic, to have had some initial experience of it akin to what I have described of my Seattle encounter with the *Star Wars* phenomenon. And if that fascination is not present, if there is not an actual visceral thrill coursing through you, it is better for you and your future audience to keep your tent folded and move on to more arid steppes of the mind, where thesis titles lie bleaching in the parched, numbing air, awaiting the eager candidate who will take them up, polish and display them.

If I possess no other qualification for the present task, I can at least admit unabashedly that I have always been fascinated with the Bond thrillers. I read the books in the sixties, I went to most of the movies in the sixties, seventies, and eighties, and now I sometimes even watch the James Bond festivals on cable (though, unlike a good friend and true Bond zealot, I do not have the complete video cassette collection of Bond movies). While unsympathetic friends have accused me of going to almost any length to rationalize my hopelessly lowbrow tastes, I find that the fun of Bond movies is inseparable from my interest in them as objects of cultural analysis. They are, or with a little intellectual obsessiveness can be made to be, instances of what the eminent cultural anthropologist Clifford Geertz has described as "deep play": amusements that issue from a people's deepest sensibilities and under-standings of itself.[2] Bond would not be such enduring fun for me or for his hundreds of millions of other fans if he did not strike a responsive chord in us all, something we hold in common despite the diversity of our experiences. This premise is enough to launch a cultural analysis of the story of Bond, for it holds out the promise that a close inspection of the saga will provide insights into the workings of our culture.

I think this process typifies the way, unscientific though it may be, that one undertakes any cultural analysis: one is initially struck by the appeal or popularity of a movie, a TV show, a sporting event, video games, purple mohawk hairdos, roller disco, rap music, or whatever, and the effect is to generate an acute puzzlement. Why in the world should *that* particular production acquire such a following? What is it about this peculiar culture of ours that installs some slipshod creation or activity at the mythic core of things? This sense of puzzlement is like an itch, and when we scratch it we discover aspects of our culture previously obscured beneath a cloud of facile, everyday assumption. I think this is where the fun of Bond leads.

Without the fascination, without the fun and thrill of Bond-watching, with only the disdain and contempt of the critic, a cultural analysis of Bond movies is inevitably mean-spirited and limited. Curiously, such treatments exhibit the very shallowness and reactionary cast their authors find so appalling in the character of Bond. They are perfect examples of how *not* to do cultural analysis.

While any number of savants and commentators have taken their crack at Bond during his heyday, it may be instructive to examine one such attack-cum-analysis that is particularly virulent, and that is, I think, one of those perfect examples of how not to do cultural analysis. It is by the well-known novelist and essayist Mordecai Richler. Writing in 1968 at the height of the Bond phenomenon, Richler was still fixated on the Britishness of Bond and couched his interpretation in that vein. It is also clear that Richler thought Fleming a pretentious hack and his books execrable writing. If the novels could not stand on their own as literature, then they must have some other, social basis for their appeal. And what might that social basis be? Richler attributed the popularity of the Bond stories to their soothing effect on the ravaged self-esteem of the English, a condition that had become acute following the second world war and the emergent hegemony of the United States and the Soviet Union.

> James Bond is a meaningless fantasy cutout unless he is tacked to the canvas of diminishing England . . . Little England's increasingly humiliating status has spawned a blinkered romanticism on the Left and on the Right. On the Left, it has given us CND (the touching assumption that it matters morally to the world whether or not England gives up the Bomb unilaterally) and anti-Americanism. On the Right, there is the decidedly more expensive fantasy that this offshore island can still confront the world as Great Britain. If the brutal facts, the familiar facts, are that England has been unable to adjust to its shriveled island status, largely because of antiquated industry, economic mismanagement, a fusty civil service, and reactionary trade unions, then the comforting right-wing pot-dream is that virtuous Albion is beset by disruptive Communists within and foreign devils and conspirators without.
>
> Largely, this is what James Bond is about. . . .
>
> It is possible to explain the initial success of the Bond novels in that if they came at a time when vicious anti-Semitism and neo-Fascist xenophobia were no longer acceptable in England, then a real need as well as a large audience for such reading matter still existed. It was Fleming's most brilliant stroke to present himself not as an old-fashioned, frothing wog-hater, but as an ostensibly civilized voice who offered sanitized racialism instead. The Bond novels not only satisfy Little Englanders who believe they have been undone by dastardly foreign plotters, but pander to their continuing notion of self-importance. (*James Bond Unmasked*, 350–4)

"Largely, this is what James Bond is about. . ." I was incredulous, downright flabbergasted when I read this. When I came across Richler's essay I had already begun thinking about the mythic nature of James Bond. And, as it happened, I was living in Richler's native Montreal at the time, a city I had got to know in part from his perceptive accounts of the multicultural complexity of life "on the Main," on the little streets leading into *boulevard St. Laurent.*[3] I simply could not believe that a writer of Richler's stature and acuity could be so hopelessly wrong, particularly when life in Montreal in the sixties should have disabused him of any idea that the people around him were infatuated with things English. This was one of my first lessons, as I began to slip into the quicksand of popular culture studies, that prejudice and invective which would not be tolerated by educated, thinking persons were the topic, say, ethnic relations or Indian land claims, are righteously unleashed against the enjoyments of the masses. Being "black" (whatever *that* might mean) will get you lots of liberal understanding, but really *liking* James Brown and, worse, wanting to talk about his music. . . sorry, but it's time to draw that line in the sand. In Richler's terms, it is terrible to imply that someone is a wog, but quite all right to pillory him as a wog-hater.

Unless Richler was simply trying to appease his *quebecois* drinking buddies (an effort he stridently abandoned in his recent diatribe against Quebec nationalists in *Oh, Canada! Oh, Quebec!*) it is impossible for me to understand how he could have arrived at such a skewed interpretation of a craze then sweeping North America and much of the Third World. Even in 1968, when his essay originally appeared in *Commentary* (it was reprinted in book form in 1971), Ian Fleming's novels and several Bond movies had reached an immense audience across the seas from the "Little England" Richler excoriates. Did he really suppose that the seventeen-year-olds thronging movie theatres in (our favorite town!) Topeka, Seattle, Boston, and even his native Montreal had gone to watch Agent 007 do battle with Rosa Klebb and Doctor No in order to revive their faith in a diminished England? The idea seems as improbable as Fleming's characters.

It may well be that Richler's virulent reaction to the Bond phenomenon is simply an extension of his obvious distaste and contempt for Fleming's work — the characteristic scorn a first-rate novelist visits on the second-rate. However that may be, he should not have tarred the movie-phenomenon and Fleming's books with the same brush, for the two are worlds apart.

You can confirm this for yourself over the course of a lazy weekend. Check out a copy of *Moonraker* from your friendly neighborhood Blockbuster Video store (if you don't have the complete Bond set in *your* cassette collection), make up a batch of Orville Redenbacher Microwaveable, open a Coke or a Coors (but definitely *not* a Perrier), and settle back to enjoy the thrill-a-minute rollercoaster ride that is a Bond movie. Then, in the lingering glow of that video experience, begin to read the copy of *Moonraker*-the-novel that you have retrieved from that dusty box of college books in the back of the closet or checked out of the local public library (don't even *think* of looking for it in a university library). I can almost guarantee that this little experiment will instill in you a great respect for the unheralded screenwriters who reworked the novel into a script, and for the director, actors, and technicians who gave the script life. For compared with the movie, the novel is turgid, flat, and hopelessly dated. Fleming, as Richler asserts, *is* old-fashioned, but his *Moonraker* is definitely *not* about wog-hating; it is a dreary tale about leftover Nazis trying to strike one more blow against England, a real yawner after the high-tech glitz and eroticism of the movie.

The glaring disparity between the novel-Bond and the movie-Bond, together with references in Richler's essay to Fleming's "works" and the Bond "novels," lead me to suspect that Richler did not bother to go down to one of the theatres on *rue Ste. Catherine* and actually watch a Bond movie before sitting down to write his essay for *Commentary*. Like the literary lion that he is, I believe Richler sat in his study, forcing himself to consume the hackneyed pulp of an immensely more successful writer, and becoming more and more angry as he read. That Richler could have watched a Bond movie, with its endless chases, seductions, and flippant one-liners, and come away with a gloomy vision of "sanitized racialism" and lurking Fascism defies belief. Even if Richler did not misread Fleming, he clearly failed to see — and probably even to view — James Bond, the mythic Hero of Our Age who consumes writers, directors, texts, and films in carving out his ample holographic niche in the global culture of the Dreamtime.

To do cultural analysis it is necessary to go where the beast leads you, and not to be overly concerned about what you may step in in its path. The beast that is the story of Bond clearly leads into the movie theatres and thence into the hearts and minds of many millions of people around the world. It is, of course, certainly possible to confine your analysis to Fleming's novels, or even to a single novel or a single character in a novel; whole dissertations have been written about subjects of lesser scope. In fact, Umberto Eco (another Bond fan!) has produced what is probably the definitive study of Bond-as-*text* in his essay "Narrative Structures in Fleming," published in 1979. It is what Richler might have aimed for had he had fewer demons chasing him, and been a lot more semiotically inclined. It is also perfectly feasible to undertake what would be a fascinating topic in itself: the complex transformations the novels have undergone in being reworked for film. A close study, say, of Goldfinger the novelistic character and Goldfinger the movie villain might reveal a great deal about the manifold changes and differences (those intersystems again) between recent periods of Western history.

But Eco would not, and we should not, pretend that any analysis of the novel-Bond, no matter how brilliant, can encompass the movie-Bond, which is the true medium of Bond's Dreamtime status. The writer and literary critic may decide, for obvious disciplinary reasons, to confine themselves to the printed word, but if they wish to put on the cap of cultural analyst, to say something about how the books they read tie into the world of experience, then they must put down their books and follow the cultural anthropologist into the native villages of Montreal and Topeka, where the Real/Reel People continue, after forty years of world-shaking distractions, to keep alive the story of Bond.

Gadgets and Gladiators: The Master of Machines

It is necessary to go to the movies. And when we go to a Bond movie we discover (but of course most of us already knew!) that every Bond movie is in fact two movies, or two acts, like a rock concert or a boxing match: there is a warm-up act and the main event. The warm-up act is an incredibly fast-paced action scene lasting just a few minutes and often bearing little or no relation to the main event. However jaundiced one's view of Bond movies may be, it is hard to deny that their warm-up acts have virtually perfected the dramatic device of the chase: packed into the opening minutes of every movie is enough high-speed, high-tech mayhem to fill out any conventional ninety-minute thriller.

Consider the opening scene of *The Spy Who Loved Me*, released in 1977 after Connery had regrettably, for all real/reel Bond fans, passed the torch to Roger Moore. It is a remote ski cabin, high in the Austrian Alps. Bond is making love to a beautiful woman on a pallet of furs before an open fire. Suddenly there is a clicking sound and his wristwatch begins to feed out a teletyped message: Bond has to report to duty. He dons a sleek ski outfit, pulls on a matching backpack and is off down the slope. But his amorous companion is a KGB spy, and she has summoned an assassination squad, also on skis, which is just making its way to the cabin. The would-be killers could conceal themselves and, when Bond neared, cut him in two with their automatic weapons. But, of course, they do not. Instead they give chase. The movie serves notice, if any were needed, that it is a piece of the Dreamtime.

There follows a spectacular display of freestyle skiing. Bond glisades down and through a tortuous, icy course closely pursued by the leader of the KGB squad who, incredibly, skis without poles and fires his pistol on the go. Out of the turns but still on a steep slope, Bond turns around, skiing backwards now, and carefully levels his right ski pole at his pursuer. It is a miniature rocket launcher; the KGB assassin's chest explodes in flame and he goes down. But before Bond can turn around, he goes over the edge of an embankment. A backwards somersault, a twist, and he lands on his skis — and in the midst of the remaining killers. There follows a fancy display of bodyblocking and ducking and Bond is in the clear, but this time going down a really steep slope. And there is a cliff!

There is a cliff, and that lone figure on skis is headed right for it. In one heartstopping moment the audience realizes that that is no dummy on the skis, not like the ones that took the fall off the log bridge into the ravine in the de

Laurentiis remake of *King Kong,* and there is no way out. The camera can cut, but our hero will still be hurtling down that precipice toward his death. This is the real thing. But there isn't a hint of a splice, and the figure goes over the cliff. The camera is still on, still out there shooting, apparently from a helicopter. And the skier is falling. His poles go, his skis fly away, and he drops and drops and drops toward a cloud bank (How high *is* this cliff, anyway?). Then the parachute pops open. It is a gigantic, silken Union Jack. A truly remarkable stunt.

Cut to a close-up of Roger Moore swinging lightly in a parachute harness, looking barely mussed if a little perturbed at having to interrupt his tryst. Then back to the tiny figure drifting down through the clouds, into a pair of superimposed, silhouetted feminine hands. The lyrics of Carly Simon's theme song, "Nobody does it better, 'cause, baby, you're the best," begin. It's time for the credits. As one body, the audience shakes off its tension and settles back in its seat; this was just for openers.

The scene described is one of innumerable dazzling chases that have become a signature of Bond movies and helped make the story of Bond the distinctive media-myth of our time. The movies have tested the limits and wrung out the last drop of dramatic potential of virtually every form of vehicular transport. Bond has made cars, planes, boats, motorcycles, hang gliders, and diving gear do things no ordinary, sane person would think of attempting. In *The Spy Who Loved Me* it is a superbly tricked-out Lotus that serves as the piece of equipment *extraordinaire*. Bond's prowess at the wheel of this miracle car reaches its best form when, pursued over a tortuous mountain road in Sardinia by a vixen in a helicopter gunship, he eventually reaches the Mediterranean shore, roars down a pier, and hurdles into the sea. Is James Bond going to a watery grave? Of course not! As the car sinks its wheels retract, it sprouts fins, and the dashboard rotates to reveal a submarine control panel. Bond pushes a red button on that panel, and his miniature sub launches a miniature guided missile that takes care of the bothersome helicopter hovering overhead.

In beginning to unpack the cultural significance of Bond movies, I think an obvious theme to focus on (again, no cinematological breakthrough here!) is those mechanized chases, which occur again and again and vary only according to the vehicles employed and the size of a particular movie's special effects budget. Since a cultural analysis looks for the unobvious in the obvious, we should thus consider two interrelated questions here: Why should the *chase* be such a recurrent and compelling theme in Bond movies? Why is it so mechanized?

The easy answer to our first question, which is really no answer at all, is that the chase is important in Bond movies because it is a universal theme of all drama. The Bond chases are simply recent installments of a long and memorable series including such classics as *The French Connection, Bullitt,* and, going back to the dawn of cinema, the Keystone Cops silent films. And if we broaden our scope and consider movies as only one of several genres of narrative, then we find the chase established as a major theme right at the beginning of Western civilization, when the blind bard Homer sang and told of Achilles's murderous pursuit of Hector, seven times around the walls of Troy.[4]

From Achilles through Steve McQueen, Gene Hackman, Sean Connery, and on to Harrison Ford and Arnold Schwarzenegger, the chase figures so prominently in our history, folklore, and, now, movies because we are fascinated with it. Our fascination with the chase has made it a universal theme in literature and film — that much is tautological, and so the "universal theme" answer is no answer at all. *Why* do we find the chase so compelling? Why haven't we seen enough of chase scenes after four thousand years of dramatized conflict and what seems like an even greater number of John Wayne war movies?

I think that chase scenes, like the movies which feature them, are so popular and engaging because they excite in us a deep-seated, primate-specific awareness of our peculiar place in a world made up of predators and prey. Consider for a moment exactly which chase scenes appeal to us most. Of the various possible permutations of the chase — the good guys chase the bad guys; the bad guys chase the good guys; the chaser catches and harms the chased; the chaser fails to catch the chased; the chaser catches the chased but then gets the worst of the ensuing conflict — the one that really fires our imagination, and the one Bond movies feature exclusively, is the last scenario. In the ski-parachute episode, in Bond's engagement with the helicopter gunship, and in a hundred other chases that have dazzled Bond fans through three decades of movie-going, Bond is the clever and resourceful prey who manages not only to elude a larger or better armed predator, but to turn the tables on him (or, often, her), to snatch victory from the jaws of seemingly certain death and defeat.

I refer to the appeal of this particular kind of chase as primate-specific because the processes of hominid evolution have involved casting proto-humans, yet again, in a betwixt-and-between, neither-one-nor-the-other role (another of those ambivalences that have been packed into our understandably anxious and expanding psyches). Remember, also, that I have argued through-out this book that it is more correct to say that culture generated or came up with us than to claim (in the conventional way) that we humans "invented" culture. But why didn't culture come up with, say, a society of eagles or one of rabbits? Why did culture "choose" as its raw material bands of miserable little ape-things whose recently arboreal ancestors had been forced out of the receding forests of the arid late Pliocene and onto the open savanna, to face rapidly evolving and truly formidable predators like the ancestors of today's big cats, hyenas, and wild dogs?

The answers to these questions issue precisely from our betwixt-and-between primate heritage. Culture didn't come up with eagle societies because eagles were doing just fine on their own: they are such marvelously adapted predators that a single eagle or mated pair can regularly make kills without any help from neighboring eagles. And for the individual hunting eagle, the "chase", if you can use that term to describe its lightning swift dive and kill, is a brutally simple either-or proposition: it either strikes its prey and kills it or it misses and has to fly back up and try again. And the eagle does all this without having to look over its shoulder; apart from modern humans no creature challenges or preys on it. Because the eagle is so effective and unthreatened, a society of sapient eagles would not be much interested in Bond movies: the long, drawn out chases in which the prey miraculously wins would seem absurd, if not downright troubling. Eagle movie critics would say, in effect: Why watch something that is stupid and makes you feel bad?

At the other extreme, culture didn't come up with rabbit societies because rabbits could not have done much with it.[5] If six or eight rabbits decided to stand up to the eagle's murderous dive, that would just have made things easier for the eagle, giving it several defenseless targets to aim for. Even if lots of social cooperation became possible among newly sapient rabbits, the best defense the rabbits could have would still be to run like hell when they saw an eagle. Like sapient eagles, sapient rabbits would not be very taken with Bond movies. While they would doubtlessly enjoy the idea of the prey turning the tables on the predator, the whole proposition would seem too nonsensical to entertain, even as entertainment. It would be like us getting wildly enthusiastic over a movie about seemingly ordinary people who can fly — amusing enough as an idle thought perhaps, but don't hold your breath waiting for a *Hook 15* (the big-budget bust Peter Pan movie of 1992).

Early hominids, as truly liminal figures in the evolutionary tableau of late Pliocene Africa, possessed betwixt-and-between qualities of both eagles and rabbits, and thus gave culture some promising raw material with which to work. Like eagles, and like baboon and chimpanzee groups observed by primatologists,[6] early hominids had acquired a taste for meat and with it an improving talent for predation. Although not the single-minded "killer ape" portrayed in the playwright Robert Ardrey's grippingly exaggerated but influential 1961 work, *African Genesis*, some of the australopithecine ape-things of four million years ago were probably good at killing, and getting better. Yet like rabbits, those early hominids, who weighed in as real lightweights of the predator world at sixty to seventy pounds, were themselves the prey of the larger, faster, and immensely more powerful carnivores that hunted the same savannas. The individual primate, then and now, is virtually powerless against the attack of a leopard. But as a *group* early hominids and present-day baboons were and are a much more formidable opponent than a cluster of frightened rabbits.[7] They could and can put up a fight and repel the attacking predator. In such engagements individual members of early hominid groups and of baboon bands distinguished and distinguish themselves as our first heros, on the tandem scales of the evolutionary past and the primate present.

By turning to face a more powerful adversary, those early hominid heros not only moved along the course of human evolution, they inculcated the beginnings of a feeling for the underdog that, millions of years later, continues to assert itself in our stories of David and Goliath, Jack and the Beanstalk, and James Bond. After millions of years of increasingly successful predation, we have distanced ourselves from our hominid ancestors and from our baboon and chimpanzee cousins, but we have not quite replaced the characteristically primate valorization of the underdog with an ethic of the *ubermensch*. While any kind of chase gets our attention, we still display our keenest interest in chases of the sort that Bond movies have made famous: a nimble, quick-witted, dashing character eludes his powerful pursuer and turns to dish out a little misery of his own. Somewhere in our collective grey matter is the ghost of memories of millions of monkeys over millions of years who, having just made it to the safety of the tree or cliff face ahead of the pursuing leopard, turn to hurl insults, branches, rotten fruit, and feces down on their tormentor.

This "big picture" anthropological perspective on a topic usually reserved for literary musings also sheds some light on the second, and for our purposes more critical, question I proposed above. Granted that the chase is a prominent fixture of our cultural productions, and perhaps even for the reasons I have given, why should it be so *mechanized*?

To appreciate fully why James Bond, our modern gladiator, should be so caught up in a high-tech world of gadgets, it is necessary to dwell a bit longer on the elemental predator-prey relationship we have been considering. Our everyday lives are so full of complications that we rarely give much thought to the fact that we are, after all, big, hundred-plus-pound mammals that spend most of their lives in close proximity with one another. In his later work the brilliant sociologist-anthropologist Erving Goffman made extensive use of studies of animal behavior (ethology) in his profound exploration of the basics of human life (see, for example, *Relations in Public*). His practice of looking at people as big, social animals did not endear him to his humanistic colleagues, but it did demonstrate, in my view, the absolute necessity of integrating all levels of action in any cultural analysis that strives for real comprehension.

The ethological concept that most interested Goffman, and that he made the basis for his analysis of "relations in public," was the *surround*, or *area of flight-distance*. Field studies of animal behavior have meticulously documented the fact that all mammals, particularly those subject to predation in the open field, recognize an envelope of space, a buffer zone, around themselves that is critical to their maintaining a sense of security. That envelope is elliptical in shape and varies in size with the size of the animal: the larger the animal, the larger the envelope. If you are that animal, for example, your surround is narrowest at your back, widens out along your sides, and extends to its maximum distance — the narrow end of the ellipse — directly in front of you. The evolutionary logic of the surround is clear: a social animal like a gazelle or baboon can more readily escape a predator directly behind it than one in front of it, blocking its path. It hears the predator or hears its neighbor's alarm call and bolts straight ahead, without having to zig or zag to the side.

An intriguing aspect of the surround is that it is very much an either-or proposition, an unambiguous signal, among most social mammals (one of those rare George Bush-style "line in the sand" affairs). For as a predator approaches a group of grazing antelope, they do not gradually become more and more restless until they take flight. Instead, they continue to graze as before, seemingly oblivious to the approaching threat, *until* the predator penetrates the surround of one of the animals, at which point they all bolt in a panic. The surround defines the *flight-distance* a particular species of animal normally requires to make its escape when attacked. The surround is an admirable piece of evolutionary engineering, for it balances the animal's obvious desire to escape danger with its need to graze and lead an otherwise routine life. The animal can carry on with normal, life-sustaining activities until the very moment that it becomes necessary to act to avoid a threat.[8]

Goffman's fundamental point is that a great many aspects of human be- havior, which we regard as "natural" if we think about them at all, have to be understood as the specific consequences of the mammalian complex. Perfectly ordinary activities like walking along a busy downtown sidewalk, riding a bus or subway, and catching an elevator involve a host of complexly orchestrated behavioral cues that facilitate the doing of them. Goffman's genius lay in identifying the contingency, the contrivance, the strangeness of everyday life and everyday behaviors, and his favorite research tool was a fine-grained examination of "unnatural" behaviors, of how the gossamer fabric of the ordinary is torn by even slight deviations. He was anthropology's Kafka.

Consider the scene on a busy downtown sidewalk, for example. Looked at ethologically, the sidewalk is filled with large, powerful animals travelling at some speed and in different directions — what Goffman charmingly called "vehicular units," further endearing himself to humanistic colleagues who liked to wax poetic about the wonder of mankind. But for Goffman the "wonder" was that this apparently simple slice of life goes so smoothly: the human traffic flows along in all directions and at different speeds with only a bit of jostling here and there.

The fragility, the contrived complexity of the scene only becomes apparent if a staggering drunk or a stray five-year-old happens along. Then the tiny movements and unconscious monitorings that speed us "normal" folks on our way, that "tell" others about our intended direction and inform us about theirs, abruptly fail us. We find ourselves suddenly confronted with someone — the drunk or the child — who doesn't play by the rules, whose movements we cannot interpret and who evidently pays no attention to our own subtle cues. So the traffic patterns we "vehicular units" have been following even without knowing it begin to break down: large gaps form; people bump into each other; normalcy gives way to an *incident*. In the aftermath of the brief chaos of such an incident, we may recognize the truth of Goffman's claims: we follow rules even when we don't know we are doing it, and our unconscious rule-following largely shapes the pattern of much social interaction.

The importance of the surround in regulating human behavior is most evident in situations where our movements are closely constrained. A perfect example is elevator behavior. What happens when you get on an elevator? You enter, see two or three other people there looking out at you, and turn around so that your back is toward them. In this fashion the elevator fills up in a back-of-the-head to front-of-the-face arrangement of occupants. Why don't you simply step on and continue facing in the direction of the other occupants until it is time to exit the elevator? It is an inadequate reply to say that you turn around because it is "impolite" to stare at others (and what does *that* mean anyway?), since you could avoid staring simply by averting your gaze to the floor or ceiling. You turn around to alleviate some of the stress the cramped quarters of the elevator place on your mammalian surround, and that of the others in the car with you. Were you to remain face-to-face with them, the long, tapered end of your elliptical surround would overlap theirs, producing acute discomfort in the limbic area of your brain (which you would probably attribute to the embarrassment of "staring"). By standing back-to-front, at least you have the narrow rear portion of your "area of flight distance" toward the person behind you, while the person in front of you is oriented just as you are.

We have devised this behavior to make the best of what, for any large mammal, is a bad situation: too many individuals whose intentions are unknown to you are packed around you in an enclosure from which there is no immediate escape. To appreciate how very human or cultural our elevator behavior is, try introducing six or eight baboons or a couple of dozen house cats to elevator rides — when those doors close pandemonium breaks out.

The fact that other mammals would react so differently indicates that our "culture of personal space" really doesn't make much sense when examined from a strictly biological or ethological perspective.[9] If we truly acted according to an imperative of biological adaptation, if we were mammals through and through, then elevators would be few and far between. Alternatively, if our world were starkly Hobbesian (and Hobbes did a great disservice to animals by comparing their highly regulated societies with our own), if it were a world of "all against all," it would make a lot more sense to keep your eyes fixed on a potential aggressor during that elevator ride: since escape would be out of the question, the next best thing would be to prepare for an attack head-on. The remarkable, truly wondrous thing (as opposed to human-istic schmaltz) about our elevator behavior is that we have so internalized the precepts of an unwritten social contract that we are quite prepared on a daily basis to make ourselves ideal targets of public violence. On the strength of that increasingly violated contract, we voluntarily enter a tiny enclosure containing several perfect strangers and turn our backs to them while the doors close, removing any possibility of escape.

Being willing to step onto that elevator, however, does *not* mean that we are comfortable doing it. Even those urbanites among us who get on and off an elevator several times a day must still make the small, unconscious effort required to quell that two-hundred-million-year-old mammalian voice that cries out in silent alarm each time those elevator doors close. It is the persistence of that inner voice that accounts for the strict etiquette regulating our elevator behavior: you enter and exist just so; hold yourself just so (no fidgeting!); maintain a neutral gaze on the control panel or the row of numbers above the door; and, most important of all, never, ever, make a sudden move-ment or loud noise. The elevator is one of our most sacred public places; it is a little chapel, a shrine to ethology, tucked away in the bowels of the modern high-rise apartment or office building.[10]

The elevator is waiting, and when we step inside, pretending to repudiate the very core of our own neural structure, of our keen sense of the mammalian surround, we consent to the lie that social thinkers long before Hunter Thompson have identified and lamented. Though they didn't do much meth or ether on high-speed convertible rides across the Mojave Desert, Jean-Jacques Rousseau in *Discourse on the Origin of Inequality*, Karl Marx in his early essays on the dissolution of the state, and Sigmund Freud in *Civilization and its Discontents* were keenly aware that the critical issue of human existence is humanity's war with itself, its hopeless effort to reconcile the individual with the group, the organism with the social animal. Rousseau, Marx, Freud, and even our gonzo journalist recognized the intensity and profound ambivalence of this inner struggle. Long before those late greats began pondering the human condition, however, in fact while the human condition was just taking shape, twisting and turning in its swaddling clothes of the semiotic dimensions of culture, the conflict and ambivalence that so agonized Rousseau, Marx, and Freud were already eating at the cerebral entrails of much earlier thinkers: the men and women who produced, and were produced by, the first myths.

That conflict and ambivalence are still very much with us. They are the basis of that uneasy truce we declare each time we step onto an elevator or engage in countless other perfectly "ordinary" behaviors that pit our mammalian, primate brain against our "higher" faculties in an internecine warfare that has no winner and takes only ourselves as its prisoners. Whitman said that each of us contains multitudes, but he didn't say how well those multitudes get along. That uneasy truce among our multitudes, that internecine warfare of the human spirit is precisely the point, the "problematic" a high-styling literary critic might say, of the mechanized chases in James Bond movies.

Bond is much more than a supercharged adolescent pursuing juvenile fantasies of fast cars and fast women. The mechanized, gimmicky chases that have become the signature of Bond movies are so compelling largely because they explore and attempt to resolve the same conflict each of us experiences, in our own grey and mundane lives, whenever we step onto an elevator, start up the car, and pull out of the drive, or otherwise trip the alarm wire of our mammalian surround. It turns out (hardly surprising if you have slogged through the first three chapters) that Bond is not primarily about wog-hating, adolescent sexual fantasies, or any of the other sinister interpretations he has been saddled with by academicians lusting after tenure, thick tweed, and martinis of their own (shaken, not stirred) in the Faculty Club lounges of this great land. Like all myth, Bond is about boundaries, about the ant paths and intersystems that both separate and tie us to animals and machines, friends and foes, creation and destruction. Bond is about, if you will, *bondaries*.

What Goffman did not quite get around to discussing, since he was intent on establishing the importance of the mammalian surround for understanding human behavior, is the quite evident and terrifying obstacles our own artifactual intelligence has placed within the confines of the mammalian surround. Our ability to make tools or machines inevitably poses grave problems for the animal in us that cries out, like a perpetual flower child, for its "space." The elevator, car, and countless other machines are paradoxically both a natural part of our environment (they have always been there and it is hard to imagine life without them) and a recent, entirely artificial addition to that environment. We have fashioned machines and machine-built environments that fill our lives with perfectly justified anxiety, with a chronic, muted terror that strickens our mammalian sense of self and place. The minimal space we require to respond to a potential threat is routinely invaded or subverted by machines like the elevator (that box us in) or the car, gun, and nuclear missile (that strike from afar with blinding speed). Even our supposed mechanical servants can become killers. The drunk's car, the sniper's bullet, some madman's finger on The Button, all these pose mortal dangers that overwhelm our perceptions and reflexes.

Hence the unresolvable problem, the "negative truth" of myth in Levi-Strauss's sense, that the story of Bond (like those other dilemma-ridden stories of Asdiwal, Prometheus, and Sisyphus) valiantly strives to resolve: our mammalian surround, our animal's sense of security, is perpetually and hopelessly out of whack with our cultural surround, that *Umwelt* generated by the holographic engine of the evolving human brain. As mammals, and particularly as primates with a keen sense of vision but with no overpowering physical assets, we rely on the mammalian surround for our safety while violating it at every turn with the products of our clever, artifactual intelligence. The task of myth here and everywhere is the impossible hat-trick of resolving the unresolvable. And James Bond has been given that assignment by the semiotic processes that propel the Dreamtime.

Bond is our most famous modern gladiator, an advance guard, an *agent* in literal fact, whom we send into the territory of lethal machines and machine-built environments to test the possibility of human survival in the relentlessly high-tech surroundings of daily life. The spectacular mechanized chases of Bond movies are an ideal dramatic device for realizing, through myth, virtual experiences that are scarcely realistic in a commonsense world but that express the extramundane, and wholly compelling reality of the Dreamtime.

His mission, however, is not unique. Myth, rarely very artful, repeats and aimlessly reformulates itself as it flows down through the ages and across the sea composed of billions of human consciousnesses. Among many South American Indian groups, for instance, myths of a Master of Animals figure prominently in their storytelling. The Master of Animals is described as a spirit that may assume animal or human form. It is often portrayed as a kind of guardian of animals or of a particular animal species, a guardian concerned that human hunters treat their animal prey with respect. But shown the proper respect, the Master of Animals sees to it that the animal is given over to the hunter as prey. In that sense the Master of Animals serves as a liasion be-tween the human world of hunting groups and the animal world that provides their sustenance. The complex of beliefs and rituals surrounding this spiritual being forms part of the diffuse but terrifically important phenomenon of totemism I have emphasized throughout this work. Similarly, James Bond has assumed for us the mythical status of a *Master of Machines*, a suprahuman figure who mediates the world of humans and that of the essential but powerful and potentially deadly machines around us. He is a prominent figure, along with Luke Skywalker, R2D2, and a host of other predecessors and successors, in a modern *totemism of machines* that articulates the vector space(s) humanity occupies on its tenuous voyage through the semiospace of culture.

Bond's mission as agent, not for Her Majesty (as Richler would have it) but for the cultural viability of our species in the approaching twenty-first century, is so critical because our relations with machines are so fateful and complex, and becoming more fateful and complex with each passing day. It would all be so simple if we merely wanted, in some carefree fantasy world where movies are indeed fairy tales, to have someone demonstrate the use of intricate, high-performance machines. But we have bid simplicity farewell long before now! After all, that is more or less what race car drivers do, along with the rather more pedestrian "demonstrators" of nifty household gadgets like Veg-O-Matics and crockpots who appear on those infomercials we zap with our TV clickers while surfing channels. But that is not what Bond does. To be sure, he does show us the all-out performance that can be wrung from cars, planes, boats, etc. by anyone with a great deal of skill and a socking big death wish, but he does much more than that.

Machines, even the exotic ones Bond handles, are not simply objects we like to get our hands on and make do things. While seeming to liberate us, to give us speed and power unattainable by the naked human frame, they also constrict our activities, force us into their mold, and place a host of obligations on our already overburdened lives. For those reasons, we want to do more than handle machines, to play with them: we want to destroy them as well, to see them suffer as they often make us suffer. The woodsman and his axe may, as Bateson suggests, form a little "ecology of mind," a graceful, symbiotic union of man and machine that represents a new force in the world. But try telling that to a lumberjack from a little hard-grits town in Washington (they haven't been "woodsmen" since Wordsworth's time), who has a bad back and is headed home at the end of his shift to the fat wife and four screaming rug rats. Moreover, in the words of the immortal ballad, his head hurts, his feet stink, and he don't love Jesus. Chances are he is not conducting an inner rhapsody whose theme is the poetic union of himself and his chainsaw; if he has any thoughts at all about that chainsaw, they probably run more in the mold of *The Shining* or *Texas Chainsaw Massacre* than of the writings of Gregory Bateson.

The truth, complex and soiled as always, is that the lumberjack often gets a great deal of pleasure from working with an instrument he has mastered over the years, but he also nourishes a hatred for the thing as a dead weight, a shackle that ties him to the company, his meager paycheck, the fat wife, and those squalling, ungrateful kids. The lumberjack, or various selves of his multitudes, simultaneously loves and hates his chainsaw, along with the other machines that figure prominently in his life. He is, in short, thoroughly ambivalent about them. And it is his ambivalence that is the stuff of myth, that, more than Sean Connery or Ian Fleming, calls James Bond into being.

As for the archetypical totem of our age, the car, its schismogenic profile is carved into the soul of virtually every man, woman, and twelve-plus-year-old child in America: while opening up whole new vistas of lifestyles and re-creations, it saddles us with car payments, license fees, insurance premiums, the indignities of the car dealer's lot, the dread of the law, and the terrorism of other drivers. And it does all this while assisting in the slaughter, often literally murder, of some fifty thousand of us every year, roughly our side's "body count" for the entire Viet Nam "conflict." When we watch Bond push his gimmicky Lotus past the red line on that winding Sardinian road, our thoughts are far more complex than the adolescent's "Wow (or, depending on the adolescent, *Sheee-it*), can that car ever go!" We want Bond to win, to escape the helicopter gunship, but we don't mind a bit if the Lotus is beat to pieces along the way. In fact, much of a Bond movie has the appeal of a stock car demolition derby, which is far more of a crowd pleaser than a regular race because we get to see lots of machinery being pounded to junk before our eyes.[11]

We like, in short, to see cars get theirs, to get what's coming to them for all the grief they put us through, for making us slaves at the workplace, drudges trapped in gridlock on the way to that workplace, and paupers after the finance companies, repair shops, and insurance companies get through with us. What would Allstate charge for a low deductible comprehensive policy on Bond's Lotus, anyway? The answer, happily, is: who cares? We can gleefully watch Bond triumph over the bad guys while pounding the Lotus into scrap, then chuckle at the avuncular Q's exasperation when Bond breaks the news that he has trashed another of Q's cherished spy-toys. At the conclusion of a Bond movie the scene is much like that after a demolition derby: the landscape is littered with the smoking ruins of tons of machines; the carefree hero emerges victorious from those ruins, arm around the pretty girl; and the audience is sated, content with the spectacle of prowess and destruction it has witnessed. James Bond, Hero of Our Age, is truly our modern Master of Machines, but, like the Master of Animals other totemistic peoples revere, Bond both cherishes machines and gives them up for destruction on the sacrificial pyres of our movie theatres.

Low Brows and High Stakes:
Bond Movies in a World of Consumer Capitalism

As a cultural hero who finesses and wisecracks his way through one perilous situation after another and leaves chaos and destruction in his path, James Bond has much in common with other trickster figures of mythology: Raven, Coyote, and Rabbit of American Indian myth and Spider (or Ananzi) of West African lore.[12] Bond, like these other trickster figures, is dedicated to stirring things up, making a mess of established, Elmer Fudd-style normalcy, unleashing a bit of Victor Turner's liminality and social drama on a crusty, fusty world that takes itself too seriously.

All these trickster figures, however, cannot be lumped together in a cultural analysis of their semiotic roles in the Dreamtime. To say that they are all tricksters with a generic part to play in our culture obscures the really interesting question of why particular figures appeal to particular audiences at particular times. Why did James Bond appear on the cultural stage at all, since Brer Rabbit, Bugs Bunny, and other literary and cinematic tricksters were already delighting audiences with their hijinks? What does the story of Bond say about our situation that has propelled Bond movies and novels to supergrosser status?

I believe we already have part of the answer to this vital question, but only part. As our modern Master of Machines, Bond delights us with his skillful displays, which reveal what the machines around us are really capable of doing, and with his willingness to consign them to a violent end. Machines, however, are unlike animals; in fact they are at opposite ends of the first semiotic dimension, which we encountered in chapter 3. Their origin or creation is definitely (if now usually indirectly) from human hands, and machines depend on those hands to operate them, to give them life. Yet, like animals, there is a tremendous diversity of machines: big ones, tiny ones, ones that crawl, ones that fly, etc. If Edward Wilson's "biodiversity" is now an engaging topic of talk shows and check-out stand magazines, we should add its cognate, "mechano-diversity," to the growing list of issues that appear critical to sustaining life on the planet. It follows that the actions of a Master of Machines are not just a random slapdash of mechanized derring-do; they involve the use of particular kinds of machines to accomplish particular social goals.

In pursuing another part of the answer, note that the "environment" in which Bond operates is that global system of consumer capitalism discussed earlier in this chapter. What Bond does with machines and the kind of machines he favors are explicable only in terms of that global system. For Bond's primary mission is to assist humanity in figuring out how it might, and might not, follow the road consumer capitalism lays out for it (on the way, of course, to a Something Else that neither individual humans nor the collective "capitalist ethic" much wants to think about). When we think of Bond in these terms, the silliness of the horseplay and one-liners of Bond movies, the stigma of low-brow entertainment they bear unashamedly, begins to seem less important than the very high stakes game they are playing: Bond simultaneously affirms and challenges a global economy of consumer capitalism. If Richler had not already used the phrase, for a very different purpose, I would be tempted to say that "largely, this is what James Bond is about."

If the low-brow entertainment of Bond movies indeed has these high stakes, then what precisely is it about Bond's particular use of particular machines that helps situate what we now know to be a shifting, drifting bubble of human consciousness in a specific region of the semiospace of culture? As you might expect, my answer to this question has to do with lines or boundaries, with the *differences* we see in things, and with ambivalence, with our inability to live inside the boundaries we establish, to play the hand culture has dealt us.

In looking for the particularities in Bond movies, for their relatively fine-grained structure (remember our ant paths!), the prominence of the David-and-Goliath theme I touched on earlier is striking. Like David, the gadgets Bond takes with him into the gladiatorial arena of global intrigue are just that: small, compact, toy-like marvels of sophisticated design and engineering, the kind of thing, except for their deadliness, that you find Yuppies pawing over in Sharper Image stores across the land.

In most of the Bond movies, we are even taken on a little shopping trip, not to the mall, but through Q's laboratory where the lethal spy-toys are designed and tested. There Bond is given, to Q's chagrin, *carte blanche*, and loads up on the cleverest, most expensive gadgets, which we, along with the morose Q, know are slated for imminent destruction. The ultimate in individualized toys, of course, is the customized sports car, and so every Bond movie features some version of the Lotus car-submarine that made such a splash in *The Spy Who Loved Me*. But most of Bond's spy-toys, like David's slingshot, are small, personalized items carried on his person or in his luggage. These are not, however, Old Testament times. The dynamics of the process of *mechano-semiosis*, of our inventing and giving meaning to machines and machines in turn redefining human life, have long ago pierced *that* little bubble of Biblical semiospace and propelled us into frothier realms where the slingshot has given way to Bond's own favorite implement of destruction, the nine-millimeter Beretta or the Walther PPK (depending on which incarnation of Bond we are attending).

Despite the tremendous importance of the introduction of the handgun for the configurations of the Dreamtime (a subject pursued in the next section), the parallel between David and Bond remains close in another critical aspect: both employ their small, gimmicky weapons against an enemy who greatly outmatches them in physical and numerical strength. I cannot stress too strongly the fact that Bond does not simply put his toys on display, does not just perform incredible feats of machine mastery for the gawking throngs in the audience to admire; he uses his puny, personalized gadgets to overcome and frustrate powerful adversaries who bristle with firepower and who command enormous financial resources.

For who are Bond's enemies? Definitely not the wogs and communists Richler found thinly disguised in Fleming's books, nor even the Nazi stragglers Fleming himself described in *Moonraker*. Bond's enemies, the enemies of the movie-Bond, of the Hero of Our Age, are a grotesque, Fellini-like assortment of megalomaniac scientists like Stromberg in *The Spy Who Loved Me*, shadowy international gangsters like Dr. No, Goldfinger, and Katanga, the equally shadowy international crime cartel of SPECTRE these super-gangsters run, and physical freaks like Oddjob and Jaws (Richard Kiel outfitted with some formidable chrome-plated dentures) these gangsters employ as their heavies and hit-men. In the service of a culture of (post?)modernity, Bond takes on these hulking Goliaths and their Philistine armies in battles that reveal, to our now thoroughly gimleted, cultural analytic gaze, a great deal about the disputed contours of our *fin de siecle* existence.

In a stunningly paradoxical twist, Bond finds himself doing battle with some of the same high-tech corporate enterprises whose appearance and domination on the world stage have made his character so appealing. SPECTRE, the satellite research and development plant of *Moonraker*, Stromberg's shipping and sea lab empire of *The Spy*, and Dr. No's monstrous projects are all (slightly) distorted versions of the multinational corporation: giant, unfeeling, scheming organizations that exist to consume more and more of the world's resources while making wage slaves of the multitudes and fat cats of the coterie of CEOs and executive vice presidents who run things. It is no accident that Bond's career parallels the postwar growth and ascendance of those corporations and of the economic superpower nation states which nurture them. For what we ask of Bond is a feat more daring than David's going out to meet Goliath: we want Bond to take on Exxon, IBM, Sony — the multinationals that dominate a new global economy — and save us from their now largely executed threat of dominating our individual lives as well.

In the final years of the twentieth century, business is not simply big; it is colossal. The enormous capital base of the larger multinational corporations, coupled with the millions employed by them and a global communications system that keeps the branch office plugged into corporate headquarters and the individual worker plugged into his supervisor, have created a world unthinkable when the century began. The adult occupants of that world, you and I, are now members of groups — offices, networks, task forces, committees, all the way up to societies — that originated with the giant corporations and now overwhelm our lives. Nothing like these groups has existed before: not in the forty thousand years or so that we have possessed a more or less fully formed language, and certainly not in the one hundred fifty thousand years or so that we have been biologically modern *Homo sapiens*. Humanity's present version of culture (and culture's present version of humanity), that little fleck caught in the dimensional fields of the semiotic polarities, took shape, found its location and contours in a world without management training workshops, executive retreats, and motivational enhancement seminars, in a world where people were *different* (those ubiquitous lines again!), where the basics of their identity had not been put through the corporate Cuisinart.

And so we find ourselves, again and always, in the maze of one of those tangled intersystems we encountered earlier. A very few of us, the farmers and poets among us,[13] are holdouts, misfits, or failures, presapient forms whose remains are destined for the same museum storage rooms housing Neandertal crania and *Homo erectus* mandibles. A similarly tiny majority of us, the Lee Iacoccas and Warren Buffetts of the world, have turned out to be virtuosos in the new domain of corporations, assimilating its style and outlook as a polyglot absorbs a language. But most of us, like our young intersystemic friend from Topeka, fall somewhere in between, which we now recognize really means *betwixt and between*. Neither rebel poets nor corporate raiders, we are just plain folks struggling to get through another day at the office or factory and maybe, just maybe, in the process of surviving to comprehend what is happening around us.

The central economic fact of life for us struggling multitudes, caught up as we are in this brave new world of corporate culture, is that major, life-altering events happen suddenly, unexpectedly, and with sometimes disastrous effects. A corporate merger engineered by backroom arbitragers and toupeed whiz-kid stockbrokers (another slice of real/reel life chronicled in *Other People's Money*, only Danny DeVito doesn't have Michael Milken's bad hairpiece) closes down several factories and puts thousands out of work. A board of directors, anxious over a deteriorating bottom line, installs a trouble-shooting CEO who proceeds to decimate the ranks of middle management, sending dozens of fortyish executives back to the suburbs to contemplate their multiple mortgages from the seats of their riding mowers. Eight thousand years of urban life and cultural evolution have left us with a cultural surround, an *Umwelt*, in which our "area of flight-distance" stops at, or really, considering the invasive techniques of medicine and psychotherapy, within, our own skins, and in which reaction time is nonexistent. It is enough to make us long for those easy times back on the Pleistocene savannas of East Africa, where our ancestors usually had at least a couple of panic-stricken heartbeats between them and the leopard's tearing claws.

Who can anticipate the radical twists and turns of events that have become a signature of modern corporate culture, so much a part of things that they seem to belong to a new and thoroughly counter-intuitive class of "natural" disasters? A couple of generations ago, economic calamities of the magnitude now commonplace were tied much more closely to truly natural processes: floods or droughts that spelled ruin for thousands of families and sent shock waves throughout a national economy. But in either case, corporate or natural disasters, there is really no one to blame; putting Michael Milken in jail for a few months does nothing to soothe the frayed nerves of millions who live on the edge of the abyss carved out by the corrosive hunger and competitiveness of corporate Goliaths.

Corporations, in short, are a very scary fact of life. Many of us depend on them directly for our survival, and all of us are affected in countless ways by their activities and products. Yet they are so big, so impersonal, and so downright rapacious that the best we can hope for from them is an uneasy truce: we will yield to Caesar what is Caesar's and hope that Caesar stays the hell out of our living room and backyard. But of course he doesn't: the family TV and even barbeque that dominate those areas are prominently embossed with his corporate logos. And to their tremendous economic clout, which constantly threatens to squash us like bugs, there is the added danger that corporations employ, and embody, the scientist, or Scientist, that necessary, dread being who cuts so large a figure in Dreamtime imagery. Big business and big science, along with big government, form a coalition that penetrates and dominates virtually every avenue of contemporary existence: the magnates set their R&D divisions to work on a project, often with government contracts to pay for it, and their Scientists create for them things that either control us directly, through their awesome firepower, or indirectly, as consumer items that we feel we must acquire and so pay the price that is demanded.

With our cultural surround, our *Umwelt*, appropriated and reshaped by the unholy alliance of business, science, and government, we latter-day primates can only react with the ambivalence that is our cultural birthright. Wanting and needing the things and jobs that corporations and their scientists provide, yet fearing and hating them for their control over us, we are driven to resolve the tension that gnaws at the heart of our consciousness. And so we — not Ian Fleming, Sean Connery, or Harry Saltzman, but the collective *we* of a distinctively human, myth-making Dreamtime intelligence — have called James Bond into being, that trickster figure *extraordinaire*, and sent him out to take on crazed megalomaniac scientists like Stromberg and ruthless gangsters like Dr. No while tweaking the noses of his superpower bosses. Bond's adolescent nature, the basis of so much critical contempt, turns out to be the adolescence of our species: a young, vital, growing thing reacting awkwardly to the constraints of its environment and sensing somehow, dimly, that the future holds Something Else unimaginably alien, final, and *old*.

Folklore Past: James Bond, Wild Bill Hickok, and John Henry

James Bond's heroic battles with the corporate giants and their behemoth machines that hold the planet in a vise-like grip do more than display Bond's virtuosity while dulling our perfectly justified anxiety. They help to situate and move humanity within the swirling vortices of semiospace (specifically, within a region of that space we like to call "history"). The process of mechanosemiosis that impels that movement operates in two directions: we invest meaning and even confer identity on machines through what we do with them and what we think about them, and machines in turn transform the basis of our relationships with other humans. Machines thereby transform at the most elemental level what it means to be human. Those movements or vectorial forces along the first semiotic dimension of Animal <------> Artifact/Machine make themselves felt, as we have seen, in the second semiotic dimension of Us/Self <------> Them/Other, where images of the individual and the group, of self and other continuously form, dissolve, and reform. The individual's relation to the group, whether a hunting band, a rural village, a multinational corporation, or a nation state, and hence his fundamental sense of Self and Other are shaped through and through by what he does with machines and what machines do to him. One semiotic dimension provides the ground or field in which the other operates.

To answer the question how Bond movies generate images of the place of the individual in a national State will involve assembling a rather unlikely cast of characters: Wild Bill Hickok, Billy the Kid, John Henry, Joe Montana, O. J. Simpson, the Beatles, the Rolling Stones, Michael Jackson, and others. If there is any validity in my claim that Bond movies operate in part on a fundamental cultural level, then it should be possible to establish connections between them and other elements of American folklore and popular culture. If the story of Bond has cultural significance, it did not spring full-blown onto our cultural stage, a happenstance creation of a disillusioned English bureaucrat holed up in his north shore Jamaican retreat. Who/what are the ancestors and cousins of Bond? What are his roots and family? And who are his heirs as the ever-changing flux/froth of the Dreamtime carries us into the next century?

Bond's roots are readily identified when one recalls the opening minutes of every movie: the silhouette of Bond, seen through a gun barrel, crosses the screen, whirls, and fires directly toward the viewer, the barrel casing framing the figure runs red with blood. First and last, Bond is a gunfighter.

And, whether we like to admit it or not, the gunfighter is without doubt the preeminent folk hero of American culture. From Wild Bill Hickok, Billy the Kid, and Wyatt Earp of 1880s dime-novel fame through all the cowboys and secret agents of mid-century movies, and on to the Stallone, Schwarzenegger, and Seagal bloodbaths that are closing this troubled century, we have cherished them all and begged for more. The unprecedented slaughter of two world wars, including the mind-numbing deaths of sixty million persons in the second world war alone, the Korean and Viet Nam "conflicts," and the brush fires of Grenada, Panama, and Iraq have not been enough to satisfy our appetite for the spectacle of armed combat. To understand the story of Bond, a gunfighter who opted for a Beretta automatic over the old Colt 45, it is necessary to understand something of the appeal the gunfighter has exercised in our popular culture.

A thorough study of this subject would be a book in itself (and an excellent one already exists in Will Wright's *Six Guns and Society*). Here I would like to focus specifically on those aspects of Bond's character that develop the two principal themes of this chapter: the mechanosemiotic complex of human-machine identity, and the Self-Other relationship of the individual to the State.

Although Western cultures have valorized hand-to-hand combat at least since the days of the *Iliad* and the Colosseum, a significant change in that tradition occurred toward the middle of the nineteenth century, when James Colt introduced a repeating sidearm that was sufficiently light and accurate to enable an *individual* to achieve virtuosity in its use. Unlike earlier dueling pistols, which were cumbersome and fired only a single charge, the Colt "Peacemaker" could be used outside the elaborate ritual setting of eighteenth-century duels. Gary Cooper needed only to step out into the street at *High Noon* and the gladiatorial event was begun.

The repeating pistol thus helped shape a new kind of gladiatorial hero, a Master of Machines whose mastery consists in his personal, highly skilled control over a complex piece of equipment. A gun, unlike a sword, lance, or bow and arrow, is an assemblage of multiple pieces, each of which must be manufactured with exacting precision. Paradoxically, the introduction of this complex machine, rather than negating individual differences in skill at arms, actually amplified them. History has not recorded the names of Napoleonic masters of the eight-inch cannon, for the very good reason that those weapons were too big, clumsy, and inaccurate and required too many people to operate them. True virtuosity was beyond the design capability of the instrument. But the names of Wild Bill Hickok, Billy the Kid, Wyatt Earp . . . and James Bond are known to one and all as masters of the deadly art of the sidearm. That art consisted in the operation of a machine that could be carried anywhere — strapped on a hip, thrust into a belt, snugged under a pillow — and used at a moment's notice with a degree of accuracy that depended only on the user's competence and cold-bloodedness.

The gunfighter's skill inevitably posed problems for him as an individual bound to a State. The legendary killers from Hickok to Bond, besides being masters of machines, share another characteristic: their skill inevitably places them on the fringes of a social group, makes them liminal figures who exercise their deadly art in a no-man's land between one group and another, or between the law and lawlessness.

Wild Bill and 007, James Butler Hickok and James Bond, meet different fates (the media moguls of the Bond industry are unlikely to follow Conan Doyle's example and allow their Sherlock Holmes to be killed off as Hickok was). Their Dreamtime personae, however, remain strikingly similar: both are talented, sexy, and highly unorthodox individuals who must come to terms with the mundane demands of the State. Although both Wild Bill and 007 possess enough aggressiveness and pride to make them permanent social outcasts, psychopaths waiting to happen, they nevertheless place their deadly talents at the service of a constricting State. If 007 is, like Wild Bill, a murderer on the loose, Hickok is also, like Bond, an agent of the State in time of war. Ironically, their individuality, the natural gifts and charm they possess, makes them particularly appropriate as a semiotic device to explore the twists and turns of the boundary that at once separates and joins Individual and State, Self and Other, Us and Them in an America rapidly transforming itself from a pre-industrial to a post-industrial society.

Bond and Hickok are casual, even flippant, about their responsibilities to the State, but they discharge their duties with a remarkable flair that sets them apart from an ordinary soldier or bureaucrat. Because they serve the State with such a distinctive and heroic touch, they provide a rationale or model for us other, plodding souls who struggle, in our ambivalent, schismogenic way, to reconcile our own individuality with the increasingly oppressive demands of a State-based society. In the very act of rebelling against the hidebound conventions of office they personalize the State, making it seem an amusing, ineffectual old fuddy-duddy (a case being the great fun Bond has with the fat buffoon figure of the southern sheriff in *Live and Let Die*).

As we have seen, the odds Bond faces are even more formidable than the McCanles gang, for he must confront the mercenary armies and massive firepower of one megalomaniac after another: Dr. No, Goldfinger, Katanga, Stromberg, Blofeld. These villains represent the underbelly, the Dark Side, of a national State that expends enormous resources to keep its citizens alive even as it tightens the noose that strangles them. They are the cinematic embodiment of the State's and its multinational corporate minion's high-tech evil, of the power a complex organization has to do mechanized violence in an unjust cause. Dr. No and the others equip themselves with colossal weapons, including missiles, nuclear submarines, supertankers outfitted as battleships, and plan crimes on an equally grand scale. To combat those villains Bond employs their own technological products, but always small, highly personalized devices, ones often crafted for his express purposes by technicians in Q's lab.

In being so much a man of gadgets and in having so little personal depth to him (particularly in the movies Bond's personality consists of little more than a string of atrocious puns), Bond actually personalizes his machines while minimizing his own human character. Our Topeka teenager, before that lad headed for the intersystemic West Coast, left the theatre thinking more about Bond's Lotus and his women than about the character of Bond himself. After all, Bond is 007, a bureaucratic convenience and job description that need not have any particular name or personality attached to it.

Something of our species' vectorial movement through the semiospace of the Dreamtime may be seen in the changing of the guard from Hickok to Bond. For although both are deadly Masters of Machines, both generic gunfighters, the semiotic landscape of Hickok's America is much simpler than that of Bond's. Although neither is a one-woman man, Hickok is very much a one-machine kind of guy: barring the incidental knives and blunt instruments he used on the likes of the McCanles, it was his set of pearl-handled revolvers that made him what he was. And those, unlike Bond's disposable spy-toys, were enduring, iconic representations of Hickok's character. They possessed an appeal that some of us may still recall: the thrill of unwrapping that Christmas present and discovering (what else!) those very (imitation) pearl-handled (cap) pistols nestled in their holsters, ready for the lightning draw and thundering explosion.

The personality or, as Tracy Kidder would have it, *soul* of a machine is an issue of fundamental importance in the identity-building, culture-generating semiotic processes of the Dreamtime. When Hickok passed his revolvers along to Bond and they transmuted into the latter's Beretta automatic, he also signalled a transformation in our relations with machines in an emerging national State. Hickok foreshadowed the world of Bond, and left us with a certain nostalgia for earlier, simpler (if still deadly) times as we contemplate daily what it is like to live in Bond's world. Bond, rather than Hickok, now stands in for each of us in our efforts to come to terms with machines in an increasingly mechanized world.

And those efforts nearly always involve our individual relationship with the State, for the first and most elemental question we ask ourselves in coming to terms with a particular machine is "Is it ours or theirs?" Is the machine one of us, a friend ready to come to our assistance, or does it belong to some lurking enemy waiting to zap us? Bond's character and actions neatly fix and offer to resolve this lingering dread. Indeed, he seems to say, some machines are evil — those employed by unfeeling totalitarian rulers or psychopathic geniuses — and could easily finish us off were he not there to throw himself between us and the technological menace. And in saving us from mechanized destruction, Bond reveals the other face of the machine world; he jokes and plays with dazzling technological toys while pulling the world away from the brink.

Americans' relations with their machines have a long, complex, and, as I have insisted throughout, thoroughly ambivalent or schismogenic history, so it is not surprising that their Dreamtime heroes should be mythic embodiments of that complexity and ambivalence. If Bond and Hickok invest their machines with their own flamboyant personalities and treat them as toys that double as weapons in triumphing against overwhelming odds, the results for other heroes of the American Dreamtime are not so happy. Bond eludes lethal machines that often succeed in destroying his companions, but Dreamtime figures like John Henry, that steel-driving man, and Casey Jones, that brave engineer, are themselves tragic victims of the products of American technology. These folkloric heroes thus provide a semiotic counterpoint, a pull versus a push, to Bond and Hickok in the ever-changing, shifting fields of human-machine and individual-State relationships that are basic to our society.

Bond and Hickok are winners; even though the latter died by the gun, he was not beaten at his own game. In stark contrast, John Henry and Casey Jones are losers, victims of machines they sought to challenge or control.

The stories of John Henry and James Bond embrace a set of oppositions that actually serve to generate a slice of what we call "history." In stark contrast with James Bond, John Henry is lower class and black vs. upper class and white; rural vs. urban; manual laborer vs. bureaucrat; physically immense and powerful vs. mentally quick and supple; master of a simple tool (the sledge hammer) vs. master of complicated gadgets; victim of impersonal technology (the Company's steam-driven hammer) vs. victor over impersonal technology.

To an unrepentant, pre-postmodern structuralist looking for Levi-Straussian "binary opposites" with which to construct structural models, this set of, quite literally, black-and-white contrasts should be a blessing. There is, however, a catch (another of those infernal complications to which we have grown accustomed!): the structural oppositions that hold between the stories of John Henry and James Bond do not represent Culture A and Culture B, *the* Bororo and *the* Timbira, say, but *virtual states of the "same" culture* — the good old USA. Rather than keeping separate from history, we see again that myth actually encodes events that we take to be part of an historical process. "History" in this perspective is not a chronicle of "events" (whatever *they* might be), but movements in the vector space of the Dreamtime. The stories of John Henry and James Bond represent two states of that vector space, two domains of semiospace, in which the critical push-pull factor is the different ways we react to different stages of a rapidly maturing technology. We do not remain "we" when the machines that play a critical role in making us "us" are undergoing their own fundamental transformations.

As social beings we are continually faced with the task of figuring out what our lives are about; even the most complacent and conservative among us have to react constantly to an ever-changing set of circumstances. Life is far more complicated than the Marxians or cultural materialists, with their wistful credos of determinism and causality, would have us believe: far from being "determined," we have to make Us up as we go along.

The business of comprehending ourselves, of constructing our experience, is made increasingly difficult by rapidly accelerating changes in the production techniques and products that transform our physical and social environments. Throughout the kaleidoscopic prehistory of the hominid line, the one constant has been this accelerating pace of technological change. The australopithecines used their simple pebble choppers for a couple of million years, until that technology ever so gradually gave way, along with the australopithecines themselves, to the Acheulian hand axes employed by the earliest representatives of the *Homo* genus. That industry in turn persisted for some one million years, until its relatively rapid replacement one hundred thousand to two hundred thousand years ago by a much more diverse Middle Paleolithic stone tool industry developed by archaic *Homo sapiens*. From that time until the present, the pace and diversity of technological changes have increased exponentially, to the chagrin of Anthro 101 students who walk into the exam room with a buzzing headfull of dates, foreign-sounding tool type designations, and Latin labels for sort-of folks who once lived and loved and died.

Now, in what would have been a mere heartbeat in the long, tedious evolutionary process leading from *Homo erectus* to *Homo sapiens*, the transition from John Henry's America to the global corporate culture of James Bond seems like eons to us. And the torrent of change only continues to intensify. The car in my driveway is such an ancient relic that it is already paid for, while the computer on my desk, just a few years old, is a living fossil staring back at me from a bygone technological era. Caught up in this tempest and struggling to survive while clinging to a shred of sanity, we need as much help from our myths as we can get.

From the pebble chopper and the cooking fire to the Walther PPK and the nuclear reactor, our ancestors and ourselves have had to adapt to a world we created. Mythic figures like John Henry and James Bond distill this complex and murky interaction into discrete sets of decisive characters and events. Through this process of the *mythification of complexity*, "history" comes to assume the form not so much of a flow of events as a set of stark, stroboscopic images that convey essential if often contradictory information about what it is to be alive in a particular society at a particular time.

Viewed from a contemporary perspective, with our magazines filled with personal computer ads and the streets and malls of our cities humming with the indescribable din of video game arcades, the figure of John Henry evokes acute nostalgia. He represents a (Dream)time when American technology was young enough to take on bare-handed, when a poor black man could still swing his sledge and beat the Company's mechanical monster — even though the struggle would kill him. His death is instructive; it ratifies a transformation in American life from a manual to a machine-based existence. Because John Henry's battle has been fought and the result has been so decisive, it is difficult to imagine a current supergrosser rendition of his story. It belongs to another domain of the American Dreamtime, another fleck of semiotic froth, sealed off from the present by its already congealing membrane.

In the vectorial flow of things the story of John Henry is a prologue to the story of Bond. In company with other tales of cowboys, lumberjacks, brave engineers, and assorted rogues, the story of John Henry forms part of an inseparable corpus: the intersystem or intertext of American mythology.

If John Henry and James Bond are binary opposites in most respects, they are complements in one critical area. Both do battle with vastly superior mechanical adversaries while accepting, and even glorying in, the technological world they inhabit. John Henry was that "steel-drivin' man" who was "born with a hammer in his hand" and loved to swing his sixteen-pound sledge with the work crews that fashioned what was at the time probably the world's grandest engineering project ever: the American railway system. Like Bond, John Henry personalizes a technological order too vast and complex to comprehend in detail. And in personalizing it, in touching it with their own charm and dynamism, they rationalize a State that bends the individual to a cruel yoke. John Henry, whose attributes could easily be those of the leader of a slave rebellion, expends his enormous energies in the white man's workplace. As an exemplary worker he validates the technological State in the very act of challenging its machine. In similar fashion Bond, the exemplary agent, carries out his supervisor's assignments while making light of their instructions. In one of the several paradoxes that gnaw at the core of civilization, the heroic and rebellious individualist affirms the bonds that tie all ordinary individuals to the State.

Folklore Present: Secret Agents, Football Players, and Rock Stars

If the themes of human-machine identity and individual-State relationships are integral to the structure of our culture, to the American Dreamtime, then the stories of Bond and John Henry should feed into social institutions other than those we (often derisively) describe as "folklore" or "myth." To understand how the Dreamtime temple of the movie theatre empties out into the street, into the highways and byways, the hearts and minds of us all, it is necessary to examine how legendary heroes of folktale and movie are related to living, breathing folk heroes who every weekend dazzle tens of millions of Americans watching them in coliseums and TV rooms across the land. Two categories of popular entertainer spring to mind here: football players and rock musicians.

To invoke our Martian anthropologist once again, a short time spent among us natives of America, watching our TV or wandering our streets, would suffice to alert it (certainly *not* " him" or "her") to the mass appeal and, not infrequently, collective hysteria of two distinctively late twentieth-century rituals: the football game and the rock concert (or, increasingly, the MTV video). The phenomenal numbers of people drawn to those rituals and the intensity of their involvement in them would indicate to our extraterrestrial visitor that the natives of this peculiar land find them essential to their enjoyment of life. Inquiring into the cultural significance of football and rock is, therefore, a means of identifying basic organizing principles in American society. If nearly every American has heard of James Bond, Joe Montana, O. J. Simpson, Elvis Presley, John Lennon, Mick Jagger, and Michael Jackson it must be because they represent areas of experience and states of consciousness (some definitely altered!) that are fundamental to us all.

But in the spirit and program of cultural analysis, we need to ask what *specifically* does James Bond have in common with such diverse personalities as Joe Montana and Elvis Presley? Clearly all are cultural heroes of a sort, but apart from that general affinity how are their several stories specifically linked within a cultural structure? How do they map out some of the twisting contours of a particular domain of semiospace?

In "Professional Football: An American Symbol and Ritual," William Arens argues that the tremendous surge of interest in football since the end of the second world war is linked to the emergence and phenomenal growth of a corporate culture in the postwar United States. As chagrined owners of major league baseball teams can attest, football has steadily gained ground in attendance and, far more important, TV ratings over our formerly undisputed National Game. As Arens cogently observes, baseball is a pastoral game, played on an irregularly shaped field (any pasture or sand lot will do) by relatively few players, all of whom need to perform several functions well: batting, running, fielding, throwing (we will not talk about the American

League's desperate effort at specialization, the designated hitter). Arens claims that baseball, as a free-wheeling, bucolic game of summer, suited a younger, less complicated America. The compatibility or fit between ritual and society thus helps explain baseball's exalted status during the early decades of the century, when the Sultan of Swat held court on the diamond. That postulated compatibility also helps explain the decline in the game's popularity as the century wore on and it became increasingly difficult for sports fans to see anything of their own high-pressure, high-stress lives in the languid game.

In sharp contrast with baseball, football is played on a rectangular, lined grid of unvarying dimensions by players who clump together around the ball (even a wide receiver plays in the middle of a crowd in comparison with a center fielder). And football players have such specialized functions that it is something of a fiction to refer to them as a "team" at all, since they are divided into offensive, defensive, and special units that take the field at different times. Many veteran team members have never been on the field together during a season, which makes their "team" a rather abstract entity.

Arens maintains that the incredible specialization involved in a game that pays men huge sums of money to be full-time nose guards, tight ends, and running backs betokens a transformed and immensely more complex America. In the postwar era corporate giants like IBM and General Motors have expanded to the point that each occupies dozens of skyscrapers in as many cities around the world and employs tens of thousands of workers. And, like professional football players, each of those workers is locked into a specialized corporate structure bristling with highly technical job description forms, a business climate that would have been difficult to imagine when Babe Ruth (who started out as a pitcher!) was thrilling the Saturday afternoon crowds at Yankee Stadium.

As a dominant ritual of American culture, football derives its compelling appeal from its ability to organize and choreograph both the nagging complexities of daily life and the elemental dilemmas of existence into a tight, dramatic presentation that can be comprehended as a whole (and ideally in a single sitting, although the notorious "TV time-out" has made a mockery of the sixty-minute football game). The anxiety-ridden junior executive at IBM knows he has to perform in a highly competitive and complex corporate jungle, and yet usually does not know just how well or how poorly he is doing. How is his work being evaluated on the upper floor? How much damage is that s.o.b. who wants *his* next promotion doing behind his back? Will the Japanese clobber the whole American computer industry over the next few years and put him in the unemployment lines?

These imponderables of corporate life, together with the unnerving certainty that decisions will be and are being made about one's personal fate, impart an ill-ease in corporate America that cries out for resolution and release. And so we watch and, in a way, worship football, particularly the Sunday afternoon NFL professional variety.

The high-powered, high-priced NFL game brings our disguised corporate anxieties out into the open for all the world to see, pitting highly paid and trained specialists against one another in a public, TV-saturated arena. And the beauty, the fascination, the sheer *power* of the game, is that it is so much more vivid and *real* than the murky doings of life itself. After all, there are referees, a clock, endless video images with instant replay, and, most important of all, a final score (which itself comes buttressed with a veritable spreadsheet of instant statistics on first downs, yards rushing, yards passing, etc). The game unfolds in the compressed temporal and spatial dimensions of ritual and yields a result with a definitiveness that acts like a balm to the frayed corporate psyche of modern America.

The ritual costumes of American sport, particularly the old favorites of football and baseball, reveal something of the changing culture they represent. Even in today's media-saturated big leagues, baseball uniforms remain almost the same casual garmets they were a century ago. And the men who wear those uniforms retain their individuality: they are easily recognized by sight and not just by position or number. Television brings the faces of Reggie Jackson, Jose Canseco, and Gary Carter into our living rooms and makes them familiar, makes them personalities. Football is a different story. Players' bodies are grotesquely distorted by their gear: they are padded, helmeted, visored, face-masked, and mouth-pieced to the point of being unrecognizable even in TV close-ups. From the distance of the bleachers, all that signifies their personalities on the field is a set of numbers. Like the corporate executive and worker, the football player is virtually faceless; his individuality has been consumed by the voracious demands of his function.[15]

If the football player is a helmeted gladiator who embodies the peculiar mix of self-effacement and in-your-face competitiveness that characterizes corporate America, then the rock musician is his antithesis. Glorying in the wildest displays of egotism, the rock star screams for the death of the corporate State. In "Football Games and Rock Concerts: The Ritual Enactment" Susan Montague and Robert Morais portray football players and rock musicians as contradictory "models of success" in American society. Articulating the principal theme of this work, they suggest that American society does not operate with a single, internally consistent image of success, but continually struggles to embrace mutually incompatible goals. From our earliest years we are inculcated with the value of teamwork and led onto the football fields of childhood. But at the same time we are urged to achieve as individuals in competition with others: report cards, honor rolls, who has a good job, who has more money, who is more attractive — all are hierarchical devices that instill in us a strong sense of ourselves as self-determined, driven individuals in a world of other similarly motivated persons.

Paradoxically, the rock star appears to trample on all these social hierarchies and yet achieves for himself a degree of success denied the humdrum multitudes that dutifully peck and scratch their way up the social ladder. As a star, he is a kind of individual in the raw, whose appetites and excesses only enhance his reputation as one who drinks life to the dregs. He is part of no institution; his stature is determined solely on the basis of popular appeal. The coliseums fill up, the records sell, and the money pours in. Formal acknowledgement of his stardom consists simply in appearances on television and in the popular press; in the words of Dr. Hook's song, he gets his picture on the cover of *Rolling Stone*.

Given the stylized, idiosyncratic identities of rock star and football player, what possible affinity can either have with James Bond? I believe the answer lies in the power the story of Bond has to bridge or mediate the contradictions generated by the antithetical images of American life embodied in rock star and football player. Those contradictions in turn are the very stuff of the semiotic polarities we have been considering throughout the last two chapters: the continuous, culture-generating tension between our disparate identities as animal and machine, self and other. Bond is obviously neither football player nor rock star, but possesses attributes of both and so serves as a powerful synthesis that knits together incompatible, unresolvable elements of the Dreamtime.

The rock star, for instance, is not so independent of the corporate State as his behavior would indicate. Although the embodiment of all that is wild and free in the human spirit, he is inextricably tied to modern technology: his artistic expression, the essence of his public image, requires truckloads of electronic equipment manufactured by large corporations and operated by a small army of technicians. Elvis Presley's and Mick Jagger's primal energy would die a few yards from their bodies were it not for the microphones they hold, the banks of amplifiers and speakers surrounding them, the mixing labs, the television cameras, stations, satellites and sets, the cassettes, CDs and video tapes, the myriad factories where all this equipment is manufactured, and the stores that sell all the products.

And like Bond, the rock star's ties to technology are more than a passive dependence. If there is any implement besides the gun and car that permeates American culture, it is the electric guitar. How many video, photographic, and concert images exist of the rock musician on stage, gyrating, howling, and clutching his guitar-cum-penis as the instrument and totem of his raw sexuality, his primal energy? The gun and the electric guitar are easily the two most popularized hand-held instruments of American culture, which has somehow managed to impart a similar function to these utterly dissimilar artifacts. The similarity is recognizable at any rock performance, where the guitarist cradles his instrument like an automatic weapon, which doubles also as a penis, and projects his music as though it were a burst of gunfire or semen. He is animal and machine, creation and destruction in one frenzied packet of energy.

The rock musician uses his instrument as if it were a weapon; Bond uses his weapon with the finesse and precision of a musician. American culture is obsessed with this conundrum of the simultaneous creativeness and destructiveness of machines, and that obsession more than any other factor calls into being our culture heroes, the secret agent and the rock star. The two represent modes or, to continue the quantum analogy, amplitudes of the human-machine relationship that alternately oppose and complement one another. Those amplitudes build and sustain the tremendous tension that runs through the seemingly flaccid institutions of our popular culture.

We think, whether we recognize it or not, so often in riddles, and we do so because the reality we experience is itself enigmatic. James Bond, Elvis Presley, Michael Jackson, and the rest are part and parcel of our everyday experience because they help us frame implicitly the questions we struggle to articulate: How is it that we are so intimately bound to such dissimilar beings as animals and machines, as families and the State? And why, if those beings are so utterly unlike one another, do they seem to become a single entity that embraces all the animate-ness and meaningfulness of existence?

I submit that the puzzling resemblance between the secret agent and the rock star consists in both being Masters of Machines, virtuosos whose power to fuse human flesh and metal or plastic into a dazzling synthesis of form and motion transforms our habitual conception of the machine as something apart, to be picked up and put down and used, in a word, mechanically.

Like Bond, the rock star is a Master of Machines. But unlike Bond, the rock star in exercising his mastery utterly alienates himself from the State that provides his equipment and audience. His electric guitar and the lyrics it accompanies are weapons aimed at the heart of the State, an organized mediocrity and sobriety that represent everything his Dionysian spirit opposes.

There is an intolerable dilemma here, one of several that make the Dreamtime an unending battleground of ideas. The rock star takes up the sophisticated product of the State, but he continues to fight John Henry's battle against the Company. Although its message is far more ambiguous, rock's ties to southern blues are no historical accident, for both confront the perpetually vexing question of how men are to deal with The Man. And while Elvis Presley and Michael Jackson have certainly won far more acceptance from society than the old blues men, they have still had to walk a fine line.[16] Bond, of course, deals with The Man by becoming His joke-cracking agent, although as a secret agent he has considerably more latitude to express his individuality than the conventional desk-bound office worker. Bond's gun shoots bullets, not musical notes, and is trained at the enemies of his employers. But in taking up the machine in Her Majesty's Secret Service, he personalizes it and demonstrates that mechanical expertise need not be the sole prerogative of an anonymous apparatchik.

If Bond is a bit like and a bit unlike the rock star, he is also a bit like and a bit unlike the football player. His forty-year career from the fifties into the nineties significantly coincides with the emergence of rock and football as our national obsessions. And with reason. If rock and football, at least from the perspective of cultural analysis, exist to explore the complex boundaries between animal, human, and machine identities, if, that is, they function as mediating devices, then we are left to wonder how these devices are themselves connected. The answer lies with Bond, whose cipher-like identity is a distilled study of boundaries or, again, *bondaries*. Bond mediates the mediators, tying into a single if highly dynamic cultural structure the disjointed figures we create to represent and wrestle with the contradictions of human existence.

The second-order mediation Bond represents is complex, for the human-machine and individual-State relationships involved in the story of Bond are not articulated separately but, as we have seen, as a whole. Bond thus provides an instructive lesson in composite identity, in the Whitmanesque multiplicity of selves. He shows that cultural processes are not one-dimensional affairs. Like the football player, Bond is a highly trained and specialized team member whose energies are all directed to beating the other side. But unlike the football player, Bond wears no uniform (and his number, 007, is invisible), nor does he disguise his personal identity with a helmet, shoulder pads, etc. Although he retains his civilian appearance, Bond in an evening jacket is every bit as dangerous as a blitzing linebacker. Football players give up their individuality and rely on their similarly robotic team mates to accomplish feats of physical prowess; the well-oiled human machinery of a professional squad is also a mountain of muscle. But Bond mocks the team he serves so well, flaunting his individuality while relying, like the rock star, on State-produced gadgetry to perform his acts of technical wizardry.

Bond's physical attractiveness both complements and opposes the physical might of the football player, which is itself already anomalous: the football player confounds the animal-machine opposition because his superb physical conditioning is the result of monotonous routine. In becoming physically perfect he is forced to abandon a supposedly animal spontaneity in favor of mechanical regulation. As we will see in chapter 6 this anomalous synthesis of animal and machine, which is a function of the two lying at the poles of a semiotic dimension, characterizes all our fateful cultural interactions with animals. The tension or ambivalence that issues from this supreme antinomy of culture is probably behind the curious inconsistency in the names of NFL teams, some of which bear traditionally "totemic" animal designations (Dolphins, Rams, Broncos) while others have function labels that identity them within the other totemism of occupational and ethnic groups (49ers, Packers, Steelers, Redskins).

Bond's animal nature is signed directly by his sexuality, to the point that his women have become a trademark of both the movies and the novels. His endless flirtations, which strike so many of us gender-polarized postmoderns as gratuitous if not contemptible, actually mask a complexity that emerges clearly when one considers the sexuality of his tandem characters, the rock musician and football player. Both figures are sexual blurs, distortions, juxtapositions of anything that could be construed as a charter of socially endorsed sexuality. The rock musician, a technical wizard at the guitar, indulges every animal appetite. He is expected to run amok; his unrestrained sexuality and drug use are devices that define and reinforce the State in the act of negating it.

Note that it would be ludicrous for the media to feature an expose of drug use by rock musicians, for that excess is theirs by right; it is almost their assigned function in a State that has made them emissaries of an emerging technological culture. Drug use in professional sports, however, attracts tremendous media coverage: those fine, upstanding young athletes should do nothing to impair their magnificent bodies or disciplined training. And the sexual taboos of the locker room are an article of faith among coaches from junior high to the NFL; the supremely conditioned animal cannot aspire to the unregulated public sexuality of his opposite number, the rock musician. A six-foot-six, three-hundred-pound tackle is already so overwhelming a physical force that any further stimulation of his physical nature, whether by drugs or sex, would make it impossible for him to function as a cog in that penultimate Dreamtime machine, the football team. In contrast to both football player and rock star, the sexual style Bond affects is to cultivate a flamboyant but seductively cool manner that both affirms and denies his animal self. Bond is that quintessentially modern figure: a technician of passion.

Animal and machine, individual and State, are oppositions whose solitary expression is impossible in a pure, unmediated state. As Descartes observed long ago, nothing can be purely animal without conforming to notions of mechanistic behavior that negate its animal status. The very existence of culture depends on a principle of semiosis by displacement: A thing acquires meaning by pointing at what it is not, by its vectorial movements within the countervailing fields of semiospace. Our cultural heroes exemplify this principle. For a close inspection of the semiotic processes underlying the phenomena of football and rock reveals that, far from being consistent stereotypes, each is a profoundly contradictory enterprise. The secret agent, however, goes the football player and the rock musician one better: he mediates these mediators. James Bond, as our archetypical secret agent, combines and confuses elements of both.

This mediation is a generative process, for in combining unresolvable opposites he sanctions their continued operation in everyday life. In short, we would not have animals and machines, individuals and the State, were their category boundaries not already intricately tangled and contaminated. There is probably no better term than "agent" to describe Bond's distinctive role, unless one borrowed from chemistry the notion of "reagent," for his presence hastens and intensifies events whose nature is generally obscure outside the Dreamtime setting of our movie theatres. The critics are right in a sense: Bond *is* empty, devoid of character, no more than a cipher whose mission carries him from situation to situation, woman to woman, group to group, category to category. Essentially devoid of content himself, he can take on that of others in operating in his chosen field, for he is, after everything else, undercover, a spy.

The Story of America

It is all too easy to adopt the refined views of an intelligentsia (Tom Wolfe's cultural mavens) and dismiss football, rock music, and secret agent thrillers as acts in a modern day Roman Circus that the masters of our society put on to amuse and pacify the mob. Too easy, and too cynical, for such an attitude rejects the possibility that simple tales and rituals may contain profound meaning and that the mob, lacking in education and sophistication, may still grasp at an intuitive level the vexing dilemmas of human existence. Faced with the unsurpassed popularity of NFL football, Michael Jackson concerts, and James Bond movies, the cultural anthropologist, if not the philosopher and literary critic, has no choice but to treat them with the utmost seriousness.

When we approach the story of Bond from the perspective of cultural analysis it yields important clues about how our culture is put together and where it appears to be headed. In the story's context of an American Dreamtime the fundamental categories of identity which, I have claimed, operate in all human societies — animal, machine, individual, group — assume stark, dynamic configurations that surely have existed in no other society, ever. While we have wrestled with the conceptual implications of our relationship with artifacts long before "we" came into being as *Homo sapiens*, it is only in the last few decades that we have had to deal with technological change of such a phenomenal order. A striking feature of the Dreamtime in its present highly charged and unstable state is our simultaneous valorization of the individual and the machine, categories that appear incompatible in principle and that in actual daily life generate a tremendous antagonism.

The ultimate signified and puzzle of the American Dreamtime, in which the story of Bond figures so largely, is the concept-myth of America itself. Our movie screens, TV sets, and supermarket novels are filled with secret agents and private investigators — James Bond, Sam Spade, Travis McGee, Smiley, Jim Rockford, Harry O., Barnaby Jones, Thomas Magnum, Rick and A. J. Simon, and many others — because they offer the illusion that there exist discrete, bounded societies, groups, or situations which the clever agent can infiltrate and set right or wrong. But despite the best efforts of Bond and his imitators, that illusion of fixity, of a clear and distinct boundary separating Us from Them, remains an illusion. The United States at the end of the twentieth century is a land of such sprawling diversity and festering antagonism that it can be fashioned into that storied land of *America* only through the continuous activity of a myth-making intelligence. That intelligence, an essentially *artifactual* intelligence, creates the disparate cultural heroes and spectacles that attempt to confer a uniform meaning on our fragmented, conflictual experience.

The semiotic construction of America is a function of those universal processes of cultural generativity identified in the previous chapter. Residents of the United States and of all the lands it influences are together in their restless efforts to comprehend their ever-changing lives. The semiotic antipodes of animal-artifact and individual-State are not static oppositions, but evolving processes of cultural formation. The apparently superficial Fleming narratives and Sean Connery movies thus lead into the most profound theoretical questions surrounding the nature of culture. To be human, as to be American, is never naturally (or divinely) to be such-and-such, for what we call "humanity" or "American" is a process through which the symbol-using, myth-making intelligence picks its way back and forth across the category boundaries it has itself erected. On that tortuous journey the mind, that strange place, must fashion its own trail markers, which may take the form of cultural heroes whose actions exemplify critical juxtapositions or transformations of elemental categories of identity.

These abstract considerations have in addition a highly personal side, for they figure directly in our individual daily lives. We are all, like it or not, akin to secret agents in that we find ourselves over the course of our lives belonging to diverse, incompatible social units. The family of our childhood memories becomes unrecognizable and disintegrates, peer groups form and reform with different codes as well as different members, loves and marriages occur with sometimes dizzying abruptness, children become if not strangers then at least . . . different. *Difference* — you and I, us and them — how naturally these terms of belonging, of innate identity, spring to our lips and yet how artificial and contingent they are. Belonging to a group, being a *this* rather than a *that*, is at once critical and problematic; there is simply nothing fixed about this whole enterprise of identity.

5

Metaphors Be With You
A Cultural Analysis of *Star Wars*

[The mathematical physicist] von Neumann sometimes spoke of a "complexity barrier." This was the imaginary border separating simple systems from complex systems. A simple system can give rise to systems of less complexity only. In contrast, a sufficiently complex system can create systems more complex than itself. The offspring systems can beget more complex systems yet. In principle, any set of physical laws that permits complex systems allows an unlimited explosion of complexity.
— William Poundstone, *The Recursive Universe*

SAL-9000:   *I would like to ask a question.*
Dr. Chandra: *Mmmhm. What is it?*
SAL-9000:   *Will I dream?*
— *2010: Sequel to A Space Odyssey*
(Dr. Chandra has just informed the SAL-9000 computer of his intention to disconnect some of its higher associative circuits)

A Bookstore Browse

When *Return of the Jedi* was released in May 1983, its promoters were ready with everything from TV ads boosting the movie to wind-up toys of its main characters. In previous years model kits of tie-fighters, replicas of R2D2 and C3PO, Darth Vader helmets, E. T. dolls, and dozens of other gadgets and gimmicks based on earlier supergrossers had made millions, and so the avalanche of *Jedi* by-products was to be expected. But lost in this avalanche, buried beneath the more expensive and exotic novelties, was an item I do not recall from the earlier supergrossers: *Return of the Jedi* bookmarks, featuring cut-out pictures of the cast (Luke, Han, Leia, Chewy, Jabba, and others).

These bookmarks might be considered a nice complement to the *Return of the Jedi Storybook*, which was rapidly moving up the best-seller list during the summer of '83 (in sweet, bizarre tandem with Umberto Eco's *The Name of the Rose*). They might be considered in that way, but for the curious fact that these bookmarks became minor cult objects in their own right among the sub-teenybopper crowd — Hollywood's effort to muscle in on the lucrative sports card market. And like those memorabilia, these *Jedi* cards were eagerly bought and collected by kids who weren't interested in reading anything, even the *Jedi Storybook*.

For example, I observed the following scene while browsing in a Burlington, Vermont, bookstore one afternoon. This bookstore, which actually stocked a fairly serious collection, had the Jedi figures in a countertop display case beside the cash register, right up in the front of the store. A woman entered with her three children in tow, a little girl of three or four, and two boys around six and eight. They circulated among the display cases at the front of the store for a few minutes without showing much interest in anything in particular. On the point of leaving, Mom and the kids simultaneously spotted the Jedi figures. They rushed up to the box and began a lively conversation, the kids badgering Mom to buy the whole set (there were about a dozen figures at eighty-nine cents a crack) and Mom countering with the suggestion that each child pick his or her favorite. To the little girl: "I know which one you'll pick. You'll pick Princess Leia" (which turned out to be wishful stereotyping on Mom's part: the morbid little tyke picked Jabba the Hut). The little boys decided, more predictably, on Han and Chewy. Their purchases made, they exited the store without a backward glance at a book.

Where were these kids headed, with their little package of bookless bookmarks? When they left the bookstore, which cultural world did they re-enter and what future culture were they in the process of creating? To approach these questions from the perspective of cultural analysis is to address a topic that has already attracted enough attention to become an item of popular culture in itself, the topic of innumerable magazine articles and TV talk shows: the status of language and literacy in an emerging electronic age that replaces printed pages with digitized disks and reading with listening to or viewing audio/video productions and interacting with video games. I believe that a cultural analysis of the *Star Wars* trilogy can provide useful insights into this broad and popularized issue by concentrating on specific thematic developments within the movies and thereby avoiding the kind of conventional breast-beating and cliche-mongering that have come to characterize discussions of the "demise of literacy."

Those whose business is the unraveling of hidden patterns in society (policy analysts, newspaper and TV commentators, literary critics, even cultural anthropologists and semioticians) are generally unwilling to confer on productions like *Star Wars* the dignity that serious examination bestows.

Considering the little episode I witnessed in the bookstore, I find that disdain itself significant. It seems to issue from a source far deeper than the petty snobbishness of intellectuals. The dons (sadly including even anthropologists, whose charge is ostensibly the science of *the people*) have largely shied away from popular movies, as they have from other crazes of the modern era such as disco, football, and video games. I think they have done so because they perceive in Bond, *Star Wars*, and the rest a thinly veiled threat to the whole academic enterprise: the movie houses, sports arenas, and video arcades of our cities are harbingers of the death, or at least fundamental transformation, of literacy. The intelligentsia look at the crowds thronging those places and see a world made up of people walking around with bookmarks without books, trafficking in images of make-believe characters on celluloid and cardboard, slipping tokens into the insatiable maws of video games, watching a thirty-second Bud commercial during the Super Bowl that cost more than it takes to run a small university department for a year. They see all this and, quite naturally, it scares them stiff.

In a world of words and things, commentators, critics, and even anthropologists tend to emphasize the power of the former over the latter. We confer on our verbal and written accounts the authority of primary, organizing actions that make sense of the mute and often intractable things we deal with daily. In the beginning was the Word. The supergrosser success of *Star Wars* flies in the face of this usual arrangement by focusing everyone's attention on the myriad fateful ways our interactions with machines shape the course and substance of our lives. Luke Skywalker is an interpreter of the world, just as literary heroes are, but the world he interprets is inhabited by the postliterate moms and kids who like their bookmarks without books. This should not be construed as an indictment of the unenlightened masses, for it makes perfect sense that contemporary cultural productions should interpret our relations with the tremendously important animate-but-voiceless things in our lives. Watching Luke Skywalker team up with R2D2 to destroy the Death Star is informative and interpretive of our own, less exalted doings in today's high-tech world, where we are often called on at a moment's notice to enter into a complicated relationship with a machine without benefit of a prior reading of the relevant operator's manual.

As an epic in the totemism of machines, *Star Wars* sketches a few contours of that complex dimensional construct, humanity, as our (quasi)species twists and turns in the fields of the three semiotic dimensions. How does the movie accomplish that feat? How does the maudlin character Luke Skywalker achieve a new definition of humanity? Attending to this question is obviously our first priority, but if we reach even a partially satisfying answer another major issue immediately presents itself. Unless we are content to dwell within the cinematic framework, it will be necessary to examine in detail other, noncinematic cultural productions and phenomena that have something to do with machines and to determine precisely how these are tied to the human-machine theme developed in the *Star Wars* trilogy. An adequate cultural analysis of the movie(s) thus leads to insights into the current status of human-machine relations outside the movie theatre.

Inside the Theatre: Semiosis in *Star Wars*

While the tendency in discussions of the role of technology in modern life is to emphasize the novelty of our situation, marvelling at the sensational implications of innovations in biotechnology and computer science, I feel that this popular obsession is simply an outgrowth of a long-standing interest in the mechanical properties of the human body. The body as mechanism has been a significant concept in Western thought at least since the time of Leonardo, whose anatomical studies paralleled his experiments in mechanical design. And Descartes, intent in his *Discourse on Method* on establishing the unique-ness of mankind, details the point-by-point similarities between animal behavior and mechanical motion and thus implies that humans could be inter-changeably animal or machine without their unique gift of conceptual thought and consequent self-knowledge. It is arguable whether George Lucas and Luke Skywalker belong in the august company of Leonardo and Descartes, but I think their cultural production, the *Star Wars* trilogy, supercedes the two great thinkers' learned discourse on the nature of machines.

Star Wars, as any film critic or even cinema enthusiast is quick to point out, suffers from minimal character development: Luke, Han, and Leia would be better served by bubble captions taken from a comic strip than by the dialogue supplied them in the movie script. But such carping misses the essential point that the characterization of *machines* in *Star Wars* is unsurpassed by any other movie (and equaled only by a few written works of science fiction, for example, Isaac Asimov's *I, Robot*). Leonardo and Descartes were prepared to consider some of the implications of people-as-machines, but were not charitable enough to the predecessors of our tinny friends to consider the semiotics of machines-as-people. This is precisely what *Star Wars* does.

I have argued throughout the book that myth, which is simply a shorthand term for the culture-generating faculty of the (for now) human mind, operates by subjecting our most cherished ideas to stress along the several semiotic dimensions that intersect to form semiospace. The pushes and pulls of the resulting vectors move the contour or boundary of humanity, of a group, or of an individual in the direction of one or other of the juxtaposed identities that lie at the extremities of the semiotic axes. In this fashion the boundary conditions of ideas that comprise our cultural bedrock, ideas of home and family, love and hate, human and inhuman, are explored and mapped by the holographic engine of our minds. For example, the experiential domain, "machine," can be explored only by investigating the significative functions of particular machines in real/reel-life situations.

Characterization in *Star Wars*, so weak where its human actors are concerned, is amply detailed for its mechanical and quasi-mechanical protagonists. The interaction of human, mechanical, and quasi-mechanical characters establishes a system of representations that gives form and meaning — new meaning — to the identities "human" and "machine." That system of representations I term *mechanosemiosis*. The effect of scrambling human and mechanical attributes in particular characters (notably R2D2 and C3PO but others as well) is to produce a cast whose characters and actions are often anomalous. Those anomalies are generative — culturally generative — for they encourage the moviegoer to examine his assumptions regarding the difference between himself and the machines in his environment. Again, the fact that viewers of *Star Wars*, like the audiences of "primitive" myth-tellers, are usually children or adolescents only amplifies the movie's importance, for their minds are still actively sorting out the cultural categories that will become the unquestioned assumptions of their adult lives.

Children's literature has traditionally focused on relationships between young people and animals, the theme of "a boy and his dog" being a perennial favorite. With *Star Wars* the central theme becomes "a boy and his droid," for much of the drama springs from Luke's interactions with R2D2. Indeed, it is often difficult to decide who (which) is playing the supporting role. But as the trilogy unfolds through *The Empire Strikes Back* and *Return of the Jedi*, Luke is clearly the central character, and particularly in *Jedi* R2D2 is shamelessly upstaged by the teddy bear Ewoks. In *Star Wars*, however, R2D2 is in its element, and a close examination of its several roles tells a lot about the movie's contribution to a totemism of machines.

If *Star Wars* is about our relations with machines (that is, about our mechanical alter-egos), the fundamental issue it must explore is how people and machines communicate. Phrased differently, the issue is the signifying practices that link persons and machines.[1] The movie is about ways of signifying, and R2D2 is a central character (quite apart from its cuteness) because it is capable of "conversing" with the widest range of entities.

R2D2 engages in four types of "conversation" (it would be more accurate here, particularly given our theme of the transfiguration of language, to say "animation"): with people (usually Luke or Leia); with the anthropomorphic droid C3PO; with assorted other droids and organics; and with the computer banks of the Death Star. R2D2's beeps and whistles somehow possess for human listeners (those in the audience as well as those on screen) a distinctly emotional, endearing quality; people have no difficulty attributing moods and motivations to the charming little cylinder. At the same time, C3PO, whose official function is translation (he continually boasts of his fluency in three million languages), is on hand to render R2D2's electronic beeps as human speech. Luke, Leia, Han and, by extension, the audience thus have the dual ability to react directly and emotively to R2D2's machine noises on a mechanosemiotic channel and to comprehend their "literal" meaning on an anthroposemiotic channel through C3PO's translation. No other film goes so far in exploring the communicative interaction between human and machine; it is one of the firsts that puts *Star Wars* on the cinematic map regardless of its box office.

With its faithful droid companion translating at its side, R2D2 thus maintains two open channels between itself and its less articulate human friends, Luke, Han, and Leia. Through these channels R2D2 transmits information it acquires from conversations, or *animations*, with nonhuman interlocutors. The most important of these are the Death Star computer and, in *Jedi*, the computer of the Imperial Guard base. It is quite remarkable that just as the personal computer craze was getting under way, Lucas presented the world with a character that is a perfect interface: R2D2 is every hacker's dream of a user-friendly, dynamic little fellow that has at its receptacle tips all the computing power of a latter day Armonk mainframe. It is probably too extreme to claim that the personal computer phenomenon that followed on the heels of *Star Wars* is a case of life imitating art, but the coincidence of the two does show that Lucas's characterization of R2D2 touched an exceptionally responsive nerve in the formative minds of the movie's juvenile audiences.

Here it is useful to recall the episode of the bookstore. Like Jabba the Hut, R2D2 attained star billing without speaking a word of English (or any other human language). If we except Lassie's seminal barks, Flipper's thought-provoking whistles, the Black Stallion's meaningful whinnies, and that ilk of anthropomorphized animal communication, we could search almost fruitlessly in the history of film for a star that lacked an intelligible voice (agreeing not to count Victor Mature's cave man impersonation in *One Million B. C.*). R2D2's remarkable ability to communicate in electronic beeps and whistles (foreshadowed by Harpo Marx?) taps the same vein as the mystification adults feel before their children's easy acceptance of electronic media of all sorts, particularly the home computer the kids have talked their folks into buying. Although the marketing folks at IBM and Apple will not come right out and say it, in a world of bookmarks without books the computer as an accessing device with instant graphics and menu-driven programs resembles the bookmark more than the book. And there is little doubt which the young audiences of *Star Wars* and the child browsers in my bookstore found more interesting and communicative.

These remarks should not be taken as yet another verse of the intellectual's familiar dirge mourning the death of literacy. It is rather that the signifying practices employed by R2D2 and his interlocutors in *Star Wars* represent a novel form of semiosis, one quite distinct from that installed in the dominant complex of writing-printing-reading. This form of signifying practice, again, is what I have termed *mechanosemiosis* (the way out of pedantry here seems to spawn yet more pedantic terms). Whatever we choose to call it, mechano-semiotic communication does not replace conventional language but grafts onto it to form a hybrid semiotic system (much in the way that linguistic communication has grafted onto a rich nonverbal substratum of expression and gesture to form the currently dominant anthroposemiotic mode of sign production). As the pioneer of this new mix of communicative channels, R2D2 already has the ability only dreamed of by present day hackers to combine three-dimensional visual and graphic displays with its aural productions (a vivid example being the holographic message R2D2 delivers from Leia in the first movie). Now that multimedia programs operating in a Windows environment (we humans do not have a lock on virtuality!) have made their way onto your or, at least, your neighbor's CD-ROM drive, it seems inevitable that children of the twenty-first century will learn their ABCs (which will no longer be ABCs, but elements of the new hybrid semiotic system) at the consoles of machines capable of assembling word, image, and schematization into a communicative form substantially different from our present written language.

It is only some five thousand years since the Sumerians or their mysterious neighbors began scratching cuneiform word-signs on clay tablets.[2] And it is only some three thousand years since the Phoenicians developed a phono-gramic syllabary (that is, a system of writing that represents the common vowel sounds as well as the less variant consonants) from which our own alphabet derives. Given such a shallow history in comparison with the much deeper past of fully human aural language, why should we expect the "written" language of 7000 A.D. to resemble today's phonogramic printed texts any more than those resemble Sumerian cuneiform or Phoenician script? If anything, grammatologists of the distant future are likely to regard our abstract, image-bereft phonetic transcription as an impoverished aberration in the history of writing. They may well see our cherished writing-printing-reading complex as an unfortunate lapse in the history of human semiosis, a Dark Age of a few thousand years, which separated the early and late expressive, iconic forms of Egyptian hieroglyphics and future multimedia software. For both those representational systems succeed in combining abstract phonetic symbols or word-signs with visual images or displays of the subject matter.

You're wringing your hands that Johnny can't read, that SAT scores continue to decline nationwide? Well, maybe Johnny's little cerebrum is not just atrophying as he slaps away at his SuperNintendo joystick; maybe it is being sucked into the maw of Something Else, some strange attractor that does not respect the tidy, linear boundary we habitually erect between writing and visualizing, that instead gravitates around the process of *narration-as-knowing* described in chapter 2. From this perspective, the teamwork exhibited by R2D2 and C3PO in *Star Wars* would seem both prophetic and indicative of a critical period — our own — in the (d)evolution of language, when people-speak and machine-speak began to fuse into a hybrid anthropo-mechano-semiotic.

The users of language (who are also its producers) are not, however, attuned to these speculative refrains; they are not grammatologists nor philosophers of language. For the most part they are ordinary people living ordinary lives, people who build houses and people who (as Merle Haggard would say) still keep them, people who watch an *awful* lot of TV, and people who take their kids to movies like *Star Wars*. The world of the movie theatre they enter is not a sedate realm of theoretical discourse regarding the nature and evolution of language; it is an active, noisy world of presentation and spectacle. What they spectate, however, may well be symbolic distillations of critical theoretical issues. Ironically it is those plain folks, who do more chatting and rapping, shucking and jiving than "discoursing," and who spend more time using tools and manipulating joysticks than composing on a word processor, who will determine the future of language.

R2D2's antics are just the kind of seminal spectacle that provides a sense of direction, an orientation, for people adrift in a situation of rapid linguistic transformation. And R2D2's antics are far more instructive than a programmer's manual for individuals, especially very young individuals, just awakening to the possibilities offered by the host of clever machines that surround them. While computer use and computerese will not replace our existing languages any more than speech has erased the play of features on the human face or writing silenced the daily flow of speech, the interfaced teenager of the near future *will* be communicating in a mode fundamentally different from his paper-bound ancestor of the twentieth century. What did Sumerian grandfathers and grandmothers think of their grandchildren's peculiar scratchings way back at the dawn of writing? Some of us may have a pretty good sense of that experience right now.

What might be called a "hardware bias" or, perhaps, a *mechanotropism* (a malapropism?!) in *Star Wars* is evident in the contrasting characterizations of R2D2 and C3PO. Before the advent of personal computers and video games, movies handled machines and, implicitly, the topic of mechanosemiotics by the familiar device of humanizing the machine: robots were given arms, legs, facial features and a voice that was recognizably human (and English-speaking). One of the more memorable figures of this kind is Robby the Robot, featured in the 1962 classic, *Forbidden Planet*. But now, in just a few frenzied decades, the ground rules for machine representation have changed dramatically. The proof of this sea change is that C3PO, anthropomorphic and articulate though it is (cast in the mold, so to speak, of Robby the Robot), has second billing behind R2D2, who/which lacks most of the standard humanized robotic features of yesteryear. R2D2 does not have a face.

Although the media has not quite faced up to it (it currently has its hands full with the gender issue spawned by another liberation movement) we are experiencing, in the waning days of the twentieth century, the early throes of another movement: machine lib. The transition from Robby to R2D2 demonstrates that machines can now assert their own identities with pride and need no longer masquerade their silicony inner selves beneath layers of makeup and prosthetic devices designed to lend them a counterfeit human appearance.

Perhaps the next phase of this new movement (once past the bra-burning period) is an intensified assault on those inchoate pronouns whose tremendous metaphoric power has been aptly described by James Fernandez. The little words "he" and "she" have become almost indigestible for us (post)moderns, who agonize over the ideological implications of using one or the other in speaking or, especially, writing about situations in which the subject is not specifically gender-marked. So we are forced into circuitous barbarisms of language:

> The writer should take her or his inspiration from events she or he has experienced herself or himself and describe their effect on her or him to the best of her or his ability.

Yet lost in all the eggshell-walking and consciousness-raising of the last twenty-plus years is the anonymous, unheralded third-person pronoun, the very type case of inchoateness: the impersonal *it*.

Paradoxically, as we lavish more and more attention on the insidious gender biases in our daily speech and behavior, as we strive to level the playing field on which men and women must live and work, we push all the myriad *its* in our lives further back in the shadows. Bill Murray and Richard Dreyfuss got us to wondering *What about Bob?*; in this work I want to get us wondering *What about It?* I think this project is supremely important, maybe even more important than Bob, for our ideological slighting of impersonal things bizarrely parallels their ever-increasing importance in our lives.

It is safe to say that a great many of us *fin de siecle* (post)moderns spend more of our waking hours staring into a computer monitor than into another human face, and more time touching its keys and massaging its "mouse" than caressing another human being. And when we finally break away from the enchanting, demanding Cyclops on our office desk and make our way through the gridlocked streets choked with (what else?) other machines to our condo apartment, the warm, affectionate being waiting to greet us and give us unequivocal love is as likely to have four legs as two. Machines and animals, these parameters of modern existence, assert their presence in our lives as never before. They have emigrated from the factory and barnyard, where they could be kept at arm's distance and treated as objects, forced to labor or slaughtered at our whim, to the core of our domestic world — into our homes, our hearts, and even our beds. With the Shih Tzu or Siamese snuggled next to us and the TV clicker resting on the other, empty pillow, we end our day, drifting in and out of consciousness, with Leno or Letterman, and are roused from sleep the next morning by Katie Couric's chirpy, cheerleaderly exclamations on the *Today Show*.

We have seen this pattern of attraction-avoidance, love-hate before: our shunning the impersonal *its* in our lives while establishing increasingly intimate ties with them is yet another schismogenic principle that fuels the crushing ambivalence of the myth of America. Even without reading a lot of paleontology, we somehow know that the machine is part of our innermost self, that it has participated in the birth of our species. Yet this truth weighs heavily on a consciousness awash in ideas about human uniqueness and human control of the environment. And so we react with horror to the urgings — the voice, if you will — of the machine-selves stirring within us, eager for their time of release from the bondage of inchoateness. C3PO and R2D2, with their contrasting mechanical and human attributes, show the way through a part of this labyrinth, and point us in the direction American movie-myth, in the instances of *Terminator* and *Terminator 2*, is taking us through the frothy reaches of semiospace.

C3PO fails to win the hearts of the audience precisely because it is presented as too artificially human. Although it possesses a human form, it also parades those traits of stiffness and preciousness that make us say of some people that they "behave like machines." Conversely, the secret of R2D2's charm (mobile trash can though it is) seems to reside in its ambling, lackadaisical manner, one that we associate with someone who is relaxed and "acting natural." R2D2's spontaneity, affability, and loyalty are attributes we increasingly look for in the machines that enter our lives. An earlier, tremendously popular quest for a compatible and fulfilling human relationship (the great *R*-word enshrined in California culture), conducted in innumerable counseling and encounter sessions across the land, has given ground to the search for truly user-friendly machines and programs. The turbo-charged joys of your new 325i or 486DX may not be true love, but they are a marvelous distraction until that (or the *Repo Man*) comes along. Caught up as we are in that distracted quest, R2D2, C3PO, and by extension the entire *Star Wars* trilogy stand as a beacon light to direct the continuing synthesis of human and machine.

The ambivalence of myth works through other combinations of human and mechanical properties found in the *Star Wars* characters representing the Dark Force: Darth Vader, Commander Tarkin, and the Imperial Guard.

The Imperial Guard, those (anomalously) white-helmeted and armored soldiers forever pursuing Luke and Han, send the simplest message in the mechanosemiotic system of *Star Wars*: Machines are hostile, impersonal instruments of our destruction. It is the eternal, paranoid fear of our deepest machine-angst: *They are out to get us*. Viewed as a metaphor of human experience, the Imperial Guard are the epitome of men in uniform: faceless, incorporeal, stripped of all vestiges of personal identity and made to function with ruthless efficiency in the service of an evil State. They are the Nazis, Japs, and Commissars we have learned to hate reflexively, throughout the endless siege of war movies: John Wayne showed the way for Rambo and Braddock (Chuck Norris's *Missing in Action* character) to follow.

Once again, however, *Star Wars* pushes a cliched image of the machine (in this case, that of mindless destroyer) into unfamiliar territory. Although they appear to be living men, the Imperial Guard are so very anonymous and servile that the strong suspicion arises in the viewer from the beginning of the movie as to whether they are human at all. It turns out that they are not. Introduced in the guise of "men in (futuristic) uniform," it later becomes clear that the Imperial Guard are another peculiarly interstitial species in the bizarre menagerie of "mechanicals" and "organics" that populates the "far, far away galaxy" of *Star Wars*. The viewer's suspicion is dramatically confirmed during one of the endless shootouts (beamouts?) between our heroes, Luke and Han, and the Guard. Luke blasts a pursuing Guardsman (Guardsit? — the impersonal pronoun asserts itself once more), who/which explodes into fragments of metallic white armor. As he gazes in astonishment at the robotic rubble, Han, more experienced in the ways of the Empire, explains to young Skywalker that there is nothing inside the lifeless armor shell of the Imperial Guard. The audience, sharing Luke's naivete, comes to realize that while certain droids (R2D2 and C3PO) may look mechanical yet have hearts of gold-plated silicon, others, like the Imperial Guard, may resemble uniformed soldiers yet contain not a shred of human flesh or feeling.

The robotic nature of the Imperial Guard serves to highlight the movies' characterizations of two other quasi-human, quasi-mechanical figures: the Imperial expeditionary force headed by Commander Tarkin, and the complex and terrifying Darth Vader. Tarkin and his staff of officers represent the conventional notion of the military in the service of a totalitarian state. They are the movies' flesh and blood Nazis, and as such are deeply etched in the cinema-going retinas of three generations of Americans. Their inhuman stiffness and blind obedience only serve to emphasize the evil side of machines (the Dark Force), which all too often manifests itself in human groups such as gangs, mobs, and military units and leads us to renounce their inhumane, mindless violence as an aspect of soulless, mechanical behavior.

R2D2 is a machine that acts like a friend; C3PO is a machine that looks like a person but that behaves pompously; the Imperial Guard look about as human as C3PO but act utterly inhuman; the military officers of Tarkin's force are men who have abandoned their personal integrity and embraced the cruelty of unthinking, unfeeling machines in the service of the Death Star and its Dark Force. What/who, then, is Darth Vader?

Vader is the sustaining enigma of the entire *Star Wars* trilogy: while Han, Leia, R2D2, C3PO, and Chewy undergo no dramatic transformation from film to film (and Luke's coming of age as a Jedi Knight is entirely predictable), Vader's identity and moral struggles are the consuming issues that drive the plot. In the first episode, Vader is introduced as little more than a high-tech black hat, a helmeted and cloaked (a la Oilcan Harry), raspy-voiced villain intent on destroying our youthful hero and a few civilized worlds along with him. There is, however, an eeriness about Vader right from the beginning that defies this easy stereotype, and that increases as the story unfolds. In the light fantastic of the mechanosemiosis of *Star Wars*, Vader is a dangerous riddle. The other characters, however anomalous with respect to "human" and "machine" domains, at least declare themselves; the audience can rely on their continuity even if it can't quite classify them.

But with Vader it is a different story. The old black hat whom we loved to hate in the first movie miraculously becomes the embattled, tragic father who sacrifices his life for his only son in *Jedi*. His rehabilitation is perhaps the most staggering, and likely the shabbiest, in contemporary film. Consider that here is a figure responsible for the genocidal bombing of entire planets, who undergoes a change of heart and ends his career as a near-saint (a member, along with Obe Wan Kenobi and Yota, of the Jedi empyrean). That Lucas succeeds in leading his young audiences from booing to cheering Vader is, at best, a frightening commentary on our moral sensibility and, at worst, an ultimate victory for the Dark Force that his trilogy purports to reject.

It would be inadequate, however, to point out the alarming implications Vader's redemption has for our moral conscience without specifying the particulars, the exact cultural basis, of his transformation. Such specifying or dissecting is always the task of cultural analysis, whether or not that involves, as in the present case, an unflinching examination of the pathology of our (post)modern lives. In *Jedi* Lucas presents his audiences with powerful reasons for believing in Vader's goodness, and a consideration of those reasons provides important evidence for the nature of cultural processes and the semiotic dimensions along which they operate.

Vader is so terribly important because his *persona* and history produce major movements or perturbations along all three semiotic axes, with the consequence that the nature of humanity is questioned and highlighted from every possible direction. The most obvious example is Vader's dramatic rejection of the Dark Force. By destroying the satanic Emperor who dwells at the heart of that satanic machine, the Death Star, he redeems his Jedi knighthood and demonstrates that the world's malevolence can be overcome by the benevolent (Life) Force.

But who/what does the overcoming? Is Vader human, machine, or even some kind of diabolically clever animal? And is he inexorably an alien Other or, improbable as it seems at the outset, might he be one of Our own flesh and blood? As an exemplary case of the ambivalence of myth, neither question has a definitive answer. For Vader is both an especially disturbing synthesis of human and machine, a cyborg, and an ambiguous combination of mortal enemy and loving father. Wrestling with these contradictions, which is the essence of myth, is what gives the trilogy its dramatic clout and audience appeal. While R2D2 also poses the puzzle of a blurred human/machine identity, Vader drives that stake into the heart of the moviegoer by showing him how a man can lose and then regain his fundamental humanity. That odyssey occupies much of *Empire* and most of *Jedi*, and takes the form of a series of glimpses into Vader's physical and psychological make-up.

The first movie of the trilogy provides only a single, chilling glimpse of Vader removing his fearsome helmet. In the half-light of his quarters and partly obscured by a wall, Vader reveals the merest flash of what appears to be a skull stripped down to raw flesh and protruding brain matter. It is just enough to set the hook of a suspicion that Vader is corporeal, unlike the hollow, mechanistic Imperial Guard whose uniform resembles his. But that suspicion is clouded in *Empire* when, during Luke and Vader's titanic struggle, Luke's light saber slashes into Vader's arm and reveals only metal, plastic, and wires. It then seems that our villain is as cold-heartedly mechanical as his actions make him appear. That feeling is strengthened by *Empire*'s most traumatic moment, which ends the fight scene: with a blow of his light saber, Vader slices off Luke's hand and our hero falls tumbling into empty space. That epic combat is rendered as Oedipal burlesque with Vader's taunting revelation, as Luke stares aghast at his severed limb, that he is Luke's father (but, but . . ., as Joe Pesci of *Lethal Weapon* might stammer, but Dad, why'd you chop off my hand?). Now the audience is really confused: the possibility that Vader is human or, again in the language of the trilogy, an "organic" seems ruled out by our look at his wiring, but then there is that shattering (if true) cruel claim of paternity. Once more, the semiotic pushes and pulls along the animal-human-artifact continuum act as vectorial processes that fix identities of Self and Other, family and enemy. Might big bad Vader be dear old Dad?

Luke's quest for his identity, which takes the form of a search for his missing father, is the driving force of *Jedi*. As the plot unfolds he is drawn to the abhorrent conclusion that Vader's taunting claim is accurate. A mysterious rapport develops between them, with each sensing the other's presence during the interstellar game of cat-and-mouse between rebel and Empire forces that occupies much of the movie. The episode of the severed hand in *Empire* reasserts itself as an emblem of similitude in *Jedi*: in Luke and Vader's final confrontation a wound opened in Luke's now bionized hand evokes paternal emotion in Vader; father and son recognize their shared identity, not as flesh and blood, but as cyborgs. It is a telling episode in the mechanosemiotics of *Star Wars*, for the initial dilemma of Vader's paternity is resolved only by Luke's meeting him part way along the road to cyborghood.

As befits a myth the time frame of *Star Wars* is hazily sketched, but one supposes that Jedi Knights (particularly Yota, who admits to being several hundred years old) have been around a long time. Vader may well be ancient, and have acquired his cyborganic features one at a time (the way E. F. Hutton measures its success with investors) in countless joustings. We are left to wonder whether, as the years go by, Luke, our towheaded, impetuous country boy, will lose other limbs in defending his new government against future eruptions of the Dark Force? And as the centuries pass will he, like his father before him, require a helmet and speech synthesizer simply to stay "alive"? Recall their deathbed scene in *Jedi*, when Vader asks Luke to remove his helmet and Luke protests, already knowing that his father's helmet is essential to maintain "his" life.

How droid-like is young Skywalker himself destined to become? Luke finds his father, and himself, but his quest takes him over the twisting, turning border of any conventional notion of humanity, in which flesh and blood beget flesh and blood in an idiom of kinship that serves as an anchor for human experience. But this unsettling discovery cannot be a complete surprise to us (or else it would not surface in myth!); similar traumatic confusions of mechanical-human identity are already being played out in the high-tech environments of our hospitals' intensive care units.

The *Star Wars* trilogy is an epic in the totemism of machines, and yet it moves, paradoxically, toward a renunciation of machines. The final minutes of *Jedi* do not feature Luke, R2D2, and C3PO in a celebratory scene of boy and droids: instead those parting shots depict a boy, his spectral father, and his newly discovered sister (Leia) with her intended, Han. The epic of machines has become an epic of family and kinship. Far from offering a resolution to the elemental dilemma of future human-machine relations, *Jedi* shamelessly retreats into nostalgia. Luke is destined to remain a sexless caricature, an impossible man-child, with the discovery of his siblingship with Leia having put to rest Han's fear and the audience's speculation that her affections were directed toward Luke rather than the swashbuckling starship pilot. And with the Empire on the run, Han and Leia can presumably settle down to perpetuating the race, like John Houseman's stockbroker, in the old-fashioned way. The fantastic menageries of the Tatooine bar and Jabba's lair, the bewildering assortment of "mechanicals" in Jabba's android repair shop, and Luke's own considerable potential as a cyborg, all these fascinating scenes and possibilities are left hanging, relegated to the status of gawping curiosities by *Jedi*'s threadbare ending.

The movie's capitulation is most strikingly apparent in R2D2's and C3PO's subordination to the Ewoks. From the novel theme of a boy and his droid, Lucas drifts into the nostalgic scenario of the teddy bears' picnic. The domesticity of animated stuffed bears replaces the technological innovation of droids, and signals an abrupt end to the movie's wondering about the crucial role machines will have in the future of an emerging cyborganic humanity. In the final scene of *Jedi* R2D2 and C3PO are left standing on the sidelines, with nothing to do but go along with the Ewoks' idea of a good time. With the battles fought and won, there is no indication of a meaningful role for the two droids in the peaceful world of home and family, where teddy bears and nurseries will presumably replace murderous engagements with killer droids in the corridors of starships. The trilogy thus ends on a flat, conservative note; all the intriguing life forms, organic and mechanical, presented in the three movies ultimately comprise only an exotic backdrop for playing out a tiresome melodrama of filial and fraternal love.

It would, however, be both too harsh and incorrect to see the conclusion of the trilogy as a meaningless flight into the fantasy of a domestic world free of intrusive machines. It is a flight, and a regrettable one for the ongoing project of mechanosemiosis, but it is far from meaningless. In relegating R2D2 and C3PO to obscurity at the trilogy's conclusion, Lucas underscores what must be *Jedi*'s ultimate point: machines in the hands of the State are so terrifying that it is best to minimize one's personal involvement with them. They are always potential traitors when ensconced around the domestic hearth. This machine-dread ushers in a paralyzing ambivalence, for so much in the three movies celebrates the intimacy of the human-machine relationship. The platonic love affair between boy and droid withers away, leaving the characters and the audience with a renewed suspicion and loathing of machines as alien op-pressors. In the glass bead game played out on the silver screens of our movie theatres, *Jedi* points the way to *Terminator*.

The trilogy's flawed conclusion only serves to remind us of the threat posed by machines in the service of a powerful and destructive State. There could be no more forceful reminder of that threat than the Death Star, the focus of action throughout all three movies. Luke pursues and does battle with the Death Star; Vader, in the Death Star, pursues and does battle with Luke; this two line summary is effectively the plot of the entire trilogy. Luke and the rebels finish off the ultimate technological horror at the conclusion of *Star Wars* only to face, in the best supergrosser tradition, a Death Star II in *Empire*.

The Death Star, as the ultimate killing machine, is R2D2's opposite number and a structural counterpoint in the trilogy's totemism of machines. Its construction and special effects rendering are among the movies' most impressive technical accomplishments, a fact all too easily lost sight of in the swirl of fantastic beings and scenes. The scale and detail of the Death Star impart a sense of overwhelming complexity; it is Hollywood's version of the biggest machine in the galaxy, presented to audiences for their comparison with the machines in daily life (including the daily life of newspaper reading and TV watching, which for a decade was filled with discussions of real-life, Ronald Reagan-style "Star Wars" scenarios).

The Death Star is the worst case of those scenarios, the projection of a machine-dread that began over two million years ago, when beings that were only on their way to becoming human first experienced the quasi-independent, action-at-a-distance effects of pebble choppers struck from the stone of Olduvai, first awakened the spark of an artifactual intelligence that would place death rays in the sky above. That image of the machine as a colossal evil, a Thanatos in stone or steel, has stalked us from those hominid beginnings to our present civilized condition in which the technological ability is present to realize our worst fears. The alarming possibility that the State and the machines it constructs are homologous, that a world capable of putting Star Wars weapons on the drawing board is fully capable of using them in an all-out global conflagration, leads us to contemplate the harsh realities that *Star Wars*, myth that it is, at once conceals and parades.

The real turning point in *Jedi*, the episode that paves the way for the movie's fatuous ending, is Luke and Vader's light saber duel in the Emperor's chamber. In that duel Vader's paternal feelings overcome his commitment to the Emperor and the Dark Force. Kinship sentiments triumph over blind devotion to the technological State and its satanic leader. Vader's change of heart, the redemption of the old genocide, is made the more dramatic by the characterization of the Emperor as a wicked old man. At the heart of the ultimate machine dwells a corporeal emblem of the Dark Force: the Emperor is not a "mechanical," nor even a master engineer of a technocratic and totalitarian society; he is a human embodiment of malign spiritual power, a sorcerer.

It is this final, stark equivalence of technology and human evil that makes it impossible for the trilogy to conclude on any kind of forward-looking view of the human-machine relationship. The evil presence at the heart of the Death Star is just a conventional, storybook boogeyman; the mechanosemiotics of an evolving human/cyborg identity is silenced by this bland device. Lucas could have made things much more interesting, and may not even have damaged his box office in the process. But inviting the audience to consider Luke's future with his droid sidekicks would raise some scary possibilities.

At the close of *Jedi* Luke is the warrior leader of a victorious armed force, which presumably will move into the power vacuum left by the destruction of the Emperor and Death Star. But that places him in a situation much like that his father, Darth Vader, faced as a young Jedi knight who proudly served a State he idealized. We have already considered the possibility that Luke will become increasingly cyborganic as time goes by; what if he becomes corrupt with his power as well? What guarantees that our young warrior will not end up as an elite member of an infernal military government, as his father did? The price paid for Vader's redemption is our incipient distrust for his son after their reconciliation: "like father, like son" is a formula still too near to mind even "long ago, in a galaxy far, far away." This is why the trilogy rejects its own impetus toward fashioning a new mechanosemiotic system of representations and peters out in the machine-rejecting, pseudo-primitivist finale of the teddy bears' picnic.

Outside the Theatre: Luke Skywalker, James Bond, and Indiana Jones in the Temple of the Technological State

An important lesson to be learned from *Jedi*'s renunciation of its own problematic is that the cultural logic, or *medialogiques*, of American movies does not generate a simple progression from minimal to maximal involvement with machines. Myth, whether in the form of movies or traditional narratives, does not follow along in the footsteps of a supposedly linear historical process, for the task of constructing history itself falls to the culturally generative interactions of identity and difference within the six semiotic domains. The distinguishing feature of myth is its restless hunting along the axes of opposing semiotic domains that bracket, instantiate, and transform human identity. Our folklore, including its celluloid manifestation in film, does not provide a consistent and sequential account of our history because neither folklore nor history is a chronicle, a transparent and linear recitation of events. Both myth and its derivative, history, are parts of a ceaseless struggle to resolve antagonistic properties of a mercurial construction, humanity, that possesses no consistency or stasis and that is always on its way to Something Else.

A principal antagonism, one that has played as large a part as any in shaping what we now call "humanity," is a love/hate triangle that has raged for ten thousand years (or as long as "civilization" has existed): the affair among the individual, the State, and the machine. Political philosophy before Marx, from Plato and Aristotle right through Hobbes, Locke, and Hegel, has focused on the abstract (and unrealistic) dyad of individual/State and largely ignored the dynamic, mechanized context in which it operates. Marxian political philosophy, while it emphasizes the mediated nature of the individual-State relationship by introducing the concept of mode of production, still denies the machine any cultural properties of its own. For Marx, who did so much to publicize the State functions of machines, the machine itself remains a mute and passive token in the implacable struggle of social classes. What would old Karl have thought about R2D2 or the SAL-9000?

The improbable contribution *Star Wars* makes to political theory, if only implicitly, is to bring home the hard fact of our deep ambivalence toward the machines in our lives. What we do with them and what others do to us using them are subjects of great concern and carry the most highly charged positive and negative overtones. Consequently, the characters of American folklore never simply accept or reject machines; they alternately glory in and smash them. In their mythologized lives, folk heroes exemplify the mixed feelings we mortals carry with us when we leave the theatre and return to our waking lives outside the Dreamtime temples of our cities and suburbs.

John Henry, Wild Bill Hickock, James Bond, and Luke Skywalker represent distinct amplitudes, or Fernandezian movements, in the mechanosemiotic processes that shape (or situate) human identity. For all their exaggerated attributes these disparate folk heroes have enough in common with our own mechanized lives to serve as dramatic tokens of the technically expert individual confronting the technological State. Taken together they chart a virtual world of possible experiences theoretically open to us all as we pursue our daily lives outside the theatre. But this virtual world is one of extremes. John Henry dies from his confrontation with the Company's machine; James Bond drifts into a flippant accommodation with the multinational corporations and superpowers that employ him; Luke Skywalker accepts bionic parts without a thought of where that might lead. Tucked among these mythic extremes are our own virtual and realized experiences with the machines produced and often run by the technological State.

Having already examined the characters of James Bond and Luke Skywalker in some detail, it is worth considering them together here. The pair represents two kinds of accommodation with the technological State. In a high-tech world, humans and increasingly complex machines are expected to form strong, constructive working relations and not, as in the nostalgic saga of John Henry, to challenge one another to a contest that can only lead to surrender or death.

Bond and Skywalker are adept at bridging the conceptual and affective abyss that constantly threatens to open between us and our silicon-based, gas-guzzling alter egos. Their talent ushers from a combination of youthful impetuousness and technical expertise, this conjunction of youth and high tech competence having become an accepted part of life in a world where there are still people walking around who were born before a twenty-two-year-old Henry Ford built his first Model A. As any oldster (meaning those decrepit old fools over forty) can tell you, if you want to program your VCR, figure out your TV remote, or (delusions of grandeur!) actually get your new computer to do something you want it to, call the kid or grandkid. Bond at the wheel of Q's miracle car, tossing off witty remarks while conducting a high-speed duel with death, is paced by Skywalker, exclaiming during a pilots' briefing on the upcoming attack on the Death Star that it will be "just like potting swamp rats in my landspeeder." Their levity and charisma demonstrate that the distinctly human qualities of individualism, flair, and humor are compatible with the sober self-restraint required of a technician.

Bond and Skywalker thus extend mechanosemiotic representation by personalizing the machine-user while demonstrating the creative uses to which machines lend themselves. And their personalities are rendered the more vibrant by pitting them against stiff, musclebound, "mechanical" opponents: Bond versus Odd Job and Jaws; Skywalker versus the Imperial Guard and its assortment of killer droids.

Although Bond and Skywalker in their role as Masters of Machines are cultural heroes of a Dreamtime world, they are sufficiently like you and me to make their personalities felt in the real/reel world (as opposed to the reel/real world of the theatre). Bond has a job and even an employee identification number.[3] And Skywalker, if the Ewoks' party ever ends, will find himself the favored knight of a highly militarized and monarchical society (if not a claimant to the throne himself: as the brother of Princess Leia, is Skywalker not a prince?).

We have seen that Bond preserves his savoir-faire by joking away his dependence on a government job. It is quite remarkable that the Bond of the movies is so glib and apolitical, so flippant about the human and social consequences of his deadly activities, for Fleming's Bond was a true Cold Warrior, constantly worrying about the Russians and brooding over the moral justification for his killings. The producer Albert Broccoli extricates himself from that character by invoking another Fleming creation, SPECTRE, the international, apolitical criminal conspiracy bent on world domination. Exit the villainous Russian spy, Rosa Klebb (*From Russia with Love*), and enter the politically cynical megalomaniacs, Dr. No, Goldfinger, Stromberg, Blofeld, and Katanga. A dramatic closure of sorts is reached in *The Spy Who Loved Me*: rather than the sexual bait of *Russia*, designed to lure Bond into a blackmail plot, the female spy of *The Spy* who loves 007 is engaged on a joint mission with him under orders from her KGB spymaster (who, incredibly, is portrayed as quite a likeable old duffer in the most recent Bond movies). Because the story of Bond is rooted in Cold War ideology, Broccoli's manipulations of Fleming's novels and Sean Connery's and Roger Moore's witticisms succeed only in neutralizing the ideological content of the films; they draw back from any political statement rather than venture out onto that risky ground.

Oddly, *Star Wars* jumps in where the Bond films fear to tread. Although Lucas insists that the trilogy's success is due to its fantastic, escapist content, its self-proclaimed fairy tale quality proves to be a license for creating a highly ideological film. Starting with a clean slate, the formulaic "long ago, in a galaxy far, far away," Lucas is free to ignore conventional political oppositions (democracy/communism, freedom/servitude) while proposing a new social order — the Empire — founded on the opposition of totalitarian technocracy versus individual technical derring-do. That opposition happens to be a foundation of American folklore, which helps explain the movie's remarkable resonance with its audiences: in a bizarre transformation Luke Skywalker appropriates John Henry's legendary status and carries on the battle against the Company's machine. The difference between the black laborer and the blond starship pilot, of course, is that the latter wins (twice, with the destruction of Death Star II) while John Henry dies with the hammer in his hand.

Adopting even a sugar-coated ideological position makes a phenomenon with such mass appeal as *Star Wars* a potent force in the world outside the theatre. And taking a position links *Star Wars* with other ideological constructs that are themselves mythic. Like Bond, Luke is David, the archetypal under-dog in an interstellar, high-tech showdown with that futuristic Goliath, Darth Vader and the Death Star. Closer to home, the trilogy is an almost trans-parent overlay on an extensive folklore of youthful American revolutionaries struggling against the repressive juggernaut of the evil King George and his contemptible, mindless Hessian mercenaries (who, however, wore red coats rather than the white armor of the Imperial Guard). And still closer, Luke's battles evoke the spirit and inventiveness of young American soldiers in the face of the war machines (appropriate phrase!) of Hitler and Hirohito. In the minds of twelve year-olds fresh from truly mythic experiences in their Ameri-can History classes, Luke and Han are unconsciously ranked with George Washington, Paul Revere, and the inevitable young soldier of John Wayne's old war movies (although he usually gets plugged toward the end of the second reel). Recalling Lucas's first hit, *Star Wars* might have been titled *American Graffiti II*.

The escapist fare Lucas claims to provide to a fantasy-starved nation is much more ideological than the politically laundered Bond movies, which give up on good guy and bad guy *sides* altogether and concentrate on the dramatic doings of the individual hero. *Star Wars* ideology, however, is far more wistful than sinister. What message do the three movies communicate to young viewers, that they can carry with them into the world outside the theatre? Not, I think, that the enemy (Russia? China? Iran? Iraq? — you fill in the blank), are inhuman fiends who deserve to be exterminated; *Star Wars* may be ideological, but it is not blatantly xenophobic.

The trilogy's message is rather a curious mix of nostalgia and fantasy: there are bad people out there who control big, bad machines and who want to hurt us, but there are also a few good, very clever people who stand ready to use their technological skills to defend us against the powerful, big-machine-wielding oppressors. An extremely simple reading of a simple tale, this interpretation identifies what I take to be the ideological appeal of the trilogy. It also shows that the media's use of the "Star Wars" sobriquet to describe Ronald Reagan's Strategic Defense Initiative is accurate only to the extent that it arouses in the TV viewer or newspaper reader the dread we feel whenever the Death Star makes its appearance in the cinematic *Star Wars*. Reagan's proposed system would have removed the last vestige of human control over instruments of global aggression, thereby moving the Earth closer to becoming the Empire. The media slogan is inaccurate, however, in that it raises the false hope that the message of the cinematic version will be fulfilled, and a flesh and blood Skywalker materialize to keep the generals' space weapons in check (even those whippersnappers Bill Clinton and Al Gore will not satisfy that forlorn hope).

Far from being a superficial endorsement of American military might, *Star Wars* is antinuke, antibig, and just plain anti-Establishment. While the movie glorifies high-tech combat, its focus is always on the individual talent of the young hero, which he possesses as an innate attribute of one in whom, as Vader says, "the Force is strong." If direct parallels between our Dreamtime myth and social institutions are to be drawn, then one might relate the immense popularity of *Star Wars* during the period 1977–83 to the renewed fear of nuclear war or accident among American and European youth and to their commitment to religious causes and movements that stress the prominence of individual experience over institutional affiliation. Luke Skywalker speaks, indirectly, to the kids who blocked the entrance to the Diablo Canyon reactor or who participate in one or other of the new "charismatic" cults.

The ideological significance of Skywalker's and Bond's adventures is couched in the Dreamtime idiom of a mechanosemiotic system of representation. That system has as its object the elucidation of the continually changing relationship between humans and machines. The stories of John Henry, Bond, and Skywalker are neither carbon copies — drab, functionalist reiterations of a social reality constituted from some other, decidedly non-Dreamtime source — nor utterly novel fabrications; they are intermeshed transformations of one another, combining and contradicting to form a complex set of virtual experiences. The play of transformations, however, is not random: on the eve of the twenty-first century humans and machines enjoy a qualitatively different form of coexistence from that of a century or even a few decades ago. It is the serious task of our unserious movies to chart the course of change in our relations with machines, and so we may expect to find something of a history, which necessarily includes a vision of the future, in the complex set of elements and themes that make up the transformations of our *medialogiques*.

The most important process here (one hesitates to call it a "progression") is the increasing interdependence, to the point of shared identity, of humans and machines. While John Henry, James Bond, and Luke Skywalker all take on some variant of the Company's (State's) machine, they incur different debts to other, different sorts of machines in the process. The story of John Henry valorizes and naturalizes a manual implement: he was "born with a hammer in his hand," and that hammer remained a physical extension of his body as he built his legend of the "steel-driving man."

This relation constitutes an elementary bionic process: it is the melding of human hand and inanimate artifact that began over two million years ago, when australopithecines first hefted the crude pebble choppers they had fashioned from the lava rock of East Africa. Those implements — the first machines — became an integral part of an elementary cyborganic or mechanosemiotic system responsible in large measure for subsequent evolutionary changes in hominid hand structure and, most importantly, brain size. The great antiquity of that system reminds us that we didn't invent tools: tools were being used and were modifying the physical and mental structures of their users two million years before "we" modern *Homo sapiens* appeared on the scene. It would be much nearer the truth to say that tools invented people.

James Bond prefers gadgets to the nostalgic hammer, but despite their technological sophistication these are as anonymous and disposable as John Henry's tool (note that the folk song refers to it as *a* and not *the* hammer). Even Bond's miracle car, a machine intimately personalized by countless teenagers over the decades, remains free of any personal familiarity or patina of use. It is merely a high-tech toy to be cast aside when the mission is completed (and eagerly so: we want to see the next batch of goodies from Q's lab). That eagerness, of course, represents a significant departure from the story of John Henry and the cyborganic system it represents, for with Bond machines have become objects of interest and desire in their own right. No one really cares about John Henry's hammer as an object, but Bond's toys help to perpetuate a dominant pattern of consumerism in contemporary culture. They are objects in what amounts to a pornography of the machine, an obsession with its physical form and movements and a consuming desire for ever changing, sensually exciting experiences with it.

We have seen that Luke Skywalker carries the ages-old mechanosemiotic system a step further than Bond: his favorite machine, R2D2, is much more than a disposable toy; it is a major personality in the trilogy. To lapse into Calspeak, Luke enjoys a Meaningful Relationship versus Bond's carnal interludes. The theme of the machine as friend and lover does not, however, capture the full meaning of Luke and R2D2's relationship (or Relationship). Luke does not direct R2D2 as John Henry does his hammer or Bond his Lotus; he enters into a partnership with it.

With himself as senior partner (*Terminator 2*, in which the Arnie-machine takes control, was still a few years in the mechanosemiotic future), Luke takes the pilot's seat in the fighter craft while R2D2 serves as his copilot. Their cooperation is such that one is led to wonder (in a mechanosemiotic vein) what separates their respective competences in doing battle with the Death Star and the Empire's minions. The actual attack sequence on the Death Star in the first movie is highly instructive here: a close examination of it tells much about the Dreamtime course of human-machine representations in future cultural productions (such as *Terminator*).

The dazzling attack scene, which consumes all of three minutes, incorporates four critical events or elements: (1) R2D2 is "injured" and forced to abandon its tasks as copilot; (2) when all appears lost, the ghostly voice of Obe Wan Kenobi urges Luke to surrender his rational, expert control over the ship and allow the Force to guide him to his target; (3) that target, the nuclear reactor that powers the Death Star, is never shown in the world-out-there, but is always depicted in computer graphics on the monitor in Luke's console; (4) the scene contains at least sixty cuts, one every three seconds, which made it a likely candidate (in the relatively easy going era of the late seventies) for the most action-packed sequence in film.

R2D2's "injury," Luke's unsuccessful effort to complete the mission on his own, and the ghostly presence of the Force together frame a major proposition in contemporary moral discourse: God is on the side not of the big battalions, but of the individual who possesses an uncanny, inspired control over his machine. That control can be won only through a Zen-like technique of abandoning conscious, deliberate thought and allowing the situation and the machine's instruments to fuse into a single, concerted action that flows from the unconscious. Though she might not have expressed it in just these terms, I believe that is precisely Brenda Howard's meaning in saying she felt "just like a machine" while bowling two straight 300 games (see the introductory quotation to chapter 4). We have heard of Zen archery; *Star Wars* is Zen rocketry (and Brenda Howard brings us Zen bowling).

When Luke yields to the voice of Obe Wan Kenobi, he does not take his hands off the instruments and let divine intervention take its course. Instead, he continues to operate the ship, but now with a mastery of the machine that is a synthesis of human, machine, and divinity. And this synthesis is more than a dramatic effect: since it enables Luke to destroy one world order and pave the way for another, it is the crucial element in the origin myth of a post-Empire civilization. The individual merges with the machine in a divinely inspired act to defeat the totalitarian, mechanized State; this is the kernel of the three minutes of cinematic Dreamtime served up in the attack sequence.

The third and fourth elements of the attack sequence have to do with the mode, rather than content, of the action. They are nonetheless at least as significant as the human-machine-divinity synthesis in charting the future of culture. The many cuts Lucas employs in the sequence guarantee that it will be perceived as action-packed adventure, but what kind of adventure actually occurs? It is the adventure of the computer monitor, in its then novel and phenomenally popular manifestation: the video game. Luke, with R2D2 looking over his shoulder and the Force guiding his fingers, is confronted with an image of the mazeway leading to the reactor and with numerous video blips representing enemy ships. His task, with the future of humanity riding on the outcome, is to operate his joystick control so that he penetrates to the heart of the maze and gets the enemy blips before they get him. The scene (with considerably lower stakes: the right to "engrave" ones initials in video on the list of top scores rather than become savior of the world) is played out tens of thousands of times a day in the video arcades of our malls, bars, and airport lounges.

John Henry valorized the manual labor of a young, vigorous America just facing up to the implications of industrialization. James Bond personifies the obsession and expertise with consumer toys characteristic of our disintegrating industrial society. Luke Skywalker represents the other face of that disintegration, the next fleck of Dreamtime froth, in which human flesh and blood and high-tech electronics are melded to form the cyborganic hero of a dawning era, a Something Else whose contours are already dimly visible through the straining membrane of the present. Luke is the video wizard, master of arcade machines, both priest and prophet of a social phenomenon *Star Wars* helped create and to which it gave some of its most popular amusements.[4]

One Dreamtime element points to another. A movie series reviled for its superficiality, but conveying important truths to those who examine it closely, feeds into a popular amusement denounced for its mindlessness. Are video arcades simply the pool halls of a new generation (and were pool halls ever "simply" pool halls, devoid of any mythic signification in a Dreamtime world?) or do they carry an important message for cultural analysis? Everything that has preceded this makes it obvious that I am inclined toward the latter possibility: any cultural phenomenon as splashy as video games must be linked in some fundamental way with the culture of which it is a (generative) part. Following up this hunch (or bias) necessitates a brief sojourn outside the movie theatre into the video arcade, temple of the technological State. That sojourn, from one carnivalesque site to another, will lead in its circuitous fashion back into the movies, only this time into the domain of one of the successors of James Bond and Luke Skywalker: Indiana Jones.

For anyone over, say, fifteen, a first experience with a video arcade can be devastating. To virtually every adult sensibility it is bedlam gone modern. The arcade is a blur of light, motion, and sound (but don't look for any printed instructions to help you through this brush up against The Membrane). And sound may be the key to the whole experience.

Try this experiment in cultural analysis. A novice to arcades, you enter an arcade with a friend. The two of you select an unattended machine and, while your friend plays and you pretend to watch, you close your eyes. You are now standing stock-still in the midst of the most incredible noise. Beeps, booms, toots, whistles, and chitterings from everywhere in the audible register come at you from every side, the products of dozens of synthesizers tortured unmercifully by the anonymous madmen who fabricated the games. In addition to the electronic scramble, you also hear the shuffling of the arcade crowd: thighs bumping against metal cabinets (more machine porn!); wrists being shaken into pre-arthritic seizures by joysticks; bill-changers dispensing an endless flow of the new casino money, "tokens."[5]

Listen to those sounds of bedlam for a few minutes (a very few, for you will probably find that time has a way of passing slowly under these circumstances), then open your eyes and leave the arcade immediately (the visual effects can wait for another visit), and find a quiet place where you can think about what you have heard.

If you are willing to grant the total effect of the arcade noises any sense whatsoever, that is, if they seem to be part of a cultural production and not a random grating of organic and mechanical parts, then the possibility presents itself that these sounds belong to a new order of experience. They may be part of a new language, or, since the term "language" is burdened with too many proprietary rights (stridently claimed by a diverse bunch that includes linguists, other assorted academics, grade school English teachers, a newspaper columnist here and there, and others), perhaps it would be better to say a new system of representation or signification (that way only semioticians and a few philosophers will get lathered up about associating the bedlam of arcades with the principles of meaning). Until a few years ago, noises like those you listened to in the arcade were heard only in the most esoteric places: electronics laboratories, recording studios, or, in the most domestic case, the home of the occasional hi-fi hobbyist. Now they flood our lives: a trip to the supermarket, a bored stroll around the airport, a drink in a bar. None of these everyday events is free of the electronic voice of the new generation of interactive machines.

While reflecting on the implications of your arcade experiment, complement it with another, somewhat more demanding investigation in the field of modern aural productions. Go down to that friendly neighborhood Blockbuster video store and rent a copy of *Star Wars*. Back at home, pop the tape into your VCR, crank up the audio so it definitely has your attention (and we won't even entertain the possibility that your system doesn't have stereo capability), then sit back with your eyes closed through as much of the movie as you can manage without real discomfort. By all means, however, be sure to close your eyes when the attack sequence on the Death Star begins. Depriving yourself of the fast-paced, circus-like visual imagery of the film allows you to concentrate on the true strangeness of its communicative exchanges (to use as general and unbiased a term as possible). This experiment allows you actually to hear some of the mechanosemiotic representations described earlier and, hopefully, appreciate the broad range of significative functions which sounds *that are part of no human language* acquire in *Star Wars*.

The engrossing (or not!) aural sensations of our little experiment pay an extra dividend: they provide direct confirmation of the similarities between *Star Wars*, particularly the attack sequence, and the countless SuperNintendo and Genesis video games that clutter our homes and the minds of our children. Luke's mission is not merely *like* playing a video game, it *is* the sensory equivalent of an arcade experience (only with a game so sophisticated that it would demand pockets full of "Replay Only" tokens before you could activate the controls of your arcade starfighter).

In the world outside the theatre, Luke's mastery of video games points the way to a close analysis of their significative function in society. In particular, his Dreamtime mastery of video game machines offers a clue to the cultural construction of his successor, Indiana Jones. The immense popularity of video games helps to explain Lucas's apparently sharp departure, in *Raiders of the Lost Ark* and *Indiana Jones in the Temple of Doom*, from his formula for success in the *Star Wars* trilogy. How is it that Lucas and the movie-going masses switched from space opera to swashbuckling adventure in one fell swoop? In answering this question we could resort to the usual jibes our social commentators inflict on popular culture: artists are continually trying something new just for the sake of novelty; the popular mind is a fickle beast; content is irrelevant because every supergrosser resorts to the same lurid sensationalism to win box office.[6]

Such knee-jerk attempts at providing an "explanation" for the thematic direction of popular movies are really efforts to dismiss the very possibility that those light-hearted productions may generate culture at a fundamental level. Besides offering the tautological solution that things happen because they happen, that one movie follows another willy-nilly, these dismissive critiques serve a major ideological function: they buttress up the comfortable old humanism's ptolemaic conception of humanity by embracing the conventional wisdom that people are fixedly and inviolably people, who may go out and do various quaint things with machines, even extremely complex machines, but who retain a basic, unchanged "human nature" from start to finish. "Men *operate* machines" is the simple credo of this centuries-old perspective on the mechanosemiosis of the species; they do not *generate experience* with machines, and they are certainly not *operated* by machines. Whether the "man" in question picks up a pebble chopper, an Acheulian hand ax, a hoe or a laser (or even fires up one of the SuperNintendo sets lying around the house for a stimulating game of Mortal Kombat), it is all the same, timeless routine of a fixed and self-determined humanity doing things with extraneous, lifeless artifacts.

The mythic processes that drive cultural generativity and that lead from John Henry through Bond and Skywalker fly in the face of the old humanism, comforting though it has been. The established and complacent view of ourselves, which has succeeded only by keeping "myth" neatly walled off from "reality" here gives way to the concept of a rootless humanity, perpetually in flux, a virtual (quasi)species that can exist at all only by continually negating and affirming its integral ties to animals and machines, kin and enemy, benevolent and malevolent forces.

Indiana Jones, of all characters (cardboard cut-out that he is), advances this new concept of humanity, but in a most curious fashion. For at first glance, Indy seems to represent a nostalgic step back into an earlier, simpler time, when our matinee heroes were cowboys and buccaneers, real swashbuckling men of action. He does not brandish a light saber or even a Beretta automatic, but relies instead on his trusty bullwhip (shades of Lash Larue, if anyone remembers him) and Wild West-style six-shooter (Wild Bill Hickock rides again). So is Indy an old-fashioned, or at least *retro* kind of guy? Hardly.

If Luke Skywalker transformed the traditional action-hero into a video game wizard, Indiana Jones takes us one more step down the road (or through another of those frothy membranes) of the mechanosemiotic process through which humanity is continuously redefined. Fast-paced and high tech as the action in *Star Wars* is, it is still strung along the line of a discernible *plot* and it still features a hero with a human past and problems that evoke a certain recognition and even empathy from the audience. But with Indiana Jones, the already fast-paced plot of *Star Wars* is kicked into warp drive, redlined past the point where it makes much sense to speak of "plot" or "character development" anymore. With Luke we still had the impression of a (very talented) individual *doing things with* machines; Indy's character and the frenetic pace of his adventures make it all but impossible to see him as much more than an animated figure in a SuperNintendo game himself, and clearly impossible to attach much importance to the "plot" of *Raiders* or *Temple*.

For not only is Indy not a retro kind of guy, he is hardly a guy at all, being more a Pac Man or Mortal Kombat animated video image than a photographed person. In his disjointedness (might we say "fractalness"?) Indy disperses the few remaining traces Luke left us of the traditional hero whose life is filled with the drama of conflicting ideals, desires, and social institutions. Indy is not so much an acted character as a reactive one.

As a video image in what amounts to a super-SuperNintendo set with a power of resolution that is still a few years away (at the most), Indiana Jones installs the pace and format of the video game within the domain of human action. In other words, the people-images on video game sets become sufficiently life-like to duplicate the actions of human actors in a movie (the movie *Looker* takes this device a giant step farther, with computer-generated video images replacing ostensibly "real" people such as presidents). The video game, however, retains its frenetic, joystick-slapping format, so that the action scenes in *Raiders of the Lost Ark* and *Temple of Doom* have one death-defying stunt following another.

Mere human behavior, even James Bond's most slapdash antics, appears pedestrian by comparison; Bond becomes the slow-walking, slow-talking old coot who is shoved aside by the homeboys slamming to rap music on their Sony Diskmans. The old-fashioned notion of motivated, goal-directed human action withers away before the rappers' onslaught, with the result that Indy's frenzied actions have no point apart from their sheer dynamism. Hence the transparent quality of the story that passes as plot in both *Raiders* and *Temple*: Indy sets out to recover some priceless treasure that possesses a vaguely religious as well as monetary value. Accomplishing that end involves him in one scene after another that is a cinematic explosion, comprising a tremendous number of cuts. The result is that an entire Indiana Jones movie proceeds at the breakneck pace of the three-minute attack sequence in *Star Wars*.

Increasing the tempo in this fashion does more than just provoke a corresponding increase in our blood pressure (those fibrillating old hearts again!). The transition from Bond and Skywalker to Indiana Jones breaks a barrier, crosses over one of those infinitely complex lines we have been considering throughout this work. That barrier, or some ragged stretch of it, is nothing less than what separates one form of humanity from another, or, just perhaps, humanity from Something Else.

Indiana Jones, then, is the next phase (or phase space) of a *Star Wars*-inspired culture. The video arcade and SuperNintendo set in your living room now become the new temples of the technological State, supplanting the increasingly nostalgic Dreamtime temple of the movie theatre. Indy's boyish folksiness and old-fashioned tastes in weapons are not signs that the pendulum of cultural change has swung back in the direction of an earlier, bucolic, normal time. Quite the opposite. The fusion of a down-home character with video arcade imagery and format is another indication that the cultural rug has well and truly been yanked from beneath our feet, that we are not so much entering the next millenium as plunging into it in free fall.

The truth that this close examination of *Star Wars* and Indiana Jones movies reveals is that there is no "normal life," no "real world" to which we can return after exiting the theatre, leaving the arcade, or simply breaking off one of our daily reveries (reveal-eries). Materialist or idealist, pragmatist or dreamer, the distinctions of *-ism* labels fall away when put in the context of several million years of a mechanosemiotic process, a dynamic system of representations, that spews out images and identities like some cerebral supernova. Those images and identities (ever-so purposeful plural here!) set the parameters of that twisting, turning, many-tendriled quasispecies it pleases us to call "humanity."

Gone to Look for (Post-Literate) America

So where, then, were those kids in my Burlington, Vermont, bookstore heading when they exited into a world whose boundaries and whose cinematic representations are undergoing such rapid changes? Where will their bookless bookmarks of Luke, Han, and Jabba take them, and what kinds of meanings will they "read" into their experiences along the way?

In concluding with a few general remarks about the dynamics of the human-machine relationship, what I have called the mechanosemiotic system of representations, the greatest obstacle I face is the extent to which that topic has already been taken up by the reportorial media and seemingly sucked dry of its implications. "Post-literacy," the "computer age," and "biotechnology," with its spectre of cyborganic men and women, are all notions most of us are bombarded with from the first cup of decaffeinated coffee and the morning paper to our Nyquil and the late evening news. I realize it is asking a lot, but I would urge you to try to put all that out of your minds for the time being, and to concentrate on what seem to be the underlying elements in this sodden mass of news about the impact of machines on our lives.

The most misleading aspect of all the reportorial hype is that it is presented as *news*: we are constantly served up shrill, breathless accounts of something dramatically new that is happening to alter our lives (and that thus deserves to count as "news"). This outlook, which inspires stacks of magazine articles, TV documentaries, and books (and the advertising dollars to back them up), misses the absolutely fundamental point that computers, biotechnology, and other gimmicky tokens of (post)modernity are an integral part of a set of cultural processes that are as old as the hills (and a good deal older than many of the quake-created hills around Hollywood). In fact, the cultural processes of what, for want of a longer word, I have been calling "mechanosemiosis," are a great deal older than humanity, since those processes were an indispensable part of its birthing. The hue and cry over "post-literacy" — our kids in the bookstore, Johnny can't read (or write, or count), the educational system is a shambles — must be put in that context.

Recall that the Sumerians introduced the first Western system of writing about five thousand years ago, mere instants on the time scale of hominid evolution. To get where we are today involved millions of years of sentient, tool-making, communicative action by individuals who had not the faintest glimmer of writing. So why make such a fuss about an item in our contemporary cultural repertoire that appeared a relatively short time ago, has transmuted beyond recognition during its brief history (from Sumerian scratchings on clay tablets through monastic scrolls and Gutenberg plates to word-processor programs), and now gives every indication of lapsing back into the specialized activity of a group of scribes who doodle away while most of us . . . do Something Else. After all, the news stories *are* accurate as far as they go: an increasing number of Johnnys can't read (the last survey I remember seeing pegged functional illiteracy among adults in the United States at around thirty percent). Our genus, *Homo*, has been nonliterate through so much of its (not "his," or even "hers and his") history, why should we now gawp and shake our heads when reporters train their myopic gaze on early indications of its incipient post-literacy? What is the big deal about reading and writing?

Considering its brief and unstable history, it seems more accurate to regard writing as derivative of other cultural processes than to treat that specialized facility as an indispensable condition of our humanity. The generativity of animals and machines, of group membership and exclusion, and of the creative and destructive forces of nature can be given expression without the use of writing. The history of our species, *Homo sapiens*, is largely a collection of just such nonliterate expressions: the Paleolithic cave drawings of Lascaux; the innumerable iconic and abstract artifacts of "primitive" peoples; the institutions of warfare and tourism; and all our monuments, shrines, and cathedrals. If semiotic or semiological approaches to culture have tended to place (a narrowly conceived) narrative and language, and almost always *written* language, at the heart of their theoretical concerns, it is because those approaches have typically taken root and flourished in university departments of comparative literature, languages, and philosophy (Roland Barthes's semiology being a prominent example). In those cloistered settings Olduvan tool kits, Paleolithic drawings, family life, and race relations are not on everyone's mind (and surely not in everyone's dissertation). *Anthropological* semiotics or cultural analysis as done by anthropologists, however, cannot afford the luxury of the narrow, "cultured" definition of the subject matter of other disciplines. It is simply impossible for an anthropological theory of culture to ignore the fact that an artifactual intelligence — a tool-making consciousness — has been around a lot longer than writers have.

The final lesson of the *Star Wars* trilogy and of the little episode in my bookstore is that the cultural processes involved in generating humanity through its relations with machines — mechanosemiosis — is an endless sorting through and rearranging of the meaningful properties of *artifacts*. Implements, shelters, clothes, as well as the generic "machines" that have come to embody artifactual activity over the last century, all these items of "material culture" once dismissed as lifeless and relegated to the museologist's shelves are the elemental stuff of an emerging anthropological semiotics. In that inventory of artifacts, writing, with all its chameleon-like properties, is one of several particularly intriguing entries. It is not, however, what impelled tens of millions of *Star Wars* viewers through the theatre turnstiles or what motivated the bookstore kids to buy their Jedi bookmarks. The movies, the bookmarks, the R2D2 toys, the Darth Vader masks, even the *Return of the Jedi Storybook* are the productions of an intelligence that never forgets its debt to the synthesis of eye, hand, and object, to the world of artifacts, of which humanity itself is a principal inhabitant.

6

It and Other Beasts
Jaws and the New Totemism

The fish moved closer, still cruising back and forth but closing the gap between itself and the boat by a few feet with every passage. Then it stopped, twenty or twenty-five feet away, and for a second seemed to lie motionless in the water, aimed directly at the boat. The tail dropped beneath the surface; the dorsal fin slid backward and vanished; and the great head reared up, mouth open in a slack, savage grin, eyes black and abysmal.

Brody stared in mute horror, sensing that this was what it must be like to try to stare down the devil.

— Peter Benchley, *Jaws*

TODAY
Jeeter the Chimp, grandson of Cheetah, of "Tarzan" fame, will appear at the Thai Orchid Restaurant, 2249 N. Palm Canyon Drive, Palm Springs, along with his trainer, Dan Westfall, to raise funds for Cheetah's star on the Palm Springs Walk of Stars. A portion of every meal served (sic?) will be donated for his star.

— "Celebrity Roundup" column in *The Desert Sun* newspaper

The Fish: An Anthropologist Goes to the Movie Studio

How deep is our involvement with animals? And how great, if the introductory quotations above are any indication, is our ambivalence toward them? The previous two chapters have attempted to provide answers to these questions where *machines* are concerned; in this chapter I explore the role *animals* play in molding the semiotic contours of our Dreamtime experience.

As befits one of the organizing principles of human consciousness, animals receive at least as much attention as machines in our popular culture. The animal-friend movies described in chapter 1, like the *Lassie* series, and the animal-enemy movies like *The Birds* and *Jaws* itself have proliferated from mid-century onward so that there is now a vast corpus of cinematic treatments of every variety of finny, furry, creepy, crawly critter. It would have given old Noah forty nights of cold sweats, the thought of being locked up with all that animal destructiveness (fortunately he did not have a VCR and a stack of tapes with him on the cruise). Nor have we (post)moderns sailed into balmier waters than those Noah had to face, for as I write the pinnacle of moviedom has just been redefined: The superest of the supergrossers, *E. T.* (also about a sort-of animal), has just been ousted from its Number One box office spot by a real rip-roaring animal-enemy movie (with lots of emphasis on the ripping and roaring). *E. T.*, move over; here comes *Jurassic Park*.

In addition to their phenomenal box office appeal, animal movies assert their importance in our culture by being recast as direct, participatory attractions in that bizarre phenomenon that has become a signature of the carnivalesque quality of American life: the theme park. The supergrosser success of *Star Wars* was soon translated into the Star Tours attraction at Disneyland, but not before the granddaddy of the supergrossers, *Jaws*, had been installed at Universal Studios in Hollywood, that writhing ganglion of the Dreamtime. With our appetite for vicarious thrills already stoked by the vivid sensations of the big screen, Cinemascope and Dolby (or Digital) inside the movie theatre, the next step in our quest for virtual experience (until, that is, the virtual-reality machines are perfected and made readily available) is for us plodding, ordinary folks actually to step into the movie set itself, or a reasonable facsimile of that facsimile. There we can experience, for a few brief minutes and on the cheap, the fantastic adventures of Luke Skywalker, Indiana Jones, and, the hero of our immediate interest, (Police) Chief Brody. The theme park is about as close as we will get to the movie coming to life — but that can *feel* pretty close when you're strapped into the Star Tours cruiser and plunging through the ice caves of Aldeban, or when, with Chief Brody, you're staring into those black and abysmal eyes of the Beast. Only in America. And, really, only in southern California.

The daily tour of Universal Studios includes a bus ride through the set of Amity Village, where Chief Brody (Roy Scheider) teamed up with ecologist Matt Hooper (Richard Dreyfuss) and fisherman Quint (Robert Shaw) to hunt the Great White Shark. I took that tour years ago, when I was just beginning to get interested in the mythic nature of popular movies. In a nice piece of irony, I was in Los Angeles to attend a meeting of the American Anthropological Association: the anthropologist goes tourist and climbs on a Hollywood tour bus; it was a lark I could not pass up (little realizing how deeply engrossed I would become in movies over the next few years). But at the time I was very involved in the interpretation of "real" myths, that is, stories told by those bona-fide exotics from far away places with strange-sounding names, whom anthropologists normally study. I had not really begun to think about "reel" myth and its implications for my esoteric vocation.

In fact, when I boarded that tour bus and we drove down the Beaver's street and past *Psycho* house on our way to Amity Village, I had not seen *Jaws* nor even read Peter Benchley's best seller. In the previous months I had been planning another research visit to Arawak and Carib villages of Guyana. These were villages without road access, located on deep, opaque tropical rivers that harbored piranha, electric eels, anacondas, and the occasional crocodile. Besides relying on these rivers for all my transportation, I also had to bathe and swim in them. With that in mind I had steadfastly avoided seeing *Jaws* or reading Benchley's novel. It seemed best not to stimulate my already overactive imagination.

So, unlike most of my fellow passengers that day, I did not know quite what to expect when I boarded the tour bus and set off for Amity.[1] The tour bus consisted of several rows of straight metal benches, three people to a bench, and open to the world except for a light canvas canopy. I was sitting on one end of a bench and looking out over the water of Amity harbor as our bus lumbered around the set and out onto a little wooden bridge suspended a couple of feet above the water. Suddenly, the bridge lurched precipitously and sagged into the water, throwing our bus at an angle and seeming to threaten a capsize into the roiled, dirty water. We tour-goers (well, alright, *tourists*) gasped and braced ourselves. Then *it* broke the water and came straight at our disabled bus: a great grey snout surrounding a red maw lined with ferocious teeth swept past us, missing the outer row of riders — which included me — by just a few feet. It seemed a great deal closer. I was at once shaken and amused by my first encounter with *Jaws*.

Considering that this shark attack was a mass-produced effect staged for hundreds of tourists every day, it was surprisingly effective drama. We, a random collection of sightseers, shared an experience like that staged for the millions of people who have flocked to see the movie: we watched as death lunged past. The shark model used at Universal is, in fact, only the studio's stand-in; nor did the studio go all out by pumping blood and gore into the water beside the capsizing bus. But the Hollywood magic was there all the same. We rode our little bus into Amity thinking "shark," and that was just what the studio served up to us.

But why do we turn-of-the-century Americans think "shark" at all? Why do we recoil in something akin to genuine horror when the studio rolls its decidedly ungenuine mechanical model past our tour bus? How is it that an unknown young director named Steven Spielberg and a virtually unknown writer named Peter Benchley (he had published an unheralded first book years earlier) concocted a fish story that gripped — no, slashed — at the collective imagination of the country? *Jaws* instantly established Spielberg as a major player in Hollywood, and saw him on his way to his present eminence. Similarly, in writing the novel Benchley hit upon the theme of mysterious doings in the sea that has propelled him through a series of best sellers: *Jaws*,

The Deep, The Island, and *The Girl in the Sea of Cortez.* These dissimilar men working in dissimilar media somehow touched a central nerve of our collective psyche: our complex and troubled relationship with animals. *That* is why *Jaws* is so gruesomely appealing.

Totemic Animals in a Technological Age

Our complex and troubled relationship with animals . . . If I were writing even fifty, and certainly a hundred, years ago, this phrase would strike most of you as very peculiar. The line (yes, another of those!) between humans and animals drawn by mid-century Americans in the lingering glow of having tamed a wild land and having just emerged victorious from an all-out, high-tech global war seemed to be straight and solid. It did not resemble in any way the tortuous, intersystemic ant paths that have worked their way, like some fiendish thing from *Invasion of the Body Snatchers,* through the equally serpentine labyrinths of our (post)modern cerebrums. And we came by this self-assured, uncluttered view of things in the easiest possible way: we inherited it. There is a broad stream of shared ideas about animals and their place in the world of humans that runs through the Judeo-Christian tradition and reaches its crest in Victorian England (whose rivulets in turn percolate through the waspish land of Dreamtime America).

These shared ideas comprise an outlook that is starkly simple: animals have their place in the world, in the Order of Creation, and we have ours — and there is precious little overlap. In fact, *they* were created separately and put on this earth by God to serve *us* (a belief that, though it may appear hopelessly passe to intellectuals, is still shared by over half the adult population of the United States). The ecology movement has a long way to go, and it is all uphill.

In the traditional view there was nothing particularly complex or troubling about our relationship with animals. They were there to be used to our best advantage; animals were, in the telling phrase, *husbanded.* If an expanding agrarian society found certain animals inimical to the husbandry of domestic breeds, if wolves and grizzly bears, coyotes and foxes *crossed the line* to prey on our cattle and sheep, chickens and ducks, then they were hunted down and destroyed. When that agrarian society began to contract into cities, first in Europe and then in America, in response to the attraction of industrialization, the separation and subordination of animals was only confirmed. Not only were they distinctly inferior to us, they were also inferior to, and much less interesting than, the machines that were beginning to fill our days. Animals still had their place, in the barnyard or the forest, but their province was greatly shrunken relative to the rapidly expanding territory occupied by factories, railroads, and shipyards. Did our Topeka teenager, growing up on the family farm, prefer working on his '57 Chevy to feeding the cows? You only get one guess.

From the perspective of what passes for an enlightened view today, it is difficult to comprehend how a people in the process of establishing the modern science of biology could give itself over to the hubris and ignorance of the separate-and-subordinate conception of animals. Even before Charles Darwin threw his large and greasy monkey wrench into the immaculate tableau of Divine Creation, all the evidence of the senses (even the fact that we *have* senses!) pointed to the inescapable conclusion that humans are a sort of animal. We eat, drink, breathe, copulate, give birth, grow old, die, and decay.[2] Surely we did not have to wait for the evolutionary biologists to determine that something over ninety-eight percent of our genetic make-up is shared with the chimpanzee before acknowledging that that oh-so mythical line separating us from animals is extraordinarily fine. In searching for examples of the power myth exerts on human thought and action, we could not find a better example than our affectation, cultivated over the entire history of Western civilization, that we are fundamentally apart from animals.

But of course things are not so tidy as this little sketch of the "history of ideas" would suggest. I would merely be leading us down one of the serpentine garden paths of the Dreamtime if I were to insist on a clear demarcation between "our" orientation to animals and "theirs", presumably meaning by the latter the conservational instincts of some untrammeled primitive society whose members are natural ecologists. Since a major purpose of this work is to get you to consider the possibility that *every significant line we wish to draw or to honor is in fact a labyrinth* — a line of infinite nestings and convolutions — I can scarcely insist here on a neat correspondence between one social group, say twentieth-century Americans, and one ideological orientation to animals. The truth, as always, is far messier and more interesting than these neat Protestant-ethic-and-the-spirit-of-capitalism match-ups that are pulled out of the professor's hat to dazzle the young minds in Anthro 101.

In using the *Jaws* phenomenon here to get at the Dreamtime-ethic-and-the-spirit-of-who-knows-what (please, oh please, let's not call it "postmodernism"),[3] I do want to suggest that there is something distinctive about our late-twentieth-century orientation to animals. After all, no other people came up with a cultural production quite like *Jaws* and flocked by the millions to see it. But I do not thereby want to suggest that the role animals play in American life and thought has somehow atrophied in comparison with their prominence in, say, a hunting-gathering society. The model developed here of culture as semiospace incorporates animals, or animal-ness, as a fundamental element of every cultural system, that is to say, of every domain, however large or small the bubble, of semiospace. Thus the intriguing thing about our present orientation to animals, and about our cultural productions which feature them, is the movement or *displacement* (that vectorial push and pull again) they represent vis-a-vis a neighboring domain of semiospace (say, American society a hundred years ago).

As we have noted in earlier discussions, the universal prominence of animals in every human society is attested in the anthropological literature. Their importance does not stand or fall on the strength or weakness of the admittedly idiosyncratic theory of culture I present here. In fact, I have argued (in chapter 2) that the true coming-of-age of anthropology was Claude Levi-Strauss's observation in *Totemism* that so-called "animal worship" is not confined to primitive, "totemistic" societies but is instead a universal principle of human thought: the propensity to *classify* the things and human groups that populate our environment and make up the raw material of our cognitized experience (or *Umwelt*). In proposing this sweeping view, Levi-Strauss sought to dislodge the parochial view we have just been considering: the insistence by Victorian English anthropologists (E. B. Tylor and James Frazer) and their successors that *they*, those primitive, colonized peoples, held "totemistic" beliefs about animals participating in a fundamental way in human life, whereas *we* moderns knew full well that animals had their separate, sub-ordinate place (like those colonized people themselves), tucked well behind the satanic mills of the young industrial revolution.

That Levi-Straussian propensity to classify, however, is a far different thing from what the phrase may seem to suggest. It does not spring from our dispassionate efforts to file away everything in our experience into its proper conceptual box, to engage, as Edmund Leach sharply criticized, in conceptual butterfly-collecting. Quite the opposite. We are driven to classify and to compose myths that serve as the vehicles for our classifications because the elements of experience do not make sense, do not have tidy little compart-ments of their own in a coherent, deterministic world. The Victorian gentleman-scholar and the Australian aborigine-hunter alike lived in a perpetual puzzle, an excruciating labyrinth of conflicting thoughts and feelings about animals, about the bearing animals' existence had on their own.

As we have seen, the question is not simply how we are like and unlike animals, but how we are simultaneously like them *and* their semiotic antinomy, artifacts or machines. We have no center of gravity in our conceptual wanderings around these polarities that constitute one of the elemental dilemmas of human existence; instead we describe a complex, weaving orbit like that of a particle caught in the chaotic field of a strange attractor. And in describing that orbit, we sketch out one of innumerable contours of that quasispecies, pictured in Figure 3.3, which we have come to call "humanity."

The work of Levi-Strauss combined with our own countless experiences with animals and animal images (probably beginning with teddy bears in cribs, long before our brains were functionally developed) point to the conclusion that "we" are at least as totemistic as "those" half-naked savages dancing around primeval campfires and waving bear skins and the like. As but one configuration among others, one fleck of semiotic froth bobbing and weaving in the cross-cutting force fields of the semiotic dimensions of culture, late twentieth-century America exemplifies a fascination — really, an obsession — with animals that it shares with humanity at large.

"Animals" long ago ceased being those furry things running around the forest that our earliest primate ancestors crudely perceived, and became mythologized elements or beings in a thoroughly cognitized *Umwelt* fashioned by an emerging human consciousness. For as long as we have been human, animals have comprised an elaborate code or symbol system articulated in countless myths, rituals, songs, paintings, sculptures, anecdotes, jokes, slang expressions, and, in the last sixty-odd years of our four million years of emerging sapience, movies. When people began to make movies, it was inevitable that Mickey Mouse, Donald Duck, Lassie, and, yes, the Great White Shark would make their appearance — old semiotic wine in the new cultural bottles of the moving picture.

Totemism, in both its old and new varieties of oral narrative and movie-myth, cultivates a particular kind of interest in animals. While hunter-gatherers and we moderns are interested in what animals are like, we are far more interested in how they are like and unlike us. It is the compelling, dramatic tension of our likeness and unlikeness to animals — again, our *ambivalence* — that grips our attention and, today, garners staggering sums at the box office. Although there are now plenty of *National Geographic* specials and Discovery Channel programs directed at our newly acquired interest in ecology, don't look for these productions to displace *Lassie, Old Yeller,* and, most especially, the *Jaws* quartet at the box office. Mickey Mouse, Lassie, Old Yeller, and the Great White Shark are not the subjects of zoological treatises; we do not watch the cartoons and movies to expand our knowledge of mice, dogs, and sharks. We watch them to learn about ourselves, to witness a dramatic display of human qualities as these are stretched and distorted, pushed and pulled, in ways that illuminate the qualities we, our friends, and our enemies exhibit in the understated, obscure domain of everyday life.

If you are prepared to grant that some of the above points are at least plausible, that only opens the door to the really important, and tough, question: Why has *Jaws* in particular been such a phenomenal attraction? If a fascination with animals is somehow an integral part of the structure of culture, why did that fascination fix on the bizarre story created through the combined talents of Benchley and Spielberg? This question poses the acid test for my preceding remarks about our "new totemism," for it is only by turning from the general, abstract issues surrounding the nature of culture to specific problems raised in interpreting particular cultural productions like *Jaws* that cultural analysis can contribute to our understanding of the world we live in. So what is *Jaws* about?

The Fish Takes a Bite: The Myth of Ecology and the Ecology of Myth

A one-word answer to the pressing question before us is *polarization* (a two-word answer is *increasing polarization*).

To begin to unpack the cultural significance of *Jaws* it is necessary to recall that animals, or Animal, represent but one of the six poles of the semiospace of culture as I have described that construct here. Every cultural production of the magnitude of *Jaws* represents a set of vector forces acting on the holographic engine of the mind as it labors to establish and reestablish the convoluted boundaries of its *Umwelt*. The identities or antinomies of Animal, Artifact-Machine, Us-Self, Them-Other, Life Force, and Death Force thus impinge on and, quite literally, *shape* our every significant thought and action. The labyrinthine matrix formed through their mutual interplay constitutes the cultural equivalent of ordinary spacetime: semiospace. At any particular point in semiospace, the major vectorial forces may be any combination of the six antinomies, weighted according to the relative strength of their attraction.

For example, *Jaws*, unlike Bond movies and *Star Wars*, obviously develops the theme of human-animal relations. The mechanosemiotic processes of those other movies — how they construct personal and group identity on the basis of our dealings with machines — give place to the *zoosemiotic* processes of *Jaws*.[4] In *Jaws* the contours of our identity are mapped or projected onto the domain, Animal.

On the face of it, this arrangement (if you are prepared to buy into it at all) might seem to suggest that some laissez-faire principle operates in our cultural productions: we have a lot to do with machines, so some movies are about the human-machine relationship; and we have a lot to do with animals, so other movies are about that relationship. And if in the real (but not reel) world we find ourselves having a lot more to do with machines than with animals, then we may expect, like Good Functionalists, to see a lot more machine movies than animal movies. That is simply not the case.

As semiotic antinomies, Animal and Machine do not lend themselves to the a-little-of-this and a-dash-of-that approach to understanding culture. The recipe for "humanity" does not call for an aggregate mixture of ingredients, like a tossed salad, but for a fused, *cooked* ensemble (something good and complex and thermodynamic like a heavy, seething stew). In fact, things are rather more extreme than these culinary metaphors would suggest.[5] Perhaps the most striking feature of humanity, the result as we have seen of some four million years of hominid evolution, is the elemental dilemma we confront in being simultaneously animal *and* machine, a fusion of unresolvable opposites.

An intriguing confirmation of this inherent polarization of our fundamental nature is found in the pattern of recent supergrossers. In this burgeoning electronic age, we might expect the popularity, and certainly the intensity, of animal movies to decline. Indeed, the wild successes of Bond movies, *Star*

Wars, and *Terminator* (I and II) would seem to support that view. But what about *Jaws* (which is really four movies) and the new, seemingly unbeatable supergrosser, *Jurassic Park,* not to mention the slew of *Jaws* imitators? These animal movies do more than balance out the machine movies: they bracket and define the entire two-decade phenomenon (1975–94) of the supergrosser. If machine movies are becoming increasingly popular, so too are animal movies. The dialectic fueled by the Animal-Machine antinomy shows no sign of cooling off; in fact, and this is a crucial fact of our existence, it is heating up.

We need to evaluate the phenomena of *Jaws,* Bond movies, and *Star Wars* as integral parts of tandem cultural processes that over recent decades have intensified a polarization in our relations with animals and machines. As the century draws to a close, we find ourselves adopting the most intensely ambivalent attitudes toward the beasts and objects in our lives.

Contemporary American society produces and consumes more pet food and more beefsteak than any other society, ever. Increasing affluence (which actually stopped increasing years ago, but it still *sounds* right) is only part of the reason behind this schismogenic trend. To affluence it is necessary to add a pervasive sense of growing isolation — from family, from spouse or lover, from community, from the workplace — that brings us to shower unprecedented affection and intimacy on creatures that are really quite insipid. And at the same time we turn a blind eye to the wanton destruction of other creatures that we classify as food, vermin, or, worst of all, merely inexpedient.

Our growing ambivalence toward animals parallels that toward machines, which we have identified as a dominant theme of Bond movies and *Star Wars.* As we enter into more and more intense and intimate relations with machines (the personal computer being the current exemplar), we regard with increasing fear and loathing the dangers technology poses to our survival, not only as individuals, but as a species. Hence the orgies of machine-destruction in Bond movies and *Star Wars.* Both animals and machines are represented in our cultural productions as gratifying extensions of oneself and one's group (Us-Self) and as mortal enemies bent on our destruction (Them-Other). Just as we glorify and denigrate machines through the characters of R2D2, Darth Vader, and the Death Star, so we glorify and denigrate animals through Old Yeller, Flipper, the Great White Shark, and the ferocious raptors of *Jurassic Park.*

The profound ambivalence we exhibit toward animals, at once loving and hating, embracing and destroying them doubtlessly has roots that reach to the earliest efforts by our hominid ancestors to mold a conceptual world, an *Umwelt,* out of their experiences on ancient African savannas. But in just the past couple of decades our ages-old ambivalence has rocketed upward in intensity, propelled by one of the more curious paradoxes of our time: the simultaneous emergence of supergrosser animal-enemy movies as exemplified by *Jaws* and *Jurassic Park,* and of the ecology movement. Seemingly in a final tribute to Gregory Bateson and his theory of schismogenesis, we whacked-out (post)moderns began flocking to movies that glorified our murderous destruction of animals, then left the theatres to ring doorbells for Greenpeace and the baby seals. As Murphy Brown likes to say, go figure.

Jaws, Jurassic Park, and the ecology movement — truly a contradiction that distinguishes our time, that pushes against the perilously thin membrane separating our little fleck of cultural (semio)space from Something Else. In seeking to understand our peculiar nature, how do we begin to explain this puzzling correspondence between the increasing popularity of animal-enemy movies and our growing awareness of the critical ecological imbalances we are creating on our planet?

One answer, easy and doctrinaire like other answers we have examined and discarded, is to claim that *Jaws, Jurassic Park*, and all the creature features that came between them are just irrelevant fluff, irritating distractions meant (depending on one's paranoia level) to conceal the terrible damage we are inflicting on the natural world. Cleaning up the environment and preventing further extinction of species, so this argument runs, are the *real* issues, scientifically documented in as much detail as one cares to have, whereas all this (reel) stuff about movies, myths, and cultural dimensions is just so much hokum. We have the clear choice of trying to preserve the planet's biological diversity or of contributing, actively or passively, to its destruction. In the words of a rhetoric itself extinct as the dinosaurs, if you're not part of the solution you're part of the problem.

An advantage this kind of answer has over my own tangled analysis of myth is, I suppose, that believing it allows us to indulge in that most American of pastimes: wallowing in *good guilt*. In my perhaps jaundiced view, the guilt many of us feel about environmental degradation and species extinction is good because in taking it on we are already in the process of exonerating ourselves of it. For in feeling guilty we are implicitly identifying ourselves with an enlightened, socially conscious faction and distancing ourselves from *those others* bent on developing the wetlands and wearing fur coats. *We* don't do those terrible things; *they* do.

Also, simply admitting our guilt is cathartic since we thereby signal at least our good intentions in the face of wildly intractable problems. How do we save the African elephant or the northern white rhino from extinction? What do we do to slow down the greenhouse effect? How can we repair the ozone layer? The modest contribution you make to the World Wildlife Fund may help pay the wages of a park ranger and thereby save a few elephant lives. It may also assist the government of Kenya or Tanzania in "relocating" a peasant village full of potential poachers further from a wildlife park, moving people who were scratching out a living on their traditional land to a harsher area where they can obligingly starve while watching from afar the photo caravans made up of Fund contributors come to enjoy the results of their good works.

You may cut down on your car trips to do your part to slow the greenhouse effect, while ignoring the incidental fact that global warming over the past ten thousand years was probably the major factor behind the rise of civilization. Running around the ice fields is okay for mastodon hunters, but those glaciers would make it a hell of a morning commute — and don't even think about what they would do to the wheat fields around Topeka.

As we know all too well from contemplating our ant path parables, things can get messy and complex in a hurry. We can approach a problem, whether measuring an ant path or something far grander like preventing species extinctions, with the best will in the world, fully expecting that rational, *scientific* investigation will move us in the direction of a solution. But then the going gets rough, unless we are prepared to rely on our strength of conviction in the rightness of a goal or the strength of an approach. Why quibble over something as important and *good* as saving a species or as incontestable as the "scientific method"? As we have seen, however, following the scientific method as it is practiced by theoretical physicists and cosmologists is a far different, and more unsettling, procedure than following that version of the method enshrined in our conventional image of Science and Scientists. It may feel good, in both the sense of morally right and scientifically correct, to indulge a righteous guilt over our current ecological crises, but in doing so we are adding to and not breaking down the enormous matrix of myth that organizes our thought.

A little section of that matrix, a tiny slice of the multidimensional whole that is Dreamtime America, is revealed by the contradiction before us: the weird, tandem popularity of *Jaws* and the rise of the ecology movement. We cannot indulge our propensity to good guilt and focus on the supposedly hard, scientific issues of ecology while dismissing the soft, subjective fare of movies for the very good reason that both the ecology movement and supergrosser movies are made of the same stuff. And that stuff is *myth* — the shifting, drifting, ever-so complexly interwoven identities of Animal and Machine, Us-Self and Them-Other, and Life Force and Death Force. Whatever the biological and climatic factors shaping the world today— and everything points to these being extremely unstable; we probably are at or near the edge of several ecological disasters — the processes through which we incorporate those arcane chunks of knowledge into a vision of a world that we both experience and believe are entirely mythic in nature. Our thoughts and actions vis-a-vis environmental degradation and species extinction issue from a *myth of ecology*, while the conceptualized context of our person-object interactions constitutes an *ecology of myth*.

These may not be happy thoughts for the Greenpeace crowd, but the evidence is all around us that we continue to situate animals and nature within a mythic system of representations, even as our ecospeak becomes increasingly shrill. The best of that evidence has to do, again, with the increasing polarization that distinguishes our contemporary relations with animals. Perhaps the best way to summarize the mass of material I have collected documenting that increasing polarization is to note the tremendous disparity between our valorization of animals, of all the good things we say and think about them, and our actual dealings with them.

Hunting or (probably more often) scavenging sustained our ancestors throughout something like 99.75% of the evolutionary development of the hominid line. Only in the past ten thousand years has food *production* from agriculture and animal husbandry first supplemented and then virtually replaced food *acquisition* from hunting animals and gathering plants. During the remaining four to five million years of hominid evolution, survival was a matter of hunting, scavenging, or scratching a living from the environment. And, despite what we now learn about the relatively large amounts of leisure time enjoyed by the few remaining hunting and gathering groups, it was a hard and demanding life, a long, tough march through the hundreds of thousands of generations from the first australopithecines to us (post)moderns.

The most important thing about that march for our purposes here is that it involved our ancestors in continual interactions and *interthinkings* with animals. Hunters do not hunt the way a factory worker clocks in at work; there is little routine in an activity that depends for its success on figuring out the elusive doings of animal prey. And when that elusive prey was finally surprised and killed in an up-close, blood-spurting, gore-dripping, eye-rolling pandemonium of shouts, bellows, slashing hooves, jabbing sticks, and flying rocks (sanitized, long-distance killing by bow and arrow did not appear until some fifteen thousand years ago), there was the butchering to do. Gutting, skinning, and hacking up a large animal carcass with stone tools was a difficult, bloody job that had to be done on a week-in, week-out basis.

Living such a life gave our ancestors a detailed, intimate knowledge of animals that is really impossible to describe from the perspective of our contemporary urban lives. Certainly the pious encomiums we hear about "primitive man's oneness with nature" do not touch that extinct consciousness which formed itself out of the experiences of countless hunts and butchering sites. There were no Greenpeacers in the caves of Upper Paleolithic Europe. Nor drunks in Wagoneers, wearing Eddie Bauer vests and cradling high-powered hunting rifles on their bloated bellies.

The transition from a hunting way of life to one based on agriculture and animal husbandry transformed our ancestors' relations with animals, but did not attenuate them. If anything, the intimacy (if that is the word for it) of those relations actually increased. Keeping animals for their labor, flesh, hides, and other by-products involved the keepers in a constant, twenty-four-hours-a-day, seven-days-a-week routine. You worked with them, often *for* them throughout the day, guarding, feeding, watering, cleaning, milking, shearing, castrating, pulling calves, and, when the time came, smashing your charges in the head with a sledge or slashing open their throats, spilling their guts onto the straw of the corral, and setting about the butchering. And at night they were still with you, often in the next room or in the stalls built below the house, where they could be kept safe from predators and thieves. Their sounds, their movements, and their warm stench were with you throughout the night, until you awoke the next morning to begin it all again.

Much of American history resembles this sketch of daily life among early farmers and pastoralists. During four hundred years of colonial settlement and national growth, the foundation of society for most of that time has been the family farm. It provided the wealth on which our cities were founded and railroads built. Even more important, it provided the people themselves: Americans who grew up on the farm doing the chores, taking in its sights and sounds and smells, learning to look at life from the perspective of an existence based on animals. Even our intersystemic Topekan friend, while still a lad growing up on the family farm, experienced some of this, absorbed some part of the earthy, rural ethos of a once-upon-a-time America before departing for the drive-by shootings of Los Angeles. To be sure, he went to school in town, hung out at the drive-in, spent a lot of his free time working on that '57 Chevy. But in the mornings before leaving for school, he still took turns milking the family cow, feeding the stock, and maybe even filling bottles with some of the warm cow's milk to nurse a couple of bum lambs.

When America moved off the farm (the end of the second world war is an approximate watershed for this protracted process) it gave up those day-to-day utilitarian activities that kept it so closely tied to the world of animals. Relinquishing those activities for the fragmented, intersystemic lives of Angelenos, Bostonians, and Manhattanites meant entering into new and sharply more polarized relations with animals.

We remember from earlier discussions how seemingly clear-cut categories can turn out to have the most confused, meandering boundaries. We are now face-to-face with another such example: Our Topekan lad going about his chores on the family farm is closer in important respects to peasants of medieval Europe than to his own reconstituted self as an erstwhile Angeleno. He is a walking, talking Whitmanesque multitude. Just as there is nothing to prevent the octopus-like tendrils of the sequence spaces of adjacent quasi-species (see Figure 3.4) from intertwining in a tangled mass that makes representatives of "different" species genotypically closer to one another than to far-flung members of their "own" species, so there is nothing to prevent the individual, multitudinous personality from assuming disparate identities that resemble "other" personalities more closely than some of its "own" Whitman-esque selves. That is precisely the situation of our Topekan-Angeleno. As he drives past the pet spas and doggie boutiques of Westwood, his memory flashes occasionally to another time and place when another lad romped in hay meadows with the family mutt after they had rounded up the cows for the evening.

The simple truth that emerges from this brush with the multitudinous-ness of life is that we used to have a lot more to do with animals than we do today. Ours was formerly very much a "hands-on" experience of a wide variety of other species. They had to be harnessed, saddled, groomed, fed, watered, doctored, herded, fished, hunted, and slaughtered on a regular basis. The grand semiotic theme of "the relation between human and animal" was thus anchored in a great deal of very earthy, concrete experience. Animals were just there — in the barnyard, the field, the woods, even the house (though farm families even today aren't great fans of Shih Tzu and Siamese). Animals were a perfectly ordinary, "natural" part of experience, and so in thinking about them and their effect on our lives, our minds did not have to run, as it were, in neutral.

It is a very different situation in these ambivalent times. Our relations with animals in the waning decades of the century have taken on a radically polarized, schismogenic cast. While Armour and Swift, A&P and Safeway put the evening roast under Saranwrap, we snuggle our poodles and kitties and settle down to watch the evening Jacques Cousteau or *National Geographic* special on the Discovery Channel. Like the rhyme about the little girl with the curl, we have come to believe that when animals are good they are very, very good, but — and we really don't like to deal with this directly — when they are bad, they are horrid.

If we once had a fairly clear and consistent set of ideas about who was who (or which was which) among the animals around us, those ideas, along with so many others, have become jumbled, *tilted* by the perplexing changes in our lives. Things have become all turned around, so that we catch ourselves harboring deep yet conflicting emotions toward animals, emotions which we can find no easy way of resolving. Are we supposed to, and do we, in our heart of hearts, *love* animals, cherish their coexistence with us, and strive to promote that biodiversity that has become an ideological slogan of the ecology movement? Then why are we so very *selective* in choosing the animals we make the objects of our adoration? If biodiversity is what we are going for, why do we seem to be headed in the other direction, not only by wiping out thousands upon thousands of species, but simply by ignoring the vast majority of species still in existence? Why do we take some animals into our homes and lavish parental affection on them while consigning others — mammals closely related to our Shih Tzu and Siamese — to the repulsive milking yards, feed lots, and slaughterhouses that have sprung up everywhere in rural America, cannibalizing the very family farms that were once homes to so many Americans (including our Topekan lad)? *These* are the questions a cultural analysis of the place of animals in (post)modern life must address.

The central argument of this book is that selectivity of the kind and degree we are now considering occurs only through the operation of cultural or semiotic processes which continuously form and transform the world humans experience. It is simply no good to fabricate some variety of materialist or determinist argument (biological, ecological, cultural, it matters little) to account for the truly bizarre twists and turns in our dealings with animals. Only a cultural analysis, an unpacking of the semiotic constructs involved, will get us anywhere near the point where we, along with William Burroughs, can see what is on the end of our forks. The layers upon layers of mythic construction, of identity-formation, that comprise experience make it impossible to scrape these away, revealing some prized gem of truth beneath the dross of myth. For human experience *is* culture, and culture is mythic all the way through.

If you are uncomfortable with this argument (which may sound like runaway idealism but isn't), then here is an exercise that will make you *really* uncomfortable. Dispensing with the frills of myth and using just good old-fashioned common sense (or bits and pieces of Dreamtime "science"), try explaining to a five-year-old that the Big Mac he or she is eating once belonged to the "moo cow" featured in a favorite storybook or song (perhaps "Old MacDonald Had a Farm"?).

"But, but (the tiny Joe Pesci might say), *how* did the moo cow *get* in my hamburger?" And there you are, staring down the length of Burroughs's fork (figuratively, of course, for you don't get a plastic fork with your Big Mac) at the hideous gobbet of flesh impaled on the end, staring at it, *seeing* it yourself perhaps for the first time, and panicking, without a clue what you will say in the next few seconds to the curious little face staring up at you. There you are, sitting square in the middle of Ronald's fun house (kids who have already finished their Big Macs are ricocheting around in a little house of rubber balls only a few feet from your table), surrounded by colorful, *fun* posters, banners, figurines, including even a couple of *Jurassic Park* dinosaurs that litter your child's tray.

And what do you say? What *can* you possibly say that will not make you in the child's eyes either an ogre or, far more likely, a stammering fool? How do you try to reconcile the incredible, absolutely irreconcilable disparities involved in bludgeoning a living creature to death, grinding up its flesh into hamburger meat, and dressing the cooked meat, not just in the Secret Sauce and Wonder Bread buns, but in clown faces and funny hats, then serving up the repulsive piece of sizzling gristle as part of the fun and games of the place where America goes to eat (*99 Billion Served* . . . and still counting)?

The answer to these vexing questions, of course, is that there are no plausible answers to them. For the questions, instigated by a five-year old who is still naive in the ways of our cultural fan dance, come straight from those elemental dilemmas of human existence we have encountered throughout this work. Remember, if culture actually made sense, if its pieces actually fit together into a coherent whole, then *we* wouldn't be here to explain ever so patiently and lucidly about the Big Mac. Something Else would have that agreeable chore, while you and I, mere human inhabitants of some other, thoroughly mixed-up world, were left to stumble through the explanation as best we could. Inevitably, the five-year-old senses our uneasiness and realizes that another adult conspiracy is about to be fobbed off on it, that it has just touched a nerve. Here, in the midst of Ronald's fun house, something ghastly is going on. And we wonder about the popularity of Stephen King's horror stories.

To insist on personifying and sentimentalizing certain animals while creating a food-processing industry whose feed lots, slaughterhouses, and fast-food chains serve up megatons of meat is to invite, not just a gap, but a great yawning chasm of credibility that cries out for some form of resolution, for some escape from the contradictions that rend our souls when we, too, have to face the five-year-old and its questions. The advent of the ecology movement offers nothing in the way of a resolution here; its strident ideology only exacerbates the dilemma by amplifying our good, righteous guilt.

Even supposing that, in a paroxysm of good guilt, most of us became vegetarians overnight, the dilemma of our relations with animals would only intensify. For with the feed lots and slaughterhouses shut down, we would then have to turn our attention to the ugly underside of our love affair with our pets: the enormous network of "puppy farms," pet shops, animal "shelters," and medical laboratories that spawn, process, and dispose of hundreds of thousands of unwanted dogs and cats every year. You thought you were in deep water at the Golden Arches? Let's hope your child's kindergarten class doesn't take a field trip to the local pound. The questions that followed *that* visit would be fearsome indeed.

Most of us, of course, will not become vegetarians overnight. Dodging the five-year-old's questions while staring into those curious eyes is certainly an unsettling experience, but when that embarrassment is past (and the little ghoul has gone back to watching *Power Rangers* on the Mitsubishi) we will slip back into our old carnivorous ways. But why not "convert" to vegetarianism? Why not at least strive to bring our good intentions, rather than our good guilt, into line with our everyday dealings with animals? Why sit down to the next Big Mac knowing in the back of our minds the ghastly business that went on to put it in its Ronald McDonald happy-face foil packet?

Well (*W-e-l-l* . . . as another Ronald used to say), it was a long haul through the Pleistocene (and Ron was around for most of it!). Tens of thousands of generations of hominids who were not-quite-Us (but, as the song goes, were getting better all the time) sat around hundreds of thousands of campfires, taking in the savory smells of joints sizzling on the coals. It was a long haul, and it has left us with something close to a Jungian memory, a residual synapse in our scent-brain that steals over us occasionally when, out walking on a summer night, we take in the heady aroma of a neighbor's barbecue. Oh, that backyard barbecue, distillation and synthesis of the shiny new (this year's model!) American Dreamtime, and of the old, old smells of the Pleistocene — for most of us it is an irresistible combination. And one that keeps us up to our eye sockets in the ambivalence of myth, caught right between the rock of the five-year-old's questions and the hard place of our salivating hunger for a taste of that barbecue. After all, who among us does not salivate just a little when we hear the lyrics of Jimmy Buffett's immortal ballad, "Cheeseburger in Paradise" (surely soon to become our new national anthem)?

It is this crater-pocked, battle-scarred terrain of our own consciousness that comprises the ecology of myth. And given the jumbled, fragmented nature of that landscape, it is little wonder that the discourse of the ecology movement is so extreme, so mythic.[7]

To understand the ecology movement we need to understand how it has taken the accumulating masses of (often conflicting) technical reports — the drossage of unlucky mud — and converted them into sound bites, how it has transformed biology into ideology. To do that it is necessary to approach the movement from the perspective of cultural analysis, to begin with the realization that biologists and those who listen to them are first of all *people*, cultural beings caught up in the semiotic frameworks we have been describing throughout this work. Consequently, the species/squiggles we select as objects of concern have more to do with the contours and forces of those semiotic frameworks that shape our lives than with any "objective" findings of biological science. When we adopt this perspective it becomes apparent that the ecology movement is a distinct cultural phenomenon, a complex, engaging *production* as worthy of study as *Jaws* itself, and for many of the same reasons. Putting on our ecologist hats (along with the nifty safari outfits that San Diego suburbanites don for their excursions to that city's famous zoo) is an activity generically akin to lining up at the theatre to see *Jaws*: both are eminently cultural pursuits.

The cultural or mythic cast of the ecology movement is immediately evident when we inspect it from our gimlet-eyed, cultural analytic perspective. For the discourse of the movement is extreme, not just in its ideological cast, but in the very subjects — the *animals* — it champions. There are uncounted millions of species out there, and among the myriad bacteria, fungi, algae, grasses, shrubs, flowering plants, ferns, palms, deciduous and evergreen trees are scattered a relatively few of those animate beings that biologists categorize as "animals." Of these the vast majority are the nondescript and often invisible amoeba, paramecia, corals, hydra, sponges, worms, spiders, insects, and so on that we nonbiologists do not think of describing as "animals" at all.

Indeed, our thinking runs in such totemistic channels — *and this is just the point* — that we typically reserve the designation "animal" for creatures much like ourselves: furry things with recognizable faces that are large enough for us to see without squinting, and that run around on legs eating, drinking, and copulating just as you or I might were it not for a few extra millimeters of grey matter and a few extra geological seconds of primate evolution. In short, when we think and talk about animals, we are usually thinking and talking about *mammals*, and not about the vastly more numerous species of fish, birds, lizards, snakes, and frogs that take up most of the space on a taxonomic diagram of the vertebrates.

It is only by qualifying through this eminently *cultural* process of classification that "animals" count for us as representatives of the semiotic polarity, Animal. And it is this cultural category of Animal that, like Vonnegut's lucky mud, we insinuate, or have insinuated for us, into virtually every discussion of looming ecological disasters and the wholesale species extinctions that will accompany them. For reasons that have nothing to do with the biota, which, as we have learned, is far too vast and uncharted to begin to comprehend as a whole, we elevate a select handful of species (*Oh, lucky species!*) to positions of prominence, not just in our minds, but in our funding of Save The Wildlife programs and of cushy, center-stage "enclosures" (*not* "cages") in our major zoos. Like God on High, we survey the multitudes of species, reach down, and pick up a few that will receive the precious gift of our breath of life. The northern white rhino (perhaps forty left alive in the world) and the panda may, along with so many other species, be on their way to extinction, but we are seeing to it that they get there first-class.

The extreme selectivity at work everywhere in our dealings with animals has thus taken on a new and even more extreme twist with the rise of the ecology movement. If the cultural category Animal is in practice a highly exclusive group, its select members must still undergo a final, merciless vetting before being admitted to the inner circle of the ecology movement's Gravely Endangered list, the first-class lounge reserved for its members' pampered use before they board that last flight to oblivion. The factors that enter into that vetting process again tell us far more about ourselves and our peculiar culture than about the surrounding biota.

Probably the most important factor here is a consideration that appears self-evident but really isn't: animals on the Gravely Endangered list, the ecology movement's supergrossing stars, must be rare. Obviously, if a species is endangered there aren't many members of it around. But as well as numerical scarcity, the gravely endangered animal's rarity is also largely a function of its exotic locale: it lives in far-away or inaccessible places seldom visited by Americans or Europeans. Most of us don't — and can't — lay out the big bucks required to take a photo safari to East Africa or a sea-mammal-watching cruise off the Chilean coast. Yet which animals, after all, capture our attention, fire our imagination, and spur our indignation over their plight? Curiously, the animals we single out as most endangered and thus most deserving of our concern are the very ones most of us would never see or have anything to do with anyway, even if there were a lot more of them than there are. Scarce or not-so-scarce, their usual domain as far as we are concerned is the very zoos, marine parks, and television specials that now herald their endangerment. Whales, dolphins, pandas, elephants, rhinoceroses, and tigers — the ecology movement's Schwarzeneggers, Stallones and Connerys — head this cast, followed by a supporting list of cheetahs, wolves, mountain lions, eagles, and, yes, even the great white shark.

Two other factors that enter into our selection or promotion of animal "stars" are paradoxically at odds: we seem to be fascinated with animals that are either fierce predators or, in the hilariously over-pronounced words of Jim Carrey (*Pet Detective*) pathetic l-o-s-e-r-s. A bizarre feature of our increasingly polarized dealings with animals is that the animals we embrace (literally in one case, figuratively in the other) are our pets and our predators. Grizzly bears, wolves, and mountain lions elicit a great deal more interest, and ecodollars, from us than a rather run-of-the-mill endangered species like the peninsular bighorn sheep of southern California. Endangered or not, anyway you slice it (but of course you wouldn't!) the peninsular bighorn is still a sheep, and as such is on the receiving end of a host of unflattering metaphors deeply embedded in our consciousness.

But the peninsular bighorn, like its desert neighbor the fringe-toed lizard and the notorious spotted owl of the Pacific Northwest, make up for what they lack in predatorial panache by the fact that they are all big-time losers in the great crap shoot of evolution. For a variety of reasons, including restrictive diet, unusual habitat, and highly specialized physiology, the range of these creatures has shrunk drastically. Isolated in tiny pockets of territory, their numbers decline to the point that extinction threatens. Then our instinctive liking for the underdog (or, in this case, the undersheep, etc.) kicks in, and we, with a lot of help from ecological activists, make heroes of these losers.

Of course, the one fatal mistake a threatened or endangered species can make is to bounce back from the brink of extinction and multiply to the point that it becomes, not just viable, but, well, a *pest*. Witness the remarkable career of the California sea lion, whose numbers had declined to the point that it was placed under the protection of the controversial Marine Mammals Act during the seventies (Free Willy! Save Flipper!). Now, twenty years later, herds of sea lions are taking over boat docks in picturesque little marinas up and down the California coast, raising a terrible racket and stench (have you ever smelled a sea lion's breath?) and making life generally miserable for the weekend Ahabs who come down to the sea to sit in the cockpits of their big, floating Chlorox bottles and soak up margaritas.

Ah, it is a tangled affair, this business of our relations with animals. In trying to figure it out we find ourselves caught up in the endless zigzags of countless cerebral ant paths that crisscross our minds, making it impossible even to find our way, let alone do the ecologically correct thing. If animals are good and we are supposed to love them, why are some animals so much better (more interesting, more exotic) than others? Why make a fuss about the fringe-toed lizard when you would probably not be delighted to find one on your bedside table? Why (wo)man the barricades to save the peninsular bighorn, then, a job well done, turn up that evening at *Auberges Aix* to savor Chef Francois's superb lamb shank? Then, of course, there are those billions and billions of Big Macs, each with its revolting piece of sizzling gristle, and each with a five-year-old waiting with those impossible questions. And whether the five-year-old nails us today, tomorrow, or next year, we know its questions are there, for they are also ours, burrowed away somewhere in our mostly carnivorous multitudes, refusing to be silent even after oh-so-many of those post-Pleistocene backyard barbecues.

At least some part of us cries out for a resolution to all this (yes, Susan, *Stop the Insanity!*), or, if not resolution, then *release*: something that, for a little while, will answer that raucous chorus of questions and doubts about our relations with animals. The Dreamtime, as ever, is obliging; that is what it does best: it offers up compelling accounts of virtual lives that triumph over the impossible contradictions of existence. The answer in this case is waiting in the Amity set at Universal Studios or, better still, at your neighborhood video store. You won't want to go near the water again: here comes *Jaws*.

The Middle-Aged Man and the Sea:
The Story of Chief Brody, the Great White Shark . . . and Flipper

The staggering success of *Jaws* and *Jurassic Park* (the movie Steven Spielberg described to Barbara WaWa on Oscar night of 1994 as his own personal *Jaws II*) issues from a staggeringly simple proposition: *Let's get even with those damned animals!*

With the World Wildlife Fund, Greenpeace, Robert Redford, Stefanie Powers, *et al* lashing away at the remaining tatters of our flayed conscience regarding animals, the only resolution or release that truly *feels good* is a drastic counterattack (there's no defense like a good offense). Despairing of ever assuaging the consuming guilt we have been made to feel toward animals, we lust for a little righteous vengeance. Enough of this shame-faced denial of our slaughterhouses, enough of trying to dodge that irritating five-year-old's questions at the Golden Arches, enough of signing petitions to save the fringe-toed lizard. We need — and we cry out for it in a silent, suffocated scream that only the likes of Spielberg can faithfully interpret — *an animal to hate*. Forget the peninsular bighorn sheep; we want a scapegoat, a true sacrificial victim for our cultural pyre. And so, enter the Great White Shark (stage left).

Just as James Bond movies and *Star Wars* free us of our customary servitude to machines and allow us to glory in their orgies of machine destruction, so *Jaws* releases us of our bad conscience regarding animals and encourages us to gratify a righteous death wish for the shark. No more beating our breasts over our own sins and failures; for once we can't wait for an animal to take it in the teeth.

As a central myth of the American Dreamtime, *Jaws* proposes a virtual world in which an animal *is* utterly animal: inhuman, mindless, and murderous. Rather than lining up on the side of the "good" semiotic polarities, the shark makes it clear that it is very much a part of Them rather than Us, a demonic representative of the Dark Force rather than another goody-two-shoes animal-friend imbued with the Life Force. By projecting this unambiguously hostile image of the shark's animal nature onto the tableau of a world that we know, in our heart, is fraught with ambiguity, *Jaws* offers a solution to the mounting problems we face in sharing the earth with other living creatures.

Rather than parade the guilt that piles up on the rotting corpses of the uncounted thousands of animals we destroy every day, *Jaws* immediately exposes us to human suffering and human gore caused by an animal in its murderous quest for human prey.[8] In daily life we carefully hide the incredible tonnage of animal gore we produce, and righteously show our disdain for those social roles associated with killing and disposing of animals (such as butcher, dog catcher, garbage collector). But in the Dreamtime world of the theatre, the drama of killing the Great White Shark is public, spread across the silver screen for all the world to see (and most of it has), and the shark's killers — Chief Brody, Matt Hooper, and Quint — are the movie's heroes.

The Great White is more than just an exceptionally aggressive animal, however. Like an earlier great white sea creature of American literature (though we will defer comparing Benchley with Melville), the shark is endowed with an evil, malignant disposition. Through the joint agency of Spielberg and Benchley the shark, like one of Stephen King's seemingly commonplace characters, becomes a demonic being unleashed from the dark recesses of the Death Force.

Their depiction of Animal as an Evil Other ravaging one helpless human victim after another completely subverts a theme near and dear to our guilt-ridden hearts: the Animal as an innately good being, an embodiment of the Life Force that is nature's creative essence and an alter ego of the simple, pure part of our own souls. We have seen this theme of the good animal and the hateful human played out in innumerable animal-friend movies. Our hearts have broken with Bambi's as the merciless hunter stalks and guns down the fawn's mother. We have cheered Lassie to victory over her tormentors. And we have applauded as *The Black Stallion* rebelled against its cruel trainer.

Jaws insists on telling the other side of this syrupy story: our abiding, and often justified, *fear* of animals. Observe a toddler coming face-to-face with a stranger's Rottweiler (the chichi "power dog" of the nineties). A look at the tyke's expression and you just know it is not thinking about how *right* the massive beast looks in the back seat of its owner's 325i; the kid is *scared*. And rightly so, just as you would be if suddenly confronted with a similar beast that could look you straight in the eye and that was twice your weight. For most of our four- or five-million-year career as hominids, we have had a lot more in common with the tyke than with the Yuppie owner of the Rotty. It was not all barbecues and brewskis out there on those African savannas of the Pleistocene and Pliocene; the hunchy little ape-things with a sapient glint in their eyes were often enough the main course for the formidable carnivores that roamed there. A great part of the appeal of *Jaws* is that it gives expression to our repressed fear — as children now grown up and as (post)moderns evolved off the savannas — of the large, powerful beast that could kill us in a heart beat (*Ba-Boom! Ba-Boom!*).

The shark is a killer, and we fear it for that. But like Melville's Moby Dick, the creature's destructiveness has a wanton, supernatural aspect. What really strikes terror in us is the sense, as we saw in the introductory quotation, that in looking into the black and abysmal eyes of the shark we are staring into the face of Evil itself. Evidence of the shark's unnatural identity is found in its peculiar behavior, which defies rational, scientific explanation.[9] In *Jaws*-the-novel, Matt Hooper, the Woods Hole ecologist, describes this terrifying aspect of man-eaters.

> "I don't want to sound like I'm making excuses for misjudging that fish," said Hooper, "but the line between the natural and the preter-natural is very cloudy. Natural things occur, and for most of them there's a logical explanation. But for a whole lot of things there's just no good or sensible answer. Say two people are swimming, one in front of the other, and a shark comes up from behind, passes right beside the guy in the rear, and attacks the guy in front. Why? Maybe they smelled different. Maybe the one in front was swimming in a more provocative way. Say the guy in back, the one who wasn't attacked, goes to help the one who was attacked. The shark may not touch him — may actually avoid him — while he keeps banging away at the guy he did hit. White sharks are supposed to prefer colder waters. So why does one turn up off the coast of Mexico, strangled by a human corpse that he couldn't quite swallow? In a way, sharks are like tornadoes. They touch down here, but not there. They wipe out this house but suddenly veer away and miss the house next door. The guy in the house that's missed says, 'Thank God.'" (218–19)

Benchley's book rode the best-seller list and Spielberg's movie became the first modern supergrosser because both impart this sense that a seemingly natural being, even something as thoroughly unassuming as a fish, may in fact be a marauding, demonic force poised to strike at each of us. At the end of the shark hunt, every reader-viewer believes that the shark is a monster.

The telling feature of *Jaws* as a core myth of the Dreamtime is that everything about it is *extreme*. The commercial success of the movie and the book were phenomenal; audience reaction to the movie was so strong that it spilled over into everyday behavior (such as going — or not going — swimming, and taking that Universal Studios tour); and the characters themselves, particularly the shark's, were so powerfully yet simply drawn. That things are cast in such extreme terms is fitting, for *Jaws*, after all, is about the increasing polarization in our relations with animals.

For this reason *Jaws* is a sea tale, a story of men who, like Odysseus and Ahab before them, have cast off the ties of a normal, settled life on land and gone out to meet unheard-of, monstrous creatures in their own tempestuous element. With the boondoggles of the Hubble Telescope and the Mars Orbiter weighting us down on our home planet, the sea with its multitudes of exotic creatures is still our last frontier, our last stage for larger-than-life performances. Life at sea is reduced to its simplest expression, and things happen in an all-or-nothing, extreme fashion. It is thus a superb theatre for Dreamtime events, in which heroic figures experience incredible adventures.

Since paradox and ambivalence are the currency of Dreamtime myth, the extreme cognitive territory of the sea is its natural home. As our last frontier, the sea terrifies as readily as it attracts.[10] Consequently, the sea and its creatures lend their all too real as well as their metaphoric power to the issue we have been considering: the polarizing effect the ecology movement has on our already rapidly changing relations with animals.

Jaws delivers a ringing slap in the face of the ecology movement.[11] For the book and movies encourage a blood lust in us in the very cathedral of Ecology: the sea. As we have seen, the animals most valorized in popular ecological literature are typically inaccessible or remote *and* effective predators in their own right. While we are distressed by the plight of terrestrial predators like the grizzly bear and mountain lion, we reserve our strongest feelings for the terrible things being done to sea creatures: whales and, particularly, dolphins. The point I cannot emphasize too strongly here is that our pro-animal, save-the-wild-things sentiments are *selectively* directed, via cultural productions (including such productions as press releases by ecological organizations), toward *particular* species, notably large, predatorial marine mammals. We may be concerned for the fate of grizzlies and cougars, but we (or the Dreamtime mechanics of the Image Industry) generally do not give them *names* or feature them as stars in major movies, television series, and advertising campaigns. Free Willy! Save Flipper! Buy dolphin-safe tuna!

The Great White Shark as an evil, malignant thing of the sea is thus exactly opposed by that good, benign being, Flipper. In the dialogue of extremes that defines our relations with animals, the Great White and Flipper stand at opposite poles. They imbue the contradictory, dichotomous elements of our thought and experience with their own tremendous metaphoric power. The semiotic antinomies of culture are unbearably *opposite* and demand, if we are to function in a world not quite mad, some promise of resolution. This is precisely the service that the Great White and Flipper perform. Through the miracle of media-myth, they give form and substance to the witheringly arid constructs of the semiotic antinomies and, most importantly, point the way to a resolution.

The Great White Shark represents a virtual world in which the domain Animal is identified with the domains Them/Other and Death Force; the animal is unremittingly hostile and malevolent. Flipper (and, of course, Willy, the friendly killer whale) represent the mirror image or holographic reverse of that world, in which Animal is identified with the domains Us/Self and Life Force. Here the animal is a friend or family member whose vitality flows directly from the source of life itself (see Figure 6.1). Both constructs are images of possible worlds, possible experiences. Both model reality in terms of the all-embracing semiotic polarities of culture. Both impose a distinct, radical vectorial movement on a particular region (yours and mine) of semiospace.

ANIMAL

Us : Life Force   **Them : Death Force**

Nature (Sea)

sea creatures as vital   sea creatures as
and interesting friends   dangerous aliens
(Flipper)   (Great White Shark)

Society

Matt Hooper,   Quint,
ecologist   fisherman

Person
Chief Brody,
social use of the sea

Figure 6.1. Semiosis at Sea: Mediating Representations of "Animal" in *Jaws*.

Because sea creatures, particularly those as exotic as great white sharks and dolphins, are so far removed from our daily existence, they are an excellent representational device with which to flesh out the conflicts inherent in our lives as cultural beings. This "fleshing-out" process is an essential first step in confronting the antinomies of culture, for it enables us to put a name, a face, and a set of behaviors on ineluctable concepts and feelings, on the animal-love and animal-dread we nourish from infancy and from long, long ago. The Great White and Flipper not only stand for the abstract semiotic polarities of human existence, they live and breathe and interact with people in highly dramatic doings that quicken our pulse (to say the least!), stir our juices, and involve us in their virtual worlds. As powerful syntheses of grand, abstract themes and immediate, visceral concerns, the Great White and Flipper are perfect examples of the *polarization of meaning* which Victor Turner identified as a critical feature of ritual symbols.

But how do we actually become involved in the virtual worlds of the shark and dolphin? How do we carry through with our urge to experience their realities, when even marine biologists specializing in those animals can get only fleeting glimpses of their lives in the wild? Here the *storied* nature of myth asserts itself: since the lives/realities of animals, spirits, and natural phenomena are incomprehensible in and of themselves, human *characters* in myth take on something of their identities. Those characters thus serve as a bridge, a conceptual mediation, between our familiar world and one that would otherwise remain unapproachably alien. We come to know the operation of the semiotic polarities by conceptualizing them in terms of the most exotic, most extreme animals: the colossal shark and the clever dolphin. And in turn we experience their inaccessible lives through the agency of human characters who personify the exotic qualities of the beasts. Through this set of nested mediations, Matt Hooper, Quint, and Chief Brody act out (within the dual frameworks of social life in Amity and life aboard Quint's fishing boat, the *Orca*) the signifying properties that situate all of us in a semiospace bounded, in one instance, by the domain Animal.

As Figure 6.1 indicates, there is something special about Chief Brody. To be sure, he is *the* star of the movie (eclipsing even Richard Dreyfuss's Matt Hooper) and the hero of the novel. But the reason *why* Chief Brody is the star/hero is a direct consequence of his peculiar role within the vectorial movements of the semiospace of *Jaws*. The character of Brody is of such pivotal importance because it provides the mediation that finally succeeds in bridging the mundane world of everyday life in Amity and the exotic world of the sea. Brody does this by serving as a foil for the other two, far more extreme characters Matt Hooper and Quint, whose exoticism puts them in touch with the contradictory properties of the sea. Brody is the star because he mediates these mediators.

Matt Hooper and Quint are opposites whose antagonistic qualities find some resolution in the actions of Brody. As extreme types, Hooper and Quint are characters whom we would not expect to pass while out for the early morning run in our Air Nikes and neon-colored exercise suits. But we are concerned now, as always, with the properties of boundaries, and so we need to look at the characters of Hooper and Quint, who live on the *edges* of things.

Matt Hooper is a wealthy East Coast preppie who carries on a love affair with the sea, and particularly with sharks. Based in Woods Hole, he roams the oceans of the world on research expeditions aboard his personal research vessel, which is outfitted (shades of James Bond) with lots and lots of high-tech equipment/toys. As the myth's ecologist, Hooper becomes involved in the Amity incidents through his desire to study a remarkable specimen, the great white shark, in action. For Hooper, the goal of killing the marauder is secondary to observing it alive.

Quint is Hooper's antithesis. A rough-hewn local fisherman who has spent his life wresting a difficult living from the sea, Quint shares none of Hooper's privileged background or idealistic sentiments. Where Hooper is urbane and witty, Quint is withdrawn and coarse — as harsh as fingernails raked across a blackboard (in one of the movie's most effective scenes). Even among the salty Long Island charter fishermen, Quint is known as a hard case. But he is not a simple man. Although early in the movie it appears that Quint's interest in the shark is solely monetary (to collect the reward for killing it), as the plot develops it becomes clear that he is driven by an obsessive hatred for the Great White Shark. We have met his character before, in another prominent myth of the Dreamtime: Quint is Ahab.

In *Jaws*-the-novel these *Irreconcilable Differences* between the worlds of Hooper and Quint are dramatically resolved: Benchley has the shark kill both men. In a scene that would have made an unforgettable moment in film, Benchley describes how the Great White smashes into the frivolous little shark cage which Hooper is using to photograph his prize specimen, crushes him in its *j-a-w-s* and devours him. The ecologist killed and eaten by the ecologized, a superbly ironic martyrdom that Spielberg did not incorporate in the movie.[12] In the movie, Hooper somehow manages to elude the shark underwater and, when Brody has finally dispatched the monster (in a scene lifted right out of a James Bond movie), gratuitously pops to the surface in his scuba gear. Semiotic processes notwithstanding, it just would not have been good box office to make shark bait of Richard Dreyfuss.

Even with a reincarnated Hooper, however, Chief Brody remains the most important character in *Jaws*-the-movie. And this alone is a remarkable fact, one of several in this remarkable movie by the remarkable Spielberg. Imagine some of the studio meetings that must have taken place over the decision to write in a plain, family-man, small-town police chief as the action hero (but not *The Last Action Hero*). Filmed with the embers of the sexual revolution still glowing, with antiwar sentiment over Vietnam still running strong among the young who make up most of a movie's audience, and with disillusion and disgust with government in general mounting with every new Watergate revelation, *Jaws* astonishingly makes a hero of a dreary, middle-aged establishment type — and a police chief to boot.

Why did Spielberg select such an unlikely character to be the hero of his slap-dash adventure story? We have already glimpsed part of the answer to this question: Chief Brody has qualities that are particularly suited to his role as mediator of the extreme, virtual worlds of Hooper and Quint. But another part of the answer has to do with the properties of Brody's world itself, taken on its own terms and not as a foil for those of other characters. And *that* raises the all-important question of how a movie, in the hands of a cinematic genius like Spielberg, grapples in its reel-world setting with the all too real-world problems of everyday existence. Brody is not the Terminator (and Roy Scheider is definitely not Arnold Schwarzenegger), and the world he inhabits is not that of the sci-fi pornoviolence we have come to expect in action movies. Brody faces dilemmas we all have to confront in our walking-around-in lives. Consequently, his actions, projected in larger than life form on the great silver screen, speak directly to our most intimate understandings of what our own lives are about.

So there are these two modalities of Brody's character: as mediator of exotic virtual worlds, and as participant in personal dramas that are very like those we all experience. The popularity — and yes, even profundity — of *Jaws* is that it unites these modalities in a single dramatic persona.

We have already seen that Brody mediates exotic virtual worlds through his relationships with Hooper and Quint, who in turn directly represent the antithetical moods of the sea. Although Brody goes aboard the *Orca* with Hooper and Quint to hunt for the shark, he shares none of their enthusiasm for or familiarity with the sea. The movie and particularly the novel make much of Brody's neurotic dislike of the water. He is a local boy, born and reared on the edge of the Atlantic Ocean, but he never learned to swim or sail. He becomes queasy just looking at the boats bobbing in Amity harbor. Yet with all this anxiety regarding his native environment, Brody did not take the expedient step and move to the heartland (perhaps Topeka?!). Quite the opposite: Benchley describes Brody as a youth wanting only to grow up to become police chief of Amity, to protect and to serve (as the slogan of another, thoroughly mythologized police department runs) the community that nurtured him.

Brody's affinity for the land does more than provide added dramatic tension for the upcoming *Great Shark Hunt* (as Hunter Thompson described it); it identifies him within the semiospace of the myth as a creature of the land, committed to its ways, its social life. After all, if Brody were a muscle-bound, cigar-chomping superhero in the mold of Schwarzenegger, going to sea to do battle with a monster would be just another testosterone-pumping test of egos. Unlike Hooper and Quint, whose diverse reasons for going after the shark are basically egotistical and antisocial, Brody pursues the shark out of a sense of civic duty. He represents the social world of families and friends that, though it may be situated on the seashore, ultimately divorces men from the sea. It is, almost, classical tragedy: if Quint is Ahab, then Brody is Oedipus. Quint's and Hooper's bravery in doing battle with the shark is less heroic than Brody's, for they have their own personal reasons for being out there on the shark hunt. They simply need to go. Brody, on the other hand, does not want to go, sees an inevitable disaster looming, and yet goes anyway because he knows he has no choice. It is his duty to go.

Thus Brody's role or modality as a mediator shades imperceptibly into his role as participant in the little dramas that constitute daily life. And here we reach a kind of semiotic bedrock. For in my opinion the most distinguishing characteristic of *Jaws*, and of Spielberg's entire corpus, is its insistence on placing the *family* at the very heart of whatever drama is transpiring. The miracle of Spielberg's success is that he turns out action movie after action movie, each a more stupendous supergrosser than the last, and yet each a little study of the workings — or the dysfunctions — of the American family.

You can see this at a glance, for there are, of all things, *children* in Spielberg's movies. And amazingly they are there in important roles, not as cute ornaments or even as foils for adult dramas. In contrast, try finding a child in any of the action movies we have been considering here, or in almost any of the countless others that are out there wallowing in their obligatory carnage. In the eighteen or so Bond movies, I can think of only one character who is less than four feet tall, and that is the dwarf (altitudinally challenged?) assistant to Scaramanga (*The Man with the Golden Gun*), played by Herve Villechaize. Similarly, in *Star Wars* the closest thing (!) to a child character is, you guessed it, our little friend R2D2. Its (remember, *its*) spontaneity, gleeful beeps and whistles, together with its small size and rather unsteady gait insinuate it into the vectorial niche in semiospace we customarily reserve for flesh-and-blood children.

In *Jaws* the most dramatic relationship to unfold on land involves Chief Brody, the shark, *and* Brody's two sons, Michael and Sean. As police chief Brody is concerned with protecting the community of Amity as a whole, but as a father he is consumed by the far more elemental need to defend his offspring against a marauding beast. Before the three adult adventurers set off on their macho Great Shark Hunt, most of the heart-stopping drama comes from scenes in which Brody is frantically trying to protect his sons from a shark attack. The most riveting action here is the shark's perverse move *into* the supposedly safe waters of Amity harbor itself, where Michael Brody is trying out his tiny new sailboat. Like the living uncertainty principle that it is, the shark bypasses the swarm of swimmers in the nearby Atlantic surf to carry its assault right into the heart of Amity — and into the heart of Brody's family life.

From a cultural analytic perspective, I believe that it is this direct assault on a particular family that makes *Jaws*, along with *Close Encounters of the Third*

Kind, E. T., and, to a lesser extent, *Jurassic Park* such powerful movies. Instead of simply adding to the dross of shoot-em-up, slash-em-to-giblets action movies, Spielberg directs productions (*cultural* productions, remember) in which *things get personal.* The Great White Shark, seemingly a random eating machine, goes out of its way to get Michael Brody, just as the mysterious aliens of *Close Encounters* are fixated on taking the toddler Robby from his anguished mother (*Save the life of my child, cried the desperate mother* ...).[13]

It is not a simple affair, however, this business of *Jaws* as a mythic exploration of American family life (we are now long past the point when we would be quick to call *anything* a simple affair). As we will see in the next chapter, on Spielberg's opus *E. T.,* the family is as highly charged, complex, and (what else?) *ambivalent* a set of social relations as we will find in contemporary life. That very complexity and emotional turmoil are why our myths engage the issue so prominently in the first place. Remember, if family life were a clear-cut matter of doing such-and-such and believing such-and-such, if the family were not so completely implicated in the elemental dilemmas of existence, then our most important myths would not engage the issue (and, again, "we" wouldn't be we and the Something Else there in our place would not possess anything like our myths).

There is, of course, a doctrinaire and highly placed element of American society that would have us believe that family life *is* a perfectly clear-cut business, that there is a single, well-defined way of being part of a family, of making the family a vital, nurturant institution. But that element does not trace its own descent from Walt Whitman's America, in which the advance of "opposite equals" is always (and always and always) a part of the "procreant urge of the world." Nor is it a part of the living, breathing, myth-making collectivity — ourselves, you and me — that has spawned and that embraces *Jaws, Close Encounters, E. T.,* and other epics of the Dreamtime. That myth-denying element is the America of Dan Quayle, of the Moral Majority, and of the legions of TV evangelists who preach Dan's "family values" between spots hawking their 800-number donation hotlines.[14] Swipe your plastic for Christ.

What the politicians and pulpitists (and, yes, this includes liberals as well as conservatives) can never get clear about the family, about parenthood and childhood, is that there is absolutely nothing clear about that inherently schismogenic, ambiguous phenomenon. Our thoughts and feelings on the subject are smeared across the continuum of the semiotic poles Us/Self and Them/Other; they comprise a major element of what Whitman, again far more eloquently than I, described as that "knit of identity" that is part of life itself.

Where our politicians, commentators, and evangelists fail us by braying messages we know to be simplistic, our myths faithfully depict the struggle and uncertainty of family life. As a superb myth of the Dreamtime, *Jaws* presents the elemental dilemma of the family with a dramatic clarity we all can grasp.

Brody is not only the pivotal mediator between antagonistic elements of the sea and its creatures, he is also a real/reel-life representation of the unstable compromise we attempt to wrest from the discordant experiences of family life and life in the wider society.

Defending his children pits Brody against that wider society, as represented by the town fathers of Amity, as well as against the shark. Although Amity's mayor has children of his own, he urges them along with other townspeople to go into the surf and enjoy themselves, thus demonstrating to anxious tourists that Amity is a safe, fun place to spend their vacation dollars. The nurturance and unquestioning love that distinguish family ties from wider social relations are constantly threatened and eroded by the demands of the community, whether defined as the village of Amity or the nation-state of the United States. The mayor capitulates to those demands and so loses the very spark and soul that binds him to society in the first place: family life. Brody, ever the tragic figure, discerns his highest duty — to protect his children — and does it, even though that brings him into conflict with the community he has sworn to serve.

The paradox here, as tough a nut to crack as Russell's paradox of the Barber of Seville, is that the family is both the "atom" or "fundamental unit" or "social glue" of society *and* a cauldron of emotion whose turbulence constantly threatens to upset the arms-length, even-keel arrangements on which society depends. The family, specifically that Whitmanesque "knit of identity" of the parent-child relationship, is an explosive, anarchic force that, if allowed to develop unchecked, would spell big trouble for any complex society such as the United States. That's why they make first grade.[15]

Society, that complicated web of jobs, offices, and responsibilities, inevitably creates soul-wrenching dilemmas for its most conscientious citizens, who refuse to abandon their all-too-real family values in favor of Dan's sickening cant while going about their lives as members of a community. Thus Brody, arch-mediator that he is, is the police chief forced to play an anti-establishment role. His concerns as a parent overcome his obligation to be a Yankee version of a good ol' boy.

To the extent possible in a contradiction-fraught world, Brody resolves the discordant domains of land and sea, of ecology and blood lust, and of family and society. He does not, however (nor could any mythic figure), silence the cries of anguish from deep within the human spirit that drive the generative processes of culture. Nor does he in fact *solve* the crucial issues he *resolves*. Despite our best ecological intentions (and elaborately choreographed charades), we continue to send countless species of living creatures to oblivion, impoverishing, perhaps forever, the biodiversity of our planet. And despite Dan's rhetoric and that of much, much wiser individuals, we continue to destroy the emotional basis of any social relation as we allow parenthood and childhood to bleed away, drop by drop, into jobs, school assignments, eight-hour-a-day television marathons, alcohol, cocaine, family counselors, and, when all is lost, divorce courts with their vicious, child-destroying custody battles (and, no, few end as positively as *Mrs. Doubtfire*). It turns out that *Jaws* features two endangered species. One, of course, is the Great White Shark. The other is the American family.

The Collapse of a Dichotomy:
Mechanistic Animals and Animalistic Machines in *Jaws* and *Jurassic Park*

> *What we are dealing with here is a perfect engine, an eating machine. It's really a miracle of evolution. All this machine does is swim and eat and make little sharks. And that's all.*
>
> — Matt Hooper, *Jaws* (the movie)

We end this cultural analysis of the *Jaws* media-myth as it began: by confronting contradiction and paradox. Our involvement with animals goes as deep as our comprehension, and then keeps on going. For the blush of sapience that tinges the human brain issues from animalian sources we all recognize (if we are not exactly quick to acknowledge). Our consciousness — quite probably an evanescent, flukish product of evolutionary and environmental circumstances impossible to duplicate — reaches through the highly touted cerebral areas of the brain to the limbic and motor cortex we share with all mammals, and on to the uncomprehending, instinctual perceptions and reactions of the reptilian brainstem. Because our involvement with animals surpasses our ability to comprehend, the profundity of our ambivalence toward them similarly knows no bounds.[16] We are simultaneously animals and their antithesis, ecologically-minded empathizers with our fellow creatures and brutal masters willing to subject them to any fate that will further whatever end we desire.

Our involvement with animals and our profound ambivalence toward them are the driving forces behind the supergrosser phenomenon of *Jaws*. Spielberg's artistry in manipulating those forces has brought the crowds thronging through the turnstiles to watch Chief Brody, Matt Hooper, and Quint do battle with the Great White Shark. But Spielberg has not willed those forces into being. *That* is accomplished through the action of the generative processes of culture, operating upon and within the semiotic polarities that circumscribe semiospace. The great white shark and other beasts are of such crucial importance to human existence because they represent or flesh out the semiotic domain, Animal. That domain in turn is a dynamic element at work, in the context of the other semiotic domains of culture, on the infinitely complex task of drawing and redrawing the boundaries of humanity, of a fundamental *Us-ness*.

A tremendous importance attaches to the antinomy Animal <-----> Artifact/Machine, for nothing like humanity would have emerged from the evolutionary stew of organisms on planet Earth had it not been a factor early in the development of the hominid line. Sapience emerged in a painfully slow, halting fashion among a succession of hominid species (the several australopithecines, *Homo habilis*, *Homo erectus*, and archaic *Homo sapiens*) whose members depended for their tenuous survival on their ability to find food and to avoid becoming food on the African savannas they shared with four-legged predators far more capable than themselves. These alimentary basics awarded credits for smarts: smarts in interpreting the actions of the many animals on the savanna, and smarts in coming up with a means of killing or scavenging some for food while staying alive to enjoy it. The conceptual surround or *Umwelt* that began to form in the mist-shrouded consciousness of early hominids (Poe has been with us for a long, long time) thus already incorporated as a major part of its framework the interlinked Animal – Artifact/Machine opposition.

The conceptual surround was a product of an embryonic *artifactual intelligence* which ever so slowly began to associate its (principally) visual perceptions of the things around it with its nascent ability to fabricate *new* things, or artifacts. Those artifacts in turn began to modify the behavior of that intelligence in significant ways. What was to become human consciousness thus evolved by building on these key modes of experience. Visual perception and muscular coordination of the hands stimulated a neurological synthesis of unprecedented importance for the future of the hominid line, an ongoing synthesis that is as crucial and as problematic today as it was on the Pleistocene savannas.

The crucial synthesis of eye, hand, and object has fueled a paradox that burns as intensely today as at any time in our hominid prehistory: Through our agency artifacts acquire a life, an *animateness*, of their own and take their place in a world populated by other animate beings, principally the *animals* that occupy so large a place in our thoughts and actions. It is impossible to conceive of a human experience of animal life without somehow invoking the artifactual basis of that experience. And it is equally impossible to conceive of a human use of artifacts that occurs outside the world of animate beings.[17]

Commonsense tells us that nothing should be simpler than keeping animals distinct from machines, yet our efforts to make that fundamental distinction — *to draw that line* — prove incredibly difficult. A sure sign of the trouble we have in bringing off the distinction is the shrillness, the ideological fervor, with which we insist on its validity. If we happen to be conservatives of one stripe or another (and Rush Limbaugh's ample frame accommodates many persuasions here), we insist on the natural, divinely ordained separation of an exalted Man and His Works from the base and, well, *bestial* world of animals. *We* possess an intelligence, a culture, and perhaps even a soul that *they* cannot begin to match. On the other hand (and here the dialectical interplay of the semiotic polarities again makes strange bedfellows!) if we happen to be liberals anxious to establish our ecological credentials, no theme is dearer to our pink hearts than what evil humans with their infernal machines do to defenseless animals struggling to survive in a "developed," civilized world. Now the shoe (damned artifactual metaphor!) is on the other foot: *we* with our machines are the mindless, impulsive louts hell-bent on destroying a natural order that *they*, in their organismic wholeness, have preserved for hundreds of millions of years.

The essence of myth is its ambivalence, its ceaseless struggle to have things both ways, to resolve unresolvable dilemmas. Nowhere is this feature of myth more evident than in the semiotic antinomy Animal – Artifact/Machine, for just as we insist on the absolute separation of these two classes of beings, so we argue that they are essentially the same. Western thought at least since the seventeenth century is infused with a naturalistic, scientific bias (which, remember, is largely the stereotypical "science" of the popular imagination, and not what living, breathing scientists do in their laboratories every day) that all life consists of physical processes which may be studied as one studies any physical system, including machines. Animals are simply very complicated machines. It is just that their parts are made of flesh and bone rather than metal and plastic, and the processes that animate them are biological and chemical rather than mechanical and electrical.[18]

And so *Jaws* is replete with the most stark, Cartesian descriptions of an animal we are likely to find in the vast corpus of our popular culture. Matt Hooper's words at the beginning of this section are one example; the passage from Benchley's novel that serves as an introductory quotation to this chapter is another. A third is again provided by the novel, whose opening lines leave no doubt as to where along the semiotic continuum Animal <-----> Artifact /Machine the Great White Shark hunts.

> The great fish moved silently through the night water, propelled by short sweeps of its crescent tail. The mouth was open just enough to permit a rush of water over the gills. There was little other motion: an occasional correction of the apparently aimless course by the slight raising or lowering of a pectoral fin — as a bird changes direction by dipping one wing and lifting the other. The eyes were sightless in the black, and the other senses transmitted nothing extraordinary to the small, primitive brain. The fish might have been asleep, save for the movement dictated by countless millions of years of instinctive continuity: lacking the flotation bladder common to other fish and the fluttering flaps to push oxygen-bearing water through its gills, it survived only by moving.

We have met this creature before, this animate, purposeful *IT* that infuses meaning and drama in every James Bond and Luke Skywalker adventure. In those movies, *it* is the host of machines, some personal and friendly, some corporate or governmental and hostile, that envelope the human spirit in their mechanosemiotic webs. In *Jaws*, *it* is the completely anonymous fish, a being without personality, without spontaneity, and seemingly without thought processes higher than mere reflex action. *It* moves by sweeps of *its* crescent tail; *its* tail drops beneath the surface; *its* great head rears up, eyes black and abysmal. *It* is a perfect engine, a killing machine. The passage could describe a nuclear submarine or an intercontinental ballistic missile as well as a great white shark, for all amount to the same thing. All are a remorseless death in motion.

Lacking a spirit, which traditionally totemistic cultures readily confer on animals but which our monotheistic culture denies them, and presumably lacking even feelings, we are free to hate the shark unequivocally, to wish to see it destroyed. Spielberg and Benchley artfully oblige us, granting us the spectacle of a bloodbath to slake our suppressed blood lust for animals, all served up in the truly mythic proportions of the giant screen with its myriad coordinated speakers. The Great White Shark thus takes its place alongside the devilish machines James Bond and Luke Skywalker confront and destroy. And when, in the final moments of the film, Chief Brody closes the collective *j-a-w-s* of civilization on the beast, the explosive sound is of the collapse of a dichotomy fundamental to our nature(s).

This collapsing dichotomy of Animal and Machine is at once an integral feature of contemporary American life and a source of its fundamental transformation. The collapse presages storm clouds, and storm clouds signify turbulence. The change that turbulence brings, of course, is chaotic, undirected, and unpredictable. *Jaws* in essence strips off the nicely tailored gloves (physical and mental) we customarily wear in our dealings with animals and goes at that delicate relationship in a raw, bare-knuckled free-for-all. In that melee a principal victim is our very concept of "animals" and how they differ from machines. *Jaws* is schismogenesis laid bare, the filmic version of Gregory Bateson's classic study of the Iatmul tribe of New Guinea highlanders in *Naven*.[19]

Jaws is thus conceptually devastating as well as emotionally draining. The fish leaves a symbolic ruin in its wake, leaves us to ponder where we can possibly go from here. Fortunately, we do not have to attempt the impossible task of predicting the future direction of Dreamtime myth's treatment of our relations with animals. Spielberg has already taken care of that. That future is upon us: not twenty years after the release of *Jaws* and its sensational reception, the nation and the world have been rocked by an even more colossal mythic phenomenon in the form of *Jurassic Park*.

A comparison of *Jaws* and *Jurassic Park* is instructive for a number of reasons. As the alpha and (for the time being) omega of supergrossers, they delineate a phenomenon that should be as interesting to historians centuries from now as to present-day film critics, social commentators, and anthropologists. Whether those historians will judge our movies to be an expression of an Age, akin to Gothic cathedrals in the thirteenth century (as I rashly suggested at the beginning of this book) or a sadistic extravagance of a deteriorating civilization — a Roman Circus in Cinemascope and Dolby — is impossible to say. In all likelihood, they will find elements of both in them, along with features we cannot begin to discern in the here-and-now.

But unless civilization gets seriously off the track in the meantime (and, no, there are no guarantees one way or the other there, either), those future historians *will* ponder our movies' cultural significance. They will attempt to reformat the archaic video cassettes and laser discs mouldering in their archives, so that they can sit back (probably with VR helmets strapped over their enlarged noggins and, alas, probably without benefit of Orville Redenbacher's Microwaveable) and see for themselves what all the fuss was about. They, too, will sail with Brody, Hooper, and Quint on the fateful voyage of the *Orca*, although their seas may be as devoid of great white sharks as our Western plains are of dinosaurs. They, too, will hear the thundering approach of the thunder-dragon itself, *T. rex*, and feel the earth shake as it walks in Jurassic Park. The sense or nonsense they make of it all (since we have no way of knowing which and how much) is not as important to us as the sense *we* have, based on how our own historians treat the past, that those movies *will* make an impression, and a large one.

America of 1975 is not the same place as America of 1994: the cultural surrounds or *Umwelten* or bubbles in semiospace are different. Thus we would not expect Spielberg's cinematic representation of our relations with animals in *Jurassic Park* merely to echo those in *Jaws*. Like the closely linked issue of our relations with machines, how we think about and act toward animals have changed a great deal over that twenty-year period.

While fundamental change *has* occurred, I would argue that its *direction* (or vectorial alignment in semiospace) has not. Throughout the earlier sections of this chapter I have argued that *Jaws* is about an increasing polarization in our relations with animals, and a correspondingly increasing guilt we bear toward them. *Jurassic Park* stretches that polarization even further, propelling us into the next millenium with a full-blown identity crisis regarding where we (whatever *that* is) stand with respect to animals and machines.

In just a few decades, we have gone from a predominantly rural and small-town people who still possessed an earthy familiarity with a variety of animals to a (sub)urban nation of commuting couch potatoes who have a hands-on familiarity with very, very few species: primarily the selectively bred cats and dogs we install as surrogate children in our homes. Meanwhile, hardly any of our actual children get up in the morning and milk the cow, feed the chickens, check on the lambs, and then saddle the horse to ride to school. Even to describe a life like that seems to lapse into wistful stereotype, to pretend that the world of *Little House on the Prairie* actually exists in our living memories, and to turn away from a harsh present-day reality in which problems getting to school on time have more to do with avoiding drive-by shootings than doing the morning chores.

But the sense of unreality we derive from such bucolic musings is due more to the blinding pace of change than to our supposed tendency to romanticize the past. The truth is that throughout most of America's brief history, our experience resembled scenes from *Little House on the Prairie* more than television news program footage from the streets of Los Angeles. And, as I have emphasized throughout this chapter, the pace of change has been particularly dazzling where our relations with animals are concerned.

Jaws is about the increasing polarization in those relations at a critical point in our recent cultural history: when the ecology movement was just beginning to apply its own formidable set of jaws to our increasingly tender sensibilities regarding animals. Most of us had already moved off the farm and lost our hands-on familiarity with animals, only to be blind-sided by wild accusations from a new breed of eco-rebel that we were responsible for the suffering of countless animals and seemed bent on destroying animal life on the entire planet. We might not be down on the farm sticking the pig, but we were sure loading up the station wagon with Saran-wrapped pork loins from (where else?) Piggly Wiggly and heading back to the ranch(er) with its double-door GE, where the nearest thing to barnyard animals were the plastic ducks from the local Home and Garden Shoppe stuck into the lawn beside the floral border.

The guilt we already had begun to feel toward animals by the early seventies as a consequence of our estrangement from them was fanned by the nascent ecology movement into a consuming inferno. And the American conscience rapidly became a great deal more schismogenic about animals. *This* is the cultural terrain on which our latest theme park of the consciousness, *Jurassic Park*, is built.

The most important points of comparison between *Jaws* and *Jurassic Park* are the extent to which animals are *distanced* and *mechanized* in the two movies. In casting for an animal enemy for *Jaws*, Spielberg selected a predator as physically and as phylogenetically remote from humans as possible: the great white shark is a solitary, mysterious, and very primitive fish — not at all like the perch and trout we pulled out of the ponds and creeks of our childhood, and certainly not like the grizzlies and mountain lions who are warm-blooded land mammals like ourselves. Since the great white shark is impossible to keep alive in captivity, only a tiny fraction of us has ever seen it in the flesh. The rest of us depend for our knowledge of the beast on the rash of *National Geographic* specials, Jacques Cousteau programs, and the like, which for the first time present us with images of the living creature. But the telling point is that these *are* images, video blips on our television screen, and our perception of the fearsome beast is a world apart from that of the diver suspended, like Matt Hooper, in his flimsy shark cage, gazing into those "black, abysmal eyes" from a distance of a few yards.

The great white shark is actually, as I have referred to it throughout this chapter, the Great White Shark, a media personality whom we know from movies, television specials, talk shows, etc., but whom we do not expect to see in what we nostalgically persist in calling "real life." Its place in American culture is very like that of Clint Eastwood or Madonna. Although (like it or not) they are an inescapable part of our mundane lives, we are not apt to run into them in the supermarket check-out line or even at our friendly neighborhood Anaheim Mobil station. And if, by some remarkable coincidence, we did suddenly find ourselves face-to-face with one of those superstars, we would probably assume that slack-jawed, vacant, gawping stare that has come to be known as being "star-struck." It is not unlike our reaction if, out with a mask and snorkel in hopes of spotting a sea lion off the rocks of La Jolla Cove, we turned to face the toothy grin and those black, black eyes of a great white shark. Like Clint and Madonna, the Great White is a superstar (even Edward Wilson treats it as one in *The Diversity of Life*). And like any superstar, the germ of physical being and personal idiosyncrasy the individual possesses is overwhelmed by his or her (or *its*) mythic aura. We expect Clint, Madonna, and the Great White Shark to be more "reel" than "real," for all are creatures of the Dreamtime.

As I have argued earlier, it is only because the great white shark is so far removed from our lives that we were able to give ourselves over to the blood lust of the hunt for it in *Jaws*. Otherwise, our newly awakened ecological conscience of the seventies would already have made us uneasy about causing an animal pain. The succeeding twenty years have now made even that arrangement untenable. Distant as the great white shark is, our ecological nerves have been scraped raw by the newfound sentiment that it is a majestic beast, an essential key to the viability of the predator-prey food chain of the sea, and, most alarming of all, itself an endangered species. If *Jaws* were released in 1994, I think it is a sure bet that it would set off a certain amount of ecological protest. Theatres would be picketed, TV talk shows would fill up with marine biologists and Greenpeace types anxious to dispel the harmful stereotypes paraded in the movie. The loud hissing sound we would hear would not just be from the pickets, it would be the sound of the fun, the release, the magical catharsis of living myth going out of *Jaws*.

And this would happen despite the fact that *Jaws* at the time was unprecedented as an animal movie which did not involve animals. Spielberg used *mechanical* models of a great white shark (one of which, remember, wound up as a tourist attraction at Universal Studios) in all the memorable close-up scenes. Stock footage of actual sharks swimming in the open ocean provided the necessary filler. Talk about collapsing dichotomies: what at the time was the animal movie of the century generated all its drama using machines.

Jurassic Park takes the next step in culture's relentless appropriation of a natural world by a technological order. In addition to mechanical models of *Jurassic Park*'s dinosaurs, Spielberg and his army of technicians broke new cinematic ground by basing entire scenes around computer-generated electronic images of the beasts. Through prodigious effort, *T. rex* and the raptors were created and animated on disk, and those images were then incorporated frame-by-frame into the "action" shots. The human actors thus found themselves playing out the most dramatic parts of the movie in the presence of phantoms: unseen electronic images that would materialize (like quantum particles from the void) only in the film laboratory. It is a long, long way from life down on the farm. And yet *Jurassic Park* has come just in time, for *images* of imaginary animals do not experience the physical suffering we have come to dread inflicting on actual, living beings — or even mechanical models of them — in everyday life.

With two decades of ecological sensitivity training behind us, we are no longer prepared to cheer Quint on as he fires harpoon after harpoon into the body of the valiant shark (after all, isn't that just how the collective, guilt-ridden "we" nearly wiped out our wise, peaceful friends the whales?). As an endangered species, the great white shark is definitely off limits for that kind of sport. But how about animals that are already extinct, and, happily, through no fault of our own? How about dinosaurs?

Here we have the perfect solution, served up to us this time through the combined skills of Spielberg and Michael Crichton. Dinosaurs are already dead, so we can't kill them or, just as hard on our eco-sensitized conscience, vicariously participate in killing them in movies. They are the perfect out, the perfect release for our guilt-ridden psyches. *Jurassic Park* depicts dinosaurs as such bloodthirsty, vicious killers that we have no qualms in giving ourselves over to the drama of the hunt: every remaining Pleistocene fiber in our pasty (SPF 15, at least!), oat-bran-crammed bodies struggles to its feet and lets outs a huge, raucous, *Yahoo!* as the movie's heroes go after The Big Meat with a murderous vengeance of their own.

As another set of jaws — the yawning, unfathomable maw of the next millenium — opens before us, it appears that we have at last found a mythic resolution (extreme as always) to the unresolvable conflicts in our relations with animals. Edward Wilson, Jared Diamond, and perhaps even Stefanie Powers have convinced us that we are the executioners in one of the major kill-offs of living things in the last five hundred million years. And while we may agonize over this sickening prospect, we realize full well that, with the human race burgeoning to a global population of six billion, we are locked in a push-comes-to-shove situation. It looks like it's either us or them (but of course, as the ecologists keep saying, if they go then we go with them: the top of the food pyramid doesn't do too well without the base).

At the same time, we expend a great deal of energy in arranging the wholesale death and suffering of countless "domestic" or "experimental" animals — all, of course, for our continued survival and pleasure. Their deaths do not diminish the biodiversity of the planet (a phrase that has become an ideological, mythic emblem in its own right), but they do leave us more blood-stained and guilt-ridden than ever. As true executioners, a part of us has come to blame the victims for their plight: if they were not somehow flawed, we would not have been placed in such a morally indefensible position. And so we come to yearn, from the depths of our souls, as black and abysmal as the shark's eyes, for revenge. We want to strike back, to get even with the animals for the pain their suffering inflicts on us. When we seek that revenge, what better animal victims to strike out at than imaginary, electronic re-creations — images — of an extinct race of monsters themselves so hideously cruel that they deserve everything we can dish out. Dinosaurs are loose in the world.

Disturbing thoughts like these should give us pause when we reflect on the remarkably wide spectrum of appeal dinosaurs have in both our popular and serious culture. They occupy the most prominent spots in our museums; they are the subjects of a welter of television nature programs, popular science books, picture books, even coloring books; they loom up in enormous concrete and plastic reconstructions at truck stops across the Western states; they are the stars of their very own television comedy series; and they inspire the "personage" that is probably the most popular character among children in the nineties: Barney, the lovable purple dinosaur. As the leading naturalist Stephen Jay Gould has summed it up in his book title, *Bully for Brontosaurus*.

Astonishingly, a race of extinct sort-of-reptiles (paleontologists are apparently still thrashing that out) has captured the imagination of an entire society. Adults who don't go near museums turn out for a lecture by a visiting dinosaur expert. And with the release of *Jurassic Park*, several of these experts, including Jack Horner and Robert Bakker, have become media per-sonalities in their own right. Imagine, a cultural phenomenon powerful enough to make celebrities of paleontologists specializing in one-hundred-million-year-old fossils. And as likely as not, the adults at the dinosaur talk have been dragged there by their kids, who turn out to be true cognoscenti of the arcane field, peppering the expert with the most detailed questions at the conclusion of his talk. For all their artistic creativity, Spielberg and Crichton hardly sparked this phenomenal interest in dinosaurs; they simply rode its coattails to the supergrosser movie and the blockbuster bestseller.

But with *Jurassic Park*, Spielberg and Crichton have given the dinosaur phenomenon a new, decidedly twenty-first century twist, and one that greatly impacts our discussion here. For whatever their animalistic or bestial qualities, the dinosaurs of the movie are not really *animals* at all. They are the cutting-edge *products* of a new field of biotechnology that makes literal truth of Descartes's prophetic remarks about the essential identity of animals and machines. Quite apart from the fact that the dinosaurs of the movie are only computer-generated images, their supposed physical beings are themselves the computer-orchestrated results of a DNA cloning experiment. They were put together on a high-tech assembly line, no different in kind from those that turn out our Mustangs and Jaguars (and with the commercial success of the movie, surely Detroit or Tokyo will come up with a *T. REX* to go with the *IROC*).

In one respect this blurring of the animal-machine boundary in *Jurassic Park* is good for our good guilt: we can purge the guilt we feel toward animals while cheering the movie's heroes on to destroy the biotech raptors because those are only counterfeit animals. In wanting to see them destroyed, we are crying out for an end to the infernal, ungodly meddling our species has begun to do with Nature and Her creatures. The raptors are abominations, straight out of Leviticus, and as such are emblematic of what animals are *not* supposed to be. In a supremely adroit bit of cerebral juggling, Spielberg and Crichton have rearranged the contours of our consciences so that we can have our cake and eat it too: we can adhere to our new-found ecological principles to respect all life while we respond to the elemental, Pleistocene thrill of hunting down and killing the raptors.

This line of analysis (as chess players say) leads into a familiar variation, for it returns us to the theme of our relations with machines and the orgies of machine destruction in James Bond movies and *Star Wars*. The fundamental dichotomy collapses (as, being dialectical, it is wont to do), so that we find ourselves facing, with Descartes, a world of undifferentiated *animateness* in which "animals" and "machines" are simply two stages of development (or bioengineering).

In another respect, however, the blurring of the animal-machine boundary in *Jurassic Park* is not very good at all for any sense of equanimity regarding our relations with animals that we might wish to carry with us into the next millenium. For the implications of the movie are deeply troubling. *Jurassic Park* somehow manages to capture, in all the heat of its fast-paced drama, the alarming possibilities that genetic engineering is already beginning to pose. If it is ungodly and unnatural to bioengineer a dinosaur, then so must it be to produce any of the numerous "designer drugs" that we already depend on as our next line of defense against increasingly resistant strains of bacteria and virus. As I write, the first bioengineered food — a tomato — is already causing a stir in the supermarkets of America (some of whose customers, while perfectly content to wolf down huge quantities of steroid and antibiotic-impregnated beef and chicken, are suddenly apprehensive about consuming this new fruit of Satan). The irony here is filled with meaning, for the very different responses individuals have to essentially the same process of modifying food sources indicates that, for them, a line has been crossed.

And since we have become especially sensitive to this business of line-crossing, we have to take notice, to try to understand the cultural principles at work in accepting steroid-soaked beef while rejecting the unassuming, if bioengineered, tomato. What is at stake here, I believe, is nothing less than the sense we have of what it means to be *alive*, to be a living being born of other living beings and not some mechanical object turned out by other mechanical objects. Faced with the anomalies of designer drugs, bioengineered plants and animals, and the spectacular dinosaurs of Jurassic Park, we can react in only one of two ways. We can dig in our heels and make a doctrinaire stand, insisting on the sanctity of a firm, straight line between "natural" and "unnatural" animals, between what is truly alive from what is some fiendish concoction. Or we can begin seriously to entertain, once again, the prospect of a world of labyrinthine lines which trace distinctions that forever cross-cut and contradict themselves, of a world in which being "alive" is an extremely complex, unnatural state.

To its great credit, this is precisely what *Jurassic Park* encourages us to do. Granted, the movie lets us sate our blood lust by going after the raptors and watching as they are destroyed. But it does not then conclude on a self-congratulatory and exhortative note of "good riddance, and let's make sure this fiendish project isn't repeated." In short, *Jurassic Park* does not conclude like *The Thing* (I), with Scotty the journalist (his McCarthyite press credentials secure) imploring us to *watch the skies* for the return of another extraterrestrial monster. Quite the opposite. In an even more unsettling conclusion, *Jurassic Park*'s paleontologist lovebirds marvel at their most important discovery: the bioengineered dinosaurs, supposedly sterile as part of their genetic design, have been hatching eggs. A living force is loose in the world, or soon will be when some nut succeeds in smuggling a few frozen embryos off the island to the mainland. Their own eggs and sperm doubtlessly stirring, the two paleontologists gaze mistily into each other's eyes and marvel at the resilience of nature: life will prevail.

In the curiously warm and tentative glow which the conclusion of *Jurassic Park* instills, we are left to contemplate a world in which the miracle of life fully accommodates whatever we can throw at it. Although this is probably an unwelcome message for doctrinaire ecologists (after all, Dan and George did not corner the market on narrow-mindedness) it is only because it insists on celebrating the open, perpetually evolving nature of those self-organized, self-reproducing complex systems we describe as being "alive." If future terrestrial organisms trace their ancestry to some ancient laboratory presided over by beings who themselves have long since gone on to become Something Else, should that fact stand as an indictment, an accusation that they are somehow inauthentic? Or, to reverse roles, if we could somehow determine that the stardust of which we and every living being on the planet are composed — the atoms of carbon, oxygen, nitrogen, iron and so on — was forged in the stellar furnaces of some ancient, pan-galactic civilization, would that realization in any way lessen the wonder we feel at the incredible generativity and diversity of biological evolution? Dinosaurs, indeed, are loose in the world.

From the perspective of cultural analysis, the extraordinary amount of attention given the bioengineered dinosaurs of *Jurassic Park* indicates that the generative processes of culture are busily at work turning out a new dominant symbol of Dreamtime America, one that will take its place alongside other icons that stand as representations of our fundamental selves. That dominant symbol is nothing short of a redefinition of the semiotic domain, Animal. We have seen in previous chapters how the semiotic domain Artifact/Machine is being radically transformed through the mythic intervention of James Bond movies and *Star Wars*; it is now evident that its opposite number, the domain Animal, is undergoing an equally fundamental transformation.

Contrary to stereotype, the supposedly archaic phenomenon of *totemism*, whose career we have chronicled here, is very much a part of our contemporary lives. Its powerful symbolic lens, capable of generating endless representations of identity, is now trained on the curious, hybrid mix of animal-like machines and machine-like animals proliferating around us. This *new totemism* is with us quite literally from the cradle to the grave, from our first snugglings with the fuzzy, stuffed toy bears and ducks that take the place of human contact, through our ersatz hunts for post-Pleistocene prey with Chief Brody, Matt Hooper, and Quint, and on to our deaths, when the true "loved ones" all too many of us childless, divorced, lonely (post)moderns leave behind will be golden retrievers and Siamese cats.

The images we carry with us, in our hearts and our minds, of the beasts in our lives, like our corresponding images of machines, are terribly important, for they are representations of what we believe the world to be about. They are also representations of what we believe ourselves to be, that shifting, drifting, boundary-hunting quasispecies we call "humanity," which is both animal and machine, and neither.

7

Phone Home
E. T. as a Saga Of the American Family

> *I bring you warning — to every one of you listening to the sound of my voice. Tell the world, tell this to every one wherever they are: Watch the skies. Watch everywhere, keep looking — watch the skies!*
> — Scotty the journalist, *The Thing*
> (member of a polar expedition that just destroyed a marauding alien)

> *Leave him alone! I can take care of him! . . . He needs to go home.*
> — Elliott, *E. T.*

From Creature Feature and Saucer Saga to *E. T.*

The flying saucer hovers menacingly over the massed troops, whose small arms, bazookas, and artillery pieces are trained on the invader. Then the thing lets fly with its death rays. The infantrymen are fried to crisps, vaporized before our eyes. Civilians run screaming through the streets. The saucer lands and the most godawful monstrosities slither out and begin gobbling up the fleeing survivors. It looks like the end of civilization for sure. The bug-eyed monsters are going to win. Then Young Scientist, our hero, hits on the Momentous Discovery: the aliens are vulnerable to fire/water/electricity/corn flakes (choose one of the above). Reinforcements are brought up, supplied with Young Scientist's critical discovery, and they set about dispatching the invaders — the bug-eyed monsters are in for a little crisping and vaporizing of their own. Our hero happily surveys this scene of carnage, with his new love at his side (who is often grouchy Old Scientist's daughter-cum-lab assistant). The alien invaders are killed or routed in this round of *Earth Versus the Flying Saucers* (but *watch the skies!*; you never know when *they* might return) and the world is made safe, at least for the time being, for the American Way.

How many movies like this have you seen (answer to the nearest dozen)? The scenario is the classic formula of fifties and sixties sci-fi, churned out by the studios and served up to a red-baiting, xenophobic audience just waking up to the horror that, after the traumas of the second world war and the Korean "conflict," they were entering an era of nuclear superpowers. From Howard Hawks's 1951 original *The Thing* through John Carpenter's gory 1982 remake (also the year of the release of *E. T.*; how's that for ambivalence?), the saucer saga or creature feature genre has reproduced itself, like one of the horrible bug-eyed mutants it depicts, in countless drive-in epics across the land. In this ocean of cinematic schlock the only variety to be found is in just what kind of hideous being is out to get us — spacemen, giant ants, sickening gobbets of slime that clamp on to the back of your neck, or just the usual bug-eyed monster — and in the character of the hero. Sometimes, in the hardcore drive-in epics, Young Scientist is replaced by Boy With Car (as in the 1958 classic, *The Blob* with Steve McQueen as BWC, which itself earned an eighties knock-off).

Intriguingly, these low-budget saucer sagas proliferated despite the release, right at the beginning of their heyday, of a highly original, pacifist, consider-the-extraterrestrials movie: *The Day the Earth Stood Still*. As I related in the introduction, had I not seen this movie at the tender age of six with my science fiction author-uncle, Roger Aycock, you would probably not be slogging through this ponderous tome. It well and truly sank the hook. *The Day the Earth Stood Still* opens with what was to become *the* stock scene over the ensuing decades: a flying saucer wobbles around the sky over the Washington Monument and Lincoln Memorial before landing near the White House, where it is received by our men in khaki, who proceed to blaze away at the alien invader. But remarkably the lone sort-of human occupant, Klatu (played by Michael Rennie), manages to escape and, even more remarkably, turns out to be quite a swell guy. He takes up residence in a boarding house where a war widow and her ten- or eleven-year-old son also live, and Klatu and the lad become great friends (does this possibly remind you of another movie?). Unlike the endless succession of bug-eyed monsters to follow, it seems that Klatu is wise and good and has come to save Earth from nuclear destruction.

This solitary and brilliant movie, unequalled in my estimation until *E. T.* came along thirty years later, made the rash of saucer sagas seen all the more alike. We became accustomed to witnessing one otherworldly fiend after another being incinerated, drowned, electrocuted, or smothered in corn flakes. And we cheered, or listened to our friends beside us cheer, as the combined might of the American military (with a little help from Young Scientist or Boy With Car) made the world safe for Mom and Dad and Buddy and Sis and the backyard barbecue. Again, this went on for thirty years with barely a let-up.[1] Our boys went out there and blew 'em out of the sky, fried the little geeks, squashed the slimy mothers, and then . . . and then came *E. T.*

What Is E. T.?

E. T. is such a sudden, dramatic change from the slew of earlier saucer sagas that we would certainly have sat up and taken notice of the movie even if it had not been a phenomenal hit at the box office. The fact that the movie was an instant, record-breaking success indicates that its novelty contained messages audiences across the land were waiting to hear. *E. T.*, like James Bond movies, *Star Wars*, and *Jaws* touched a highly sensitive nerve in our collective psyche. The movie is a key element in the complex of myths that make up the American Dreamtime, and so it is necessary to ask, as we did with those other movies, the by-now familiar, unassuming question that guides every cultural analysis: What is *E. T.* about?

Before we can properly address that question, however, it is necessary to pose an even more basic, if rather curious, question about the character itself: What *is* E. T.? The characters of James Bond and Chief Brody do not raise this sort of question, since both are flesh and blood, human heroes. With Luke Skywalker, on the other hand, this basic question regarding the character's identity does loom large. Despite his gee-whiz, country boy personality, as the *Star Wars* trilogy develops Luke begins to acquire bionic prostheses that raise the disturbing issue of just how human Old Luke will be as a venerable Jedi Knight, after two or three centuries of light saber duels with the enemies of Queen Leia's empire.

The character of E. T. confronts us with this fundamental question of identity from the very beginning of the movie. Along with Darth Vader (whose anomalous nature we discussed in chapter 5) and Bo Derek (animal, vegetable, or, most likely, mineral?), E. T. is one of the most enigmatic figures in all of American moviedom. As the movie's title indicates, E. T. is "the extraterrestrial," but that identity is simply a cipher or gateway into other, discrepant identities that negotiate portions of the complex boundary of human-ness. E. T. is several beings in one, a figure that just might have intrigued Whitman.

First of all, of course, E. T. is an extraterrestrial. By definition, saucer sagas and creature features are about strange, alien beings. They provide us with representations of the Other. Or, on a less abstract plane, they are about our beliefs and our fears of *Them* (released in 1954 and featuring twelve-foot mutant ants spawned during the atom bomb tests in the Southwest). For all their fancifulness, these movies zero in on the semiotic domain of Them/ Other, attempting to give form and substance to the ineluctable and often repressed images we harbor of what life is like *over there*, in a world defined by its absence of Us. However, writers of science-fiction novels and screenplays, like their cousins the quantum physicists, realize that it is an impossible task to represent a world that excludes us; the measurer must be there to take the measurement, the human host or victim must be there to receive the alien.

Science-fiction writers in particular recognize the dialectical nature of their subject matter: they know that images of aliens are effective only to the extent that these plumb uncharted depths of the human condition. It is the essential, *intersystemic* action between Them and Us that makes the story, that produces myth.

Still, the saucer sagas and creature features that have poured out of the studios over the past forty years have taken an extremely timid, myopic approach to their dynamic, inherently dialectical subject matter. Having introduced the alien with great fanfare, these movies make a point of keeping their distance from it, and in the process keep us in the audience distant from it as well. Generally, we are allowed to get up close to the alien only during stereotyped attack scenes, when the slathering, slithering, bug-eyed horror is coming right at us, its tentacles flopping and its multiple jaws hinging wide to devour us. But do we get to see what the *Alien* does on its coffee break, or what it does about lunch when we aren't it? Do we get to see the alien when it is just hangin' with its homeies, or when it is spending quality time with its little baby aliens? Hardly ever.[2]

The saucer sagas, although they rely on the dramatic device of strangers-among-us, carefully segregate the alien, confining it to the fringes of our experience, the exotic moments of our social life. They send it out to take on the U. S. Army or, even scarier for it, Arnold Schwarzenegger (as Dutch) in *Predator* (hands down, the best rip-snorting action movie ever made). But they never show it dropping in on the Johnsons for a beer. Or they didn't, until *E. T.* appeared with its hilarious scene of the little alien and the family mutt raiding the double-door while the family is out (E. T. pops a couple of Coors — Silver Bullets! — and gets plastered, telepathing its condition to Elliott, who proceeds to make his grade school science class a memorable event).

As I have argued with regard to *Jaws* and Spielberg's work as a whole, the truly remarkable thing about *E. T.* is its insistence on placing an ordinary American family and, particularly, its children at the very center of the action. This point informs the whole of the present chapter, but it is essential to note it here because any discussion of the character of E. T. requires us to ask how we come to know the character. If the alien spends all its time on the battlefield trading death rays for flying lead, we hardly get a chance to know it in its more domestic moments. *E. T.* is such a thorough, consummate study of an alien's character precisely because it introduces the alien into a family, where it becomes fast friends with a young boy. In the best ethnographic tradition (which the discipline of anthropology has not quite choked off entirely), we get to know E. T. through its *friendship* and, really, *kinship* with Elliott, and not through a sterile, scientistic procedure of fact-finding and analysis. As Elliott says at the crisis point of the movie, when it appears that E. T. has died despite the efforts of the medical team to revive it, "They're just going to cut him all up."

Seen close at hand, in the setting of Elliott's room and that gigantic walk-in closet the kids share, the character of E. T. is a complex and contradictory set of identities — just what we would expect from the very best of Dreamtime mythic heroes. It comprises, at the very least, the disparate roles of fairy, religious saviour or spirit, animal, Master of Machines (in the dual veins of South American Indian mythology and of James Bond and Luke Skywalker), friend, and father. Each of these needs a brief separate discussion.

E. T. has often been likened to a fairy tale, although usually with the intent of dismissing it as unworthy of the attention Serious Cinema merits. But in truth E. T. *is* much more like a fairy than it is like any of the bug-eyed monsters from *It Came from Outer Space* to *Alien* that have rampaged across the movie screens of America. Consider the opening scene of the movie. It is night in a mysterious, fog-shrouded forest, filled with strange shapes and spooky noises. There are several squat, shadowy figures moving about the forest floor, startling the resident bunnies and deer and collecting the occasional plant. One immediately thinks of wood sprites rather than man-eating aliens. Right in the middle of this whole scene is a twinkling artifact that resembles a giant Christmas tree ornament, the decidedly low-tech, nostalgic starship that has brought E. T. and its shipmates to Earth.

The entire scene conjures up images from *Peter Pan* rather than *Star Trek* or any of the other, much lower-budget saucer sagas. And this association is intensified as the sound track insinuates a musical theme reminiscent of *Peter Pan*. Then just to drive the point home, in case you were still stocking up on four-dollar popcorn, nachos, and movie weenies at the concession stand during the opening minutes of the show, there is the touching scene mid-way through the movie in which Mother Mary (Dee Wallace) is reading *Peter Pan* as a bedtime story to daughter Gertie (Drew Barrymore) with E. T. peeking at them through the louvered slats of that hurmongus closet: "If you believe in fairies, say 'Yes, yes I believe.'" And bright little Gertie, knowing a real, live fairy is only a few feet away, can respond fervently, "I believe. I believe."

E. T.'s likeness to a fairy, however, is tempered by its solemn disposition and ominous power. These aspects of the character are more closely tied to that of a religious saviour or spirit — a Messiah figure — than to a light-hearted Peter Pan-type sprite. With its glowing, pulsating Sacred Heart and its luminous healing touch, E. T. evokes strong religious associations from anyone in the audience predisposed to thoughts about Messiahs (whether in the elevated vein of God and Man touching in Michelangelo's painting or our more recent, diminished saviours in the guise of Jim Jones, Reverend Moon, and David Koresh). That we have suffered through these characters and still seem to be on the lookout for others is a chilling reminder of how deeply our longing for a Messiah figure penetrates our supposedly secular — all dressed up and off to The Mall — lives.

Intriguingly, E. T.'s Coming could not have been better scripted to reach the hearts and minds of contemporary Americans. The little extraterrestrial does not show up in Washington, D. C., with a hackneyed "take me to your leader" speech. Nor does it present itself to the savants of the Institute for Advanced Study at Princeton, or any of the other high-powered think tanks across the country (since it has the power of flight or levitation, surely it could have beamed itself across the mental desert of San Fernando Valley slurbs where Elliott lives to Pasadena, where the big thinks swimming in the tank at Cal Tech would have given it a hearty welcome). Instead, E. T.'s Coming, like Christ's, is to the common people — and a southern California stucco-and-tile tract house with its single-parent family and a ton of toys and gadgets is our version of Bethlehem, of Everyman. E. T. inserts itself right smack in the middle of that culture of consumer capitalism which is both the American Dream and, as Sly says in *Cobra*, your worst nightmare.

E. T.'s attributes of fairy and religious saviour identify it with the Life Force; it is a highly effective symbol of our inchoate sense of the power, the irrepressible animation of living things (and as such, in the quantum physics-like world of anthropological semiotics, E. T. is a kind of antiparticle version of that old avatar of the Death Force, Darth Vader). But the character of E. T. spills over into other domains of semiospace. It is, for example, in some ways an animal.

Consider for a moment what E. T. looks like. Disregarding the fact that it is supposed to be an extraterrestrial, what is its nearest living relative on earth? I would suggest that it is the Galapagos turtle, minus its immense shell. With a length of four feet and a weight of several hundred pounds, this remarkable animal has a head about the size of a child's. And that head, flattened frontally to suppress the prominent beak, is the spitting image of E. T. As a frequent visitor to the San Diego Zoo, where I go as much to witness the fascinating zoosemiotic encounters between people and exotic animals as to stand sentinel over the Great Extinction already underway, I have on several occasions observed individuals making this connection themselves. "Hey, look! It's E. T.!"

The Galapagos turtle enclosure at the San Diego Zoo is just a low wall, with a couple of dozen of those nearly extinct giants oh-so-slowly moving about their ample yard (if you're looking for action, you have to come during the spring mating season, when these giants perform some prodigious balancing acts in the name of Eros). Oddly, the turtles occasionally seem to seek out human contact — and not for tidbits of food, which are strictly *verboten* — and approach the wall to present their extended heads for human visitors to touch and stroke. Their leathery skin is surprisingly soft, and as the visitor strokes it their lambent eyes assume a very, well, E. T.-like expression. Then the head, extended on its stalk of a neck, is tentatively moved or withdrawn. It is hauntingly reminiscent of the good-bye scene in *E. T.*, when brother Michael gingerly reaches out to touch E. T.'s head and E. T. at first recoils but then allows the contact. That scene is repeated countless times at the turtle enclosure and, whatever the turtles may be experiencing, their human admirers give every indication of awe at this close encounter with an alien intelligence that gazes back at them from the perspective of a century of life on this shrinking planet.

Then there is the matter of E. T.'s voice. Whatever we may think about E. T. resembling this or that animal, there is no question that E. T. "speaks" through most of the movie in animal sounds, or synthesized renditions of animal sounds. Recall our little experiment in chapter 5, in which we closed our eyes and just *listened* to *Star Wars* unfold around us. Our ears were filled with the myriad beeps and whistles of a menagerie of droids, interspersed with the occasional inanity from Luke, Han, or Princess Leia. Particularly in the climactic assault on the Death Star, the sounds of *Star Wars* were indistinguishable from those in a video arcade. We found ourselves listening to the mechanosemiotic discourse of machines as they produced incredibly fast-paced, compellingly dramatic action *in the virtual absence of human language*. Much the same thing occurs in *E. T.*, although here the basic audio channel consists of an impressive collection of animal, rather than machine, sounds.

This comparison is hardly forced, for the same technical wizards at Lucasfilms' Industrial Light and Sound who crafted the sounds of *Star Wars* also assembled and composed the animal cries and calls that make up E. T.'s voice. We come to know E. T. by means of a remarkably wide range of snorts, grunts, chuffles, moans, and screeches that are of animal origin, however reshaped they may have been by the banks of synthesizers at Lucasfilms.

If E. T.'s appearance and voice are animal-like, so is its behavior. We are introduced to E. T. at the beginning of the movie, not as it operates the controls on the flight deck of its starship, but as it savors the organic delicacies of the forest, along with the deer and rabbit with whom it seems to share a bond of kinship. In this mode of its character, E. T. evokes in us much of the range of thoughts and feelings that Flipper, Willy, Lassie, and Bambi do: it is the sweet, adorable, and vulnerable creature of nature whose life hangs in the balance of our blindly mechanistic society. In this respect, *E. T.* has more in common with *Watership Down* than with *Star Wars* or its accompanying rash of high-tech thrillers.

Machines at Home: The Suburban Family in a Technological State

E. T.'s other attributes (those of Master of Machines, friend, and father) combine to form a principal theme of the movie: the dilemma of the American family in the technological society of the *fin de siecle* United States.

In discussing *Jaws* in the previous chapter, I argued that the family, or specifically the parent-child relationship, is a source of the schismogenesis that rends American culture. We want to believe that the parent-child bond is the very basis of every other social relation, that it is the fundamental unit of a social system, the social glue that binds the larger, more complex parts of society together. But paradoxically, as Chief Brody's tragic situation demonstrated, one can honor the commitment that fatherhood entails only by breaking the covenant that makes one a full member of a community. Face-to-snout with the Great White Shark, Brody's duty to his children conflicted with his duty to the village of Amity. As we other boundary hunters pick our way over the same jumbled, impossible terrain of late twentieth century America, we are forever confronted with this intractable centripetal-centrifugal problem.

In *E. T.* the rending force of schismogenic paradox has only grown more intense. *Jaws* at least presents us with a whole family — Mom and Dad and Buddy and Sis — just like we see in *Leave It To Beaver* and just like we read about in those insufferably boring (and unreel) introductory sociology text-books. And that whole family lives in a whole community: the village of Amity is a cozy collection of a few cottages and beach houses, where everybody knows everybody else and where we immediately get to know its mayor, the town doctor, and, of course, the police chief. The scene of the Brody family against the quaint tableau of Amity might have been a subject for Norman Rockwell — but he would probably not have painted in the fearsome thing in the water just offshore.

Elliott's family and "community" are an entirely different matter. In fact, they appear positively *alien* when placed against the backdrop of the Brody family or of Beaver Cleaver's family. Things change fast, and they change a lot. In the words of Jimmy Buffett's immortal ballad, "We are the people our parents warned us about." But that change is often not the fun and games Buffett's song makes it out to be. The father/husband has abandoned Elliott, Michael, Gertie, and their mother Mary, and run off to Mexico with some cookie named Susan. He has left behind a shocked, grieving, atomistic collection of individuals (note that the script never gives this family a last name) who hunker down in their tract house located on the edge of a sea of nearly identical, equally anonymous houses. Many of those houses in that notorious valley (Oh, my Ga-hd! You're from the Va-el-ly too! To-tal-ly awe-some!), of course, shelter equally fragmented lives. Remember, nothing is whole; it is a world of intersystems.

In that trackless wasteland, that immense sea of lights waiting just over the edge of the hill where E. T.'s starship has landed in mist-shrouded, fairyland forest, there can be no suggestion of community. We do not meet the mayor, town doctor, and police chief of Elliott's "village," much less see them as major characters in the drama that unfolds. Except for the memorable scene in Elliott's grade school science class, details of the world outside the home are provided only in the most fragmented, anonymous way, obviously choreographed by Spielberg to make his point about the nature of "community" in Elliott's southern California megalopolis.

In *Jaws* we are given enough information about the venal mayor to know him (and despise him) as a person. In *E. T.*, menacing, mysterious authority figures are forever lurking on the fringes of Elliott's family life. They are the shadowy figures in the 4x4s that initially surprise E. T. and its shipmates. They are the faceless technicians in the sinister black vans jammed with electronic easedropping equipment and parked outside Elliott's house. They are, in perhaps the most staggering scene of the movie, the spacesuit-clad figures that burst into the family's home to capture E. T. The message is unmistakable: the larger society — the people who run things — is as menacing and alien to the life of Elliott's family as any slithering monstrosity from the saucer sagas. In a stunning reversal of semiotic polarities, We (our own kind) become Them (lurking, menacing authority figures), while They (an alien from another world) become Us (a loved and trusted family member).

The strangeness and hostility of life outside the family is mitigated only by the intriguing character Keys (he does not have a name in the movie and is identified in the credits on the basis of the key ring he wears on his belt). Although Keys makes his appearance in the opening scene (he is apparently the leader of the saucer-trackers who surprise E. T. in the forest and cut it off from its ship), we see only his waist with that set of keys jangling on their ring. In his several subsequent appearances the same waist-high shot is adopted (had Keys been female, Spielberg would have been assailed for chauvinism as well as pandering to the mob). Keys acquires a face (that of Peter Coyote) only in the final episodes, when Elliott and E. T. are near death and being ministered to by the medical crew that has occupied and quarantined Elliott's home.

Keys is rather like Francois Truffaut's saucer-hunting character in *Close Encounters*: both are scientists driven by an obsession to meet aliens, and both defy the militaristic power of the State while working for it. But Keys fills other roles as well. By the concluding scene he has become a (very) tentative father/husband figure for the family abandoned by its own deadbeat dad. He and Mom look on side-by-side while the kids say their goodbyes to E. T. before it waddles up the ramp of its ship. It is a semblance of the all-American family, and as such is both a painful reminder that all is not well with Elliott's human household and a glimmer of hope that maybe, just maybe Mom will strike some sparks with this rocket scientist. Will Elliott be getting a new Dad to take the place, not only of his real father, but of his departing friend and ersatz father as well?

It is the sparks Keys strikes with E. T., however, that are of particular interest to us here. For the two characters are contrapuntal representations — two faces — of the rapidly changing role of science and technology in everyday life (Note that we never stray far from this topic!). Keys represents the impersonal, intrusive, and menacing aspect of machines under the control of a correspondingly impersonal, intrusive, and menacing State. Elliott and his family are Little People whom fate brings into conflict with Big Government and Big Machines. And while Keys is hardly a blast-em-out-of-the-skies military type,[3] the technology he commands is enough to scare *The Living Daylights* out of Elliott's family.

E. T., on the other hand, has no fleet of vans or cadre of technicians at its disposal. A striking feature of the movie is E. T.'s ability to work magic with the small, domestic machines, the heaped debris of a culture of consumer capitalism, it finds lying around Elliott's home. When E. T. conceives the idea to Phone Home (while looking at a sci-fi comic strip), the parts it uses to build a transmitter do not come from an electronics lab at Cal Tech. They are a sheet of Reynolds Wrap aluminum foil and a fork from the kitchen, a small rotary hand-saw blade from the deadbeat Dad's old workbench in the garage, and the Speak N' Spell toy ("pho-ne ho-me!") E. T. had used earlier to learn a little English.

E. T. is awash in brand name merchandise, from Elliott's first efforts to explain his life to the little visitor (when he brandishes a shiny red-and-white can of Coca-Cola and says, "See, this is Coke. We drink it."), through E. T.'s raid on the refrigerator with its six-pack of Coors, to the final close-ups of the Speak N' Spell transmitter in the woods. And these products are displayed, not, as cynics suggest, solely for the hefty endorsement fees they bring, but because they are a fundamental part of Elliott's suburban life. Spielberg succeeds so well in conveying a sense of the domesticity of Elliott's home precisely because he includes so many of the things that make a southern California house a home.

Elliott, Michael, and Gertie, like millions of other kids growing up in late twentieth-century America, are Children of the Mall, young addicts of that culture of consumer capitalism whose very essence is the spewing out of products that we want to own. Since their subdivision neighborhooods were built yesterday and have no tradition, since their Mom and Dad are always out on the endless commute, since their grandparents live a thousand miles away, and since their school is a prison sentence, our children's friendships and passions — their lives — outside the home center on the mall. There, in the nacho stands and pizzerias of the Food Court (teriyaki tacos, anyone?), the raucous video arcade, the shops with every youth accessory, the parking garage with its illicit skateboarding ramps, and, not least, the Cineplex 10 with the current batch of Dreamtime myths, these children of the mall, who are also the future of America, live out their childhood. There they acquire the going version of "humanity."

E. T. thus chronicles a fundamental transformation in our relations with artifacts: the stuffed toys, plastic soldiers, beer cans, television sets, home fix-it-up saws, and Speak N' Spell machines have *moved in*. They have filled up the domestic space of the American home, displacing in large measure the cozy family confabs and meals that once made the house alive. Watch a couple of *Leave It To Beaver* shows and then a few scenes from *E. T.* and you will see two quite distinct domestic orders, two ways of organizing the Us-ness of American culture. In *Beaver* the few artifacts given any prominence — an occasional baseball mitt, a bike — are important only to the extent that they figure into the little morality plays orchestrated by Dad (and Ward Cleaver is definitely not the deadbeat variety). In *E. T.* the whole morality play angle has been tossed out, along with the orchestrating Dad, and life before E. T. comes along is mostly a matter of kids relating to other kids through the mediating services of artifacts. Tellingly, the heart of the household in *E. T.* is not the family dinner table (where sage Wade instructed), but the kids' closet, where they can retreat to the mechanosemiotic pleasures of the stacked consumer goods, brought from Toys R Us in (Audi) carloads to fill up the absence at the center of domestic life.

At the same time, this appropriation of domestic space by machines continues and deepens a process we have identified in earlier movies: our abiding love for small, personal machines and our hatred of the large, impersonal machines that are the instruments of State suppression. In this respect, E. T. continues where James Bond and Luke Skywalker left off.

As we saw in chapters 4 and 5, Bond and Skywalker are masters of small, hand-held machines which they handle with great finesse in destroying the lumbering behemoths that megalomaniac scientists and evil emperors send against them. In this way they humanize machines, but only in the public arena of the battlefield. We never get to see whether and how artifacts are part of Bond's and Skywalker's domestic lives; in fact, we never get to see much of their domestic lives at all. James Bond movies and *Star Wars* depict machines as belonging exclusively to the public sector of life, where they figure in military battles and the corporate blood-letting of business. *E. T.* shows us that the province of machines extends into the heart of the domestic world, into the suburban family that coexists with the encompassing technological State. There their mechanosemiotic webs, the welter of human-machine interaction and interthinking, fill the void left by atrophying human emotions and relationships.

If Bond and Skywalker evoke our deeply ingrained feeling for the underdog (the David and Goliath theme) E. T. and Elliott pluck those same heart strings for all they are worth. They endear themselves by taking on an army of technicians and military security men with little more than mountain bikes and a few toys — and winning. And whereas the armed might that Bond and Skywalker faced was confined to faraway, exotic locales or the reaches of space, E. T. and Elliott have to withstand an invasion of high-tech enemies into their only retreat: their home. In this way *E. T.* anticipates the stunning porno-violence of *Terminator*, which is so terrifying because the Schwarzenegger-android searches out its victims in their homes and kills them without a second thought.

As a master of domestic machines, E. T. possesses a bag of tricks that are beyond even Bond and Skywalker. Although the rubber balls, mountain bikes, aluminum foil, and so on E. T. has to work with are pretty unglamorous when compared with Q's high-tech goodies or Luke's light saber and tie-fighter, E. T. performs miracles with them. Through E. T.'s agency the rubber balls levitate and form themselves into a miniature solar system, the mountain bikes fly, and the aluminum foil becomes part of an otherworldly communications device. E. T. (again, with its Sacred Heart) can even raise the dead: the wilted plant it restores is one of the movie's emblems of the little alien's life-giving power.

Edmund Leach, in *Culture and Communication*, argues that there is no clear-cut distinction between science and magic (thus undermining one of the cherished principles at anthropology's Victorian origins). As an example, he cites a situation in which someone from a remote, primitive village (a "native") is suddenly placed in a modern home. The individual is sitting there when his host enters the room, reaches out and touches something on the wall — and the room is instantly, miraculously bathed in light. What for the host is the reflex action of switching on a light is for his guest magic, pure and simple. Moreover, the host's efforts to "demystify" the experience by explaining to the indigenous Australian or Amazonian Indian the rudiments of electricity, power generation, and glowing filaments can only deepen the mystery from that individual's perspective. As a powerful, invisible force that acts instantaneously over a distance to produce the most dramatic results, "electricity" has to sound a lot like the white man's word for "magic."

Or, to put the matter in a temporal rather than spatial perspective, if you want to see magicians at work, come back in a couple of thousand years.

Arthur Clarke made this same point by noting that magic is simply any sufficiently advanced technology. Clarke's aphorism suits the story of E. T. perfectly, for in that movie as in Clarke's futuristic novels it is we who are the slack-jawed natives recoiling in dumb amazement when our extraterrestrial guest switches on the equivalent of its light bulb. E. T. is for us a *sorcerer*: a being skilled in techniques that achieve wondrous, supranatural effects. But unless we are prepared to believe that E. T.'s glowing "heart" is an innate aspect of its religious, Messianic nature, we have to consider that the organ is a superbly engineered energy source capable of keeping E. T. going in an alien environment while piloting squadrons of mountain bikes to boot. E. T. may "have DNA" as the medical team discovers, but it must also be a sublime synthesis of organic and manufactured parts. Whether we call it a cyborg, an android, a robot, or whatever, what we mean at bottom is that E. T., for all its lovable spontaneity, is a machine. It is R2D2 crossed with a Galapagos turtle. Perhaps that's where E. T.'s DNA came from? Or perhaps the turtle got its

DNA from an E. T. who visited the planet when the San Fernando valley was still a smoldering volcanic slag heap?

This exotic little being, whose doings have awed a generation of movie-goers, combines its disparate attributes into an overwhelmingly seductive image. E. T. holds out for us what, recalling Victor Turner's phrase, is a "realm of pure possibility," in which the shoddy, recalcitrant consumer items we enslave ourselves to own miraculously live up to their Madison Avenue billing — and more. Rubber balls and mountain bikes are shown to be capable of fundamentally transforming experience, of lifting us (literally!) from the everyday world of gut-churning anxieties — the deadbeat Dad, the whopping mortgage on that little tract-home slice of the American Dream, the coming storms of adolescence, the looming senescence of adulthood — to a magical world where things are whole, where the family is united in common cause, and where the family's closetfulls of dull possessions acquire a luster that outshines everything the menacing outside world has to offer.

Monsters at Home: *E. T.* and *Poltergeist*

It is night and everyone in Elliott's household is asleep. E. T. is stashed away in that phenomenal closet, camouflaged from Mom's prying eyes among the heap of stuffed animals. Then, as Dennis Hopper says in the Nike commercial (a long way down the highway from *Easy Rider* and *Apocalypse Now*, Dennis!), Bad Things start to happen. First E. T.'s magical, mystical "heart" begins to glow, turning blood-red. Then those sweet, lambent eyes cloud over and themselves turn blood-red. Finally that toothless, Galapagos turtle mouth opens wide and extends — not a message to pho-ne ho-me! — but an extra set of jaws armed with ferocious, venom-dripping fangs a la *Alien*.

The lovable family mutt hears the commotion in the closet and rushes in to investigate. More Bad Things happen. We hear horrible screams and thrashing sounds. Then the severed head of said lovable mutt comes sailing across the closet and hits the wall with a sickening "Thock!", smearing it with gore as it slides down to the floor. The head is followed by a pair of ragged paws, reflexively scuttling across the floor of the silent closet.

At this point the closet itself undergoes an alarming transformation: its straight lines of wood and sheetrock begin to dissolve into a convoluted, oozing passageway, like the intestinal tract of some giant beast. We know that E. T. has the power of levitation? Well, it proceeds to draw little Gertie, struggling and screaming, into this horrible, consuming maw, this gate of Hell (no more *Peter Pan* for Gertie for a while!). She disappears into the nether world of the transformed closet, and the whole house begins to shake violently. The rest of the family wake up and bolt out of the house, only noticing once outside that they are missing a couple of members.

Does this nightmarish retelling of America's favorite fairy tale/myth strike you as extreme? As a desecration of one of our holiest shrines, one we have erected to that spirit of sweet innocence which we may have lost but which we believe the movie recaptures, if only for a couple of hours? If so, then we must collectively take Steven Spielberg to task, for he has committed a strikingly similar violation of *E. T.* with his release of *Poltergeist.*

One of the remarkable things about Spielberg's ability to enthrall the American imagination is that he evokes, with *E. T.* and *Poltergeist,* completely different emotions simply by rearranging a few elements of what is essentially the same film. (Could Spielberg be an unrepentant structuralist?) Released in the same year (1982), the two movies focus on the trials a suburban California family undergoes when suddenly confronted with an alien presence in the household. They could have been shot on the same street, using the same tract house and, with a significant change here and there, the same cast of family members.

The points and counterpoints of resemblance and difference that unite *E. T.* and *Poltergeist* demonstrate how interconnected, and intersystemic, are the key myths of the Dreamtime.[4] Regardless of the theoretical spin we put on a cultural analysis of American movies, the vitally important fact is that it takes only a little twiddling of the knobs on our cerebral wiring to get us from *E. T.* to *Poltergeist.* However odd it may seem at first, *E. T. is Poltergeist,* with the pieces rearranged to produce (tellingly) discrepant messages. It turns out that individual myths, like individual persons, contain their separate multitudes.

How are these points and counterpoints of the two movies arranged? It may be helpful to outline them here.

E. T.		*Poltergeist*
visit by benevolent alien	<----->	visit by malevolent aliens
male child establishes special tie with alien	<----->	female child establishes special tie with aliens
father absent	<----->	father present
mother is ineffectual	<----->	mother is heroine
public/govt. presence emphasized	<-->	public/govt. presence deemphasized
bedroom closet as refuge	<----->	bedroom closet as danger
machines important	<----->	machines unimportant
male scientist establishes special affinity with alien	<----->	female psychic establishes special affinity with aliens
alien's goal is realized	<----->	aliens' goal is thwarted
family left in non-nuclear state	<----->	family left in nuclear state

In *Poltergeist* the "alien" presence is provided by a host of vengeful spirits of the dead: ghosts of California pioneers whose rest has been disturbed when the family's subdivision house is built on their graveyard. The family's young daughter, Carol Ann (who is the spitting image of Gertie in *E. T.*) first establishes contact with the spirits, and it is she who becomes the object of the spirits' efforts to invade the world of the living. The plot revolves around their successful attempt to abduct Carol Ann to their nether world and the family's fight to return her. In that struggle it is the mother (played by Jobeth Williams) who performs the most heroic deeds, herself journeying into the nether world to free Carol Ann from the evil spirits. She is the very opposite of Elliott's harried, distracted mother. Although the father (Craig T. Nelson) is very much a part of the family in *Poltergeist* (he is no deadbeat Dad), he is by no means a heroic, take-charge kind of guy. In fact, it is significant that the father's business dealings as an agent for a real estate developer have brought on the whole crisis; he has been selling houses built on desecrated ground and has even moved his family into one.

Next to the mother, the most effective character in the movie is the tiny female medium (Zelda Rubinstein) who guides the mother in her quest for Carol Ann in the spirit world. She is the opposite number of Keys in *E. T.* Apart from their gender difference, the significant thing about the medium is that she is innately gifted with the ability to see beyond the veil of the spirit world. Keys, on the other hand, has no such innate ability to communicate with alien intelligences. He relies instead on a battery of machines and the technicians who run them, which are furnished him by a powerful State with its own agenda.

In creating these antithetical characters, Spielberg draws on a phenomenon that will be familiar to cultural anthropologists. In societies scattered all over the globe, religious specialists who possess an innate ability to use their contact with the spirit world to do good or evil are almost always female, and may conventionally be described as *witches*. In contrast, religious specialists who depend on their acquired knowledge of techniques and implements to contact and manipulate spirits are usually male, and are called *sorcerers*.[5]

The distinction between witchcraft and sorcery here helps to make some cultural analytic sense of *E. T.* and *Poltergeist*, for the former is definitely a movie about a sorcerer while the latter is a movie about witches (yes, even lovely little Carol Ann and her doting mom). This seemingly arcane distinction helps to explain the very different roles assigned technology in the two movies. *E. T.*, as I have argued, is a veritable video Toys R Us catalog, with E. T., Elliott, and Michael relying on the machines around them to alter the course of events. That machine fetishism is notably absent from *Poltergeist*; Carol Ann, her mother, and the medium rely on nothing but their own (extra-sensory) perceptions in dealing with the evil spirits haunting the family's home.

Also, the witchcraft-sorcery distinction just may help to explain why *E. T.* was a colossal success while *Poltergeist*, by Spielberg's box office standards, was a commercial flop. Again, the arbiters of Serious Film cannot help us with this rather interesting anthropological question. For the critics who assailed the shallowness and implausibility of *Poltergeist* also leveled the same charges against *E. T.* So why did one boom and the other bust?

I would suggest that *E. T.* boomed in large part because (as I have been claiming incessantly throughout this book) late twentieth-century America is obsessed with the power and potential of machines, but is not much interested in innate aspects of individual psychology. As a sorcerer, E. T. can take its place beside other Masters of Machines — James Bond, Luke Skywalker, even R2D2 (remember, who is to say that E. T. is less a machine than our lovable little trash can?). But as witches, Carol Ann, Mom, and the medium only leave America asking the collective question: When will they *do* something about their unfortunate condition? Our concern with individual psychology itself takes a highly mechanistic turn. We want to know how to *fix* ourselves, how to tune ourselves up to work more productively, to make love more sensually, to parent more effectively. One has only to ponder the dismaying sameness of titles of nonfiction books Americans read to see that they might all be collectively retitled, in the fashion of movies, *How to Become Someone I'm Not* $(1 \ldots n)$.

Ambivalence at Home: The Myth of Family

E. T. contains another virtual movie, another arrangement of reelity that may be swept up from the cutting room floor and spliced together.

It is the movie's opening scene. The family has just finished dinner; no Domino's pizza delivery tonight, but good, wholesome roast beef, mashed potatoes, and string beans. It is Elliott's turn to take out the trash. While he is dropping the CinchSak into the trash can, he hears noises coming from the little garden shed in the back yard. He is scared and runs back inside. "Dad! Dad! I think the coyote's back!"

"Damn it," Dad says, setting down his can of Coors and getting up from the Lakers game on the big screen (did *that* little indulgence ever do some damage to the old plastic!). Dad goes into his and Mom's bedroom, fumbles around in the closet, and comes up with the family twelve-gauge and a handful of double-ought shells. Then he goes outside and approaches the shed, where he, too, hears something rustling around in there. With a shell in the chamber and the safety off, Dad kicks the door wide open and jumps inside, sighting the shotgun along his flashlight beam. And there, caught in the beam is . . . *something* that lets out a blood-curdling shriek and seems to come straight at him, somehow extending its neck to go for his face.

Dad did a tour in 'Nam and his reflexes take over. The shotgun bucks repeatedly in his hands, and through the swirling smoke and stench of cordite he sees he has blown several large, ragged holes in the little geek.

"O-o-o-u-u-c-c-h," moans the thing with its last breath.

Dad goes back inside the house and calls Encino Animal Control to come pick up the carcass, telling the kids to stay the hell away until the thing is disposed of. Then he pops another Coors to replace the one that has gone flat and sits back down in front of the Mitsubishi. Magic is hot tonight and there's still time to catch most of the fourth quarter. Thank God. Wonder what that thing was, anyways?

No, it is not an auspicious beginning for *E. T.* as we have come to cherish that movie, although just such a wham-bam opener would have fit right into all the James Bond movies and *Star Wars*. It doesn't work here for the very good reason that this hypothetical version violates one of the basic features of *E. T.* as schematized above: *E. T.*, in direct opposition to *Poltergeist*, is about a non-nuclear, "incomplete" family. The missing father, Elliott's deadbeat Dad, is not around to put a speedy end to the little alien, or to do any number of other things that would drastically have altered *E. T.*'s reception in the household. Had Elliott's Dad been part of the family, then *E. T.* would not be the movie it is (instead, it would be a semiotic amalgamation or intersystem of *Poltergeist* and *Jaws*). In chapter 3 we came to see "humanity" as an absence at the center of things; it now appears that Elliott's Dad performs a similar role in *E. T.*

E. T. is ostensibly about the little alien's efforts to Phone Home, to re-establish contact with its kind. But if we examine our feelings about the movie, and particularly the *depth* of those feelings, it is quite clear that we can have no real understanding of what E. T. is missing, of what its life aboard ship must be like. What we do know for a certainty, and what we feel with a special, wrenching poignancy is what our family life, our attempt to communicate with family members, to Phone Home, is like. Just as *Jaws* is not a treatise on marine biology, so *E. T.* is not a treatise on exobiology.

Our feelings for E. T. as it attempts to find its "home" arise from the intense feelings we all have about our own homes and families, and especially about our problems with them. It would all be so simple if our family lives (and particularly the parent-child relationship, which is as near to an "atom of kinship" as we will come) followed well-defined rules and stages. Such a "program" for kinship or parenthood-childhood could then be written on the grey disks we carry around between our ears. The program would specify that such-and-such a behavior by such-and-such a kinsperson elicit such-and-such a response when the subject (you or I) is such-and-such an age. If I am seven and see my father coming home at the end of the day, then my reaction to his arrival falls within fixed parameters, according to his behavior on entering the house.

But that program does not exist, nor could one much like it conceivably be written to run on the cerebral hardware we have evolved over the past four or five million years. A principal difficulty of writing such a program, as complexity theorists have amply demonstrated over the past several years, is that it is impossible to specify a "behavior" so exactly that Behavior X will always elicit Behavior Y, which in turn will elicit Behavior Z, etc. Little problems of interpretation (or measurement) creep in at the beginning, and those are amplified progressively as one proceeds along the behavioral chain. That smile on Dad's face as he comes through the door may be that of Ward Cleaver, happy to see his adoring brood and eager to dispense his nurturing wisdom to them. Or it may be Jack Nicholson's far more famous (and far more expensive) grin in *The Shining* as he comes through the door with something rather different in mind for his little family (but at least both scenarios involve a cleaver!). H-e-e-e-r-r-s-s-s Johnny!

Minute, undetectable differences between one situation and another lead to progressively greater differences between those situations as time goes by. As Jeff (*The Fly*) Goldblum reminded us in *Jurassic Park*, a butterfly stirring its wings in China may mean floods a few months later in the American Midwest.

But (as we have come to expect) things get more complicated still where the parent-child relationship is involved, for that happens to involve human beings locked in a most peculiar, and very highly dynamic situation. However complex is the relation between the Chinese butterfly and Missouri floods, meteorologists do not have to build into their models of weather patterns scenarios for the multiple effects those Missouri floods may have on the lives of Chinese butterflies, or for the second-order effects that changes in the populations of Chinese butterflies may have on Missouri weather in coming years. Such second-order effects (and third, and fourth, ad infinitum), however, are an integral feature of the parent-child relationship. Not only may a variety of interpretations arise from a particular action, but whatever interpretation is made provokes a particular action in response, which in turn is subject to a welter of discrepant interpretations by the original actor.

The dynamic system that forms around this feedback loop of action-interpretation-response can never settle into a stable pattern. As we have just noted, there is more and more room for novel behavior as the feedback loops cycle through their chaotic orbits.

But there is something else as well. In the parent-child relation both elements of the system are themselves undergoing significant changes that are only partly due to their mutual interaction. The child is growing, developing, its brain undergoing neurological transformations so extensive that, if we were honest with ourselves, we would take as evidence of a species difference between the child and its parent (and most certainly between the teenager and its wretched parent!). The parent in turn is shaping its understanding of the world, including its child, in response to what is going on with it in the wider world. Against the child's robust, unpredictable growth we have the parent's erratic dance around the candles of sexuality, senility and death. As their lives flash past, each party on this two-way street is remarkably acute at picking up the highly distorted messages it receives from the other.[6]

As we discussed in chapter 3, the Us-ness inherent in the parent-child relationship is both a fundamental property of culture and a staggering paradox, an impenetrable enigma. The identity of flesh and blood is contradicted by the necessity on the part of the child to divorce itself from the parent, to create that primal *boundary* from which all the others — the stuff of human consciousness — follow. Yet we insist (and we are powerless not to do so) on trying to have it both ways, trying to sustain a concept of inviolable Us-ness while living in a world rampant with sexuality, with desire for the Other. It is this unremitting ambivalence that drives us to produce and to consume, as voraciously as any fanged predator, *images* of personhood, of family life, of mothers and fathers, daughters and sons, all of which are made a part of and served up to us as myth. That ambivalence propels us through the theatre turnstiles to see E. T. and Elliott, Mom and Carol Ann, and Chief Brody and his sons wrestle with the enigma of kinship and in the process propose their own unique, and utterly discordant, solutions to this elemental dilemma of human life.

The sovereign institution that is the American family is built of this intractable, mythic stuff. The family is not a fixed entity with a discrete function in American society (however much Talcott Parsons and Dan Quayle might have wanted it to be). It is instead a writhing, Heraclitean thing whose members (you and I) find themselves caught up in the most dynamic and intense intersystemic experiences we are likely ever to know. Its dynamism and complexity insure that its properties are forever in the process of becoming, or, again in the language of complexity theory, *emergent*. The child's and parent's experiences of each other and of themselves undergo continual transformation, so that it is impossible to plot any linear "history" of the family, to recover those *temps perdu*.

It is for this fundamental reason that our myths serve up such a contradictory multitude of images of family life, all of which we multitudinous beings consume with a desperate hunger. We avidly follow the doings of Ward, June and Beaver Cleaver, of Jack Nicholson and his isolated, terrified family, of Chief Brody and his sons, of Elliott, E. T., and the deadbeat dad, and of Carol Ann and her parents because we somehow know that *all* are present within our multitudinous individual selves, a heartbeat away from erupting into action. Jack with his maniacal grin and carving knife in *The Shining*, The Great White Shark of *Jaws*, the cruel and unfeeling scientists of *E. T.*, and the malevolent spirits of *Poltergeist* are, indeed, those very "creatures from the Id" depicted in that sci-fi classic, *Forbidden Planet*. They frighten us, not because they are boogeymen waiting in the dark to jump out and kill us, but because we recognize them as parts of ourselves and our own, unfailingly troubled experiences.

Here we arrive at a central truth of cultural analysis. The representations of our lives that we enshrine in movie-myth are so discrepant precisely because our culture is itself riddled to its core with internal contradictions. We do not inhabit *a* culture, but a myriad of coexistent and mutually inconsistent *virtual* cultures that spring into and out of being in a flash, as suddenly and evanescently as quantum particles appearing and disappearing in the void. To acquiesce to the pernicious conventional wisdom that Americans share an identifiable, bounded "American" culture that possesses properties *x*, *y*, and *z* is to ignore the evidence of culture's virtuality and semiotic contrariety that pours forth from our cultural productions. The tremendous discrepancies among the movie-myths that captivate us can never be reduced to a single, plodding theme, for those discrepancies, in all their glaring and flamboyant contradictoriness, *are* the reality of the culture they depict. Those discrepancies, arising directly from the unresolvable elemental dilemmas of culture, are the message of our movie-myths. The "We" they represent so faithfully — mothers and fathers, daughters and sons — is a thoroughly liminal phenomenon, a skittering phantom caught in the swirling vortices of cultural processes that will never stop until "We" have transmuted into Something Else.

In the words of Edmund Leach, which social critics of every persuasion have not heeded, myth is not a chorus of harmony. It is a language of argument.[7] The lesson that Elliott and E. T. teach us is that the argument of myth pervades that improbable collection of individuals we call the "family." Like the culture of which it is a vital part, the family is a knot of virtuality. Anything can happen. And, as we know all too well from watching the TV news and reading the newspapers, anything does happen. Tom Wolfe's workadaddy is a heartbeat away from becoming Elliott's deadbeat dad. The mild-mannered Jack wakes up one morning with murderous thoughts obsessing him. An affable, handsome football star and corporate icon . . . The *boundaries* we traverse on our erratic wanderings through semiospace are the furthest thing from cerebral playthings — toys the symbolic anthropologist invents to amuse himself, as Clifford Geertz unfortunately characterized them in his otherwise impressive essay, "Thick Description: Toward an Interpretive Theory of Culture." Those boundaries are deadly, agonizingly serious, and always with us. And they are the reason we all find it the most difficult and ambiguous of actions to Phone Home.

8

Conclusions

They became what they beheld.
— Edmund Carpenter, *Oh, What a Blow that Phantom Gave Me!*

Oh, my God! It's full of stars!
— Commander David Bowman, *2001: A Space Odyssey*
(Commander Bowman's final transmission from the *USS Discovery*
as he inspected the black obelisk orbiting a moon of Jupiter)

Understanding Our Movies and Ourselves:
Cultural Analysis and Film Criticism

What, finally, are we to make of our movies? And what, far more impor-tantly when we veer toward cultural anthropology and away from film or literary criticism, do our movies make of us? Throughout this work I have endeavored to answer the first question in such a way that my remarks (and you, the reader) are drawn to the second. I have attempted to explore certain popular movies, not as spin-offs or knee-jerk reflexes of an American psyche or society already in place, but as fundamental elements in the continuing process of establishing and transforming that psyche or society. To this end, the premise I have adopted is that at least some of our popular movies may be studied as an anthropologist (if he is a right-thinking type!) studies *myth*, that is, as representations of what a particular people is all about, of what resides in their innermost selves.

As in the introduction, it is important in concluding to make it, as Dick used to say, *perfectly clear* that my mission here has been to use movies as a probe, as a device already insinuated by others, into the writhing body of American culture. Since I believe that procedure leads inexorably into an inquiry regarding the nature of culture itself, that is where I have followed it (and dragged you through the labyrinth of chapter 3 in the process).

In summarizing this ambitious (if foolhardy) program, I wish it also to serve as a disclaimer: whatever grandiose ideas I concoct about the nature of humanity or culture and attempt to fob off on you, I do *not* present them in the spirit of film criticism or, its literary soul-mate, narrative analysis. I think that it's perfectly okay to critique movies-as-movies, and maybe even to pretend that movies are just another kind of text which can be submitted to textual or narrative analysis. God knows there are enough people out there doing these things (so I won't be missed!). The business of film criticism and commentary is a major subsidiary of the film industry itself. We can't get through a morning news show (which, it seems, is increasingly about the *new* movies) without hearing whether Siskel and Ebert give two thumbs up to the latest blockbuster, or what the guy with the Einstein hair and thick-framed glasses thinks about it. Magazines and newspapers regularly feature "Cinema" sections or columns, some of which are serious essays in themselves (Pauline Kael's long reign and voluminous production at *The New Yorker* being an outstanding example).

And for those cerebral types among us (or, which may amount to the same thing, those of us cursed with high pain or boredom thresholds), there is a separate vast corpus of Serious Film Criticism that dissects a film (never a movie!) frame-by-frame and serves it back to us (refried filmoles) in page after page of crushingly abstract argument. Vladimir Propp started all this with his *Morphology of the Folktale* (published in the United States in 1958), and Juri Lotman has reached an even more rarefied atmosphere with *Semiotics of Cinema* and other studies. Between and after these leading savants, whole strike forces of graduate students and junior professors of comparative literature have peeled off from the air brigade cruising the lofty skies of academe and dive-bombed the surface of our planet, Phi Beta Kappa pins flashing like gun muzzles in the glaring marquee lights, surprising our hapless Topeka teenager as he exited the theatre, arm around his girl, still slurping his over-priced drink, and thinking, as they walked back to his Chevy for the late night stop at the drive-in and, just maybe, the outdoor bedroom of the local Lover's Lane, thinking of Bond's Lotus and Bond's women, of all those virtual lives out there too evanescent and too alluring to be captured and displayed by Propp, Lotman, and Company.

It strikes me that the problem with film criticism is that it takes itself far too seriously, as though self-consciously atoning for the intellectual sin of deciphering Bergman rather than Brecht by making sure that no one cracks a smile from the first ponderous analytic paragraph to the last. And, in all honesty, I must admit that some of that nervousness is justified. I have felt it myself as I began to venture outside the cloistered setting of a university department of anthropology, where, thanks to Levi-Strauss, the analysis of "primitive" myth is a bona-fide pursuit, and to experiment with the analysis of movies.

For so many movies, so much of the Discourse of Film, *is* such silly, tedious stuff, often the product of third-rate directors and actors ripping off work by second-raters who happened to rack up the boxoffice bucks. Even if you very much want to understand, for example, our evolving, complex relationship with animals (the subject of chapter 6) it's hard to sit through even a single of the *Lassie* movies from beginning to end. And if you make it all the way through the first, and by far the best epic, *Lassie Come Home*, are you then ready for back-to-back (tail-to-tail?) screenings of *Son of Lassie, Courage of Lassie, Master of Lassie, Challenge to Lassie*, and the half-dozen or so other *Lassie* movies that were simply cobbled together from old movie shorts and TV serials? I wasn't. Despite all my brave talk about movies as vital elements of the *myth of America*, I have found it impossible to review systematically productions like the *Lassie* series or the endless saucer sagas, such as *It Came from Outer Space* and *Invaders from Mars*.

Instead, in the preceding chapters I have taken the sluggard's way out and dealt exclusively with a very few movies whose phenomenal boxoffice success can only mean that they have captured, at whatever level, the imagination of the entire country and, more often now in recent years, of the world.[1] The appeal of Bond, of *Star Wars*, of *Jaws*, and of *E. T.* has been so compelling and so universal that they dispel the tediousness of their imitators, just as they negate the carping of serious students of Film that they are unworthy of analysis.

If I were a less charitable sort, I would even suspect that the film critics' and other tastemakers' dismissal of our extraordinarily successful popular movies stems not just from the movies' failure to meet their exacting aesthetic standards, but from their own failure to comprehend the American psyche and society that takes those movies to heart, that embraces them as a badge of identity. In focusing so obsessively on the first of the two questions I posed above — What are we to make of our movies? — the critics conveniently let slide the much tougher but much more important second question: What do our movies make of us? I think that this is precisely the juncture where film criticism and cultural analysis or anthropological semiotics part company, for I do not believe that the former is prepared to contemplate a humanity, the movie audience, so essentially unformed and *virtual* that it derives from movies not just a commentary on its condition but a renewal and reshaping of its very being.

If there is a single thread running through the preceding chapters it is the perspective that "humanity" is an exceedingly complex set of ever-shifting *boundary conditions*. That perspective, as I have argued, is contrary to a very well-established view of humanity as a fixed, discrete entity which has a *presence*, a definitiveness about it, and which reacts to equally fixed entities — animals, machines, etc. — around it. That view, which is at least as old as the "Enlightenment" of eighteenth-century Europe, forms the core of a conventional humanism that still asserts itself in every debate about life in contemporary America. Its signature is the classic and all too comfortable we-they formulation of social issues: How do *we* humans treat *those* animals around us? How do *we* humans treat the environment as a whole? How do *we* deal with *those* machines that surround us? How do *we* deal with *those* criminals in *our* streets who are trying to destroy *our* society? And finally, how do *we* deal, as mothers and fathers, sisters and brothers, sons and daughters with *those* others who, though our own flesh and blood, are increasingly, disturbingly *alien*?

All my discussions of James Bond, *Star Wars, Jaws, and E. T.* have had the agenda of loosening the clammy grip two-hundred-odd years of humanism has on our understanding of ourselves as a species and of the horrific problems we confront at the end of this turbulent century. We will make no progress in coming to terms with the animals and machines in the world around us until we realize that each of us, as a human being, is simultaneously also both animal and machine, that our fundamental identity is a restless mix of animal and machine attributes acquired during several million years of hominid speciation and cultural evolution. If we come to believe, with Walt Whitman, that each of us contains multitudes, we must include in those multitudes something of the "personages" of the Great White Shark and Lassie, of R2D2 and the Death Star, of the Predator and E. T.

We — you and I — are, in short, living, breathing paradoxes, ambulatory protoplasmic sacs of the most acute, the most exquisite ambivalence imaginable. It is the great pity and scandal of our time that we find intolerable the paradox and ambivalence that are our birthright. Rather than embrace the animal-us and machine-us that constitute inalienable parts of our being, we lurch from one extreme to the other, alternately glorying in the destruction of animals and machines or wrapping them in a suffocating, covetous blanket of adoration.

When the cultural anthropologist trains his flawed lens of analysis on the social issues that embroil his fellows, his distinctive contribution — and who could welcome it? — is to establish in meticulous ethnographic detail the agonizing truth that things can never be set right, that Americans will never get the good old U. S. A.'s house in order, that the problems confronting us literally will not go away until *we*, as an ephemeral instantiation of cultural processes, a bit of semiotic froth, push through the conceptual membrane separating us from Something Else.

For the one constant in the turbulence surrounding us is that the semiotic antinomies of culture, far from beginning to resolve themselves in some mushy, Clintonesque middle ground, *are becoming increasingly polarized*. Animals and machines, our group and theirs, the forces of creation and destruction are not moving toward a happy accommodation within the embracing, nurturing arms of a discrete humanity. Quite the contrary: in the waning years of the century those antinomies are pulling away from one another with incredible force, spreading or *smearing* the human quasispecies across an increasingly serpentine, disjointed configuration. The octopus arms of Figure 3.3, as they become more and more attenuated, configure or *morph* diverse, localized we-nesses — little baby humanities akin to the cosmologists' baby universes — that share little besides a genetic code and more or less similar phenotypes.

The Logic of Things That Just Happen:
The Sandpile and Cellular Automaton as Models of Cultural Process

> *When catastrophe strikes, analysts typically blame some rare set of circumstances or some combination of powerful mechanisms. When a tremendous earthquake shook San Francisco, geologists traced the cataclysm to an immense instability along the San Andreas fault. When the stock market crashed on Black Monday in 1987, economists pointed to the destabilizing effect of computer trading. When fossil records revealed the demise of the dinosaurs, paleontologists attributed the extinction to the impact of a meteorite or the eruption of a volcano. These theories may well be correct. But systems as large and as complicated as the earth's crust, the stock market and the ecosystem can break down not only under the force of a mighty blow but also at the drop of a pin. Large interactive systems perpetually organize themselves to a critical state in which a minor event starts a chain reaction that can lead to a catastrophe.*
> — Per Bak and Kan Chen, "Self-Organized Criticality"

> *The universe is a recursively defined geometric object.*
> — William Poundstone, *The Recursive Universe*

Like the myths they are, our movies lead us to agonizing reflections concerning the things we hold nearest and dearest in life. Perhaps most unsettling of those reflections is what amounts to a principal theme of this work: that our most deeply held beliefs and emotions (about animals and artifacts, family and enemy, good and evil) are in fact a shimmering web of semiotic antinomies that continuously transform our very essence, continuously transform what it is to be human. In confronting this dilemma we attempt, paradoxically, to deny myth a place of importance in our lives while clinging fast to mythic constructs that serve, for us thoroughly cultural beings, as the only possible signposts of consciousness. What we think and feel about the basics of human life, right down to our very sense of self and body, is infused with a significance that seems at once compellingly natural and utterly fabricated. Human existence is a ceaseless, tragic ballet of contingency and necessity.

The analogy I have pursued here between quantum physics, cosmology, and cultural anthropology engages that central paradox in an effort to promote a new way of thinking about culture and its current host, humanity. It is a way — the only way I can see — out of the paralyzing contradictions that issue from our simultaneous embrace and rejection of myth. The virtuality and inde-terminacy of the quantum world are, I suggest, far more characteristic of culture and humanity than are the materialist and determinist models that many anthropologists still insist on applying.

By invoking the quantum analogy here, however, I awake a dragon that most of my colleagues would be content to let sleep: the seemingly unresolv-able opposition between a powerful and exact scientific theory of the world and an existential or interpretive perspective that views events as disconnected phenomena lacking any unifying framework. It is hardly possible to overstate the importance these radically different orientations have had in shaping human thought over the few millennia that we have possessed literacy as well as sapience. Whatever labels or spins we put on it — idealism vs. realism, rationalism vs. empiricism, hermeneutics vs. existentialism, postmodernism vs. positivism, science vs. magic — and whatever vast edifices of philosophy we erect on it, this critical opposition boils down to the simple question of whether we can discern an order or pattern at work in the world around us. Is there a *logic* underlying experience or do things just happen?

Sadly, in my own field of cultural anthropology it seems that most of us in the United States have lost interest, or never had much to begin with, in this absolutely crucial issue. Rather than engage the fundamental questions that flow from it, cultural anthropologists for the most part have drawn up into tight little camps ("strategic enclaves" in the old Newspeak we remember too well) where embarrassing theoretical issues are not an appropriate subject of collegial discussion. In one of these camps, the vital and unique research program of *ethnography* — cultural anthropology's one claim to a lasting contribution to human knowledge — is treated as an interesting form of literature, as texts to be put through the postmodern grist mill for the sheer joy, apparently, of commenting on them endlessly. In another camp, scientism has choked off any truly scientific approach to the complex relation between beliefs and behavior, so that silly, pseudo-causal "explanations" are popped out of a hat and paraded as a model of theoretical acumen (Aztec human sacrifice developed in response to protein deficient diets, etc.). Elsewhere, anthro-pologists have decided that they are, after all, historians (the affinity has always been close) and plunged into their minute interpretations of the human archive. Finally, and most tragically for our young and ambitious "science of humanity," many anthropologists, despairing of finding jobs and/or inspiration in traditional departments, indenture themselves to the fields of law and medicine or to government agencies, where they serve, advertently or inad-vertently, to rationalize the pernicious doings of lawyers, doctors, and bureaucrats.

This fragmentation has dissipated the energies of a field of inquiry that still promises so much. But that is not the real loss, for academic departments and disciplines rise and fall in power and relevance over the decades and centuries.

To confirm that, you only have to visit the nearest large university and compare the luxurious digs of the Schools of Medicine and Law (the lowly bloodletters and shysters of an earlier era) with the cramped quarters of the Department of Religious Studies, whose harried members have lost the perks (and often even the faith) enjoyed by their predecessors when Theology was the summit of intellectual endeavor. Considering the vicissitudes these titans of learning have experienced, the fate of an upstart, borderline field like "cultural anthropology" is of no great significance in the broad sweep of intellectual history. But if cultural anthropology goes down the rat hole of history, it takes the concept of "culture" as a theoretical, explicatory entity with it. *That* would be the real loss to an inquiring human consciousness, for without the concept of culture it is impossible, as I have argued throughout, to begin to make sense of what people are about, of what our lives mean. It would be like trying to describe the life of a spider without mentioning its web. In their divisiveness anthropologists are at great risk of ripping out the heart of their discipline (to return to our friends the Aztecs!) for the sake of some highly dubious work in textual criticism, cultural materialism, and applied or development anthropology.

To my mind, the great power, beauty, and, yes, even mystery of the quantum analogy as applied to cultural anthropology is that it permits us (and what could be better for such ambivalent beings as ourselves?) to have things both ways. Rather than divide into snitty little factions espousing Levi-Strauss's rationalism, Marvin Harris's materialism, or the postmoderns' literary ethnography, we can take heart from the fact that quantum physics has managed to unify a staggering diversity of information within a single theoretical edifice. And it has accomplished so much because mathematical physicists like Heisenberg, Schroedinger, Hawking, and Penrose have pulled off the ultimate magic trick: they have discovered a logic of things that just happen.

In the messy, smeared, virtual world of subatomic particles, things indeed do *just happen*. Particles pop into existence from out of nowhere and then annihilate themselves; a particle can be here, there, or everywhere at once in the quantum superpositions of many-dimensional Hilbert space; a particle observed on one side of a physical barrier may mysteriously "tunnel" through it to appear on the other side. As we discussed in chapter 3, such bizarre goings-on threatened the foundations of classical physics, and classical physicists reacted as one might expect: with suspicion and disdain. Even Einstein, in what is probably his most quoted remark, affirmed his belief that "God does not play dice with the universe."

But Heisenberg, Schroedinger, and the others, if they did not have God on their side, did have a powerful ally with which to counter Einstein's doubts as well as those of lesser lights who wanted convincing. They had the formidable field equations of quantum physics, which accurately described what those mysterious particles were up to. Even if physical action on the quantum level violated common sense, the equations demonstrated that they, and not common sense, provided an accurate description of the world. The microwave you use to nuke your next burrito, the television you watch every night, and the computer you hammer away at every day all have quantum principles engineered into their designs. That's why they work, even though you and I, and most of the engineers who built them, do not grasp the mathematical subtleties embodied in quantum field equations. The astounding truth is that the esoteric mathematics of quantum theory accurately describes a physical world which should not behave as it does — except that it does. A rigorous mathematical logic exists to explain the indeterminate, virtual world of subatomic particles. It is a logic of things that just happen.

With the dazzling successes of the mathematical physicists in mind, the bedraggled, mosquito-bitten, dysentery-wracked field anthropologist might well ask, even if sarcastically, why he should not just pack it in, abandon the "natives" and go back to his university department and sip martinis in the faculty club lounge while awaiting the news that the physicists had come up with a set of equations that accurately described culture. Indeed, he might be more than a little tempted to do just that upon reading in the popular scientific press that the physicists, not content with their wildly successful theories to date, were hot on the trail of the ultimate truth, the Holy Grail, in the form of a set of equations that would wrap up all the forces of nature (electricity, magnetism, the weak nuclear force, the strong nuclear force, and gravity). While his fellow cultural anthropologists sat around querulously debating whether their very *raison d'etre*, culture, had any substance to it at all, the talk over in the physics department was about the search for the Grand Unified Theory, the Theory of Everything that would explain all of physical creation in a few lines of equations.

On the other hand, our befuddled anthropologist might decide against ordering that next round of martinis and instead get on the phone to see about auditing some math classes. If the physicists were really onto something, perhaps he could apply their high-powered approach to his theorizing about the nature of cultural systems. This is not a bad idea, but as I discuss momentarily I don't think it will fill the bill by itself. Like the American public at large, most cultural anthropologists are woefully ignorant of mathematics. Early in their undergraduate careers, if not before, they had to choose between an Arts or a Sciences curriculum, and the great majority chose Arts. Any math they picked up along the way was, in the spirit of the liberal *arts*, intended to "broaden" their minds. Nobody expected them to be building spaceships ten years down the line.

In graduate school, if any math course was required it was typically something on the order of "Statistics for the Social Sciences," and most budding young cultural anthropologists regarded it as cruel and unusual punishment inflicted by their professorial elders (and, truth to tell, the young, untenured mathematician teaching this "service" course to a lecture hall of surly, resentful Artsies probably held the same view). But even with the best will in the world, such a course would have done little to prepare the future cultural anthropologist to make a substantive assessment of possible applications of quantum theory to cultural analysis. Instead, it fostered a low-grade ability to marshall statistical arguments about the correlations of Culture Trait X with Culture Trait Y (for example, do cultures with late weaning tend to believe in benevolent, nurturing deities as opposed to evil spirits?). The whole dreary exercise of tabulating "trait indices" of cultures around the world produces anthropology that is closer to hack sociology than to Heisenberg. I would confidently wager that not one cultural anthropologist in a hundred (including myself, I am sorry to say) can find the solution(s) to a differential equation. And that level of competence would just be the gateway to beginning to do meaningful work on the topic at hand.

Fortunately, this sad state of affairs — which is merely an instance of the deplorable condition of scientific education in the United States — does not mean that cultural anthropologists have to abandon any serious effort to bring scientific thought to bear on problems in cultural analysis. In fact, help is to be found from an unexpected source: the soft underbelly of mathematical physics. Powerful as quantum mechanics is, in propounding a logic of things that just happen it does not specify exactly what *will* happen, or even what the precise connection is between one event and the next. Remember that the truths of quantum theory are expressed as probabilities or, strictly speaking, *amplitudes* that, for example, a particle x will be at point y at time t. It is a science of maybes. In this fact is, not just a straw to grasp but a socking big log for cultural anthropologists to haul themselves aboard as they enter the cerebral rapids of cultural analysis. For in cultural analysis the maybes matter.

Since I am unable to use mathematics to explore this thought (and most of you are probably unable to grasp the mathematics required),I would like to develop it, as cultural anthropologists often do, by using *models* that represent fundamental properties of culture. The models here are the sandpile and the cellular automaton.

Models are used to make sense of complicated situations (the only kind we have encountered in this book!) by identifying and isolating their key features. What *matters* about a particular case? What significance does it have for other, seemingly unrelated cases? What significance does it have for the big picture, the total system? In the topic before us — the application of principles of mathematical physics to cultural analysis — what matters is, on one hand, the notion of a "logic" at work in physical and cultural systems and, on the other hand, the notion of randomness, chaos, of "things that just happen" in those systems. The model I propose to represent and to explore the notion that "things just happen" is the sandpile. The corresponding model for "logic" is the cellular automaton.

Through a close comparison of these models, I hope to demonstrate two fundamental points. First, of course, I hope to substantiate what I have been saying throughout this book about the applicability of recent work in physics and cosmology to cultural analysis. Failing miraculous equations, analogical reasoning will have to suffice here. Second, I hope to identify a middle ground, really a *border area* (we have encountered those before!) where a cultural system paradoxically manifests logical features *and* nearly chaotic behavior at the same time. In the now much-used phrases of complexity theorists, that border area is "the edge of order and chaos" characteristic of systems that manifest "self-organized criticality."[2]

The Sandpile. The sandpile model and, as you will see, the sandpile experiment illustrate what I called the soft underbelly of mathematical physics: the job of figuring out what will happen next in a particular situation and how particular events are connected. Another name for that soft underbelly is *determinism*, the doctrine or assumption that it is possible to isolate a discrete event or condition that *causes* another, later event or condition to occur. In a determinist perspective, it is blasphemous to entertain the idea that things just happen. Events occur according to precise laws, and if you know those laws you know the entirety of a system — now, in the past, and in the future. Given a specific configuration of particles at time t, you can identify their configuration at an arbitrary point in the past or in the future.

In cultural anthropology, messy as its subject matter is, determinist perspectives have nevertheless flourished. Marvin Harris's cultural materialism (those protein-deprived Aztecs again) enjoys wide acceptance in anthropology departments across the land, and, through Harris's popular books, is far and away the dominant stereotype of "cultural anthropology" among the American public. Cultural materialism satisfies the need we have acquired at least since the time of Descartes, Newton, and Leibniz to believe that things fit together in a tidy fashion, that events follow one another in an intelligible way, that the world makes sense. In cultural anthropology that need has been particularly acute, since its intellectual charter, drafted by English Puritans and French rationalists, is to show to a doubting world that the frenzied doings of half-naked savages are in fact perfectly sensible adaptations to their physical and social environments.

As in everything else, anthropology has inherited its deterministic bias from intellectual titans of the past. Among them perhaps none stated the case in more forceful, absolute terms than Pierre Laplace, heir of Descartes's rationalism and of Newton's and Leibniz's stunning mathematical advances.

> We may regard the present state of the universe as the effect of its past and the cause of its future. An intellect which at any given moment

knew all the forces that animate nature and the mutual positions of the beings that compose it, if this intellect were vast enough to submit the data to analysis, could condense into a single formula the movement of the greatest bodies of the universe and that of the lightest atom: for such an intellect nothing could be uncertain; and the future just like the past would be present before its eyes. (cited in Morris Kline, *Mathematics: A Cultural Approach*, 448)

Today's cultural materialists would stop short of Laplace's grand proclamation of an absolutely determined world, but the ember of that idea still glows within them. And for that reason the sandpile analogy is such a valuable tool in moving cultural analysis along, out of the dead air they have created. In the sandpile experiment I am about to describe, everything a deterministically minded type might long for is provided: all the minute details about size and position of particles are known with precision; change is introduced into the system in strictly incremental quantities; and instruments are in place to measure every event to the nth decimal place. This experimental system possesses an exactness cultural anthropologists can only dream about. There is just one small problem: knowing all the facts tells us very little about what the system is up to.

In an experiment that should take its place as a milestone in physics, Glenn Held and colleagues at the IBM Thomas J. Watson Research Center constructed an apparatus to test the dynamic properties of a sandpile. They started with a precision balance, accurate to one ten-thousandths of a gram, and a supply of sand carefully screened to leave only sand particles weighing approximately six ten-thousandths of a gram each. Then they rigged a long capillary tube in such a way that by turning it a single grain of sand would fall on the small plate of the balance (mercifully, a computer was hooked up to the device to perform this tedious chore). Finally, the balance was shielded from air currents by placing a large plexiglass box over the equipment.

The experiment began. A particle of sand dropped on the plate. The computer waited for the balance to stabilize, recorded the new weight on the scale, and then caused another grain of sand to drop. After some thirty-five thousand grains of sand had been released in this fashion, the experimenters stopped to examine their results. Not exactly Indiana Jones's kind of science, but the findings were conceptually more spectacular than anything Indy ever pulled off.

At first, as we might expect, most of the individual grains of sand collected on the plate, with some bouncing off the plate and some knocking other grains off the plate as they fell. Gradually the fallen sand assumed a familiar conical shape with low, sloping sides: a sandpile. Then things started to get interesting. With gravity tugging at the collected particles, the sides of the sandpile could not get appreciably steeper. Some particles had to go. The questions were, which particles and how many at a time?

The experiment was designed to answer these very questions. A new particle would fall on top of the pile from the capillary dispenser and it would either lodge in place or fall off, perhaps knocking other particles off as well. After each event the computer would let things stabilize and then calculate the number of sand grains, if any, lost over the side of the balance plate. Sometimes no particles were lost, sometimes only a few, sometimes dozens, and occasionally a major avalanche of several hundred grains cascaded off the sides of the pile.

Is there a way to tell when a grain falling from the dispenser will lodge in place, dislodge only a few other grains, or set off an avalanche? All the equipment is in place to measure and analyze this imminent event. The ghost of Laplace, and perhaps even Marvin Harris, are gleeful at the prospect of a finely tuned, deterministic system producing well-defined, predictable behaviors. Alas, though, in a blinding flash of deja vu we find ourselves back at our earlier and far more modest experiment of measuring ant paths (only in this case the experimental system *does* something; it does not just sit there like the drawings of the ant paths). A grain of sand falls; it is exactly like the grain that fell before it and the grain that will fall after it. But whereas a thousand grains fell before it and did no more than knock off a few dozen particles among them, *this* grain sets off an avalanche! Hundreds of particles cascade down the sides of the pile and spill off the scale. And when the very next grain falls, it too may touch off an avalanche almost as large. It seems that anything can happen.

This insignificant little sandpile (in the experiment it never exceeded one hundred grams) is bad news for any physical or social theory that harbors the slightest vestige of determinism. If sensitive laboratory equipment and lots of computing power cannot enable us to find a determinate pattern in events touched off by the falling particles of sand, it is foolish to expect to find such patterns in systems as large and complex as the cosmos or human culture. Laplace's vision of a supreme intelligence that possesses every iota of knowledge about the past and future of the universe now seems like the delusional ravings of a deeply disturbed soul.

Moreover, the uncertainties inherent in the sandpile experiment are disturbingly like those that appear to prevail on a much larger scale, namely the behavior of the earth's crust along its major fault lines. As I write these lines I am sitting at home, six miles away from the San Andreas fault, and still nursing bad memories of the early morning of June 28, 1992, when the Landers quake (7.5 on the Richter scale) and the Big Bear quake (6.6) struck without warning within three hours of each other. About eighteen months later the Northridge quake, of somewhat lesser magnitude but far more devastating to human life and property, awakened me as a series of ominous spasms (not shaking jolts this time; I was too far away) coursed through my home. Somewhere close, I knew, something awful had happened.

In both cases, of course, and particularly in the wake of the Northridge disaster, the media swarmed all over the seismologists at Cal Tech, who in recent years have outfitted a nifty show-and-tell media room for just such traumatic occasions. But for all the computer monitor displays and tight focus shots of seismograph needles going crazy, there was little to report. The scientists dispensed what southern Californians have come to recognize as seismobabble: pearls of wisdom to the effect that if we've just had an earthquake we'll probably soon have another, and that if the earthquake we just had is smaller than the next one (whenever *that* will be) then it's probably an aftershock of the one before it (unless the next one is really big, in which case the preceding quake was probably a foreshock).

When you live on a large sandpile and lack even the rudiments of control over your environment (the Cal Tech seismologists didn't even know the faults existed that caused the Landers and Big Bear quakes), you come to have a visceral appreciation for the truths that the sandpile experiment teaches. To be told, as the seismologists are fond of doing, that there is a thirty or forty percent chance of a major quake occurring on the southern arm of the San Andreas sometime in the next twenty years or so does nothing to answer your most pressing questions: When will the Big One hit? Will it hit near me? The seismologists do not release specific information about a determinate system because their subject, the earth's crust, is not such a system. And, just as with Humpty Dumpty, all the State's computers and all the State's technicians will not enable them to tell you much more about the Big One. Indeed, seismologists' "forecasts" are little more than actuarial tables like those your insurance agent refers to in writing up your life insurance policy. You know you're going to die, but it makes a bit of a difference whether that happens today or twenty years from now.

The sandpile experiment, then, well and truly extinguishes the last spark of wishful thinking that determinate answers exist to seemingly straightforward questions about the connectedness of events in the innumerable dynamic systems that make up daily life. So does that mean that the dialectic we have been considering between "logic" and "things that just happen" collapses? That the by now all-too-familiar tension of wanting to have it both ways dissipates and we are left to contemplate life in a world of sheer randomness and chaos, a world devoid of logic or pattern, a world where things just happen? Intriguingly, and as you might expect from everything that has gone before, the answers are "yes" and "no."

In their theoretical discussion of the sandpile experiment, Per Bak and Kan Chen make the profound suggestion that the sandpile is neither a determinate, logical system nor an utterly random one, but something *in between*. Although their argument is couched in the terms of mathematical physics, the concepts it evokes are stunningly like those developed throughout this book: virtuality, liminality, intersystem, continuum, mediated semiotic polarities. Stripped of its determinate, functionalist (mis)interpretations, human culture appears to possess the critical features Bak and Chen attribute to every dynamic system, whether physical or social.

> An observer who studies a specific area of a pile can easily identify the mechanisms that cause sand to fall, and he or she can even predict whether [very small, localized] avalanches will occur in the near future. To a local observer, large avalanches would remain unpredictable, however, because they are a consequence of the total history of the entire pile. No matter what the local dynamics are, the avalanches would mercilessly persist at a relative frequency that cannot be altered. The criticality is a global property of the sandpile.
> Even though sand is added to the pile at a uniform rate, the amount of sand flowing off the pile varies greatly over time. If one graphed the flow versus time, one would see a very erratic signal that has features of all durations. Such signals are known as flicker noise, or $1/f$ noise (pronounced "one over 'ef' noise"). Scientists have long known that flicker noise suggests that the dynamics of a system are strongly influenced by past events. In contrast, white noise, a random signal, implies no correlation between the current dynamics and past events.
> Flicker noise is extremely common in nature. It has been observed in the activity of the sun, the light from galaxies, the current through a resistor and the flow of water through a river. Indeed, the ubiquitousness of flicker noise is one of the great mysteries in physics. The theory of self-organized criticality suggests a rather general interpretation: flicker noise is a superposition of signals of all sizes and durations — signals produced when a dynamic system in the critical state produces chain reactions of all sizes and durations. ("Self-Organized Criticality," 48)

I find these remarks brilliantly suited to our quest after the meaning of movie-myth in American culture for two reasons. First, erratic as sandpile avalanches and the themes of Hollywood productions are, they are not quite random, not the white noise of chance or the "booming, buzzing confusion" of William James's theory of perception. Things do not just happen — but almost. Instead, things follow an elusive, mathematical pattern, "flicker noise," which, I would argue, is an excellent operational definition of what I have called a "logic of things that just happen." Second, the non-randomness of flicker noise is difficult to discern because flicker noise in fact consists of *multiple patterns* formed, as Bak and Chen claim, by a "superposition of signals of all sizes and durations." It would be difficult to find a phrase more suited to the welter of themes or meanings contained in our movies.

Like quantum superposition, the superposition of signals in a critical, macroscopic system, whether physical or social, requires that individual elements of that system ("cultures," "persons," "social institutions," or whatever) exist in a dense cloud of *virtual* states. A particular movie, or an individual frame of a particular movie, does not have a single clear and distinct meaning, does not emit a single "signal," but multiple meanings. These meanings in turn relate to people's lives, to what is going on outside the theatre, in multiple, complex ways. But they *do* relate to people's lives; it matters that we have James Bond, *Star Wars, Jaws,* and *E. T.*, and not some other, utterly different movies — or no movies at all. Yet the project of determinism (which is also the project of functionalism) can never succeed: the univocal meaning or function of a movie, how the movie ties into our actions and beliefs, can never be spelled out precisely. Consequently, the next twist or turn in the semiotic ballet of our movies, like the next particle to fall on the sandpile, may touch off an avalanche, reversing a long period of steady, uneventful accretion. Who knows, even in this era of the pornoviolence of the machine, Hollywood might come up with a new release of *Lassie?*

The Cellular Automaton. Bak and Chen's analysis of Held's sandpile experiment establishes that non-random, complexly patterned behavior typifies that physical system. And they go on to claim that such behavior characterizes a great many systems, perhaps all that have evolved to the critical state at which an event is sensitively affected by another event. But what of the other pole of the dialectic I proposed at the beginning of this section? Is there any place for a concept of logic, or inherent pattern, in a world where, as we now know, things *almost* just happen? Why even worry about the possibility that a "cultural logic" might underlie the scrambled patterns or flicker noise of our lives?

The nice thing about models is that they allow us (math dunces though we may be) to cut to the chase. The sandpile experiment showed us how a tiny slice of nature actually behaves when it is constructed in the most deterministic manner possible. In the experiment the empiricist in each of us is given free rein to exclude all the messy imponderables that intrude on daily life; events are put under a microscope and regulated and measured obsessively. Despite that obsessive scrutiny, the sandpile serves up an astonishing result: we can never know enough about the state of the system to know what it is doing. Although we did everything possible to exclude them, those messy imponderables still turn up in the end. All the philosophical argument of the rationalists from Descartes on cannot overturn the results of this simple experiment, which, artificial though it is, accurately models the world we inhabit.

It is still possible, however, to come at the matter from the other direction. The sandpile experiment does not automatically silence the logician in each(?) of us who wants to believe in a world ruled by a few unambiguous laws precisely applied: the world of Descartes, Newton, and Laplace. Experience is confusing, even experience of a simple little thing like the sandpile experiment, but, so we might claim, if we only knew the underlying laws governing experience then everything would be clear. How do we explore things from this angle? One way, following Laplace, would be to indulge ourselves in ponderous hypotheticals about the Intrinsic Order in the Universe and the Omniscient Being who could grasp that order. Another way is to employ a model. Rather than maunder on about a world governed by Intrinsic Order, let us (in the best American tradition!) slap just such a world together and see how it works. Enter the cellular automaton.

Like any good model, the cellular automaton collapses complex situations and interpretations into a simple, manageable package. The first surprise it offers those us befuddled by too much philosophical reading and thinking is that there is no great trick to putting together a world that is precisely regulated by known laws. Rather than saddle ourselves with Laplace's conundrum of knowing the Mind of God, all we have to do is decide to play God ourselves and make up a world run by laws that we create. Then, like the sandpile, we can sit back and observe just how events in that law-governed world unfold.

A cellular automaton is sort of like any board game, such as Monopoly, checkers, chess, or Go, but without the idea of opposing sides. Take a chess or checker board, for example: sixty-four squares arranged in an eight-by-eight configuration. For simplicity, make all the squares one color, say white. Then place at random a handful of twenty or twenty-five tokens, say black poker chips, on the board, one token per square. We now have the "world" of our model. Not exactly an event to celebrate with paintings on the ceiling of the Sistine Chapel, but the world thus formed is perfectly serviceable for our purposes.

To animate the world of our model we need to come up with some "rules of the game." We can make these whatever we want — remember, we are playing God and this is our Universe. For example, we could make up the following rule or law:

> Begin in the upper left-hand square and proceed square-by-square to the right. At the end of the row of eight squares, return to the left-hand edge of the board, go down to the next row, and proceed as before. For each square visited, if that square is occupied by a token, move that token one square to the left. If the token already occupies a left-most square, then remove it from the board. After visiting all the squares on the board, go back to the original square in the upper left-hand corner and repeat the procedure as specified above.

Proceeding with a square-by-square search according to this rule, each time we encounter one of the tokens randomly placed on the board we move it one square to the left (or off the board if it is already on the edge). Since the world we have created has only eight-square rows, all the tokens placed on the board will disappear off the left-hand edge after eight cycles of following our rule. However, the fact that the board is empty — that the world is a void — does not affect the application of the rule. We would have to go on inspecting the board square-by-square forever; we just wouldn't run into any more tokens.

That is why such a world is called a cellular automaton. It consists of separate, discrete regions or *cells*, each of which has the potential of being in at least two (and perhaps many) *states*. In our example, these states are simply Token Present and Token Absent. As the system develops, the state of each cell is determined by a rule or law that is followed universally and, unless the rule itself specifies a deadline, ceaselessly. The rule-following is automatic, and hence the system it governs is called an *automaton*.

The cellular automaton we have just constructed, of course, does not do much. The random pattern of tokens placed on the board at the beginning persists through the eight cycles as it runs off the left side of the board. The position of tokens vis-a-vis one another never changes; it merely shifts one square to the left. For the brief period of its existence, then, the pattern created remains constant. And when the tokens are gone, the only "pattern" that remains is nothingness — forever.

We could make our world a bit less boring by modifying its rules so that all the tokens do not fall over the edge after a few run-throughs. For example, we could specify that on the second cycle each token encountered is moved to the square above it rather than to the left of it. On the third cycle each token is moved to the right, and on the fourth cycle each token is moved to the square below it. On the fifth cycle we return to our original rule of moving tokens to the left. And so on ad infinitum. In this way, the token's movements describe a neat little square, endlessly overdrawn.

Note, however, that in order to move a token to the right or down we will need to introduce a kind of "wait-state" to prevent us herding tokens off the right-hand or bottom edges of the board in a single cycle. Now rather than move the token immediately after reaching a particular square, we will simply make a note of where the token is to be at the end of the cycle, whether left or right, above or below its present position. Then at the completion of the cycle we will go back over the board, using our notes, and reposition each token. Thus instead of the action (such as it is!) occurring sequentially, everything is shuffled around in one fell swoop at the completion of the cycle.

Following our modified rules, most of the tokens (except for those that started out on the edge of the board) never leave the board, no matter how many cycles the system experiences. Instead, the original pattern of tokens is seen to shift all at once, first to the left, then up, then to the right, then down, at which point every token is back in its original position.

By now you have probably tossed your note pad into a corner (perhaps along with this book!) and, rather than keep track of all those tokens shifting around the board by making sketches and notes, have dashed off a few lines of BASIC and set your trusty PC the task of operating our modest cellular automaton. With your new program up and running, you can sit back and watch the cellular automaton go through its motions. Depending on the speed of your computer, each token seems to revolve in a tight square (perhaps it is just a blur if you are Pentiumed and Turboed to the max). The overall pattern formed by the tokens, however, remains constant.

Although the little world we have created here is pretty unspectacular (to say the least), it is intriguing to note that it is already close to the level of complexity beyond which Laplace's vision of a perfectly determinate, predictable universe begins to blur. So far, though, our automaton still has not strayed into that crucial boundary region where order gives way to chaos. In fact, it still manifests a kind of celestial order that Newton might have enjoyed watching on his Apple monitor. Like the solar system, the automaton's overall pattern does not vary: the tokens, like the planets, retain their fixed orbits. And like the solar system, it is possible to predict exactly where a particular token or planet will be at any given time. We can identify the square token x will occupy (and hence the state of that square) ten cycles from now, a thousand cycles from now, or a million cycles from now. Laplace would be proud of our little cellular automaton.

There is a good reason why our automaton is so thoroughly predictable (and it is not because we have lucked out on our first try and tapped into the Mind of God!). The tokens of the automaton move around but they never *interact*. What one token does never influences what another token does. Again like the planets, they revolve in individual orbits that never intersect (or, in the case of the planets, never get close enough to each other to influence one another to any significant degree). If interplanetary gravitation were powerful enough to overcome the effect of the sun's gravitational field, the solar system would be a very much more dynamic system indeed. It would be so dynamic, in fact, that we, or any other life form, would not be around to contemplate the wonder of a determinate universe.

Just such dynamism characterizes most of the systems we experience on a daily basis. The traffic on the morning commute, the weather that morning, the earth's crust precariously supporting the freeway on which we drive, and the television shows — and movies! — which we watch that evening all share the property of the modest sandpile in being composed of multiple elements that interact with one another in multiple ways. The problem of knowing what the system is doing stems from having to keep track of all those individual interactions.

Still, very simple forms of interaction among the cells of our automaton are broadly predictable, and so do not make Laplace's idea completely unworkable. For example, we might be interested in how the occupied (Token Present) cells of the automaton might be made to increase in number or "breed." To that end, we can require the automaton to stop at each square or cell it visits and inspect the immediate environment of that cell. Since every cell not on the edge of the board has eight cells adjacent to it (three above, three below, one on the right, and one on the left), the automaton checks these eight cells to determine which, if any, are occupied by a token.

Adopting this procedure, we might modify our set of rules so that if at least two cells adjacent to cell *(x, y)* are occupied by a token, then on the next cycle the automaton sees to it that cell *(x, y)* also has a token, regardless of whether it had one before. The automaton "switches on" or produces a "birth" at cell *(x, y)*.

Although tokens are sparsely distributed on the board at the beginning of our world-building session (remember that we started by randomly scattering twenty or twenty-five tokens over the sixty-four square board), if just one square or cell has two neighbors, then the fate of our model is sealed. Each cycle will see the birth or switching-on of new tokens, which in turn will enable new births on the next cycle. Depending on the original distribution of tokens, the board will probably start to get crowded after a very few cycles, and after a few more almost all the squares will be occupied. The inevitable result of this sort of interaction is that every square will have a token on it: our little world (like our own planet) will be filled to capacity. Growth, and any other form of interaction, will cease, but the automaton will go on inspecting cells forever. With our automaton set up in this way, we might dub it the "Malthus" model.

A broadly predictable result can also be had by specifying rules that produce the opposite kind of interaction: a decline, rather than increase, in the number of tokens on the board. For example, when the automaton stops at a square we can instruct it to determine whether that square has a token on it (whether that cell is "on"). If a token is present, we can instruct the automaton to select another cell at random and to determine whether that cell is "on." Then at the end of the cycle, we can instruct the automaton to remove from the board or "turn off" any tokens or cells it has found through its random selection process. In this fashion, tokens are weeded out as the system goes through its cycles and the board becomes more and more sparsely populated. Eventually, probably after a great many cycles, there will be only a single token remaining on the board. We might call this version of our automaton the "Highlander" model (after the four Christopher Lambert movies of that title).

The weeding-out process of the Highlander model will require many more cycles than the growth process of the Malthus model, but both are interacting, weakly dynamic systems whose outcomes are known in advance with just a little intuitive reasoning. Thus both are broadly predictable. To what extent they are predictable in detail is an interesting question, but one I will not pursue much here. If asked to say whether a particular square will be occupied by a token at the end of the fifth cycle of the automaton's operation under the Malthus rules, you or I would probably throw up our hands. However, a chess or Go grandmaster might well come up with the right answer (the Highlander model, since it involves so many random choices, would defy even these experts). Similarly, a mathematician could probably write a neat equation that we could use to determine future states of the Malthus model.

Both models, though, are special, limiting cases of interaction systems. The Malthus model is all growth, whereas the Highlander model is all decline. As we know all too well, real/reel life consists of an endless round of give-and-take. Erratic spells of growth are punctuated by declines that may be just a few (figurative) grains off the pile or a major avalanche. Thus if our cellular automaton is to model faithfully any aspect of the real/reel world, it too should have built-in tendencies to grow and to decline. This is easily achieved by a little more tinkering with the rules we have been making up for the automaton to follow.

Suppose we start just as we did with the Malthus and Highlander models. The automaton proceeds cell by cell and at each cell it stops to determine how many (if any) of the cells adjacent to its present location are occupied by a token or are turned on. It notes that information in its memory and moves on to the next cell. At the end of the sixty-four-cell cycle, it reviews these notes and makes the following changes to its constituent cells:

> If a cell has two occupied cells adjacent to it (two squares with tokens) then that cell is left alone. That is, if the cell happens to be occupied by a token, then that token is left in place during the next cycle of the system. If the cell happens to be empty, then it remains empty during the next cycle. However, if a cell has *three* occupied cells adjacent to it, then that cell will have a token on it during the next cycle regardless of whether it has one on it now or not. In all other cases — in which a cell has 0, 1, 4, 5, 6, 7 or 8 occupied cells adjacent to it — the cell will be unoccupied during the next cycle. In those five scenarios, a presently occupied cell loses its token and starts the next cycle as an empty cell.

We have now performed another small modification in the original rules we devised for our automaton. Whether we have kept using the cumbersome note pad or have written a very short computer program to operate the automaton, it is clear that we are dealing with an extremely rudimentary system, one not far removed in terms of its formal rules from the first (and completely uninteresting) automaton we designed a few pages earlier. So how does our slightly retooled system behave?

It is a wonder of Creation, a model of Generativity.

The modified system I have just been describing has an intriguing name and a brief but rich history. It is the Game of Life, developed in the late sixties by the mathematician John Conway and incorporating related work by Stanislaw Ulam and John von Neumann. The fascinating story and cell-by-cell account of the Game of Life are given in William Poundstone's thought-provoking *The Recursive Universe*, which provides an opening quotation to this section.

Conway called his cellular automaton "Life" because it displayed a completely unanticipated propensity to create separate, distinct patterns (or "organisms") and to undergo a complex evolution. When you set the automaton in motion (ideally on a peppy PC and with a "board" of eight hundred to one thousand cells rather than sixty-four), the most amazing things start to happen. Since you have seeded the system with a random distribution of tokens (Xs or Os on the computer monitor), at first you see these winking on and off in a seemingly meaningless pattern. You might suppose that you have merely concocted a batch of video snow, except as you continue to watch the "snow" dissipates and identifiable figures emerge. Squares of four tokens, lines of three or more tokens, open boxes and ovoids of a varying number of tokens, T-shaped, R-shaped, and U-shaped figures all begin to populate regions of the screen, displacing the video snow. This is the euphoric shout of "Eureka!" that comes with scientific discovery: you begin to observe a thing with no great expectations (and perhaps even with disdain), and then it surprises you, does something completely unexpected and fascinating. It sets you thinking about issues far more exotic and profound than, in the present case, a batch of dots blipping on and off on a computer monitor.

Observing Life closely reveals more than interesting patterns of tokens: individual figures of only four or five tokens undergo complex sequences of evolution requiring hundreds of cycles to complete. The original figure fragments into others — sometimes dozens — and each of those subsidiary figures goes through its own evolutionary process. Life is not just a kaleidoscope, not just another screen saver. Moreover, a few of the figures seem to *move*. The simplest and most common of these mobile figures is a five-token object called a "glider" (Life aficionados have coined a long and colorful bestiary for the figures that appear on screen). The glider goes through a series of transformations during successive cycles that culminate in its reconstituting its original form, only displaced by one square from its starting point. On a fast display, it literally appears to be "gliding" across the screen.

Computer scientists have done astonishing things with this astonishing phenomenon. They have discovered patterns, imaginatively called "glider guns," that themselves *generate* gliders and send them off into infinity. Happiness is a warm glider gun. Their discovery makes clear that "Life" is more than a catchy name to attach to Conway's creation. As we sit watching our monitors, we observe an amorphous, seething stew of video blips or tokens, from which small, stable patterns begin to emerge and to interact. Moreover, this mix never settles down (if our automaton is large enough), for a new pattern (a migrating glider) eventually comes drifting in to mix things up.

What do we call such an evolving, self-reproducing system that is always the same (in terms of its internal mechanisms) and yet always different (in the configurations of distinct patterns or entities it generates)? If that system involves mobile assemblages of organic molecules which form and reform into distinct kinds of beings (species) according to rules encoded in DNA, we have no qualms in saying that we are in the familiar territory of *living* things. But if, as in the present case, video blips replace organic molecules and the rules of the system are simple instructions we ourselves have jotted down, then we draw back, perhaps with a shudder of excitement or dread, from calling that system "alive." The Thing has escaped its Arctic tomb and is multiplying, not on human blood but on the computer monitors of hackers across the land. This staggering breach of one of our most cherished boundaries, the line we insist on drawing between "living things" and "inanimate matter," is the subject of the concluding section of this book.

In taking up the question of what a "logic of things that just happen" might look like, our models of the sandpile and cellular automaton have much to teach us. Perhaps the most surprising truth they reveal is how easily and naturally complex behavior arises from the simplest conditions. The sandpile's flicker noise, produced by a superposition of many discrete signals, could not have been anticipated on the basis of a commonsense knowledge of the elements of the experiment. Yet once the experiment is begun, the complex pattern of signals seems irrepressible: it somehow has to arise. Similarly, the cellular automaton's multiple evolving patterns are the last thing we might have expected from the extremely simple and tedious rules Conway devised to switch cells on and off. We might have expected to see a meaningless scrabble of tokens __ video snow __ or even some frozen, crystalline structure, but not the "birth" of discrete, interacting patterns. Both models, once they are started up, miraculously assume lives of their own. Like the cultural systems we have been considering throughout this book, these simple models reveal the operation of generative processes that cause events to unfold in ways that are at once novel and patterned. Culture, sandpiles, and the Game of Life are all emergent systems.

We are accustomed to thinking of ourselves as the pinnacle of creation because our brains are so intricate, our genomes so astronomically large, our societies so complicated. Surely such complexity must spell uniqueness, if not Most Favored Species status in the eyes of Mother Nature? Here, as before, our answer to this question has to be "yes" and "no." Humans, with their big brains and specialized societies, *are* a wonder of Creation (and it has been the joy and shame of cultural anthropology to have such an intriguing subject and to analyze it so poorly). But the sandpile experiment and the Game of Life impart the sobering realization that our vaunted complexity is nothing special: if things are left to develop, it seems they inevitably become complex, self-organized, critical systems in which a grain of sand, a stray video blip, or a casual glance can precipitate the most elaborate behaviors.

With the sandpile, we did everything in our power to insure a predictable, determinate, *safe* result. And yet even under the uniform stimulus of precisely weighed grains of sand falling in a slow, synchronized cadence, the pile began to act up, to produce an unwieldy, messy set of signals in the form of irregular avalanches of all sizes. Perhaps even more remarkably, the cellular automaton —*for which we wrote the rules* — slipped the leash of our rational intellect and began to produce patterns of extraordinary intricacy. In both models the "logic" we introduced at the outset to control the system gets fuzzier and fuzzier as the system evolves. It soon becomes irrelevant whether we have the sandpile under our empiricist's microscope or whether we are the author of the rules governing the cellular automaton. Both models defy those original constraints and proceed to dazzle us with their inventiveness, their generativity. They make us humble observers of miniature worlds in which events outstrip rules, of worlds in which things just happen.

Something Else

In this book I have focused (obsessively!) on the phenomenon of *boundaries* — that property of sentient life that discriminates between a this and a that, a here and a there, a now and a then. Although boundaries are in a sense the most natural and omnipresent aspect of life, they are also, for us humans, the most puzzling and agonizing. If we were only capable of forming clear and distinct concepts of the entities around us (Hume's frustrated dream which, alas, seemed so modest), we would not be so haunted by boundaries. But such a capacity does not reside within us. As I have argued in the preceding chapters, what makes us human is our uncertainty or ambivalence over the very distinctions that matter most to us: animal and machine, family and enemy, benevolent and malevolent forces of nature. The paradox that is our trademark and destiny is that we, like those elusive subatomic particles of quantum mechanics, are forever shifting our elemental identities and somehow managing to fuse discrepant natures into a single entity.

In searching for a graphic representation of that mercurial entity we call "humanity," I have found most persuasive Manfred Eigen's depiction of the sequence space of a viral quasispecies (see Figure 3.3). Eigen constructs his model in much the same way that we put together our various cellular automatons. Take a tiny bit of data from a large collection (in Eigen's project, the genome of a single virus in a population of viruses; in our case, a single token in a collection of scattered tokens) and assign a precise geometric function to it. Then repeat the procedure for the next item, until all items have been fit into a spatial array. Just as we were surprised by the resulting patterns of the Game of Life, so Eigen's model surprises us with the bizarre shape and fantastic detail a population's genome assumes when mapped onto multi-dimensional space. Whatever we may have expected from Eigen's arcane mathematical exercise, it was not the eerie, octopus-like thing that emerges in Figure 3.3. Yet that thing is a precise, rigorously defined map of a population's genome; it is what the "species" looks like.

I am suggesting that Eigen's map is also an analytical picture of what our "species" looks like. Like the virus, the boundaries of our cultural productions do not form a coherent pattern. Rather, as we have seen in detail with movie-myth, they run off in all sorts of cross-cutting directions. To remain true to the suggestive imagery of Eigen's model, we would have to say that our cultural productions are like a tangled mass of interconnected tentacles. And yet they *are* interconnected, just as two points within a labyrinth are connected.

Eigen's principal conclusion is that it is often misleading to say that a population of viruses belongs to the same species, for its members may vary so extensively in genetic makeup that they behave very differently as, for example, pathogens. Hence his proposal to adopt the notion of "quasispecies": a highly diverse population that nevertheless seems to have a number of relatives in common (those near the nucleated core of the octopus-like entity). In the sequence space mapping of that entity, one specimen may be represented near an end of a far-flung tentacle while another specimen may be near the end of a tentacle that meanders off in a completely different direction. What they have in common is not some overarching set of universals or "invariant properties," but a pathway of transformations — a line sketched in the labyrinth — that connects one to the other.

It is this kind of connectedness (and this aspect of speciation) I sought to emphasize in my discussion in chapter 3 of the intersystem and cultural continuum as vital features of the semiospace of human culture and personality. Our Topekan lad has so many problems adjusting to life in the warm California sun because he keeps running up against intractable *differences* between himself and others and between conflicting attributes of his own identity. These will simply not go away, no matter how many Clintonesque flips he makes in an effort to achieve consensus. And they will not go away because our Topekan lad has very little in common with a Malibu real estate wheeler-dealer, a Laotian Hmong immigrant, or a gang-banger from South Central. Moreover, in the very act of adjusting to life in the staggeringly diverse City of Angels and Teriyaki Tacos, he stretches his own psyche into new, fantastically contorted shapes. Like those virtual particles of quantum physics, he becomes another commuter on the Intersystem, another committee of resident aliens.

The all-important phenomenon of boundaries is given its due in Eigen's model and, I would hope, in my own. The paramount goals of analysis now are to represent as accurately as possible the convolutions of the beast — the extent of its internal variation — and to sketch some of the myriad connections it has with its neighbors. Under this program as applied in cultural anthropology, it is no longer enough to wax eloquently about the integrality of this or that primitive culture or the psychic unity of humankind. Rather, it becomes essential to *show*, in visual, graphic form, just how two "species," two "individuals," or two "cultures" articulate or intertwine with each other.

And therein lies a most important tale. Eigen's model, and my own attempt to sketch out the parameters of semiospace, do not describe isolated populations. They deal with *interacting* elements, some of which are members (however "membership" is defined) of the population under study, and some of which are not. Viruses, human individuals, social groups, and cultural productions (particularly movies) consist of a great many such interacting elements that impinge on one another in complex ways. Indeed, if they were not like this, i.e., if they existed in tidy, self-contained worlds of their own, they would be nothing like they are. They would be like the thoroughly predictable, and boring, cellular automatons we considered before taking up Conway's dynamic, ever-changing Game of Life automaton. All these very different systems get their vitality from interaction and its effects.

In order to interact, it is necessary for two elements to be different. That much, certainly, is a truism. But *how* different? As different as twins — biological replicas? Or as different as enemies squared off and ready for mortal combat (or Mortal Kombat)? *That* is the question Eigen's model addresses for viral "species" and it is the question my discussions of intersystem, cultural continuum, and semiospace address for the human "species" and for human individuals. In both cases, the answer is that the individual elements can be very different indeed. So different, in fact, that one individual may well have less in common with its distant neighbor of the "same" class or type than with another individual of a supposedly distinct class. In the marvelously helpful imagery of sequence space or semiospace, the octopus-like entities representing various viral quasispecies or various human societies/ individuals are entangled in such a way that it often happens that subject A is closer to subject B, located on the tentacle of another entity, than to subject C, which is much further away from A but still a member of the "same" entity.

As I have argued from the beginning, this business of how lines are drawn and crossed is absolutely critical in developing a theory of culture. Sadly, the topic of *variation* has not figured prominently in cultural anthropology (for a number of reasons too involved to discuss here). We anthropologists have been too ready to search for patterns of uniformity, to stress the supposedly shared nature of culture, and have thus neglected the divisiveness and, frankly, horror that await us whenever we enter the field to conduct ethnographic research. Eigen's work, coming from an exotic mix of mathematics and biology, is free of anthropologists' disciplinary blinders and so provides a refreshing stimulus here.[3]

For me the most intriguing feature of Eigen's model is thus not its emphasis on internal variation (Darwin had already done that, if you allow my reading of him), but its ability to unite information and dimensionality in a presentational whole, *to present the meaningful in terms of a geometric array*. From everything that has gone before, it is clear that I attach a fundamental importance to this relationship between sentience or knowing and dimensionality. The notion of semiospace put forward here is an (inexact) application of this principle as it is embodied in various works reviewed earlier: Eigen's sequence space, to be sure, but also Penrose's phase space and Hilbert space, and Conway's cellular automaton.

Although these several models address different phenomena from the perspectives of very different disciplines, I believe they share a profound similarity. By insisting both on the dimensional properties of sentience and the sentient properties of dimension, they dissolve one of our most cherished (and mistaken) dichotomies: the strict separation between mind and matter, thought and action.

Common sense teaches us that we live in a world of things, and our unbounded pride tells us that we, perhaps alone in the universe, also produce thoughts, symbols, representations of those things. Shoot a cue ball into a rack of pool balls and watch the result as the balls ricochet around and come to rest at specific locations on the table. Here we seem to have perfectly uncomplicated action in a physical world, which we happen to be observing. Apart from shooting the cue ball (which could have been done remotely), we didn't need to be there for the balls' movements and collisions to occur. And surely we didn't *will* the three-ball to strike the eight-ball, or determine where the balls would come to rest. Their physical motion and location are independent of our observation.

But now suppose (the last of these "supposes"!) that on closer inspection we discover that the pool table is divided by cross-cutting lines into an array of cells, each just large enough to accommodate a ball. And further suppose that some mad engineer, unbeknownst to us, has installed some equipment and circuitry beneath the table which tidies up after the break by adjusting each ball so that it just fits into one of the cells. Finally, let us suppose that our mad engineer — a fanatical hacker when he is not tampering with pool tables — has designed his circuitry so that it begins to adjust the position and presence of the balls according to the simple rules of Conway's Game of Life.

Now what do we have to say about our pool table? That it is still a physical system composed of material objects which someone has outfitted to run on its own? That the Game of Life "beings" — the blinkers, gliders, beehives, tetronimos, and so on — are, while interesting shapes, still merely physical collections of individual balls? That those "beings" still depend on us and our minds to "read" some pattern (how we cling to that analogy!), some *meaning* into them?

Now suppose just a bit more (I lied!). Suppose that our cellular automaton-cum-pool table were enlarged to cover, say, all of North America, and that the number of balls present at the initial break were correspondingly increased. Uncounted billions of cells and millions of balls would now be in play, far too many for any of us to keep track of. What could we say about the behavior of balls in far away or inaccessible places like the frozen lakes of Manitoba or the carousels of Michael Jackson's Neverland?

Since we are humans with keen minds and the power to reason (to use our minds over matter), we have already determined that the behavior of balls in our immediate vicinity conforms to specific rules, that orderly, patterned behavior is occuring. We observe blinkers, gliders, and so on interacting and we cleverly (scientifically) piece together some of the sequences in their evolution. But we soon recognize that there are severe limits to our powers of observation and inference. A glider or some other mobile form comes drifting in from the uncharted frontier and upsets the scheme of things in our locale. Such surprises force us to admit that, although we are quite certain orderly behavior is occuring out there in Manitoba or Neverland, we cannot say just what it is. Things are just happening out there.

So we find ourselves staring out over an endless plain of cells, dotted here and there by balls that jump around, appear, and disappear. Perhaps somewhere out there, in all those billions of cells, the Game of Life has spontaneously generated what computer whizes at the M. I. T. artificial intelligence lab have managed to engineer into it: the ability not just to reproduce itself but to build its own computer, forming logic gates out of precisely arranged glider guns. In that event, we might expect to be sitting on the front porch of the little cottage in Topeka one day and receive a message, not on the Internet but on the Intersystem of the cellular automaton: "It's mighty cold in Manitoba; how's the weather where you are?"

The content of that message might be considerably different if we were to extend the parameters of our cellular automaton a bit more, say ten or twelve billion light years in every direction — more or less to the limits of what we parochially call the "known" universe. We would also want to give the automaton a few billion years to settle down and start generating signals after the largest pool ball break ever (which we provincials might call the "Big Bang"). Granted all that (since this has been our very last "suppose," I have made it a whopper!) the message we receive one day might inquire about something other than the weather in Topeka. It might ask: "What are you? Are you alive?" Or even, following in the footsteps of the SAL-9000: "Do you dream?"

Fanciful as all this appears (and what better note to close this work on the seriousness of unserious things), it is fairly faithful to deeply serious discussions in theoretical physics about the possibility that the universe may be an evolving, self-reproducing cellular automaton. That the universe may be, in a word, *alive*.[4]

Some years ago the eminent physicist John Wheeler anticipated the current theoretical debate by posing the question in what, even for a physicist, must be a model of brevity. He asked whether we get Bit from It or It from Bit.

In the universe of Descartes and Laplace, the one most of us common-sensical moderns have inherited, we unquestioningly believe that we get Bit from It, that the physical world is mutely, implacably *there* and we proceed to compile information (bits) about it, aided perhaps by science or by God. If we are smart enough or faithful enough, we eventually discover those very laws Nature or God put there, laws determining where everything was, is, and will be. Our information about the world out there — the dimensional world — is strictly derivative; even if we have a hint of what is in the Mind of God we remain voyeurs of a physical reality that is indifferent to our prying ways.

As we have seen, though, this seemingly unshakable order has been rocked to its foundations by developments in theoretical physics and cosmology over the course of this waning century. Relativity and quantum mechanics have given us a world from the other side of Alice's looking glass,[5] a world in which the observer is as necessary as the object in fixing the nature of reality. In Wheeler's terse formulation, in that world we get It from Bit. Or, a little more precisely and more long-winded, we can get at the It-ness of things only because they already incorporate some form of sentience, some Bit-ness. Note that the Bit-ness of things need not issue from the human mind (that un-bounded pride again!) but somehow inheres in the most elementary actions, as when physicists speak only partly metaphorically of a photon "knowing" whether to present itself as a particle or a wave.

The heady thought that the universe as a whole incorporates some form of Bit-ness in its physical organization is the basis for contemporary discussions regarding its being alive and sentient, a kind of immense cellular automaton. That thought brings us, finally, to the phantom that has haunted these pages from the outset: the specter of a Something Else that is alive, sapient, *generative* in the deepest meaning of that term, and that hovers at the edges or nestles in the crevices of "humanity" as it is presently constituted. The extraordinary processes of cultural generativity have catapulted us former ape-things an extraordinary distance in a few million years, and unless it all hits the fan they will continue to do so. At some point on that frenzied ride, and we have seen intimations of it in our movies, we will confront directly, as physical beings, the tortuous boundary separating our flesh-and-blood sapience and generativity from a sapience and generativity more characteristic of the cellular automatons we have been considering. What are you? Are you alive? Do you dream?

The universe, as William Poundstone claims, may be a cellular automaton, a "recursively defined geometric object." If so, it — or very localized regions of it — has the capacity to assume highly complex forms. This is the essence of the It from Bit credo: that physical reality (at whatever level of complexity) is composed of units (bits) of information. In a far more literal than usual sense, the world is a book (but a very special sort of book — one that does things, that is a machine, a *device*). Scattered among the galactic voids there may occur tiny pockets of exceptionally complex organization, as in the cerebral and manipulative equipment of an otherwise undistinguished creature inhabiting, for a brief time, a small, rocky planet orbiting a similarly undistinguished main sequence star. Or there may be, wandering somewhere among Jupiter's moons, an enormous black obelisk whose cellular structure recapitulates or "stores" the information necessary to reproduce a good-sized slice of the universe, information that can be accessed if just the right party (one Commander David Bowman) wanders by and does just the right thing. Oh, my God! It's full of stars! And then . . . But, as we say in postliterate America, yah had ta of seen the movie.

Notes

Chapter 1: Introduction

1. We shall hear more about schismogenesis in American culture in chapter 3 and in the topical essays that follow. In the meantime I cannot recommend too strongly that you go to the trouble of locating a copy of Bateson's hard-to-find early masterpiece *Naven*, a theoretical monograph on the Iatmul people of New Guinea and their elaborate rituals celebrating homicide and head-taking.

2. At last count about five hundred million globally, almost all of which may be found chugging out ozone on ramps of the southern California freeway system.

3. Stanley Kubrick's famous subtitle to *Dr. Strangelove*, "How I Learned to Stop Worrying and Love the Bomb," might serve as the epitaph of the Pepsi/Star Wars generation.

4. Including those of the Australian aborigines as described by William Stanner in the epigraph to this work.

5. Who, on their way to associatedom, apparently discovered that Film presented more opportunities for original criticism than the hallowed literary ground of Chaucer, Shakespeare, Faulkner, and company.

6. The international successes of television serials like *Dallas* and *Dynasty* and supergrosser movies like *Star Wars* are cases in point.

7. The literature on science fiction film and novels is already so voluminous that a sharp focus on particular productions is required to skirt the mass of tangled argument that has grown up around the field.

8. Long a popular theme in Hollywood, the interplanetary visitor appears in movies from the early fifties onward. In fact, my first experience with science fiction, at the tender age of six, was a memorable (and probably life-altering) trip with my uncle, Roger Aycock, himself a prolific author of science fiction, to the theatre to see an all-time classic, the true but, I think, unrecognized predecessor of *E. T.* released in 1952: *The Day the Earth Stood Still*. While the vast majority of "e. t." movies feature menacing, revolting creatures (what my archeologist friend and fellow student of cinematic culture, Michael Bisson, calls "bug-eyed monster movies") that have to be dutifully squashed by an obliging American military, *The Day the Earth Stood Still*, like *E. T.* itself, features an interplanetary visitor who actually settles in to live with an American family. I examine some of the parallels between the two movies in chapter 7, but it is worth noting, and lamenting, here the unfortunate rarity of their common theme of even a tentative understanding between sapient species. With the exception of Spielberg's own *Close Encounters of the Third Kind* (itself more than a little ambiguous), most recent interplanetary visitor movies continue in the depressingly paranoid, xenophobic vein of the Cold War "bug-eyed monster" movies of the fifties and sixties. This heterogeneous corpus includes: *Invasion of the Body Snatchers* (II); *Superman* (I, II, III, and IV); *The Thing* (II); *Starman*; *Predator* (I, II); *Terminator* (I, II); and that nightmare inversion of *Close Encounters*, which takes up the big question of what happens to people *inside* the saucer, *Fire in the Sky*. All these movies fall within that middle ground between space opera and incredible adventure. And in the Dreamtime world of the theatre, the fantasy

element in these movies induces audiences to suspend everyday criteria of what is plausible long enough to ponder the truly mythic problem of nonhuman intelligence and the possible relationships that humans and technologically advanced nonhumans might establish.

9. If there is a single, critical weakness to this work of which I am aware (as opposed to all the other damning flaws of which my author's blind spot makes me blissfully ignorant), it is skirting the horror movie. Here I can only offer the lame excuse that the techniques of a cultural analysis of movies I have laboriously come by in thinking and writing about James Bond, Luke Skywalker, and Indiana Jones have up to now been too frail instruments to employ in a full treatment of the horror movie. The material itself is so gruesome, and the implications of the tremendous popularity of the genre so alarming, that it requires a future, full-length study of its own, and one conducted in the discourse of a cultural analysis that has developed critical skills (and a stronger stomach) through examining less frightful productions.

10. *Jaws*, which quickly spawned a II and then a 3-D and a IV, shares the supergrosser list with *Star Wars*, *E. T.*, James Bond, and Indiana Jones. As with space operas, the box office glitter of *Jaws* has enticed other studios and directors to repeat the formula for incredible adventure movies featuring dangerous animals, and so the serious student of the unserious fare of popular movies must now subject himself to the vicarious thrill/horror of being torn apart and eaten by a whole menagerie of nasty critters. *Grizzly* (aptly dubbed "Claws"), *Tentacles*, *Piranha*, and *Swarm* are typical of the adrenalin-pumping, gore-dripping, post-*Jaws* creature features. Intriguingly, just as *Star Wars* appeared years after Kubrick's serious *2001* had come and gone, so *Jaws* developed an earlier idea of that old master of suspense Alfred Hitchcock, in *The Birds*, which was released in 1963.

11. For the official pronouncement, and denouncement, by the dean of American folklore studies, see Richard Dorson's 1975 work *Folklore and Fakelore*.

12. An anthropologist going to the movies to do anthropology inevitably subverts the practices and assumptions of a traditionally conceived ethnography. Popularity, in the form of supergrosser status, becomes the imprimatur of the genuine that strangeness and remoteness were for the old ethnography. And commercialism, that index of popularity in the capitalist world system, becomes a major topic of investigation and not a mark of that pariah "fakelore."

Chapter 2: The Primacy of Myth

1. Instead, we reserve our adulation for another Dreamtime phenomenon: Hollywood stars, our homegrown brand of royalty.

2. It is the impossibility of having it both ways, coupled with the prevailing assumption that myth is uncritical stereotype, that accounts for the great divergence in approaches to myth in modern social thought. And while one encounters numerous twists and turns of interpretation in the works of the several theorists reviewed in the following pages — Roland Barthes, Gregory Bateson, James Fernandez, Marvin Harris, Edmund Leach, Claude Levi-Strauss, Thomas Sebeok, and Victor Turner — all of them can be arranged roughly into two camps. In one camp, represented by the theory, if not of Marx then of a conventional Marxism, and by the American-style materialism of Marvin Harris, is the approach which regards myth as stereotype or *mystification* that must be debunked and dispelled. This approach rests on the pervasive view that social thought, including cultural anthropology, is or should be *social science*, and science, as everyone is presumed to know, is antithetical to myth. In the other camp of theorists, represented by the works of Bateson, Fernandez, Levi-Strauss, Sebeok, and Turner as well as by this book, is the approach that treats myth as inherently constructive and distinctively human — so much a part of the human condition that it both generates and reflects the problematic, ambivalent nature of its subject.

3. A concept developed by Dean MacCannell in his pioneering study *The Tourist*.

4. Which means not burying myth in a mess of platitudes that merely serve to explain it away: myth A "serves to promote" condition X in Society Y, etc.

5. One variety or other of the materialist perspective is to be found in the works of a wide range of social thinkers influenced by Marx and/or by the disciplines of economics and ecology. We shall encounter one particularly esoteric brand of it in the following section, where I review Roland Barthes's early contribution to cultural analysis.

In the United States, the banner of *cultural materialism* is carried high by Marvin Harris, whose popular introductory textbook (*Culture, People, Nature*) and other widely read works (see, for example, *Cannibals and Kings: The Origins of Cultures* and *America Now: The Anthropology of a Changing Culture*) have established him as one of only two cultural anthropologists since Margaret Mead to acquire a truly public voice. (In a fine irony, the other is the materialists' nemesis, Carlos Castaneda.) In my (doubtlessly jaundiced) view, the popularity of Harris's work stems in part from the intuitive resonance he establishes with American readers: as anthropology's Rush Limbaugh, he tells them what they want to hear. And, following on our earlier discussion of the *myth of America*, you will understand that what they want to hear is that culture, particularly its frothier components such as myth and ritual, is simply a kind of cerebral window dressing on a rock-solid tableau of down-to-earth, practical considerations. Why did Aztec religion emphasize human sacrifice and cannibalism? Well, you see, there were an awful lot of Indians in central Mexico back then (before Cortez and his henchmen showed the Aztecs what bloodletting was really all about) and there were very few local sources of animal protein, so the folks in the next valley started looking *pretty* tasty. Why do Hindus regard cattle as sacred, when people could more rationally get rid of the cows and use the grain they consume to feed themselves? Well, you see, if you do a nutritional calculus of village life in India, you discover that it makes good sense to keep cows around for the milk, butter, and fertilizer they produce, so the ancient priests figured they would gull the rube farmers, who otherwise might put a quick end to the pesky critters, with a little sugar-plum fairy tale about how the deities love and protect cattle.

6. And this is a large "suppose," which materialist theories manage by making large and unproven generalizations about the circumstances of cultural origin.

7. Authors and directors are not exempt from this *uncenteredness of meaning* of movies, even when they happen to be the sole or principal creative agent at work in a particular case. For example, George Lucas, the creator and director of *Star Wars*, offers an interpretation of his creation that goes only part way toward explaining its popularity.

> I've always loved adventure films. After I finished *American Graffiti*, I came to realize that since the demise of the western there hasn't been much in the mythological fantasy genre available to the film audience. So, instead of making "isn't-it-terrible-what's-happening-to-mankind" movies, which is how I began, I decided that I'd try to fill that gap. I'd make a film so rooted in imagination that the grimness of everyday life would not follow the audience into the theater. In other words, for two hours, they could forget. . . .
>
> I'm trying to reconstruct a genre that's been lost and bring it to a new dimension so that the elements of space, fantasy, adventure, suspense and fun all work and feed off each other. So, in a way, *Star Wars* is a movie for the kid in all of us. (*Star Wars* — the book, page four of photo insert section)

While I can certainly embrace Lucas's assertion that *Star Wars* is mythological, it is clear that he uses the term in a more restricted sense than I. The problem here is not just a quibble over how to use the word, "myth," but is rather Lucas's assumption that a film "so rooted in imagination" offers an escapist fantasyland in which "the kid in all of us" can "forget." His view that the popularity of the movie is due to its escapist plot, its ability to provide a simple fairy tale with a happy ending, is no doubt shared by many who have seen the movie or been exposed indirectly to the phenomenon of *Star Wars*. Yet things are not so simple that they allow a clear distinction between an often unpleasant "real" world of everyday experience and a charming fantasyland of the screen. *Star Wars* succeeds, apparently despite its director's intention, in touching a nerve that is very much alive.

Lucas correctly claims that people grow tired of going to the movies to see more of their familiar, depressing, conflict-ridden lives. Will Jill Clayburgh find happiness as *An Unmarried Woman*? How many ways will Woody Allen and Mia Farrow find to make each other miserable? What will happen to the *Rich Kids*, Frannie and Jamie, and their newly divorced, hopelessly screwed-up parents? People sometimes go to the movies to see more of their daily lives, but increasingly, with the proliferation of space operas, disaster films, killer-animal movies, horror shows, and Schwartzenegger, Stallone & Company adventure sagas, they go, as everyone (including George Lucas) says, to escape. The question, however, is whether they are escaping *from* something in the movie theatre or escaping *to* an underlying reality — a *Dreamtime* — that is only intuitively sensed in ordinary life? I think that they are doing the latter and, moreover, that what really packs them in is a movie's resonance with the irreducible problems, dilemmas, tensions in that, really not so "ordinary," life. Movies as myths do not avoid the drama of life; they amplify and embody it.

8. Levi-Strauss's treatment of myth is developed in the context of his theory of structuralism, which is not only a prominent feature of anthropological thought but of discussion and debate in several branches of the humanities and social sciences. Levi-Strauss's own writings are so extensive and introductions and commentaries on his work and on the field of structuralism so numerous that I will not attempt anything like a comprehensive treatment of the structural analysis of myth in this work. I am more interested in borrowing from his work where it aids the purpose at hand — a cultural analysis of popular movies — while pointing out aspects of his thought that sometimes distract from the interpretation of modern culture. For reasons not really central to this topic, it would be inaccurate to describe my treatment of a popular movie as a "structural analysis." Suffice it to note here that I treat Levi-Strauss's monumental works on mythology as a starting point and constant inspiration for my analysis of movies, without being greatly concerned with the exactness of fit between the two approaches.

9. See *A Course in General Linguistics*, p. 16.

10. The crux of the difficulty in Barthes's treatment rests right at the heart of his concept of myth, of his notion of how myths operate to produce meaning. Working from his recent reading of Saussure and within the context of literary studies, Barthes was understandably interested in the place *language* would occupy in an emerging (general) semiological science. The basis of Saussure's theory lay in his concept of the *linguistic sign* as a synthesis of *signifier* and *signified*, the former being a fixed *utterance* (like saying the word "tree") and the latter the *concept* with which that utterance is associated (the class of large leafy objects growing out of the ground) by speakers of a particular language, in this case English.

11. I realize that many Americans may have difficulty with this example, for a dominant theme in American culture is that people are either "black" or "white." It is important to recognize, however, that this simplistic view is not typical of a majority of the world's societies, and that it has been the basis of much of the racial discord that has blighted American life. "Race" is as much a cultural construction, and subject to as much cross-cultural variation, as "nationality" or "brotherhood" and requires the same close, ethnographic attention to content and context if we are to understand its meaning in a particular case.

12. At least until *Return of the Jedi* came along, but that was six years in the future.

13. "Imaginals" in Mary Watkins's evocative term, as used in her *Waking Dreams*.

14. See James Gleick's very accessible *Chaos: Making a New Science* for a discussion of this major development in modern science. Gleick's work opened a floodgate for popular treatments of chaos and complexity theory.

Chapter 3: A Theory of Culture as Semiospace

1. As I discuss in the following sections, such drastically different actions arise because of the starkly incompatible but dialectically fused constructs of an Us and a Them, kinship and ethnicity, that together stake out a major semiotic dimension of culture.

2. It is intriguing, and highly ironic, to contrast these state-of-the-art views theoretical physicists and cosmologists have of the near-mystical nature of their craft with the dominant stereotype in American culture of science as an implacable grinding away of the unknown and mysterious, replacing the emotional and religious with the cold, intellectual, atheistic truths of a transparent, verifiable body of logical statements. My earlier comments about the "myth of America" as a practical, down-to-earth place and people, and about the internal contradictions and deep ambivalences in myth are relevant here: we cloak ourselves in the image or stereotype of practicality and realism, yet recoil from those among us — scientists — to whom we ascribe the very qualities we profess to admire. This is Bateson's schismogenesis in action. As I attempt to show in the topical chapters that follow on James Bond, *Star Wars*, *Jaws*, and *E.T.*, this ambivalence about science and scientists (our modern Masters of Machines) and by implication about the scientists lurking within ourselves and our "loved ones" is a foundation — a "key myth" in Levi-Strauss's sense — of the American Dreamtime. It is a myth that generates as much self-contradictory love-hate and desire-loathing as any in our culture.

A particularly ironic aspect of our stereotype of science and its lack of fit with what those exemplars of science — physicists and cosmologists — actually seem to be up to is that, quite apart from the lay public, the stereotype plays well (actually, great) among cultural anthropologists, those academe-bound neighbors of the very scientists I have been discussing. It is both ironic and disturbing that cultural anthropologists for the most part seem to be blissfully unaware that the "science" they castigate for its outmoded insistence on an "objective" world and its denial of a complex, intersystemic or intertextual world of many realities is only their own, hopelessly antiquated boogeybear, a relic of distorted memories of high school (or grade school) science classes and of God-only-knows-what personal phobias. The physicists were working that rich, "intertextual" ground when anthropologists, to their lasting discredit, were out in the field busily putting an academic veneer on the politics of racism and colonialism. Einstein, Bohr, Heisenberg, and Schroedinger practically opened the century with a flurry of new concepts and theories of nature whose pale reflections are only now being seen in the works of cultural anthropologists. If anything, it appears that the deep, unconscious appeal of the Dreamtime image of science and scientists (as a calling that requires its practitioners to be completely objective and rational, and thus inhuman and evil) has seduced our postmodernist anthropologists, so that they, elaborating on the awe and dread of science in their brain marrow, denounce the objective, inhuman menace. Rather than leading an intellectual vanguard into the next century, they are only serving as apologists for the last.

Lest symbolically-oriented colleagues protest that I have singled them out for unfair criticism, I should hasten to add that, in my opinion, a truly flagrant hoax has been played for decades by those decidedly *non*-postmodernist anthropologists — all healthy-minded believers in down-to-earth realism — who denounce the "fashion" of an intersystemic world of virtuality and parade (or parrot) a threadbare version of a "science" that, if it ever existed, vanished along with Bacon. In the name of anthropology-cum-science, these workers produce an endless deluge of statistical surveys (the "coital frequencies" of Haitian women) and "development" studies (how to turn Maasai nomads into ranchers), unfailingly written in the stupefying prose of a C-minus sociology major and dedicated to a doctrinaire belief that they are furthering the cause of an empirical "science." Bohr and Schroedinger, the discoverers of a world of virtuality, are spinning in their graves, while those disciples of a "scientific" anthropology carry on through the years, taking up precious university positions and, a thousand times worse, forcing their claptrap on young and vulnerable graduate students.

3. Even the metaphorical thrust of "culture" is wrong: it directs us to the *agri*-culture of an earlier, *cultivated*, bucolic life just as we are thrashing about in the machine-angst death grip of computers that can trounce us at chess, after they've taken away our jobs.

4. Although there are truly exceptional exceptions in which the topology of culture asserts itself in Leach's analysis. See, for example, his brilliant essay, "Anthropological Aspects of Language: Animal Categories and Verbal Abuse."

5. It will be convenient here to summarize and quote at some length Roger Penrose's account, in *The Emperor's New Mind*, of these concepts, both to establish something of their specific content and applicability to my argument regarding the spatial nature of culture, and to provide readers as mathematically unsophisticated as myself a glimpse into the remarkable complexity of the physical world as elucidated by the true myth-makers of our age: theoretical physicists and cosmologists.

> Try to imagine a 'space' of a large number of dimensions, one dimension for each of the coordinates $x1, x2, \ldots p1, p2, \ldots$ (Mathematical spaces often have many more than three dimensions.) This space is called *phase space* . . . For n unconstrained particles, this will be a space of $6n$ dimensions (three position coordinates and three momentum coordinates for each particle). The reader may well worry that even for a *single* particle this is already twice as many dimensions as she or he would normally be used to visualizing! The secret is not to be put off by this. Whereas six dimensions are, indeed, more dimensions than can be readily(!) pictured, it would actually not be of much use to us if we were in fact able to picture it. For just a room full of air molecules, the number of phase-space dimensions might be something like
>
> 1000000000000000000000000000000
>
> There is not much hope in trying to obtain an accurate visualization of a space *that* big! Thus, the trick is not even to try — even in the case of the phase space for a single particle. Just think of some vague kind of three-dimensional (or even just two-dimensional) region. . . (176–7)

A highly unusual "space" to be sure! Yet this is just the sort of thing I have in mind in proposing that culture is a semiospace. As conceptualized here, semiospace is *not* a physical gridwork composed of intricately arranged components (on which the "new ethnographers" of a bygone era could perform their "componential analysis"). It is a highly complex *domain of possibilities for the evolution or transformation of sentient, message-bearing entities*. To map a "point" onto phase space or semiospace is to describe one possible arrangement of the total system: "[a single point] *Q* represents our entire physical system, with a particular state of motion specified for every single one of its constituent particles" (177). That point occupies a region of phase space containing a number of other such points, each of which describes an arrangement of the system much like that of the original point.

The really interesting question is what happens to such a well-defined, tightly bounded region as the system of phase space or semiospace develops over time? Does it remain fairly cohesive, and hence coherent, or does it fragment into indecipherable labyrinthine shapes? Note that as far as *phase* space is concerned, this question is a perfectly straightforward problem in classical mechanics. It has none of the smoke and mirrors of a literary or philosophical argument, none of the trappings of interpretivist or "postmodernist" cultural anthropology. Yet the answer to that straightforward question strikes at the heart of any positivist anthropology. For the truth — the *physical reality* — is that even the most simple, uniform arrangement of elements does not evolve in a stable, deterministic fashion. It soon becomes an untraceable labyrinth.

However, this [presumption of stability in the system] is deceptive, and on reflection we see that the very reverse is likely to be the case! In Fig. 5.14 I have tried to indicate the sort of behaviour that one would expect, in general. We can imagine that the initial region R_0 is a small 'reasonably' shaped region, more roundish in shape than spindly — indicating that the states that belong to R_0 can be characterized in some way that does not require unreasonable precision. However, as time unfolds, the region R_1 begins to distort and stretch — at first being perhaps somewhat amoeba-like, but then stretching out to great distances in the phase space and winding about backwards and forwards in a very complicated way. The volume indeed remains the same, but this same small volume can get very thinly spread out over huge regions of the phase space.

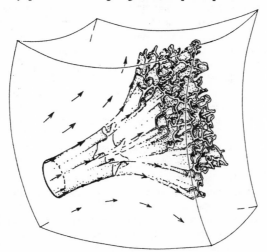

Fig. 5.14. Despite the fact that Liouville's theorem tells us that phase-space volume does not change with time-evolution, this volume will normally *effectively* spread outwards because of the extreme complication of this evolution. (181–2)

. . .

We may ask, in view of this spreading throughout phase space, how is it possible at all to make predictions in classical mechanics? That is, indeed, a good question. What this spreading tells us is that, no matter how accurately we know the initial state of a system (within some reasonable limits), the uncertainties will tend to grow in time and our initial information may become almost useless. Classical mechanics is, in this kind of sense, essentially *unpredictable*. (pages 182–3)

The properties of semiospace that I explore in the remainder of this chapter have much in common with Penrose's account of phase space. If, by introducing a physical sciences analogy, I distort the nature of my subject matter, I believe that distortion is much less serious than what positivistically-inclined anthropologists do routinely: in the name of "science" they describe a social world of cause-and-effect that bears no resemblance to Penrose's account of physical reality.

As conceptualized here, semiospace is highly sensitive to minute changes in the initial conditions of a system; it is an *emergent* or *generative* phenomenon. It shares these properties with phase space. But semiospace, by definition, is infused with sentience, and it allows for seemingly contradictory arrangements of elements, not just physical differences. Semiospace is not only an exceedingly intricate, labyrinthine world, it is a domain where possibility or *virtuality* reigns. These attributes ally semiospace with the quantum world(s) of subatomic particles — world(s), however forbidable their mathematical descriptions, that seem to accommodate the myth-maker more than the laboratory scientist. In the quantum realm, it is Hilbert space rather than phase space that provides the geometric bearings.

The puzzling feature of quantum reality — namely that we must take seriously that a particle may, in various (different!) ways 'be in two places at once' — arises from the fact that we must be allowed to add quantum states, using complex-number weightings, to get other quantum states. This kind of superposition of states is a general — and important — feature of quantum mechanics, referred to as *quantum linear superposition*. It is what allows us to compose momentum states out of position states, or position states out of momentum states. In these cases, the linear superposition applies to an *infinite* array of different states, i.e., to all the different position states, or to all the different momentum states. But, as we have seen, quantum linear superposition is quite puzzling enough when applied to just a *pair* of states. The rules are that *any* two states whatever, irrespective of how different from one another they might be, can coexist in any complex linear superposition. Indeed, any physical object, itself made out of individual particles, ought to be able to exist in such superpositions of spatially widely separated states, and so 'be in two places at once'! The formalism of quantum mechanics makes no distinction, in this respect, between single particles and complicated systems of many particles. Why, then, do we not experience macroscopic bodies, say cricket balls, or even people, having two completely different locations at once? This is a profound question, and present-day quantum theory does not really provide us with a satisfying answer ...

Recall that in Chapter 5 the concept of *phase space* was introduced for the description of a classical system. A single point of phase space would be used to represent the (classical) state of an entire physical system. In the quantum theory, the appropriate analogous concept is that of a *Hilbert space*. A single point of Hilbert space now represents the *quantum* state of an entire system ...

The most fundamental property of a Hilbert space is that it is what is called a *vector space* — in fact, a *complex* vector space. This means that we are allowed to *add* together any two elements of the space and obtain another such element; and we are also allowed to perform these additions with complex-number weightings. We must be able to do this because these are the operations of *quantum linear superposition* that we have just been considering. (256–7)

In what follows I hope to persuade you at least to entertain the possibility that semiospace, or culture, has much in common with Hilbert space.

6. In fact, phase space, in modelling the Hamiltonian equations, subsumes all of classical mechanics (and in the process rigorously demonstrates the undecidable, chaotic implications of that field, which "scientific" anthropologists and other social thinkers have routinely lauded as a model of objective truth).

7. From this mythic perspective, scientific rationality can only be *made to fit* people's lives by imposing it in the form of an authoritarian, even totalitarian regime. Note that the villain of many, many movies over the past four decades has not been the Nazi or the Commissar, but the Evil Scientist (or, if not quite evil, then the "mean scientist," who won't let E. T. hang out with his mountain-biking buddies in peace). As we have seen, anthropologists and other social thinkers are not immune to the attractions of myth, and so it is not surprising that they should bristle at the nightmarish Dreamtime image of men with crew cuts and lab coats coming through the door with rulers, compasses, and other equipment to measure and dissect the elusive "wonder that is man" (or the wonder that is E. T.).

Remarkably, the wonder that Penrose and other writers of (sort-of) accessible books on the inaccessible topics of quantum mechanics, cosmology, nonlinear mathematics, and fractal geometry let us glimpse is that the practitioners of those arcane fields abandoned their rulers and compasses long ago, with hardly a backward glance, and set off to explore worlds of infinite dimensions, multiple realities, turbulence, and byzantine labyrinths that make the exotic doings of the anthropologist's "natives" pale in comparison. Lacking actual flesh-and-blood villains to dread then, we are left with a sort of "dentist fear" of those mysterious mathematician-scientists and their terrifying, contemptible rulers and compasses. But when we finally see them in action we discover they have traded those medieval instruments of torture in for Cray computers, graphics software, and radio telescopes.

8. Some of the very straightest coming from "arrow cane," a relative of the sugar cane plant found in upriver areas of the Guianas and Amazonia).

9. "So pack your ermines, Mary. We're getting out of here. Ten thousand years in show business. The public is going to tear the place apart."

10. Which also happen to be fractals. See Prusinkiewicz and Lindenmayer's *The Algorithmic Beauty of Plants*.

11. See Talcott Parson's *The Social System*, the 1954 codex (which has yet to be translated into English) for a generation of social scientists on both sides of the Atlantic.

12. See "The Serpent's Children: Semiotics of Cultural Genesis in Arawak and Trobriand Myth," and "Jonestown: An Essay in Ethnographic Discourse."

13. After long years of mulling it over, I have more or less decided (and you are free to reject the outlandish analogy) that the tenets of structural-functionalism have a hold on anthropology like that of the President Kennedy assassination on the American public at large. The mountains of literature documenting a conspiratorial cover-up, the endless frame-by-frame replayings of the Zapruder film that have been burned into our retinas, and, to top it off, Oliver Stone's Dreamtime version of the event in *JFK*, have all combined to instill grave doubts in many of us that the official lone-assassin, single-bullet story describes how the president was killed. We all, or many of us, take a swipe at the official version, but thirty years of relentless criticism have left it intact. It is really quite remarkable: you can't find anyone whose opinion you value to unequivocally endorse the Warren report, and yet the years go by and the official version persists. It is much the same with structural-functionalism: everyone you, as an anthropologist, talk to claims either never to have endorsed it or long since abandoned it in favor of newer, zippier theories, and will usually take *their* gratuitous swipe at the old doctrine while they are at it (functionalist-bashing has been in vogue for decades). Yet the basic core of the doctrine does not go away. The old habit of thinking about a diverse human population as a "society" whose members hold a set of integrated, fairly stable beliefs and values, or "culture," like the old habit of thinking about lines with fixed lengths and a space with absolute, intuitive dimensions, persists in the face of massive evidence all around us of the circumstantial, evanescent, and tremendously complex nature of those "elementary" concepts.

14. Do not, however, let my cavalier attitude dissuade you from consulting Turner's impressive works, where you may find much that is familiar from your readings here.

15. As I acknowledged earlier, you would probably not be wading through this chapter on the peculiar topic of "culture as semiospace" if I had not had the opportunity, as an impressionable graduate student, to attend Turner's seminars and devour his then recently published works.

16. Caught like deer in the headlights of an onrushing semi(otic)!

17. If you are interested in pursuing this topic in a bit more detail, I suggest two essays of mine: "The Cultural Continuum: A Theory of Intersystems," which draws heavily (steals) from Derek Bickterton's superb theoretical monograph on Guyanese speech: *Dynamics of a Creole System*; and "Are There Cultures to Communicate Across? An Appraisal of the "Culture" Concept from the Perspective of Anthropological Semiotics."

18. This impetus to identify a core of underlying regularities in the dross of speech has been with linguistics since its beginnings: Ferdinand de Saussure, whose contributions I touched on in chapter 2, sought for the principles of phonology and syntax (*la langue*) and discounted the bothersome speech (*le langage*) of individuals.

19. The figure, my impressionistic adaptation of a drawing by Jared Schneidman, is inspired by Eigen's article, "Viral Quasispecies," in the July 1993 issue of *Scientific American* (pp. 42–9). I would ask you to spend some time reflecting on its implications for our present discussion, for Schneidman's figure, together with Penrose's drawing of the multiple foldings of phase space, are the best visual representations I have found of the ideas I am developing in this work.

Here is Eigen's account of the basics of Schneidman's figure:

How to Construct a Sequence Space. One way to study the diverse nucleotide sequences in the genes of viruses is to map them into a multidimensional matrix called a Hamming sequence space. In this space, each point represents a unique sequence, and the degree of separation between points reflects their degree of dissimilarity. The space can be most easily drawn for short sequences consisting of binary digits. For a sequence with just one position, there are only two possible sequences [0 or 1], and they can be drawn as the end points of a line. For a sequence with two positions, there are four permutations [00, 01, 11, 10], which form the corners of a square. The variations on a three-digit sequence become the corners of a cube [000, 001, 011, etc], and the variations on a four-digit sequence are the vertices of a four-dimensional hypercube. Each higher-dimensional space is built iteratively by drawing the previous diagram twice and connecting the corresponding points. The sequence spaces for viral genomes are far more complex than these simple figures because they involve thousands of positions that can each be occupied by one of four different nucleotides.

Population Dynamics of a Virus depend on the error rate of its replication process. These figures are highly simplified representations of the sequence spaces that might contain a viral population. If the replication process of a virus were perfectly accurate, all the viral offspring would occupy the same position in sequence space [represented by a tiny, dense spheroid in the middle of the sequence space]. If replication were highly imperfect, mutant viruses would soon occupy every position in sequence space [represented by the space being filled with a uniform, diffuse cloud] and the viral population would lose its integrity. At some intermediate error rate, however, the viral population would become a coherent, self-sustaining entity that resembles a cloud centered on the original consensus sequence [see Figure 3.3 in text]. That cloud is a quasispecies. (44–5).

It is crucial to note that the "sequence space" of the figure, like the phase space of Penrose's drawing, is multidimensional, so that the twisting, turning pseudopods of the "quasispecies" describe an incredibly convoluted labyrinth, a great, fuzzy "cloud" to use Eigen's term. Yet each point within the cloud represents a distinct arrangement, or sequence, of elements (strings of code such as nucleotide base pairs or grammatical features). The fundamental point here is that the constituent elements of the "system" do not share any discrete common property, any "Englishness" or "Spanishness" (or, the idea I want to drive home, any "humanness"). Nevertheless, elements *are* connected to one another by the set of transformations (or intersystems) required to get from one place in the labyrinthine sequence space to another. (Note that the application of this model to the paleontological dispute raging over multiregional evolution vs. an "out of Africa" theory of human origins would do much to clarity that issue.)

20. As a fieldworker studying American culture this is quite okay; lurking and voyeuring have been ethnography's key "methodological tools" since anthropology began.

21. And as unpredictable. The folks in Des Moines and Saint Louis didn't hear much from the Cray supercomputers at the National Weather Bureau in late June 1993, when the Mississippi and Missouri — surely among the most monitored and controlled rivers in the world — were a few weeks away from record flooding.

22. On this topic see Deborah Tannen's popular study *You Just Don't Understand.*

23. In the lyrics of the tops-in-pops ballad from the early years of Vietnam: "Men who mean just what they say. Those brave men of the Green Berets."

24. The 1966 product of a decidedly unholy cinematic alliance between the eminent Huston and Dino de Laurentiis.

25. This short-lived series chronicled the doings of (who else?) Anthro, an exceedingly bright cave lad who looked a lot like a Zuma Beach surfer (or Kato Kaelin). As in my little just-suppose sketch above, Anthro went around noticing things and acting on them (a good man of few words and large deeds): he noticed that people were having a hard time chewing their raw food, so he made the first cooking fire; he noticed that it was hard to throw a spear far enough to bring down a juicy boar for the new barbeque, so he invented the bow-and-arrow. He continued in this vein at breakneck speed until, after just a few issues, there seemed to be nothing left for him to invent short of a particle accelerator. At that point in his meteoric career as culture hero *extraordinaire*, Anthro and *Anthro* comics were mercifully retired — to the chagrin of surrealist-prone young anthropology graduate students, who were waiting for Anthro to become a sort of early day Magritte, pushing at the limits of conventional thought. But even they could see the inevitability of the end of this pop culture totem of their discipline, *for there was nothing more for Anthro to accomplish.* All the major social institutions and cultural productions of early humanity had been handily slapped together in the space of a few issues of the comic book, so that its plot and character were exhausted.

26. "Our time" being, as Dean and Juliet Flower MacCannell have called it in their book title, *The Time of the Sign.*

27. Recall that even chimpanzee and human chromosomes differ by only about two percent).

28. Other peoples, for example Bronislaw Malinowski's classic Trobrianders, have very different ideologies of kinship in which descent is traced exclusively through women (the hallowed "matrilineal descent systems" of Anthropology 101 lectures) and the physical role of the father in conception is flatly denied. Trobrianders, in common with Australian peoples, believed that a woman became pregnant when a totemic or ancestral spirit entered her.

29. *Easy Rider* dramatizes, but hardly exaggerates, the intensity of feelings about hair length and appearance that raged in late twentieth-century America. "Beatnik" and "hippie" became emblems of ethnicity that cut as deeply into the psyches of some Americans as the identities "Serb" and "Croat" or "Tutsi" and "Hutu" do for others today.

30. A fact now widely known, which dispels their stereotypical image as peaceful fruit-eaters.

31. See Gregory Mahnke's *Signs of the Unself* for a profound analysis of the implications of cloning for our institutions and beliefs that center on "kinship."

32. See "The TransAtlantic Nanny: Notes on a Comparative Semiotics of the English-Speaking Family."

33. On the fundamental nature of the face : ass opposition in Western art and philosophy, see Octavio Paz's remarkable little volume, *Conjunctions and Disjunctions*.

34. Is it the only way? I don't think so, but that gets a bit more complicated!

35. The thrown together piece of work that is the human spine also explains why most of us have bad backs.

36. If very slowly: perhaps on the order of a tablespoon of grey matter every one hundred thousand years, according to the eminent biologist Edward O. Wilson.

37. Some archeologists have sketched grislier scenarios, which have those proto-folks cracking open the long bones and splitting the skull to get at the juicy marrow and brain matter of the dear departed.

38. Remember (and who could forget) Hannibal Lecter's parting words in *Silence of the Lambs*: "I'm having an old friend for dinner."

39. The discoverer and excavator of the Shanidar site, Ralph Solecki, made this finding the basis of a popular book (published two years after Woodstock) which suggested that these Neandertals had anticipated the American cultural movement of the late sixties: *Shanidar: The First Flower People*. Intriguingly, Solecki's work and that of other archeologists who studied the Shanidar material inspired Jean Auel to write *Clan of the Cave Bear*, which acquired true Dreamtime status first as a runaway bestseller and then as a movie of the same title starring Daryll Hannah (its producers apparently rejected more descriptive titles like *Unusually Articulate Malibu Blond among the Dark Hunchy People Who Make Weird Grunting Noises*). Like those twists and turns of our ant path, the routes through the semiospace of Dreamtime America are indeed convoluted and bizarre — but much more interesting!

Representations of protohuman hominids in popular movies is a fascinating topic with much material for the cultural analyst to examine, beginning with the dawn of cinema and D. W. Griffith's 1912 classic *Man's Genesis*. To date I know of only one manuscript on the subject, by the archeologist Michael Bisson. Another archeologist, Erik Trinkaus, whose *The Shanidar Neandertals* is the definitive monograph on that subject, has also coauthored, with Pat Shipman, a fascinating intellectual history of Neandertal studies: *The Neandertals: Changing the Image of Mankind*. In their final chapter, "Created in Our Own Image: 1984-1991," Trinkaus and Shipman make a solid contribution to the fledgling field of the anthropological semiotics of Dreamtime America (though they stop short of diving into the novel-movie *Clan of the Cave Bear* and its cinematic predecessors and successors!).

40. As the ad mavens at Virginia Slims would have told Immanuel Kant, "You've come a long way, baby!".

Chapter 4: The Story of Bond

1. Keeping company with works by Stendhal and Churchill; the president's taste in literature was as democratic as his taste in women.

2. See Geertz's essay, "Deep Play: Notes on the Balinese Cockfight," in his modern classic, *The Interpretation of Cultures*.

3. See, for example, *St. Urbain's Horseman*.

4. In fact, the *Iliad* would probably lend itself rather well to the supergrosser attentions of a top screenwriter and some big-name talent. Arnie, in a sort of retro-*Conan the Barbarian* role, could play Achilles. There would be enough lopping-off of limbs and slicing-open of entrails to

keep even *Predator 2* fans happy. And, to top it off, to give the movie that redeeming quality Tipper Gore would endorse, there would even be the social drama of the warrior Achilles, bravest of the brave, fiercest of the fierce, living happily in his army tent with his homosexual lover, Patroclus, leaving his arms only to go out and do some more lopping-off and slicing-open of the Trojans. Supergrosser treatment of Western civilization's first war-hero-cum-gay-in-the-military might not play well with the Joint Chiefs of Staff or the ranking members of the Armed Services Committee, but I believe that at least the chase scene of *Achilles the Gay Barbarian* could rank right up there with the best of recent action movies.

5. Short of some incredible event orchestrated by an Anthro-Bunny comic book character who gives rabbits automatic weapons or death rays overnight.

6. See Shirley Strum's *Almost Human: A Journey into the World of Baboons* and Jane Goodall's *The Chimpanzees of Gombe*.

7. Who, as Strum notes in *Almost Human*, have to make it on the same open savannas that provided the stage for human evolution.

8. As we might expect, the advent of *Homo sapiens* and culture has done some interesting things to the mammalian surround, which we will examine in a moment. But culture has not wiped the slate clean where deep-seated mammalian behaviors are concerned. A couple of millimeters of grey matter deposited atop the cerebral cortex in modern humans (the so-called "higher associative areas") have not erased neural structures built up over two hundred million years of mammalian evolution. Evolution takes what it is given and works with that; it is a classic tinkerer.

9. The study of which Edward Hall has called *proxemics*. See his *The Silent Language* and *The Hidden Dimension*.

10. As Goffman would have insisted, the unspoken intensity of the code regulating our elevator behavior is best demonstrated by little incidents in which that code is breached. Here it is possible for you to engage in a little mischievous field research of your own into the bricks and mortar of the American Dreamtime, to conduct a little exercise in what, in the heady days of yesteryear, was called "experiential sociology" or "experiential anthropology": exploring your culture by messing with it.

A simple, harmless version of the experiment is just this: Wait for an elevator with four or five people inside; step aboard; but *do not* turn around. Continue facing toward the rear of the car, not intentionally making eye contact with the other occupants but not avoiding it either. Observe the effect of your little transgression on the other occupants. Better yet, since they will doubtlessly attempt to conceal their discomfort from you, arrange to have a shill aboard when you enter — a friend who is among the passengers. Have the friend stay aboard after you exit and note the behavior and remarks of the other passengers. The chances are good that even in that constrained setting the other passengers will do or say something that indicates their relief at the harmless conclusion of your little breach of the public order.

Such mild-mannered tinkering, however, does not get to the bedrock of our mammalian faith in the surround, however distorted that faith may have become by a few million years of cultural evolution. To do that, you need to go from mischievous to malicious experiential anthropology, which may land you in jail but stands a good chance of cutting through the layers of conditioning that usually prevent us from an honest expression of our gut feelings. Consider, for example, reenacting a scene from a classic work on American culture by the masterful ethnographer and dean of gonzo journalism: Hunter Thompson's *Fear and Loathing in Las Vegas: A Savage Journey to the Heart of the American Dream*.

Choose a hotel filled with conventioneers (poetic justice would make the convention that of the American Anthropological Association, but virtually any group — Jaycees, Insurance Underwriters, whatever—will do). You and a very large friend (Thompson's companion was his three-hundred-pound Samoan attorney) prepare in advance for your experiment in elevator behavior by choosing something like biker regalia — lots of denim, leather, rivets and chains — and dousing these outfits in a mixture of cheap red wine (a gallon of Gallo will do nicely) and pizza topping (extra anchovies!). When this brew congeals it gives the nice effect of an alcoholic's dried vomit. Dressed in these laboratory togs, wait in the hotel lobby for an elevator with a few good citizens filing in. Both of you enter, talking in yells, reeking to high heaven, and face the other passengers who have dutifully turned to face the doors. When the doors close and the car begins to ascend (no way out now!) your large friend flies into a paranoid rage, screeching "Somebody looking at me?" "Somebody looking at me?" in the faces of the now-terrified passengers. Then comes the *coup de* (not so) *grace*: pretending (in order, maybe, to stay out of jail) to dig in his pocket for a blade, your maniacal companion fixes the most terrified passenger with his red-eyed stare and growls, "Somebody wanta get his face cut?!"

Your experiment is guaranteed to produce either absolute, shrieking bedlam or ice-cold catatonia in its hapless victims. Either result demonstrates the unspoken, sacred power of elevator etiquette, of the uneasy truce our mammalian brain has worked out with the forces society marshals against it. Hunter Thompson's account of his visit to Las Vegas is so outrageous, not just for its language or now rather wistful evocation of a drug culture, but because it touches a nerve, one of the main ones, probably the spinal cord itself, of human existence: *social life is a lie that must be accommodated because there is no real alternative, no life outside society that would be conceivably human.*

11. See Tom Wolfe's perceptive early essay on this very topic, "Clean Fun at Riverhead," in *The Kandy-Kolored Tangerine-Flake Streamline Baby.*

12. Of these, general readers in the United States are probably most familiar with Joel Chandler Harris's *Uncle Remus* stories, an artful retelling of African- and American Indian-derived trickster tales featuring that irrepressible mischief-maker, Brer Rabbit. A much larger audience (in these postliterate times) knows the Disney animated version of Uncle Remus, and Brer Rabbit's Looney Tunes cousin, that "wascally wabbit," Bugs Bunny.

13. But *not* the agribusinessmen whose subsidized rural factories produce our chickens, milk, and vegetables, nor the English professors whose occasional poems merely break the cadence of their computer-generated paychecks, which come with their pension plan payments conveniently deducted.

14. After Lewis and Clark's expedition, the western mountains beckoned to men who could find no place in the confining cities and towns of the East and the Prairie States. Hunting, trapping, and brawling along the rivers of Colorado, Wyoming, Kansas, Texas, and New Mexico, the mountain men lived their lives by their own rules. To this unregulated life was added a further upheaval: the Civil War. The war caused many of the mountain men to choose sides and filter back to the border states, where they served as scouts, hunters, and even spies. In the excitement and turbulence of war they found, for a time, an outlet for the lust for adventure that first propelled them into the mountains. And when the war finally ended, they drifted among the social debris left in its wake: Springfield, Abilene, Dodge City, Deadwood. In the saloons of those frontier towns and on the dusty streets outside their doors, Yank and Reb refought that traumatic, fratricidal war countless times.

The energies of those restless, deadly men were suited to their time and place, so that even the more sociopathic among them sometimes found themselves wearing a badge and charged with maintaining a semblance of order in the anarchy of cattle and mining towns. Witness the Old West's most notorious killer, William Bonner — Billy the Kid — who was deputized by the cattle czar Chisholm to enforce his brand of justice west of the Pecos. If group identity, the difference between Us and Them, is a fundamental dimension of culture, then it is hard to imagine a more dramatic setting for its operation than the frontier towns that inherited all the confusion and bitterness of the Civil War.

The career of James Butler Hickok developed in those turbulent war and postwar years, and for that reason resembles the career of a later veteran turned agent, James Bond. Hickok's career is just as much a part of the American Dreamtime as Bond's, owing to the sensationalized, quintessentially mythic accounts by which we know, not the history, but the *histoire* of Hickok.

According to the story of Hickok, he was born and reared near the edge of established society, in La Salle County, Illinois, but at the age of twelve or so was unable to suppress an innate restlessness that made him a runaway. For fifteen years he lived in the mountains, growing strong, developing his woodcraft, and honing an amazing ability as a natural, "dead" shot.

> I allers shoot well; but I come ter be perfeck in the mountains by shooting at a dime for a mark [from fifty paces] at bets of half a dollar a shot. And then until the war I never drank liquor nor smoked . . . War is demoralizing, it is.
> (In George Nichols's 1867 essay, "Wild Bill," *Harper's New Monthly Magazine*, p. 278)

With the outbreak of war Hickok joined the Union army and served with distinction as a scout and spy, sometimes donning a Confederate uniform to penetrate Rebel lines and carry back intelligence on troop movements and munitions stores.

As a master of small, maneuverable, sophisticated machines, Hickok, like Bond a century later, got into terrible jams that only his extraordinary abilities allowed him to escape. Perhaps the definitive tale in the story of Hickok is the McCanles massacre. In the best James Bond tradition that was to come, the army scout and spy was taking a little time off to visit a lonely widow in her small, isolated cabin. Since he was on a social call, so the tale goes, Hickok took only one of his customary two six-shooters with him. His visit was rudely interrupted by the arrival of David McCanles and nine of his gang, all armed desperados and sworn enemies of Hickok. The ten killers cornered Hickok in the cabin and stormed the place. The room filled with gunsmoke and the smell of cordite, knives flashed, fists flew, and when it was over Hickok staggered out of the cabin, bleeding from a dozen wounds and leaving ten dead men behind. After that, so the legend goes, people knew what homicidal rage lay waiting to be kindled beneath the gentle features of the army scout. "Wild Bill" Hickok left that scene of carnage.

After the war, Hickok drifted from town to town, from gunfight to gunfight, until that fateful July day in 1876 when the coward Jim McCann shot him without warning in Carl Mann's saloon in Deadwood, South Dakota.

15. The media finds itself in an odd predicament here. It has hyped a sport in which increasing anonymity is the rule, and yet it needs stars and superstars to continue hyping the game. So John Madden and Al Michaels talk (and talk, and talk) about the personal lives of the players and besiege them with uncomfortable questions in sideline or locker room interviews. The sideline shot of the player off the field and out of his all-obscuring helmet is a favorite supplemental device for imparting personal identity to men who perform their exploits as numbers.

16. So fine, in fact, that both superstars tragically fell off it. Graceland was an early grave, and there will be no more Super Bowl half-time shows for the man with one glove.

Chapter 5: Metaphors Be With You

1. What Thomas Sebeok, following on a distinction between "anthroposemiotics" and "zoosemiotics" in his essay "Zoosemiotics," might have termed *mechanosemiotics*.

2. As discussed in Ignace Gelb's 1962 classic, *A Study of Writing*.

3. Alhough *007* has become an icon of intrigue in itself, its Bondesque allusion intensified by the bizarre coincidence of the 1984 tragedy of Korean Airlines Flight 007.

4. In fact, it is now possible to walk into a video arcade, climb into the cockpit of a starfighter, feed it a few tokens, and relive from the pilot's seat Luke's dizzying assault on the Death Star.

5. "Tokens," not chips (those are all inside the machines) that are inscribed "For Replay Only — No Cash Value." Those tokens go chunking down the slits of apparatuses that are designed to provide, depending on one's level of play (or "replay"), perhaps a sixty-second experience.

6. Jibes inflicted because, I think, they dimly perceive the murky depths stirring beneath the shallowness — and that worries them.

Chapter 6: It and Other Beasts: *Jaws* and the New Totemism

1. This is, however, entirely in keeping with the anthropologist's usual role in a "native" community, where his combined ignorance and peskiness typically make him something akin to the village idiot.

2. Like bears, we sometimes even shit in the woods (though bears, as Senator Proxmire would have noted, do not award themselves National Science Foundation grants to document their *toilette*).

3. Please, oh please, don't trow me in dat briar patch!

4. Again, this term, if not quite its meaning, is taken from Thomas Sebeok's essay *Zoosemiotics*.

5. With all due respect to Levi-Strauss's *The Raw and the Cooked*.

6. Even more telling for our immediate concern with *Jaws* as cultural production is the fact that the same growing shrillness, the same increasing polarization, we find in machine movies is also present between the two sorts of animal movie we identified earlier: animal-friend and animal-enemy movies.

Suppose that our old friend, the Martian anthropologist, landed its (again, *not* "his" or "her") spacecraft beside the Washington monument today. Instead of blowing anthropologist and spacecraft to smithereens (Bill & Hil figure there will be plenty of room to reach a compromise with it), the National Security Council turns the matter over to a panel of leading exobiologists (that branch of biology with an as yet undocumented subject matter: life on other worlds). These experts decide, for whatever peculiar reason (after all, we figure *they* must be pretty peculiar to spend their time studying something that nobody knew existed) to isolate the extraterrestrial and show him only a collection of popular animal movies.

Bring on *King Kong*, Mickey Mouse and Donald Duck cartoons, the *Lassie* series, *Jaws, Flipper, Old Yeller, Free Willy, Milo and Otis* (yes, even *Milo and Otis* — cultural analysis has no gag reflex!), and, to top it off, *Jurassic Park*. The Martian takes all these in, thanks its hosts, and tells them it will be beaming back its report (turns out the Martian anthropologist is one of those applied types who works for the Agency for Interplanetary Development, which finally got around to our backward little planet). Then, with its lavish expense account about to run out (applied anthropology is the same everywhere), the Martian warp-drives out of Washington air space before Bill has his usual second thought and orders the Patriots to draw a bead on the Martian ship. Now, what would that report contain?

Assuming a very great deal about our interplanetary visitor (for example, that it is even capable of perceptually differentiating between bizarre Earth creatures that resemble each other as closely, say, as dolphins and sharks), its report might well resemble those sent back by our own early explorers about their first encounters with the native peoples of Australia and the Americas. Those explorers, all staunch Victorians with visions of steel mills dancing in their heads, found remarkable the pervasive, intimate, and manifestly irrational ties their "discovered" peoples had with animals. Through garbled translations they found that Arunta and Assiniboin apparently believed that animals were, or were once, just like people, that animal species were the ancestors of existing social groups, and that individual people regularly established profound spiritual relationships with particular animals. As these accounts filtered into discussions in the new discipline of anthropology, they formed the basis for the still entrenched view that native peoples enjoyed a special, "totemistic" bond with animals.

The anthropologist Lucien Levy-Bruhl, continuing the tradition of Cartesian rationalism, did E. B. Tylor and James Frazer one better: native peoples not only possessed the "animistic religion" of totemism; they actually thought in a fundamentally different way from enlightened, scientific moderns (see his *How Natives Think*). Their close association with the animal world, to the point of melding human and animal identities, was the consequence of their possessing a "pre-logical mentality" based on a sense, not of Descartes's differentiating *cogito*, but of a *mystical participation* in the world. The poor sods couldn't quite tell the difference between humans and animals (without industry they lived so close to nature anyway) and so they enshrined their conceptually blurred vision in beliefs and behaviors that equated people and animals. Clearly Lucien had never hopped in his Mustang, checked that his Garfield stick-on doll was adhering properly to the rear window, and driven past the endless strip of Piggly Wiggly and El Pollo Loco stores on his way to take in a Rams-Dolphins game.

For these reasons I think it likely that the Martian's report, based on similarly fragmentary information, might have much in common with the explorers' tales. And back on the Red Planet, in the plush offices of AID, there might even be a hotshot young Development Officer waiting, like Lucien in the sky with diaphanous tentacles, to infer from the second-hand accounts of Lassie and Flipper that the primitive natives of Earth felt a mystical bonding with animals. Or some animals, at any rate. What would our tentacled Lucien make of Jaws and Jurassic Park?

I think it likely that Lucien, if it were given at all to theorizing in its Project Analysis, would come up with ideas strikingly similar to those of our own, earth-bound Lucien. If Earthlings bonded mystically with creatures like Flipper and Willy (which, after all, is a *killer* whale), and at the same time vented such murderous rage on a seemingly identical creature, the Great White Shark, it could only be because they were afflicted with a form of "pre-logical mentality" that produced an incredible irrationality in their thought and behavior (and so, rather than try to "develop" these wretched creatures, it would be better to put them out of their misery and grind them all up for mulch to grow the savory fungi the first Martian colonists would crave). What goes around comes around.

The Martians would actually have stronger grounds for rationalizing their colonial endeavours than nineteenth-century Europeans, for the staggering contradictions in our own relations with animals indicate a mentality that is far less "logical" than that of the Arunta and Assiniboin. The yawning gulf between representations of animals in our animal-friend and animal-enemy movies is part of a widespread trend toward an increasing polarization in all our dealings with animals.

7. To be sure, the environmental devastation our species is wreaking on the planet and its creatures is alarming. If authorities like Edward Wilson (*The Diversity of Life*) and Jared Diamond (*The Third Chimpanzee*) are at all accurate in their somber assessments, we are in the midst of the largest mass extinction of species since the dinosaurs went under sixty-five million years ago. Wilson's and Diamond's estimates are particularly grim, for they make the disturbing argument that most of the species we are wiping out haven't even been officially "discovered" yet. While biologists have documented the existence of some two million species of living things (everything from bread mold to that pinnacle of evolution, *H. sapiens*), their sampling procedures of selected biota indicate that some thirty to one hundred million species are actually out there.

Diamond's depressing prognosis is that about half of those will become extinct in the next century, before most of them even receive a Latin name to carry with them into oblivion.

But even the prospect of this global calamity, involving numbers of species and a wealth of biodiversity that numb the mind, does not account for the particular direction the ecology movement has taken over its brief career since the late sixties. Curiously, the sheer scale and technical intricacy of species extinction and environmental degradation are so intimidating that they actually impede our efforts to see the problems and, like any good, practical-minded American, fix what needs fixing. Few of us have the training and vision to grapple with the issues as Wilson and Diamond do. And even if we had, we would discover that tackling the issues head-on or "objectively" leads us right back to our old nemesis: that intractable class of problems that includes our earlier project of measuring those infernal ant paths.

Do we spend all day or even all year focused on the one tiny squiggle a single species represents in the vast biotic scheme of things, trying in this case not to come up with a precise measurement *per se* but to save one among the millions of (mostly unidentified!) species from extinction? If so, how do we make the call as to just which squiggle/species we will select from the vast array of other squiggles, other species that might draw our attention? It is like God standing on the river bank, about to fashion Man in His own image from a bit of clay He takes from the bank. But *which* bit? Of the miles and miles of river bank He has created, of the tons and tons of clay in them, which tiny piece will He select to fashion into the Wonder of Creation? Or, as Kurt Vonnegut put it in *Cat's Cradle*, "Oh, lucky mud!," to be that infinitesimal handful that receives the spark of life among all those tons that had to go on being just plain, dead mud.

8. In an opening scene and musical score — *Ba-Boom!, Ba-Boom!* — that have become an immortal piece of cinema, right up there with the shower scene in *Psycho*: *Eeeh! Eeeh! Eeeh!*

9. Intriguingly, South American Indians say very similar things about how they know when a certain animal is in fact a spirit, or a Master of Animals.

10. If *Jaws* makes you uneasy about your next trip to the beach, be grateful that Spielberg has not tried his directorial hand with John Wyndham's terrifying classic about monsters from the deep, *The Kraken Wakes*.

11. Perhaps one reason why this powerful movie, first of the supergrossers, did not get very far in the Politically Correct Sweepstakes (otherwise known as the Academy Awards).

12. Perhaps wishing to avoid further irritating the profound ecological sensibilities of his Hollywood colleagues (but sorry, Steve, still no Academy Award for you!).

13. In making this claim, I am once again revealing my anthropological prejudices along with my inadequacies as a film critic, for the critics have reviled all four of the *Jaws* movies for having plots based on the absurd belief that a creature as mindless as a shark could seek revenge on a particular family. But the critics, intent on defending their exacting standards of cinematic aesthetics, here miss the all-important point that humans are deeply affected by anything that brings them face-to-face (or face-to-snout) with the parent-child relationship. That relationship is a powerhouse of emotion, an anchor or polarity in the swirling turbulence of our individual lives and of the semiospace of culture. Everything in life that bespeaks an Us-ness resolves to that fundamental relationship between child and parent, and so the critics should not be surprised when, unmindful of their contemptuous reviews, the masses flock to movies that unashamedly put children on center stage. Anthropologists, on the other hand, have made kinship their stock-in-trade from the beginning (and so they have an even poorer excuse than the film critics for not seizing on representations of the family in *Jaws* and searching out their implications in American society at large).

14. In the absurd and vacuous world of American politics, nothing of recent vintage can surpass Dan Quayle's attack on the *Murphy Brown* television series for its "glorification" of unwed motherhood and its insult to "family values" (this came at a point in the 1992 presidential

campaign when Dan and George could already see the lounge chairs beginning to slide across the deck of the listing *Titanic*, and so they were out on the hustings taking some pretty wild swings). Between their political addresses, George was hopscotching around the globe aboard *Air Force One*, putting the finishing touches on his "new world order" (while the real/reel world he could never see was busily fragmenting itself into a tormented jumble of warring, starving splinter groups). Busy with his world tour, George left the sagacious Dan to preside over a domestic policy that was completing its gutting of every major social program, and in the process wrenching apart uncounted thousands of families. But *Murphy Brown*, now *there* was a real threat to family values.

15. And that's why the last thing George and Dan would have wanted was a real triumph of family values in a properly Republican America. They didn't even care for the little taste of it provided by *Roseanne*.

16. We are back to feeling our way through Edgar Allen Poe's "fog" of the mind.

17. Although, again, developments in the field of "virtual reality" are pushing at the membrane separating animate beings inhabiting a physical world from computer-generated animate beings inhabiting a world of cyberspace. To anticipate the discussion just a bit, that is why we have gone from *Jaws*, with its evocation of Nature red in tooth and claw, to *Jurassic Park*, with its bioengineered, theme park dinosaurs brought to "life" through a complex process of computer animation.

18. I have not dealt very charitably with the writings of Rene Descartes in this work, but the very section of his *Discourse on Method* that contains his (in)famous doctrine of the *cogito* also has a remarkable argument for the essential identity of animals and machines. Published in 1637, the ideas in the passage (if not its prose style and its pious suckups to the Inquisitors who were then giving Descartes's contemporary Galileo such a rough time) may be found in thousands of scientific and popular works of our own century. They constitute, in fact, the kernel of a scientific world view that permeates even our most ordinary thoughts and assumptions about the nature of life and about our relationship with animals.

> And afterwards I had shown there, what must be the fabric of the nerves and muscles of the human body in order that the animal spirits therein contained should have the power to move the members . . . [and by] distributing the animal spirits through the muscles [they] can cause the members of such a body to move in as many diverse ways, and in a manner as suitable to the objects which present themselves to its senses and to its internal passions, as can happen in our own case apart from the direction of our free will. And this will not seem strange to those who [know] how many different *automata* or moving machines can be made by the industry of man, without employing in so doing more than a very few parts in comparison with the great multitude of bones, muscles, nerves, arteries, veins, or other parts that are found in the body of each animal. From this aspect the body is regarded as a machine which, having been made by the hands of God, is incomparably better arranged, and possesses in itself movements which are much more admirable, than any of those which can be invented by man. Here I specially stopped to show that if there had been such machines, possessing the organs and outward form of a monkey or some other animal without reason, we should not have had any means of ascertaining that they were not of the same nature as those animals.

According to this view, animals are just very well-made machines and, correspondingly, machines are just very crudely executed animals. Its general acceptance is a signature of the modern, scientific outlook on the world, including its animal species. We thus find it everywhere, and particularly in our key myths, whose function (like particle accelerators of the mind) is to isolate pure "particles" of thought, pure ideas (would Kant critique the *reinen*-sound of this?), along with their opposing "anti-particles" and smash them together to see what happens.

19. In which Bateson was so indiscreet as to describe and theorize about the horrid, grisly business of routinized murder and head-taking among that little band of Nature's children. One only wonders if Kevin Costner could pull *their* fat out of the fire, along with that of the gentle Lakota Sioux, in a *Dances with Wolves II*.

Chapter 7: Phone Home: *E. T.* as a Saga of the American Family

1. Is *2001* an exception? Maybe, but *just* maybe; it's hard to say anything definite about that thoroughly ambiguous movie.

2. *Aliens* (the first of two sequels to *Alien*) is a memorable exception.

3. He would not have fared as well as Scotty if hauled before the vindictive old fools of an earlier generation's House Committee on Unamerican Activities).

4. This property of American myth validates, in my view, the (rather peculiar) use I have made of Levi-Strauss's structural analysis of myth throughout this work.

5. The innate vs. acquired feature seems so locked into the gender distinction in cultures around the world because women in and of themselves possess the generative power of giving birth, whereas men can transform social relations only through their instrumental actions. Since, as we have seen, the Life Force is dialectically paired with the Death Force in the semiotic of cultural generativity, it follows that if women control one they must have some strong association with the other. Thus widowed, embittered old women are feared for what they are: foreboding reminders of the inherent malevolence of existence. Isolated, grouchy old men, on the other hand, are feared for what they may do: their antisocial behavior is translated through spirit familiars into deadly attacks of sickness.

6. Much as the spacetime travelers in Einstein's special theory of relativity receive "information" about each other's lives (such as how rapidly each party is aging) that does not correspond at all with the experience of the sending party.

7. See Leach's classic monograph, *Political Systems of Highland Burma*, p. 278.

Chapter 8: Conclusions

1. Witness the instant, well-oiled global marketing campaign that catapulted *Jurassic Park* to the top of the supergrosser charts in a few short weekss. Such a system was nonexistent when James Bond first appeared in *Doctor No*.

2. See, for example, M. Mitchell Waldrop's *Complexity: The Emerging Science at the Edge of Order and Chaos*.

3. The problem of boundaries and variation, however, was already at the forefront of the work of Eigen's predecessor, Charles Darwin. In this world of paradox, it is delightful to realize that *The Origin of Species* is a colossal misnomer, for the book has less to say about "species" than about the problem of understanding variation. Edward Wilson, in his ongoing eulogy to the "species" concept, would do well to reconsider Darwin's message, which, for all its doggedly methodical presentation, is amazingly (post)modern in its concern with the fragmentary and fragmenting minutiae of life.

4. See John Gribbin's *In the Beginning* for a thought-provoking statement of this view.

5. And Michael Herzfeld has even given us *Anthropology through the Looking Glass* •

References

Ardrey, Robert
1961 *African Genesis: A Personal Investigation into the Animal Origins and Nature of Man*. New York: Atheneum.
Arens, William
1981 Professional Football: An American Symbol and Ritual. In *The American Dimension: Cultural Myths and Social Realities*. 2nd edition. W. Arens and Susan P. Montague, ed. Pp. 1-9. Sherman Oaks, Calif.: Alfred Publishing Co.
Asimov, Isaac
1991 *I, Robot*. New York: Bantam.
Auel, Jean
1980 *Clan of the Cave Bear*. New York: Crown.
Bak, Per and Kan Chen
1991 Self-Organized Criticality. *Scientific American* (January). Pp. 46-53.
Barthes, Roland
1973 (1957) *Mythologies*. Annette Lavers, trans. and ed. London: Granada.
Bateson, Gregory
1958 (1936) *Naven: A Survey of the Problems Suggested by a Composite Picture of the Culture of a New Guinea Tribe Drawn from Three Points of View*. 2nd edition. Stanford, Calif.: Stanford University Press.
1972 *Steps to an Ecology of Mind*. New York: Ballantine.
1979 *Mind and Nature: A Necessary Unity*. New York: E. P. Dutton.
Benchley, Peter
1974 *Jaws*. Garden City, NY: Doubleday.
1976 *The Deep*. Garden City, NY: Doubleday.
1979 *Island*. Garden City, NY: Doubleday.
1982 *The Girl of the Sea of Cortez*. Garden City, NY: Doubleday.
Bickerton, Derek
1975 *Dynamics of a Creole System*. New York: Cambridge University Press.

Bisson, Michael
    1987 Archeology and Symbolism: Images of the "Cave Man" in Popular
        Movies. Paper read before the seminar, "Rendering Culture:
        Anthropological, Journalistic and Literary Approaches to Ethnographic
        Discourse." Department of Anthropology, McGill University.
        Montreal, Quebec.
Black, Max
    1962 *Models and Metaphors: Studies in Language and Philosophy*. Ithaca,
        NY: Cornell University Press.
Brydon, Anne
    1991 *The Eye of the Guest: Icelandic Nationalist Discourse and the Whaling
        Issue*. Ph. D. Dissertation, Department of Anthropology, McGill
        University. Montreal, Quebec.
Burroughs, William S.
    1959 *Naked Lunch*. Paris: Olympia Press.
    1964 *Nova Express*. New York: Grove Press.
Capra, Fritjof
    1991 *The Tao of Physics: An Exploration of the Parallels between Modern
        Physics and Eastern Mysticism*. 3rd edition. Boston: Shambhala
        Publications.
Carpenter, Edmund
    1972 *Oh, What a Blow That Phantom Gave Me!* New York: Holt, Rinehart
        and Winston.
Darwin, Charles
    1954 (1859) *The Origin of Species*. New York: Modern Library.
Davies, Paul
    1991 *The Mind of God*. New York: Simon and Schuster.
Descartes, Rene
    1952 (1637) *Discourse on the Method of Rightly Conducting the Reason*.
        Elizabeth S. Haldane and G. R. T. Ross, trans. Chicago: William
        Benton.
Diamond, Jared
    1992 *The Third Chimpanzee: The Evolution and Future of the Human
        Animal*. New York: HarperCollins.
Dorson, Richard
    1975 *Folklore and Fakelore: Essays toward a Discipline of Folk Studies*.
        Chicago: University of Chicago Press.
Drummond, Lee
    1978 The Trans-Atlantic Nanny: Notes on a Comparative Semiotics of the
        Family in English-Speaking Societies. *American Ethnologist* 5: 30-43.
    1980 The Cultural Continuum: A Theory of Intersystems. *Man* 15: 352-
        374.

1981 The Serpent's Children: Semiotics of Cultural Genesis in Arawak and Trobriand Myth. *American Ethnologist* 8: 633-660.

1984 Jonestown: A Study in Ethnographic Discourse. *Semiotica* 46: 2/4: 167-209.

1987 Are There Cultures to Communicate Across? An Appraisal of the "Culture" Concept from the Perspective of Anthropological Semiotics. In *Georgetown University Round Table on Languages and Linguistics 1986*. Simon P. X. Battestini, ed. Pp. 214-225. Washington, D. C.: Georgetown University Press.

Eco, Umberto

1979 Narrative Structures in Fleming. In *The Role of the Reader: Explorations in the Semiotics of Texts*. Bloomington: Indiana University Press.

1983 *The Name of the Rose*. William Weaver, trans. San Diego: Harcourt Brace Jovanovich.

1991 *The Limits of Interpretation*. Bloomington: Indiana University Press.

Eigen, Manfred

1993 Viral Quasispecies. *Scientific American* (July). Pp. 42-49.

Emerson, Ralph Waldo

1990 (1838) *Essays*. Cambridge, Mass.: Belknap Press.

Fernandez, James

1971 Persuasions and Performances: Of the Beast in Every Body . . . and the Metaphors of Everyman. In *Myth, Symbol, and Culture*. Clifford Geertz, ed. New York: W. W. Norton.

Fleming, Ian

1953 *Casino Royale*. New York: Macmillan.

1955 *Moonraker*. New York: Macmillan.

1957 *From Russia With Love*. New York: Macmillan.

1958 *Doctor No*. New York: Macmillan.

1959 *Goldfinger*. New York: Macmillan.

Freud, Sigmund

1961 (1930) *Civilization and Its Discontents*. James Strachey, trans. and ed. New York: W. W. Norton.

Geertz, Clifford

1973a (1972) Deep Play: Notes on the Balinese Cockfight. In *The Interpretation of Cultures*. Pp. 412-453. New York: Basic Books.

1973b Thick Description: Toward an Interpretive Theory of Culture. In *The Interpretation of Cultures*. Pp. 3-30. New York: Basic Books.

Gelb, Ignace

1962 *A Study of Writing*. Chicago: University of Chicago Press.

Gleick, James

1987 *Chaos: Making a New Science*. New York: Viking.

Goffman, Erving
1971 *Relations in Public: Microstudies of the Public Order*. New York: Basic Books.
Goodall, Jane
1986 *The Chimpanzees of Gombe: Patterns of Behaviour*. Cambridge, Mass.: Belknap Press.
Gould, Stephen Jay
1991 *Bully for Brontosaurus*. New York: W. W. Norton.
Gribbin, John
1984 *In Search of Schroedinger's Cat: Quantum Physics and Reality*. New York: Bantam.
1993 *In the Beginning: After COBE and Before the Big Bang*. Boston: Little, Brown.
Hall, Edward
1966 *The Hidden Dimension*. New York: Doubleday.
1973 *The Silent Language*. New York: Doubleday.
Harris, Joel Chandler
1982 (1880) *Uncle Remus: His Songs and His Sayings*. Robert Hemenway, ed. New York: Viking.
Harris, Marvin
1977 *Cannibals and Kings: The Origins of Cultures*. New York: Random House.
1981 *America Now: The Anthropology of a Changing Culture*. New York: Simon and Schuster.
1992 *Culture, People, Nature: An Introduction to General Anthropology*. 6th edition. New York: Harper and Row.
Hawking, Stephen
1988 *A Brief History of Time*. New York: Bantam.
Herzfeld, Michael
1988 *Anthropology through the Looking Glass: Critical Ethnology in the Margins of Europe*. New York: Cambridge University Press.
Kael, Pauline
1968 *Kiss Kiss Bang Bang*. New York: Atlantic Monthly Press.
Kidder, Tracy
1981 *The Soul of a New Machine*. New York: Atlantic Monthly Press.
Kline, Morris
1962 *Mathematics: A Cultural Approach*. Reading, Mass.: Addison-Wesley.
Leach, E. R.
1964 Anthropological Aspects of Language: Animal Categories and Verbal Abuse. In *New Directions in the Study of Language*. Eric H. Lenneberg, ed. Pp. 23-63. Cambridge: Massachusetts Institute of Technology Press.
1965 (1954) *Political Systems of Highland Burma*. Boston: Beacon Press.

1966 (1961) *Rethinking Anthropology*. New York: Humanities Press.
1976 *Culture and Communication*. New York: Cambridge University Press.

Levi-Strauss, Claude
1963a (1958) *Structural Anthropology*. Claire Jacobson and Brooke Grundfest Schoepf, trans. New York: Basic Books.
1963b (1962) *Totemism*. Rodney Needham, trans. Boston: Beacon Press.
1966 (1962) *The Savage Mind*. Chicago: University of Chicago Press.
1969 (1964) *The Raw and the Cooked: Introduction to a Science of Mythology (Mythologiques I)*. John and Doreen Weightman, trans. New York: Harper and Row.
1988 (1985) *The Jealous Potter*. Benedicte Chorier, trans. Chicago: University of Chicago Press.
1995 (1991) *The Story of Lynx*. Catherine Tihanyi, trans. Chicago: University of Chicago Press.

Levy-Bruhl, Lucien
1966 (1910) *How Natives Think*. Lilian A. Clare, trans. New York: Washington Square Press.

Lieberman, Philip
1991 *Uniquely Human: The Evolution of Speech, Thought, and Selfless Behavior*. Cambridge, Mass.: Harvard University Press.

Lotman, Juri
1976 (1973) *Semiotics of Cinema*. Mark E. Suino, trans. Michigan Slavic Contributions, No. 5. Ann Arbor: University of Michigan.

Lucas, George
1976 *Star Wars: From the Adventures of Luke Skywalker*. New York: Ballantine.

MacCannell, Dean
1976 *The Tourist: A New Theory of the Leisure Class*. New York: Schocken.

MacCannell, Dean, and Juliet Flower MacCannell
1982 *The Time of the Sign: A Semiotic Interpretation of Modern Culture*. Bloomington: Indiana University Press.

Mahnke, Gregory N.
1981 *Signs of the Unself: A Semiotic Analysis of "Clone" as a North American Cultural Construct*. Master's Thesis, Department of Anthropology, McGill University. Montreal, Quebec.

Malinowski, Bronislaw
1961 (1922) *Argonauts of the Western Pacific*. New York: Dutton.

Mandelbrot, Benoit B.
1983 How Long Is the Coast of Britain? In *The Fractal Geometry of Nature*. Pp. 25-33. New York: W. H. Freeman.

Merleau-Ponty, Maurice
1964 (1946) The Primacy of Perception and Its Philosophical Consequences. In *The Primacy of Perception*. James M. Edie, trans. and ed. Pp. 12-42. Evanston, Il.: Northwestern University Press.

Milton, Katharine
1993 Diet and Primate Evolution. *Scientific American* (August). Pp. 86-93.

Montague, Susan P. and Robert Morais
1981 Football Games and Rock Concerts: The Ritual Enactment of American Success Models. In *The American Dimension: Cultural Myths and Social Realities*. 2nd edition. W. Arens and Susan P. Montague, ed. Pp. 11-25. Sherman Oaks, Calif.: Alfred Publishing Co.

Nathanson, Paul
1991 *Over the Rainbow: The Wizard of Oz as a Secular Myth of America*. Albany: State University of New York Press.

Nichols, George
1867 Wild Bill. *Harper's New Monthly Magazine* 34: 273-285.

Parsons, Talcott
1951 *The Social System*. New York: Macmillan.

Paz, Octavio
1974 (1969) *Conjunctions and Disjunctions*. Helen R. Lane, trans. New York: Viking Press.

Penrose, Roger
1989 *The Emperor's New Mind: Concerning Computers, Minds, and the Laws of Physics*. New York: Oxford University Press.

Poundstone, William
1988 *The Recursive Universe: Cosmic Complexity and the Limits of Scientific Knowledge*. New York: William Morrow.

Powter, Susan
1993 *Stop the Insanity!* New York: Simon and Schuster.

Propp, Vladimir
1958 *Morphology of the Folktale*. L. Scott, trans. University Research Center in Anthropology, Folklore, and Linguistics. Bloomington, Indiana.

Prusinkiewicz, Przemyslaw, and Aristid Lindenmayer
1990 *The Algorithmic Beauty of Plants*. New York: Springer-Verlag.

Reynolds, Vernon
1976 *The Biology of Human Action*. San Francisco: W. H. Freeman.

Richler, Mordecai
1971 James Bond Unmasked. In *Mass Culture Revisited*. B. Rosenberg and D. White, ed. Pp. 341-355. New York: Van Nostrand Reinhold.
1992a (1971) *St. Urbain's Horseman*. New York: Viking Penguin.

1992b *Oh Canada! Oh Quebec!: Requiem for a Divided Country.* Toronto, Ontario: Penguin Books.
Rousseau, Jean-Jacques
1994 (1752) *Discourse on the Origin of Inequality.* Franklin Philip, trans., Patrick Coleman, ed.   New York: Oxford University Press.
Russell, Bertrand
1919 *Introduction to Mathematical Philosophy.* New York: Macmillan.
Sahlins, Marshall
1976 *Culture and Practical Reason.* Chicago: University of Chicago Press.
Sapir, Edward
1951 Culture, Genuine and Spurious. In *Selected Writings of Edward Sapir in Language, Culture and Personality.* David G. Mandelbaum, ed. Berkeley: University of California Press.
Saussure, Ferdinand de
1959 (1916) *Course in General Linguistics.* Wade Baskin, trans. C. Bally and A. Sechehaye, ed. New York: McGraw Hill.
Schneider, David
1968 *American Kinship: A Cultural Account.* Englewood Cliffs, NJ: Prentice-Hall.
Sebeok, Thomas A.
1977 Zoosemiotic Components of Human Communication. In *How Animals Communicate.* Thomas A. Sebeok, ed. Bloomington: Indiana University Press.
Solecki, Ralph
1971 *Shanidar, The First Flower People.* New York: Alfred A. Knofp.
Stanner, W. E. H.
1965 (1956) The Dreaming. In *Reader in Comparative Religion: An Anthropological Approach.* 2nd edition. William A. Lessa and Evon Z. Vogt, ed. Pp. 158-167. New York: Harper and Row.
Strum, Shirley C.
1987 *Almost Human: A Journey into the World of Baboons.* London: Elm Tree Books.
Tannen, Deborah
1990 *You Just Don't Understand: Women and Men in Conversation.* New York: William Morrow.
Thompson, Hunter S.
1972 *Fear and Loathing in Las Vegas: A Savage Journey to the Heart of the American Dream.* New York: Random House.
1979 *The Great Shark Hunt: Strange Tales from a Strange Time.* New York: Summit Books.
Trinkaus, Erik
1983 *The Shanidar Neandertals.* New York: Academic Press.

Trinkaus, Erik, and Pat Shipman
  1993 *The Neandertals: Changing the Image of Mankind.* New York: Alfred A. Knofp.
Turner, Victor
  1967 Betwixt and Between: The Liminal Period in *Rites de Passage.* In *The Forest of Symbols: Aspects of Ndembu Ritual.* Ithaca, NY: Cornell University Press.
  1969 *The Ritual Process: Structure and Anti-Structure.* Chicago: Aldine.
  1974 *Dramas, Fields, and Metaphors: Symbolic Action in Human Society.* Ithaca, NY: Cornell University Press.
Vonnegut, Kurt Jr.
  1963 *Cat's Cradle.* New York: Dell.
Waldrop, M. Mitchell
  1992 *Complexity: The Emerging Science at the Edge of Order and Chaos.* New York: Simon and Schuster.
Watkins, Mary
  1984 *Waking Dreams.* Dallas, Texas: Spring Publications.
Wheeler, John A.
  1991 Questioning the "It from Bit." In Profile: Physicist John A. Wheeler. By John Horgan. *Scientific American* (June). Pp. 36-38.
Whitman, Walt
  1942 (1855) Song of Myself. In *Leaves of Grass. The Selected Poems of Walt Whitman.* Pp. 25-110. Roslyn, NY: Walter J. Black.
Wilson, Edward O.
  1992 *The Diversity of Life.* New York: W. W. Norton.
Wolfe, Tom
  1977 (1965) Clean Fun at Riverhead. In *The Kandy-Kolored Tangerine-Flake Streamline Baby.* Pp. 24-30. New York: Bantam
  1982 *The Purple Decades: A Reader.* New York: Farrar, Straus and Giroux.
  1988 *Mauve Gloves & Madmen, Clutter & Vine.* New York: Farrar, Straus and Giroux.
Wright, Will
  1975 *Six Guns & Society.* Berkeley: University of California Press.
Wyndham, John
  1962 *The Kraken Wakes.* London: Penguin.

Index of Movies

Alien (I, II, III) (1979, 1986, 1992) 13, 244–5, 253, 310
American Gigolo (1980) 115
American Graffiti (1973) 188, 292
Apocalypse Now (1979) 253
Bambi (1942) 16
Batman (I, II, III, IV) (1943, 1966, 1989, 1992) 10
Battlestar Galactica (1979) 13
The Bible (1966) 91
Bill and Ted's Excellent Adventure (1988) 12
The Birds (1963) 199, 292
The Black Hole (1979) 13
The Black Stallion (1980) 219
Blade Runner (1982) 68
The Blob (I, II) (1958, 1988) 242
Buck Rogers in the Twenty-Fifth Century (1979) 13
Bullitt (1968) 138
Carrie (1976) 14
Casino Royale (James Bond) (1967) 128
Challenge to Lassie (1949) 263
Clan of the Cave Bear (1985) 302
Close Encounters of the Third Kind (1977) 10, 62, 226, 249, 291
Cobra (1986) 246
The Color Purple (1985) 17
Colors (1988) 115
Conan the Barbarian (1981) 302
Courage of Lassie (1946) 263
Dances with Wolves (1990) 310
The Day the Earth Stood Still (1951) 242, 291
Doctor No (James Bond) (1962) 128, 310
Dr. Strangelove (1963) 291
Dumbo (1941) 16

E. T. (1982) 10, 13–5, 17, 25, 35, 77, 107, 123–4, 131, 200, 227, 241–51, 253–7, 259, 263–4, 275, 291–2, 295, 310

Earth Versus the Flying Saucers (1956) 241

Easy Rider (1969) 253, 301

The Empire Strikes Back (*Star Wars* II) (1980) 10, 123, 173, 181, 183

Encino Man (1992) 86

The Exorcist (I, II, III) (1973, 1977, 1990) 14

Fire in the Sky (1988) 291

Firestarter (1984) 14

Flipper (1963) 306

Forbidden Planet (1956) 176, 259

Free Willy (1993) 306

The French Connection (1971) 138

Friday the Thirteenth (I–VII) (1980–9) 14

From Russia With Love (James Bond) (1963) 128, 187

Grizzly (1976) 292

Halloween (I–V) (1978–89) 14

Hangin' with the Homeboys (1991) 115

High Noon (1952) 154

Highlander (I, II) (1986, 1990) 279

Hook (1991) 140

Indiana Jones and the Temple of Doom (1984) 10, 194–5

Invaders from Mars (1953) 263

Invasion of the Body Snatchers (I, II) (1956, 1978) 202, 291

Irreconcilable Differences (1984) 224

It Came from Outer Space (1953) 14, 245, 263

Jaws (I, II, III, IV) (1975, 1978, 1983, 1987) 10, 14, 16, 17, 18, 25, 48, 77, 102, 107, 124, 199, 200–9, 215, 218–29, 232–5, 243–44, 247–49, 257, 259, 263–4, 275, 292, 295, 306, 308–9

JFK (1991) 299

Jurassic Park (1993) 200, 207–8, 213, 218, 227, 229, 231–4, 236–40, 258, 306, 309–10,

King Kong (I, II) (1933, 1976) 138, 306

Lady and the Tramp (1955) 16

Lassie Come Home (1943) 199, 205, 263, 275, 306

The Last Action Hero (1994) 224

Lethal Weapon (I, II, III) (1987, 1989, 1992) 181

Live and Let Die (James Bond) (1973) 156

The Living Daylights (James Bond) (1987) 250
The Loved One (1965) 121
The Man with the Golden Gun (James Bond) (1974) 226
Man's Genesis (1912) 302
Master of Lassie (1948) 263
Milo and Otis (1993) 16, 306
Misery (1990) 14
Missing in Action (I, II) (1984, 1985) 179
Moonraker (James Bond) (1979) 13, 135–6, 150
Mrs. Doubtfire (1993) 229
My Stepmother is an Alien (1988) 96
Nashville (1975) 17
A Nightmare on Elm Street (I–VI) (1984–93) 14
Old Yeller (1957) 205, 306
The Omen (1976) 14
One Million B. C. (1940) 174
Other People's Money (1991) 152
Pet Detective (1993) 217
Pet Sematary (1989) 14
Peter Pan (1953) 245
Piranha (1978) 292
Poltergeist (1982) 14, 15, 17, 253–7, 259
Predator (I, II) (1987, 1990) 10, 35, 244, 291, 303
Psycho (1960) 201, 308
Raiders of the Lost Ark (Indiana Jones) (1981) 10, 194–5
Rambo (I, II, III) (1982, 1985, 1988) 10, 35
Repo Man (1984) 178
Return of the Jedi (*Star Wars* III) 10, 123, 169, 173–4, 180–5, 294
Rich Kids (1979) 294
Rocky (I–V) (1976–90) 10
Rosemary's Baby (1968) 14
The Shining (1980) 14, 147, 258–9
Silence of the Lambs (1990) 302
Sleepless in Seattle (1993) 82
Son of Lassie (1945) 263
Son-in-Law (1992) 86
The Spy Who Loved Me (James Bond) (1977) 18, 44, 107, 137–8, 150, 187
Star Trek (I–VI) (1979–91) 13, 245

Star Wars (1977) 1–5, 9, 10, 12, 13, 14, 17, 18, 25, 35, 44, 45, 48, 77, 97, 104, 107, 119, 123–4, 131, 133, 169–96, 198, 200, 206–7, 218, 226, 238, 240, 243, 247, 251, 257, 263–4, 275, 291–5

Starman (1984) 291

Superman (I, II, III, IV) (1978, 1980, 1983, 1987) 10, 291

The Swarm (1978) 292

Tentacles (1976) 292

Terminator (I, II) (1984, 1991) 10, 178, 183, 190, 207, 251, 291

The Texas Chainsaw Massacre (1974) 147

Them! (1954) 243

The Thing (I, II) (1951, 1982) 239, 241–2, 291

The Turning Point (1977) 17

2001: A Space Odyssey (1968) 12, 91, 115, 120, 261, 292, 310

2010: Sequel to A Space Odyssey (1984) 169

Uncle Remus (1960) 304

An Unmarried Woman (1978) 17, 294

Watership Down (1978) 247

A Wedding (1978) 17

What about Bob? (1991) 177

When Harry Met Sally (1989) 90

The Wizard of Oz (1939) 3

Index

'57 Chevy 49, 59
1975 10, 103
1977 1
academic irrelevance 7
academics 18
Acheulian artifacts 52, 94
advertisements 25
advertising 9, 41
Agency for International
    Development 7
alcheringa 12
alienation 3
aliens 10, 48, 89, 264
Allen, Woody 17
Altamira 48
Altman, Robert 17
ambiguity 29
ambivalence 2, 6, 17, 25, 26, 27, 28,
    29, 60, 76, 89, 92, 264, 284
America/Americans 2-4, 9, 10, 11,
    14, 15, 19, 20-21, 23, 24, 25, 28,
    58, 80, 86, 261, 263, 264, 269, 271
American anthropologists 7
American audiences 17, 41
American culture 1, 11, 14, 18, 19,
    28, 263, 275
American Dream 82
American Dreamtime 11, 19, 59,
    70, 108
American Indians 37, 38
American myth 8, 24, 26, 60
American practicality 28
Amerindian 31
Amish 7

amplitudes 270
Anaheim, California 82, 83, 89
angeleno 83, 84
animal movies 14-17,
animals 5, 15-17, 26, 30, 38, 43, 48,
    92, 97, 100, 104-108, 263-265,
    284
ant 51, 65
ant path 62, 64, 65, 68, 70, 81, 84,
    85, 95, 98, 102, 103, 106, 108, 109
Anthro comic books 93
anthropological semiotics 8, 19, 29,
    37, 38, 42, 87, 94, 96, 108, 263
anthropologists 2, 6, 10, 11, 17, 18,
    21, 23, 26, 36, 38, 44, 52, 55-57,
    60, 66, 67, 91, 93, 94, 96, 103,
    261, 267, 269, 286
anthropology 7, 10, 15, 31, 32, 49,
    51, 54, 55, 61, 70-73, 79, 262
    applied 8, 9
    cultural 2-7, 11, 12, 14, 15, 17,
        19, 41, 45, 47, 49, 51, 54, 94, 96,
        100, 105, 261, 264, 265, 270, 272
    development 8, 9, 72, 268
    "economic" vs. "symbolic"
    opposition 8
    symbolic 8, 19, 51
antiquity 31
antistructure 73, 75
Apollo Creed 13
Arawak 5, 6, 48
Arawak myth 7
architecture 8
art 8, 96

artifact production 45
Artifact/Machine 100
artifacts 5, 8, 26, 90, 92, 97, 104, 107, 108, 265
artifactual intelligence 46, 93, 95, 101
artifactual processes 29, 91
audience 36, 263
Australian aborigines 5, 9, 20, 37, 38, 49
Australian languages 5
australopithecines 46, 52, 104, 107
Aztecs 267, 271
baby universe 103, 265
Bacon, Francis 53
Bak, Per 265, 274, 276
Bambi 16, 17, 36
Barcelona 84
Barthes, Roland 37-39, 42, 43
Bateson, Gregory 3, 52, 59, 92
Bedouin social organization 7
Beemers 105
belief system 38
Bennett, John 48
Bennett, Lynette 48
Bergman, Ingmar 262
Beverly Hills High School 42
Bickerton, Derek 79
Big Bang 288
Big Bear earthquake 273
Bigfoot 24
biology 287
biotechnology 94
Boas, Franz 32
Bond 263, 264, 276
Bond, James 10, 13, 14, 17, 18, 25, 31, 36, 45, 48, 52, 97, 263, 264, 276
Borneo ritual 7
Bosnia 78
boundary/boundaries 19, 62, 65, 81, 98, 263, 283-285, 290

Bowman, Commander David (*2001*) 261, 290
boxoffice 263
brain 49, 54, 79,
Brecht, Bertolt 262
Brody, Chief 10, 36
Buck Rogers 12
bug-eyed monsters 13
Bugs Bunny 36
built environment 4
Burroughs, William 57, 58, 67
Busch Gardens 105
C-Span 9
C3PO 2, 3, 45
Cal cuisine 89
Calamity Jane 25
California 11, 13, 82, 83, 100, 274, 285
California Institute of Technology 100, 274
Calspeak 77
calypso 80
camshaft 79, 80
capitalism 20
Capra, Fritjof 53
Carib Indians 5, 6
Caribbean 80
Carpenter, Edmund 9, 261
categories of identity 41
cellular automaton 270, 271, 277-289
chaos 66, 68, 89, 270
chaos theory 49
Chaucer, Geoffrey 87
Chen, Kan 265, 274, 276
chess 281
Chevy 81
Chewy (Chewbaca) 2
children 15, 77, 89
Chomsky, Noam 21, 49, 79, 80
Chung, Connie 21
Cinemascope 4, 103
cinematic ethnography 17

cinematology 6
class conflict 34
classical mechanics 67
classificatory thought 38, 41
Clinton, Bill 264, 285
Club Med 18
cogito ergo sum 95, 103
colonialism 80
comic books 9, 93
comic strips 13
commercialism 18-20
commodity value 8
common sense 8, 21, 29, 61, 65, 70,
    81, 269, 287
Communist Manifesto 21
communitas 73
comparative religion 23
complexity 60, 67
complexity theory 26, 66, 68, 271
computers 48, 66, 94, 272, 274, 279
Congressional Record 21
consciousness 4, 25, 26, 58, 59, 70,
    75, 89, 90, 92, 93, 95-97, 102-105,
    107, 108, 265, 268
Constitution, U.S. 21
consumer capitalism 25, 28
continuum 56, 59, 76, 77, 79, 80, 82,
    87, 88, 95, 104, 106, 107, 275
contradiction 76, 266
Conway, John 282, 286, 287
cosmologists 53, 60, 265
cosmology 26, 49, 51, 53, 54, 57, 67,
    100, 101, 103, 265, 271, 289
cosmology of consciousness 100
cosmos 273
Couric, Katie 21
creation 26, 108, 264, 281, 283
creationists 91
creativity 91
creature features 14
creole linguistics 79, 80, 82, 87
cubano 84
cuisine 8

cultural analysis 3, 4, 6, 8, 9, 10, 12,
    14, 15, 17, 19, 21, 25, 29, 31, 33,
    37, 52-54, 76, 77, 90, 103, 263,
    270-272
cultural change 80, 86
cultural continuum 285, 286
cultural dimensionality 75-77, 79
cultural evolution 264
cultural framework or pattern 3, 11
cultural generativity 10, 47, 90, 92,
    94, 95, 289
cultural identity 16
cultural materialism 268, 271, 272
cultural processes 15, 40, 75, 78,
    88, 90, 92, 95, 109, 264
cultural production 3, 8, 17-19, 29,
    37, 38, 44, 51, 52, 54, 70, 97, 285,
    286
cultural system 3, 34, 35, 40, 49, 55,
    67, 103, 271, 283
culture 1, 8, 9, 11, 17, 18 , 23, 25,
    28, 29, 32-36, 38, 43, 47-49, 51-
    57, 59, 60, 70, 71, 73, 75, 77, 78,
    88, 90, 91, 93, 95, 101, 103, 104,
    107, 108, 261, 262, 264, 267-273,
    275, 285
Cushing, Peter 2
cyborgs 10
da Vinci, Leonardo 11
Dallas 18
Dalton, Timothy 13
dance 48
Darth Vader 2, 4, 45, 48
Darwin, Charles 76, 105, 287
Davies, Paul 53
Death Force 14, 97, 100
Death Star 2, 4, 21, 45, 264
Declaration of Independence, U.S.
    21
denotative message 41
deracinement 10, 70
Descartes, Rene 95, 104, 271, 276,
    289

desirability 34
destruction 26, 108, 264
determinacy 66
determinism 271, 276
dialect 80, 81, 84, 85
dialectic 108, 274, 276
dichotomy 19
dietary system 58
dilemma 3, 8, 28, 265
dimensionality 54, 55, 59-61, 65-67, 70, 72, 81, 84, 85, 87, 88, 90, 109, 287
Disney movies 17
Disney period 16
Disney, Walt 16
Disneyland 20
divorce lawyers 24
Dolby 4, 103
dolphins 16
Donald Duck 16
Dorothy (*Wizard of Oz*) 3
drawing 48
dream 1
dream factory 9
Dreaming 5
Dreamtime 5, 9, 11-14, 17, 20-22, 26, 31, 36, 42, 47-49, 54, 61, 65-68, 70-72, 75, 76, 81, 86, 89, 90, 105
Dreamtime America 31, 82, 88, 91
Dreyfuss, Richard 62
drive-by shootings 77, 78
droids 2, 3, 45, 48, 52,
drug trade 20
Dude (speech) 86
Dumbo 16
Dynasty 18
E. T. 10, 17, 48, 264
earthquakes 274
Eco, Umberto 37, 88
ecology 9, 32, 90
ecology of mind 52, 59,
economics 33-35

economy 19, 90
eidos 11
Eigen, Manfred 85, 97, 284, 287
eighteenth century 94, 263
Einstein, Albert 61, 63, 65, 71, 262, 268
elemental dilemmas 36, 45, 48, 90, 92, 95, 107
elitism 18
Elliott (*E. T.*) 10, 13
emergent systems 283
Empire, The 36
empirical research 19
empiricism 267
English (language) 80-82, 84
enigma 5, 58
Enlightenment 19, 94, 263
Enterprise, U.S.S. 36
entertainment 20
entertainment industry 8
environment 59, 82, 92, 274
environmental movement 10
environmental processes 33
ethnic group 26
ethnic identity 41
ethnic relations 10
ethnicity 16
ethnography 7, 18, 19, 72, 73, 267, 268, 287
Euclid 65, 68
Euclidean geometry 68
Europe 9
evangelists 92
event 73
everywhen 26
Evil Empire 20
evolution 91
existentialism 267
extraterrestrial movies 13
extraterrestrials 13
fairy tale 3, 4, 12
fakelore 18

family 10, 15, 23, 24, 30, 109, 265, 284
family therapists 24
fantasy genre 12
fantasy movies 12, 14, 17
fashion 8, 9
faxes 105
Fernandez, James 56, 59, 76, 77, 105
fetishism of commodities 8
field 72, 75
field equations 269
field work 18
film 10, 12, 17, 20, 36
film criticism 2, 6, 7, 14, 17, 18, 108, 262, 263
Flash Gordon 12
flicker noise 275
folk production 6
folklore 18
folklorists 6
food and non-food 58
football games 10
Force, The 20
Ford, Harrison 81
forms of life 102
fractal geometry 67
fractals 65
frameworks of understandings 29
Franklin, Benjamin 25
Frazer, James 38
Freddy Kruger 14
freeway shootings 77
Freud, Sigmund 18
functionalism 275, 276
Future of America 86
Galileo, Galilei 95
Game of Life 282-288
games 8
gangs 77, 78
Garfield the Cat 16, 105
Gauss, Karl 70
Geertz, Clifford 48

gender 10
generative processes 97, 108, 283, 289
generativity 27, 28, 52, 54, 106, 108, 281, 284
genesis of culture 33
geometric array 287
geometry 55, 60, 65, 66, 76, 287
gesture 48
Gleick, James 68
glider 282
glider gun 288
global cultural system 28
gluons 53
gnosis 47
Go (game) 281
Gore, Al 87
Gothic cathedral 11
Grand Moff Tarkin 2, 4
Grand Unified Theory 269
Great White Shark 17, 36, 264
Greenpeace 108
group 5, 32, 109
Guinness, Alec 2
Gutenberg 48
Guyana 5, 6, 48, 83
Guyanese Creole 82
hackers 67
Harris, Marvin 268, 271, 273
Harris, Zellig 79
Hawking, Stephen 53, 268
Heisenberg, Werner 71, 268, 270
Held, Glenn 272, 276
Hell's Angels 7
Hendricks, Joe 48
hermeneutics 267
Hero of Our Age 13
Highlander model 280, 281
Hilbert space 49, 59, 65, 66, 76-78, 87, 97, 103, 268, 287
Hispanics 82
history 90, 267, 268
Hmong 285

Hobbes, Thomas 34
Hollywood 6, 14, 19, 21, 275, 276
holograph 47, 49, 54
holographic engine 49, 52, 54
holographic image 58
hominid evolution 45, 46, 93, 106, 264
hominids 27, 47, 57, 93
Homo erectus 102
Homo habilis 102
Homo sapiens 15, 45, 46, 48, 92-95, 104
horror movies 14
human evolution 91, 105
human experience 25, 31, 35
human identity 4, 8, 35, 90, 95, 104, 106
human nature 28, 90, 91
human-animal relationship 15
humanism 94, 263, 264
humanity 3, 25, 27-32, 43, 52, 55, 88, 90-97, 102, 104, 262-264, 267, 284, 289
Hume, David 284
Humpty Dumpty 36, 274
hunting and gathering groups 5
Huston, John 91
IBM Thomas J. Watson Research Center 272
idealism 267
identity 89
identity crisis 45
ideology 19
image 20
Imperial Guardsmen 2
incest 30
inchoateness 77
incoherence, of existence 3
incredible adventure movies 12, 13, 16
indeterminacy 65, 267
Indiana Jones 7, 13, 272
individual 88, 89

Industry on Parade 4
insectoids 4
intergroup relations 8, 93
internal contradiction 72
internal variation 286, 287
internal variation 80, 85, 87, 286, 287
interpretivism 51, 52
intersystem 53, 72, 76, 77, 79, 80, 82, 83, 85, 87, 88, 96, 106, 108, 275, 285, 286, 288
intertextuality 106
invariant properties 81, 85, 285
It from Bit 289
J. R. Ewing 18
Jackson, Michael 288
Jakobson, Roman 79
Jamaica 83
James, William 275
Jason (*Halloween*) 14
Jawas 2, 4
Jaycees 79
Jedi 20
jokes 18
Jonestown 78
Kabakaburi 6, 48
kachina figures 39
Kael, Pauline 262
Kafka, Franz 10
King, Stephen 14
kinship 16, 26, 23, 32, 51
Kirk, Admiral James T. 36
kiva 39
Kline, Morris 69, 70, 272
Koresh, David 78
Kubrick, Stanley 12, 91
Kwa language group 80
Labov, William 80
Lambert, Christopher 280
Landers earthquake 273
language 30, 32, 39, 40, 42, 44-46, 49, 51, 52, 55, 57-59, 79, 81-83, 85, 88, 90, 95, 106, 109

Laplace, Pierre 271-273, 276, 277, 279, 289
Larsen, Brooke 96
Lascaux 48
Lassie 264
Leach, Edmund 54, 55, 59, 70, 72, 76, 105
Leia, Princess 2-4, 36, 45
Leibniz, Gottfried 271
Levi-Strauss, Claude 15, 32, 35-44, 49, 55, 59, 72, 73, 76, 79, 91, 96, 105, 262, 268
Lewin, Kurt 75
Lieberman, Philip 46, 52, 55
Life Force 97, 100
life-crisis rituals 73, 75
Limbaugh, Rush 21
liminality 72, 74-79, 275
line 64-66, 84,
linear equations 68
linguistic change 86
linguistic continuum 80, 83
linguistics 44, 48, 56, 79, 81
literacy 267
literary criticism and critics 6, 18, 37, 44, 51, 261
literary semiotics 42
literature 8, 267
Little Old Woman Who Lived in a Shoe 36
Little Woman, The 25
Lodge Boy 31
logic 270, 271, 274, 276
logic of things that just happen 26, 275, 283
Lorenz, Edward 49
Los Angeles 77, 78
Lotman, Juri 262
Lowe, Charlie 48
Lucas, George 11, 12, 76
M. I. T. 79, 288
machines 2-5, 26, 45, 46, 49, 59, 79, 104-106, 263, 264, 276, 284

magic 267
Magritte, Rene 100
Mahnke, Gregory 51
Makunaima 36
Malibu 285
Malinowski, Bronislaw 38
Malthus model 280, 281
Mandelbrot line 102
Mandelbrot set 66, 67
Mandelbrot, Benoit 49, 64-66, 81, 106
Manitoba 288
Martian anthropologist 19
Marxism 9, 20
materialist account of cultural origin 34
materialist critique of myth 31, 33, 35, 39, 90, 267
mathematicians 64, 66, 68-70, 270
mathematics 26, 52, 55, 59, 60, 65, 66, 68, 70, 269, 287
Maxwell Smart 61
McDonald's 86
Me Generation 24
Mead, Margaret 7
meaning 35, 40-42, 54, 58
measurement 64, 85
media-myth 19
mental constructs 58
Merleau-Ponty, Maurice 57
mesons 53
metalanguage 40, 42, 43
metamorphosis 102
metaphor 56, 57, 59, 77
Michelangelo 11
Mickey Mouse 16, 36
Middle English 87
Mighty Sparrow, The 80
migration 80
mind 38, 44, 46, 49, 51, 52, 54, 55, 57, 66, 289
mind and matter 287
Mind of God 277

models 270, 276, 277, 283, 284, 287
Moore, Roger 13
Mortal Kombat 286
Mos Eisley 2
movie industry 11
movie-myth 20, 30, 31, 97, 275, 285
movies 2-6, 8-14, 17-21, 23-25, 28,
    29, 31, 35-37, 39, 46, 48, 70, 72,
    75, 77, 91, 96, 103, 105, 108, 261,
    262, 265, 276, 286
multiple realities 26, 49, 52, 53, 72
multiplicity of selves 87, 88, 103,
    108
multivocality 72
music 8
mystification 33-35
myth 2, 4-6, 8, 10-12, 16, 17, 19, 21,
    24-35, 38-44, 48, 49, 51-55, 61,
    65, 71, 73, 81, 89-92, 95, 97, 103,
    106, 108, 261, 262, 265, 267
myth of America 25, 26, 60, 81, 88,
    263
myth of humanity 71
myth, "primitive" 5, 6
mythic processes 25, 108
mythology 30, 32
myths of clan origin 5, 11, 31
narrative 4, 6, 28, 31, 44, 45, 47, 48
narrative analysis 262
Nathanson, Paul 3
National Bureau of Standards 62
native peoples 11, 18, 23, 25, 26, 49
"natives" 52, 71, 73, 269
nature 43, 59, 106
Ndembu 72, 73, 76, 78, 79
Neumann, John von 282
Neverland 288
New Guinea 80
New Guinea Pidgin 82
New York 18
New York Times 21
Newspeak 267
Newsweek magazine 21

Newton, Isaac 70, 271, 276, 279
Nietzsche, Friedrich 95
non-Euclidean geometry 67, 70
nonlinear equations 68
nonlinear mathematics 67
Northridge earthquake 273, 274
Nova Mob 67
novels 21
Nutcracker 3
Obi-Wan-Kenobi 2, 4
Oedipus, Joe 31
Old English 87
oscillation of the void 53
Pacific islands 80
painting 48
Palm Canyon Drive 59
parable 28
paradox 21, 32, 71, 107, 108, 264,
    265, 284
particle-wave 88, 103
particles, elementary 52, 53, 89,
    268, 284, 289
Pasadena 100
pebble choppers 46, 52
Peirce, Charles S. 37
Penrose, Roger 53, 59, 60, 65, 66,
    76-78, 85, 97, 98, 103, 268, 287
people movies 12, 17
perception 57, 90
performance 48
personal trainers 24
pets 16, 39, 105
phase space 49, 59, 60, 65, 66, 76-
    78, 85, 97, 98, 287
phenomenology 47
philosophers 44, 51, 53
philosophy 267
photon 51, 87, 289
physical reality 26, 53, 59, 67, 76
physicists 269, 289
physics 49, 59, 66, 70, 75, 79, 271,
    275, 289
plants 5

plastic surgeons 24
Platonists 65
Poe, Edgar Allen 101
poetry 48
Polanski, Roman 14
polarization of meaning 72
political organization 32
political reality 21
popular culture 6, 10, 11, 13-15, 17, 37, 38, 42,
popular film 17
positivism 30, 51, 267
postmodern/postmodernism 7, 51, 52, 77, 89, 267, 268
Poundstone, William 265, 282, 290
Predator, The 264
prehistory 19
primacy of myth 57, 92
primates 46
primitive culture 286
"primitives" 15, 18, 28, 38, 39, 76, 262
print 20
printspeak 80
process 73, 76, 78
processual analysis 72, 73, 77
processualism 72
Prometheus, Joe 30, 31
Propp, Vladimir 262
protoculture 48, 93
ptolemaic conception of humanity 94
quality space 56-60, 77
quantum linear superposition 53, 268
quantum mechanics 26, 51-54, 57, 59, 67, 70, 87, 100, 101, 103, 265, 268, 270, 284, 286, 289
quantum multiplicity 78
quantum world 49
quarks 53
quasispecies 85, 97, 265, 284, 285
R2D2 2, 3, 4, 45, 49, 264

race 23
Radcliffe-Brown, A. R. 32, 38
Rambo 13, 25,
randomness 270
randomness 52
Rastas 83
Rather, Dan 21
rationalism 267
reading 47
Reagan, Ronald 20, 21
Real People, The 18
realism 21, 26
realism 267
reelity 9, 49, 101
reflectivist perspective on myth 32-34
relations of production 34
Relativity 289
relativity 68
representation 284, 287
representation 3, 15, 16, 29, 38, 41, 43, 45, 64, 70,
representations 261
Riemann, Bernhardt 70, 71
ritual 2, 9, 32, 48, 51, 76, 79
ritual symbolism 72, 73, 75
ritual value 8
robots 3, 4
rock concerts 10
Rockwell, Norman 89
Rocky 13
Rose Bowl 100
Russians 20
Sahlins, Marshall 35
Samsa, Gregor 89
San Andreas fault 273, 274
sandpile experiment 270-272, 274, 276, 283, 284
Sankoff, Gillian 80
Santa Claus 24
sapience 15, 92, 95, 267, 289, 290
Sapir, Edward 18
Saussure, Ferdinand de 37, 39, 42

scale 66, 81, 85, 86
schismogenesis 3, 92
Schroedinger, Erwin 71, 268
Schutz, Alfred 47, 54
science 26, 51, 52, 60, 67, 70, 79, 82,
     267
science fiction 12
science of humanity 15, 19, 70, 267
Scientific American 53
scientific method 53
scientism 28, 267
Sea World 105
Seattle, Washington 1, 2
Sebeok, Thomas 37, 47, 54
self-organized criticality 49, 78,
     271, 284
semantic processes 42
semiology 37, 42, 43
semiospace 32, 33, 35, 51, 54-6, 72,
     75, 87, 88, 90, 92, 95, 97, 101,
     103, 285-287
semiotic dimension(s) 16, 54, 58,
     60, 72, 76, 77, 90, 95, 97, 105,
     264, 265, 275
semiotic processes 35, 47, 56, 107
semiotics 25, 36, 37, 39, 43
semiotics of modern culture 37, 39,
     93, 94, 96
sentience 287
sequence space 85, 97, 284-287
Seurat, Georges 96
sexuality 10, 30
Shore, Pauly 86
Sierra Club 108
sign 42
signified 39
signifier 39, 41
signifying practice 28
silk-cotton tree 36
Siskel and Ebert 262
Sistine Chapel 277
Skywalker, Luke 2, 4, 10, 13, 18, 20,
     31, 45, 48, 52

slang 81, 85
slasher movies 14
slavery 80
Sly (Stallone) 13
smeared reality 53, 88, 103, 264
social change 5
social differentiation 34
social drama 73, 75, 77, 78
social organization 32
social reality 20
social thought 37
solar system 279
Solo, Han 2
Something Else 27, 79, 88, 95, 96,
     102, 264, 289
song 21, 48
South American Indian myth 44
South American Indians 5, 6, 36
space 61
space opera 4, 12, 13
spacetime 54
Spanish 81-84, 89
species 102, 264, 285, 286
speech 48, 79, 81, 86
speech community 80
Spielberg, Steven 10, 11, 14, 15, 76
spin doctors 21
sports 8, 37
Spring Boy 31
Stanner, William 5, 20, 26, 49, 105
strange attractor 49
structural analysis 44, 59
structural functionalism 71, 72, 79
structural linguistics 55, 79, 80, 81
structural model 55, 61
structural transformation 73, 77
structuralism 37, 54, 55, 72, 73
structure 73, 75
Sue Ellen *(Dallas)* 18
supergrosser era 10
supergrosser movies 6, 10, 13, 18,
     21, 31, 48, 91, 94, 105, 109
supergrosser novels 14

symbol 19, 42, 43
symbolism 9, 72
symbolization/conceptualization
   processes 33, 44, 46, 47, 49, 52,
   56
system of differences 43
system of meanings 8, 35
Tatooine 21
technological change 27
technology 46
television 1, 4, 7, 10, 14, 20, 21, 25,
   37, 77, 83, 103
teriyaki tacos 89, 285
text 38, 47, 51, 73, 100, 262, 267
The New Yorker 262
Them/Other 100
theory of culture 6, 19, 24, 51, 72,
   75, 78, 286
Theory of Everything 269
theory of myth 24
Third World 6, 7, 9, 48, 73
thirteenth century 11
Thomas, Dylan 106
thought 5, 39, 43
tilt of consciousness 77
time 21
Tin Man 3
tool 81
Topeka 76, 82, 84, 89, 262, 285, 288
topological anthropology 72
topology 76
Toronto 18
totemic ancestors 5
totemism 15, 16, 38, 43, 105
totemism of machines 105
Toto 3
tourism 8, 18, 20, 37, 68
TransAm 83
truth 89
Turner, Victor and Edith 72, 73,
   75-79
Tusken Raiders 2
twentieth century 11, 26, 35

Tylor, E. B. 15, 105
Ulam, Stanislaw 282
Umwelt 47, 49, 54, 57, 60, 90, 102,
   107
uncertainty 52
Uncle Remus 71
undecidability 68
United States 19, 21, 22, 25, 68, 85,
   262, 267
universe 89, 273, 279, 287-289
unpredictability 68
Upper Paleolithic 48
Ur-mythe 14
Us/Self 100
value 34
vampire movies 14
variation 19, 286
Variety 11
vector 66, 72, 75, 93
vectorial processes 49, 76, 86, 90,
   97, 98, 105
Viet Nam 10
virtual beings 87, 88
virtual experience 20, 49, 54, 76
virtual particles 53, 66, 285
virtual worlds 31, 49, 53
virtuality 26, 49, 52, 53, 66, 72, 75,
   89, 263, 267, 275, 276
virus 85
visceral understanding 57, 274
Volkswagen 63
Waco, Texas 78
Walters, Barbara 21
wave function 53
Wayne, John 89
Welk, Lawrence 101
West Africa 80
Western thought 19
whales 16
Wheeler, John 289
Whitman, Walt 87, 88, 103, 108,
   264
Williams, Charles 48

Wills, George 21
Wittgenstein, Ludwig 27, 102
Wolfe, Tom 11, 24
Wookies 2, 4
World Bank 7
World Dawn 5
world historical irony 95
writing 47, 48
writing-printing-reading complex
     48
Yuppies 105
Zambia 72, 78

Note on the Author

Like other boundaries explored in this book, the line between cultural anthropology and philosophy is infinitely complex. I know something of its contours, for I have wandered over that contested terrain since undergraduate days at Reed College, where I pursued an interdivisional major in anthropology (in the "division" of the Social Sciences) and philosophy (in the "division" of the Humanities). Following Reed, I studied anthropology at the University of Chicago, where I received a couple of degrees in the subject.

I have conducted fairly traditional ethnographic research among Arawak and Carib groups of Guyana and the Guyanese-Brazilian border. I have also done somewhat less traditional ethnographic research in several Caribbean locations, and carried out what some would doubtlessly consider downright wacky field work in the San Diego Zoo, Sea World, Disneyland, and, of course, movie theatres across the country.

Since 1988 I have been director of the Center for Peripheral Studies, P. O. Box 477, Palm Springs CA 92263. The Center is a little think shop I have operated when I am not out delivering pizzas, selling houses, running a small hotel, or otherwise engaged in the business of living. The work of the Center is along two broad (and, of course, highly convoluted) fronts. One front is the theoretical enterprise of understanding the nature of sapience, particularly in the guise of an artifactual intelligence (our own, parochial version of sapience). In the glory days of philosophy, this enterprise went under the heading of the "theory of knowledge." But that was before they dug that fateful scrap of typescript out of the rubble of writings Wittgenstein left at his death: "*Der Irrtum ist zu sagen, Meinen bestehe in etwas.*" Not a very comforting parting thought there, Ludwig! So if the mistake is to say that meaning consists in something, then we are left with the diminished task of saying what we can about the general activity and grounding conditions of sapience. I make a stab in that direction in the book before you, and continue to plug away at it in two electronic, word-processed *Zettel* always underway: "Culture, Mind, and Physical Reality," which applies cultural analytic thinking to the debate now raging over the nature of consciousness; and "Where Is Everybody? Cultural Anthropology and the Search for Extraterrestrial Intelligence," which (like Barry Sadler's song) is pretty much about what it says.

The other front of research, thinking, and writing at the Center has to do with *practice* (as the Marxists used to like to call it): locking horns (in an intellectual and not-so-intellectual way) with what is actually going on around you, trying to figure out what makes turn-of-the-century America (or, at any rate, its bizarre, southern California version) really/reely work. Here reelity continually overwhelms reality, for vast structures of posturing and "spin" utterly take over the flow of events in what was once fondly called the "real world." Unless you happened to be orbiting Neptune at the time, you, too, witnessed the famous "low speed chase" of O. J. Simpson and the carnivalesque events that followed, and know exactly what I am talking about. So we here at the Center — our thronged, Whitmanesque multitudes — are up to our hair implants in The Trial, and are beginning to fold an account of it into other ongoing studies of the Super Bowl (the magical XXX is almost upon us!), Shamu's Night Magic at San Diego's Sea World, and the bonobo enclosure at the San Diego Zoo.

These latter topics obviously build on the cultural analysis of the ecology movement presented in the present work, particularly in chapter 6. And, you may be relieved to learn, here at last cultural analysis reveals its practical, "applied" side. For we are now very much engaged in two ecological campaigns for the next millennium.

One, the Save the Smelts Foundation, aims at restoring the numbers and, just as important, the dignity, of a much-ignored, much-abused species. If you have ever visited San Diego's Sea World and lined up at one of the concession stands dotted around the theme park to buy dolphin and walrus treats, you know what I am talking about. You pay your dollar and you get, served up in a red-and-white checked paper container just like ballpark weenies come in, an entire little family of smelts — Mom and Dad and Buddy and Sis Smelt — their cold, dead eyes gazing up at you in the silent ignominy of bait, lying there waiting to become tidbits for far luckier species to munch upon.

The Center's other campaign/project is the Chicken Oasis, modeled after the many "pet oases" that have sprung up across the country to save abandoned dogs and cats. The Chicken Oasis will be a sanctuary for the hundreds of thousands of "layers" that live a hellish life in the egg factories (*not* farms) that dot formerly rural America. Now, rather than being destroyed at the end of their useful lives and pureed into the fecal sludge served up in our TV dinners and chicken soup, these wretched creatures will be granted a reprieve. At the Chicken Oasis, they will live out their few remaining days happily scratching in the soil and socializing with their fellow survivors.

This, at any rate, is our vision. But it will take your contribution (preferably in large, unmarked bills) to make it come true. So open your heart — and your wallet — dear reader, and give so that we might heal. Yea-ah! Yea-ah! Hee-al! Hee-al! *S-a-v-e* the Smelts and the Chickens! God loves you. We love you. Hallelujah! Cowabunga! Aloha!